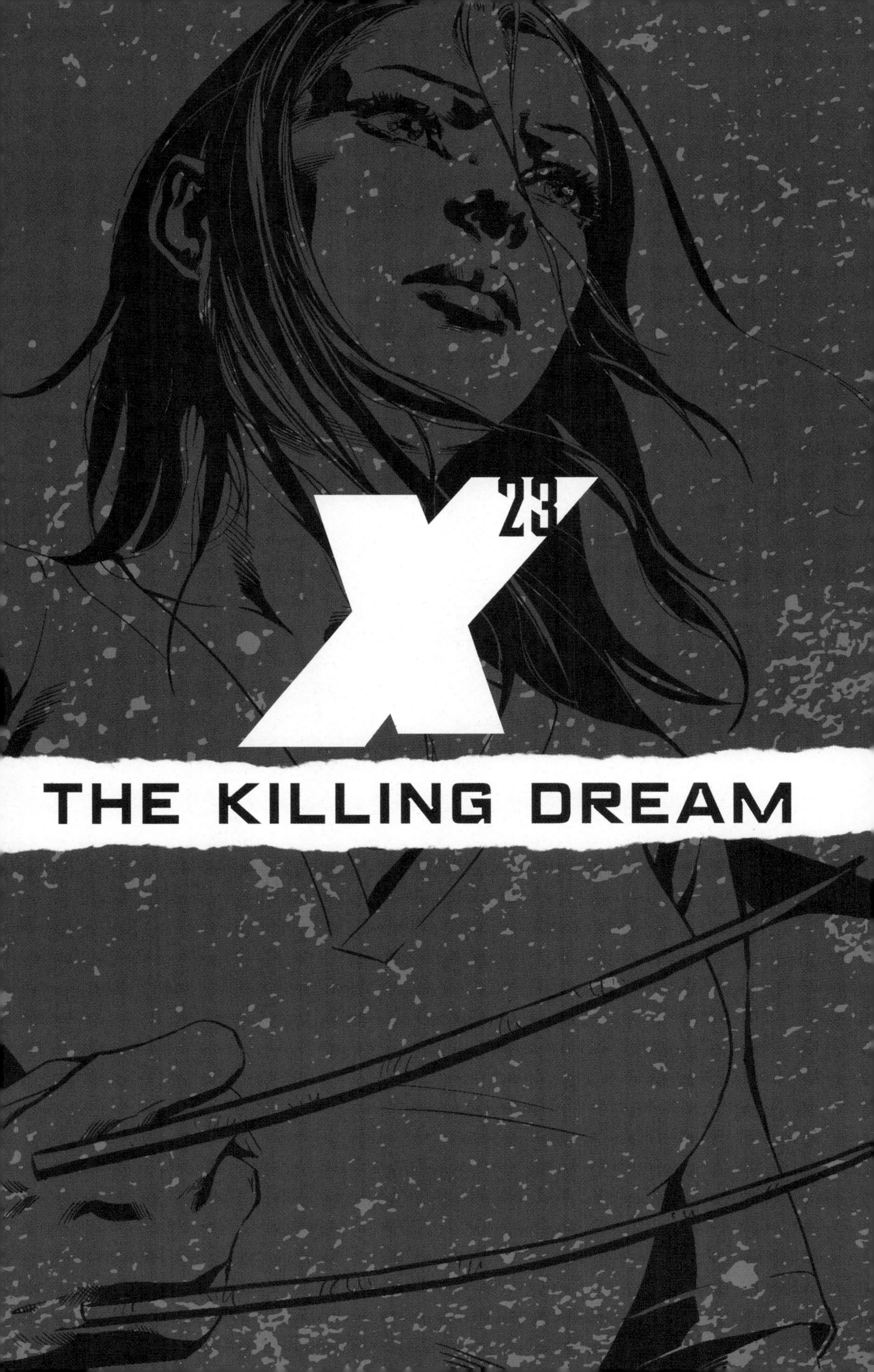
X23
THE KILLING DREAM

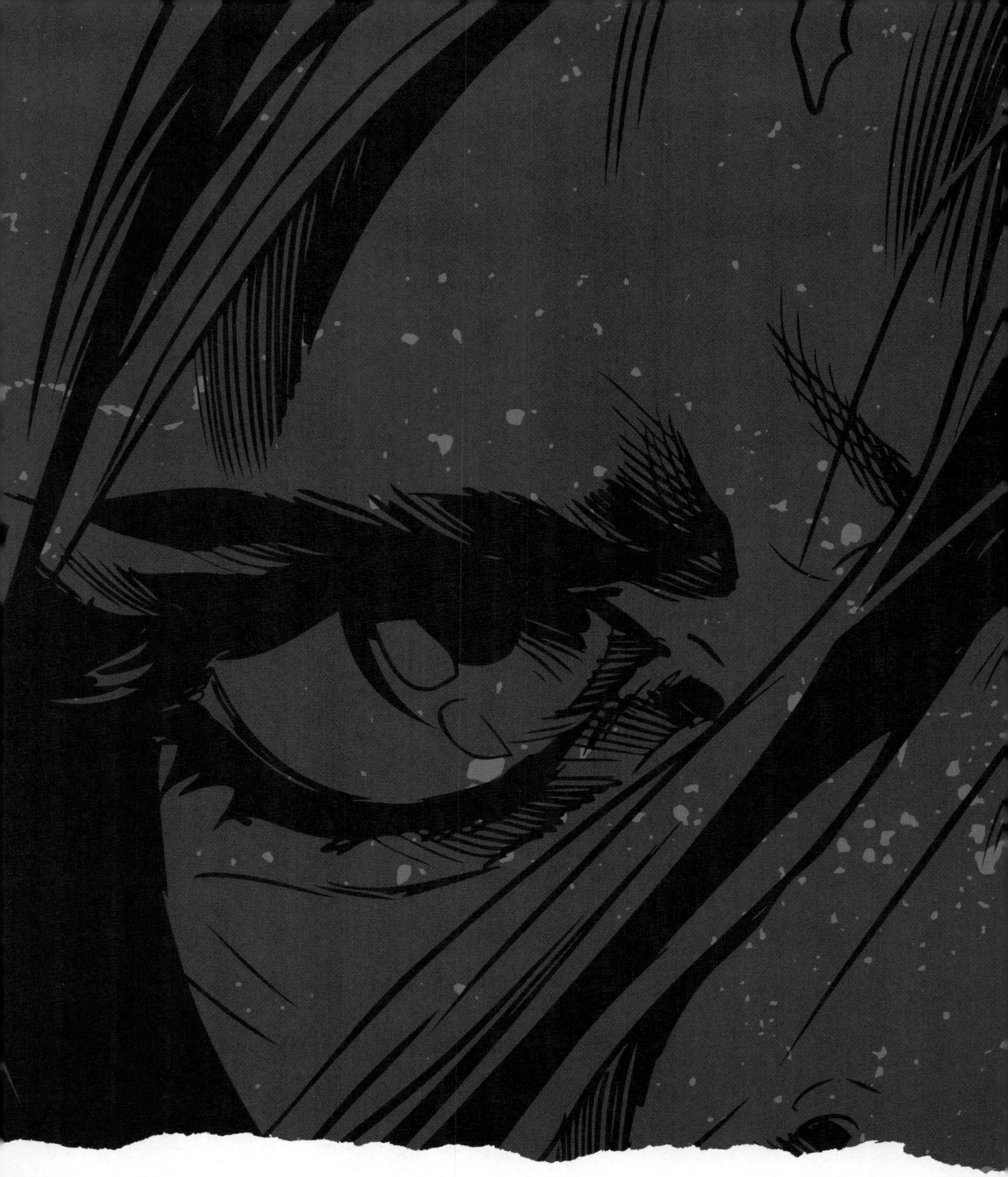

WRITER
MARJORIE LIU

ART
WILL CONRAD WITH
SANA TAKEDA
[ISSUE #3]
MARCO CHECCHETTO
[ISSUE #4] AND
DAVID LÓPEZ & ÁLVARO LÓPEZ
[ISSUES #5-6]

COLOR ART **JOHN RAUCH**

LETTERS **VC'S CORY PETIT & CHRIS ELIOPOULOS**

ASSISTANT EDITOR **JODY LEHEUP**

COVER ART **DANNI SHINYA LUO, LEINIL YU & JASON KEITH** AND **KALMAN ANDRASOFSZKY**

EDITOR **JEANINE SCHAEFER**

X²³

THE KILLING DREAM

Collection Editor **Jennifer Grünwald**

Editorial Assistants **James Emmett & Joe Hochstein**

Assistant Editors **Alex Starbuck & Nelson Ribeiro**

Editor, Special Projects **Mark D. Beazley**

Senior Editor, Special Projects **Jeff Youngquist**

Senior Vice President of Sales **David Gabriel**

Book Design **Jeff Powell**

Editor in Chief **Axel Alonso**

Chief Creative Officer **Joe Quesada**

Publisher **Dan Buckley**

Executive Producer **Alan Fine**

X-23 VOL. 1: THE KILLING DREAM. Contains material originally published in magazine form as X-23 #1-6 and ALL-NEW WOLVERINE SAGA. First printing 2011. Hardcover ISBN# 978-0-7851-5295-8. Softcover ISBN# 978-0-7851-4797-8. Published by MARVEL WORLDWIDE, INC., a subsidiary of MARVEL ENTERTAINMENT, LLC. OFFICE OF PUBLICATION: 135 West 50th Street, New York, NY 10020. Copyright © 2010 and 2011 Marvel Characters, Inc. All rights reserved. Hardcover: $19.99 per copy in the U.S. and $21.99 in Canada (GST #R127032852). Softcover: $16.99 per copy in the U.S. and $18.50 in Canada (GST #R127032852). Canadian Agreement #40668537. All characters featured in this issue and the distinctive names and likenesses thereof, and all related indicia are trademarks of Marvel Characters, Inc. No similarity between any of the names, characters, persons, and/or institutions in this magazine with those of any living or dead person or institution is intended, and any such similarity which may exist is purely coincidental. **Printed in the U.S.A.** ALAN FINE, EVP - Office of the President, Marvel Worldwide, Inc. and EVP & CMO Marvel Characters B.V.; DAN BUCKLEY, Publisher & President - Print, Animation & Digital Divisions; JOE QUESADA, Chief Creative Officer; JIM SOKOLOWSKI, Chief Operating Officer; DAVID BOGART, SVP of Business Affairs & Talent Management; TOM BREVOORT, SVP of Publishing; C.B. CEBULSKI, SVP of Creator & Content Development; DAVID GABRIEL, SVP of Publishing Sales & Circulation; MICHAEL PASCIULLO, SVP of Brand Planning & Communications; JIM O'KEEFE, VP of Operations & Logistics; DAN CARR, Executive Director of Publishing Technology; JUSTIN F. GABRIE, Director of Publishing & Editorial Operations; SUSAN CRESPI, Editorial Operations Manager; ALEX MORALES, Publishing Operations Manager; STAN LEE, Chairman Emeritus. For information regarding advertising in Marvel Comics or on Marvel.com, please contact Ron Stern, VP of Business Development, at rstern@marvel.com. For Marvel subscription inquiries, please call 800-217-9158. **Manufactured between 2/28/2011 and 3/28/2011 (hardcover), and 2/28/2011 and 9/26/2011 (softcover), by R.R. DONNELLEY, INC., SALEM, VA, USA.**

10 9 8 7 6 5 4 3 2 1

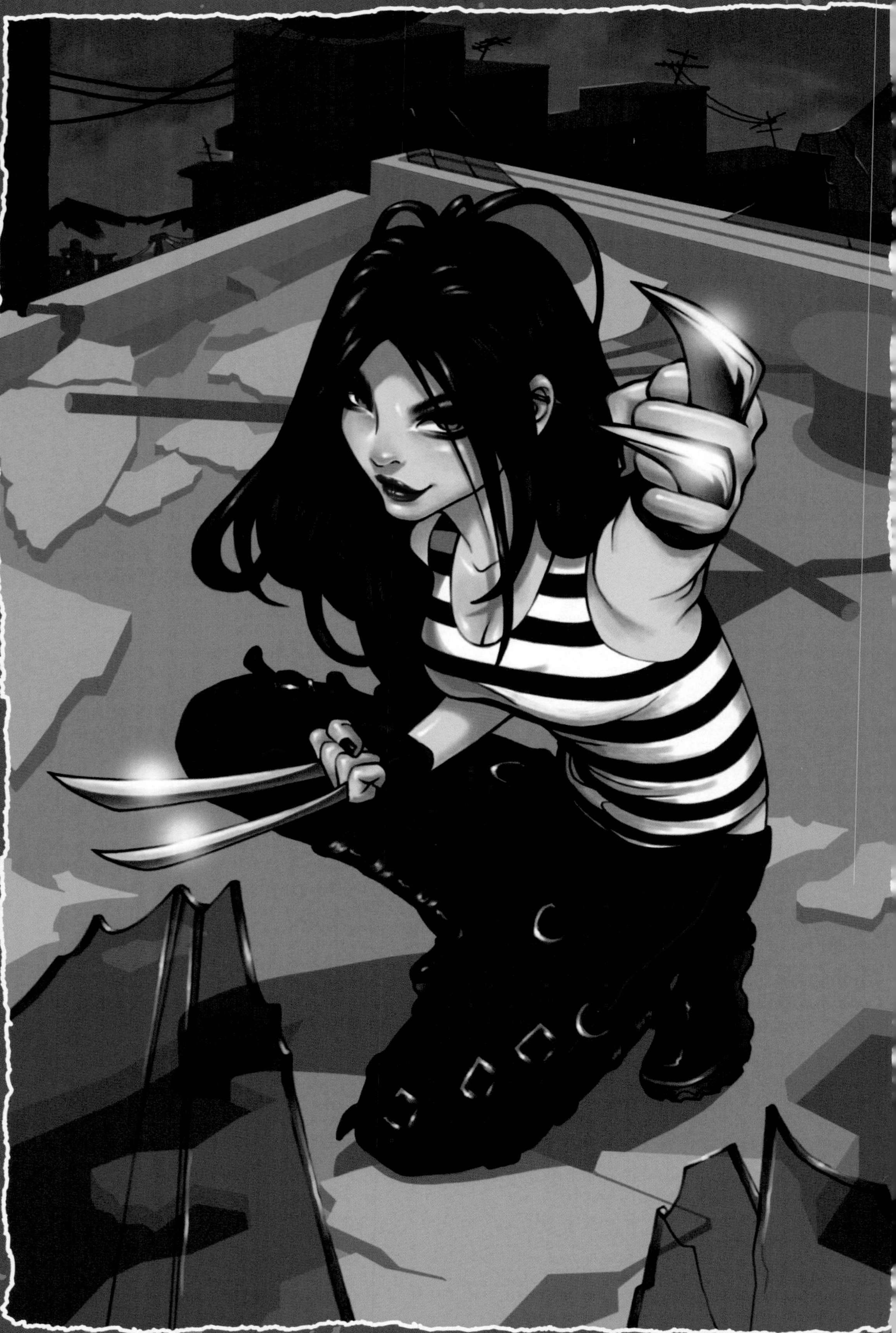

ONE

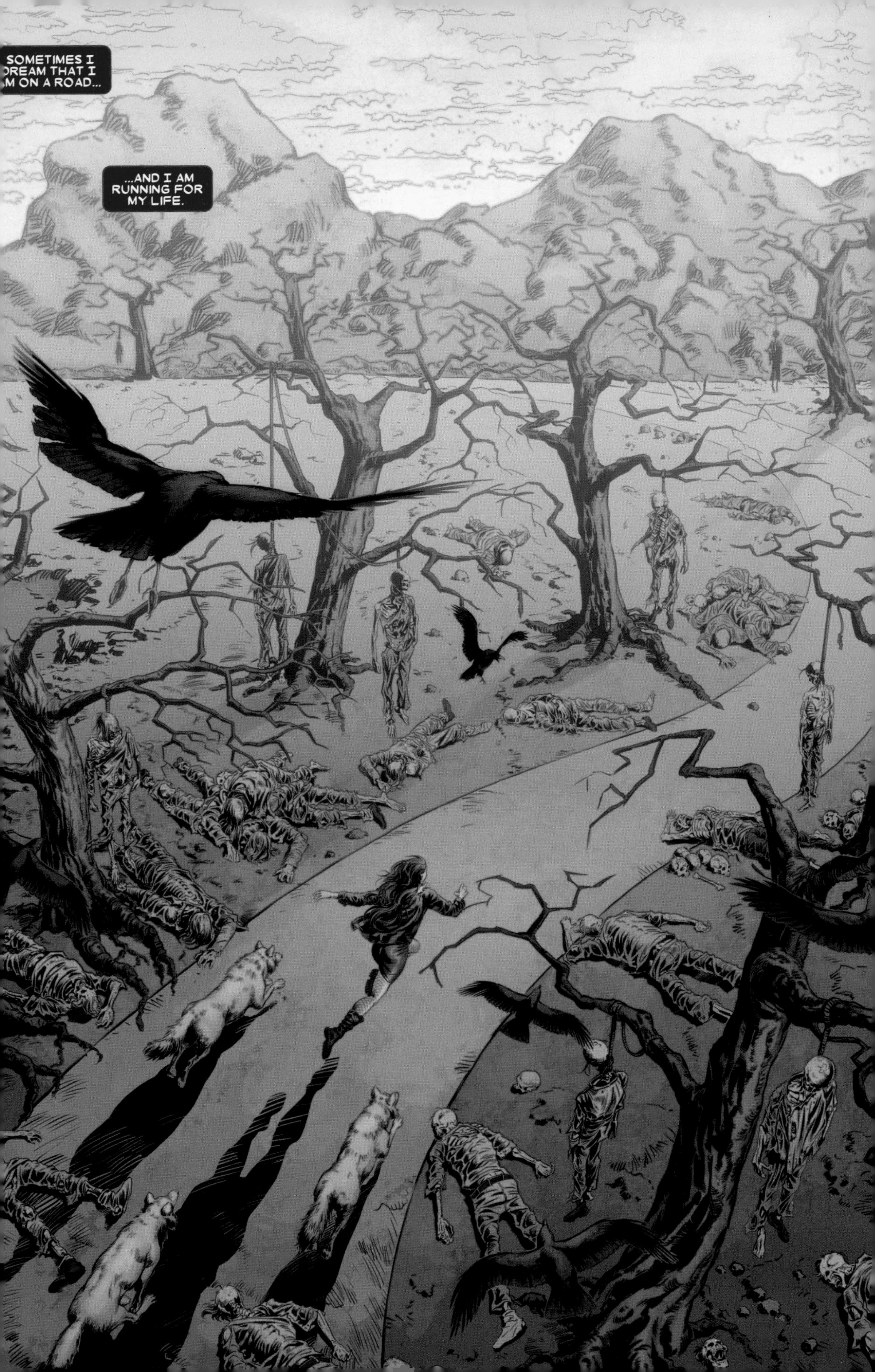
SOMETIMES I DREAM THAT I AM ON A ROAD...
...AND I AM RUNNING FOR MY LIFE.

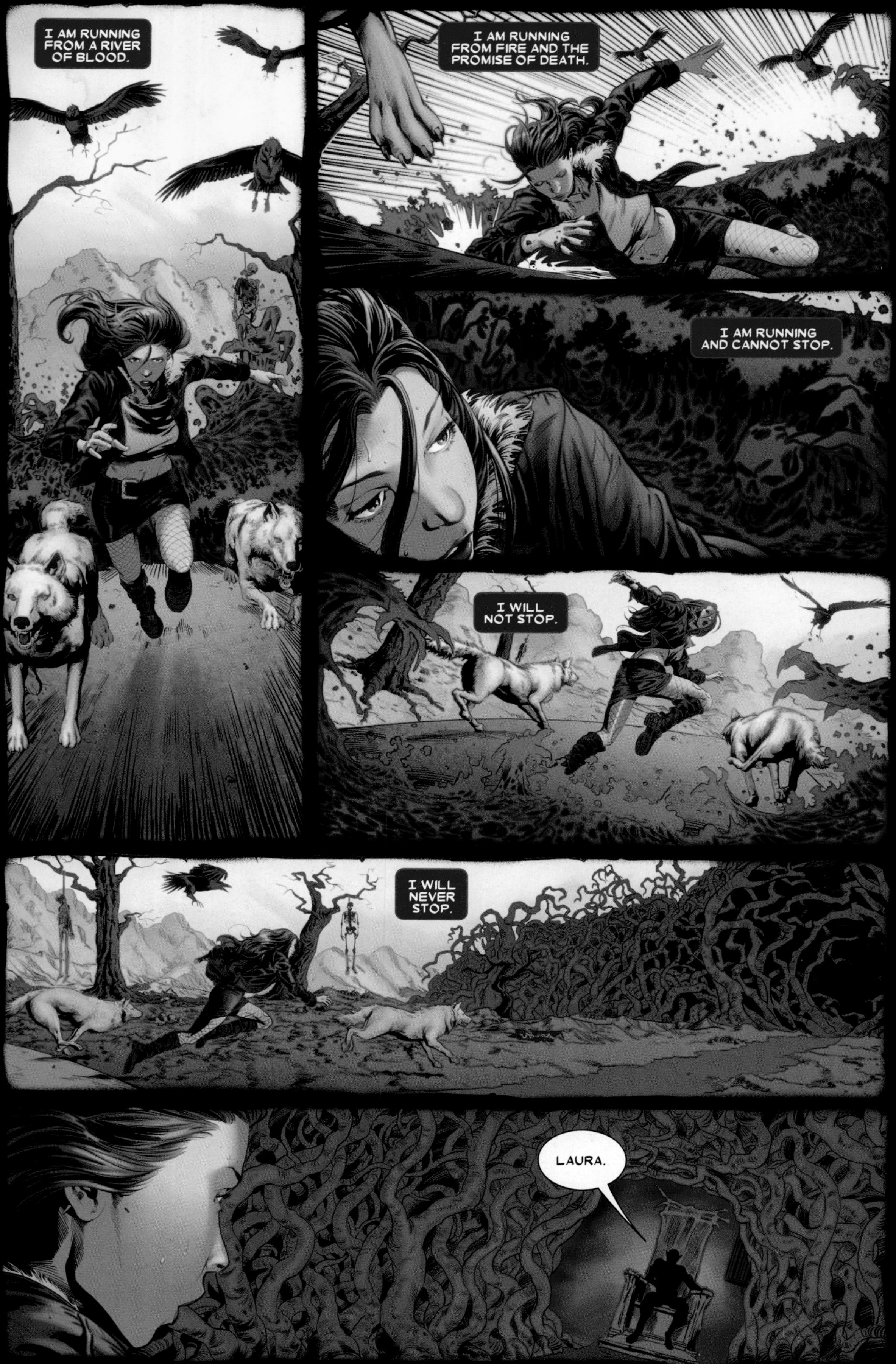
I AM RUNNING FROM A RIVER OF BLOOD.
I AM RUNNING FROM FIRE AND THE PROMISE OF DEATH.
I AM RUNNING AND CANNOT STOP.
I WILL NOT STOP.
I WILL NEVER STOP.
LAURA.

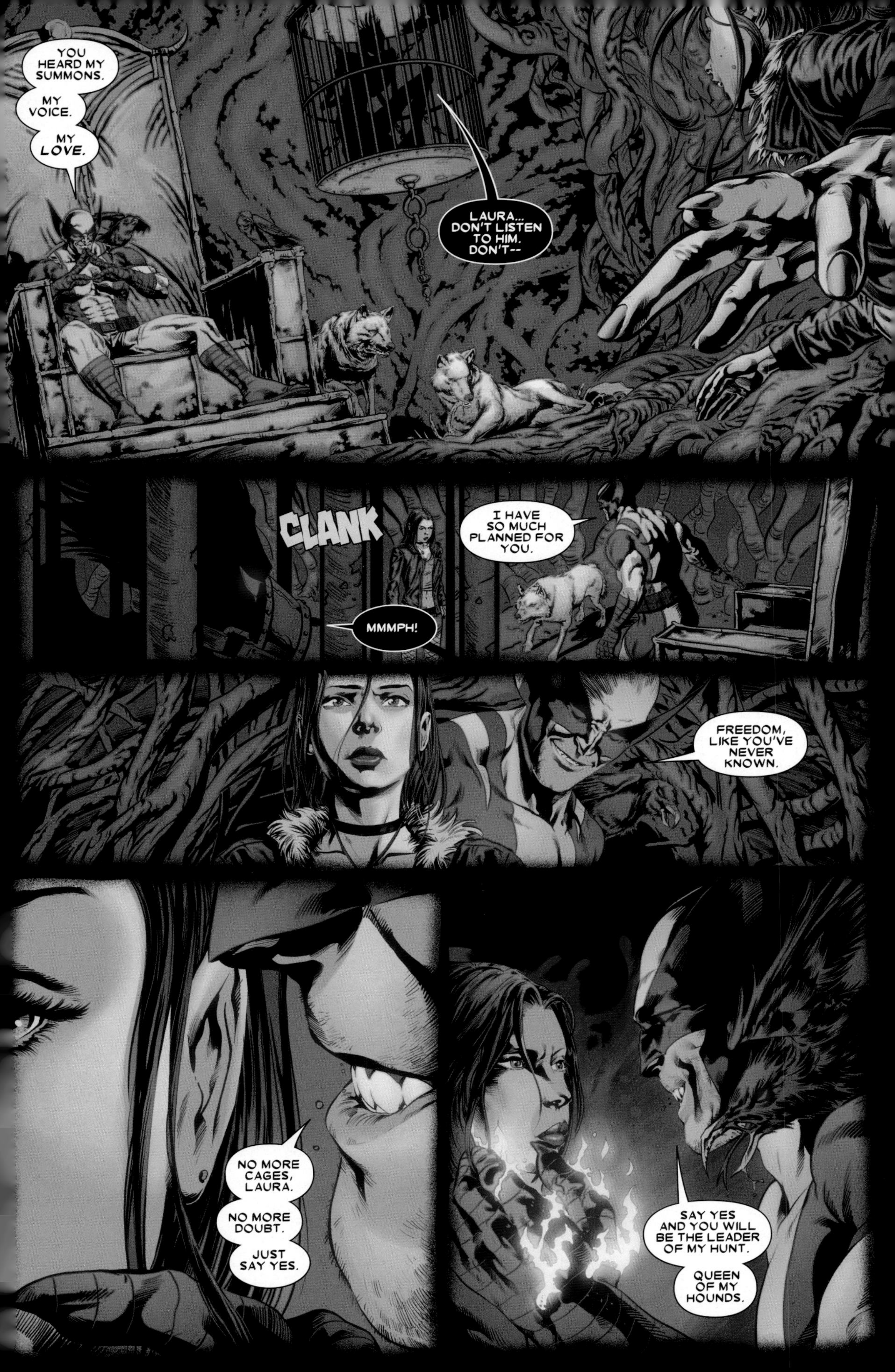

YOU HEARD MY SUMMONS.
MY VOICE.
MY LOVE.
LAURA... DON'T LISTEN TO HIM. DON'T--
CLANK
I HAVE SO MUCH PLANNED FOR YOU.
MMMPH!
FREEDOM, LIKE YOU'VE NEVER KNOWN.
NO MORE CAGES, LAURA.
NO MORE DOUBT.
JUST SAY YES.
SAY YES AND YOU WILL BE THE LEADER OF MY HUNT.
QUEEN OF MY HOUNDS.

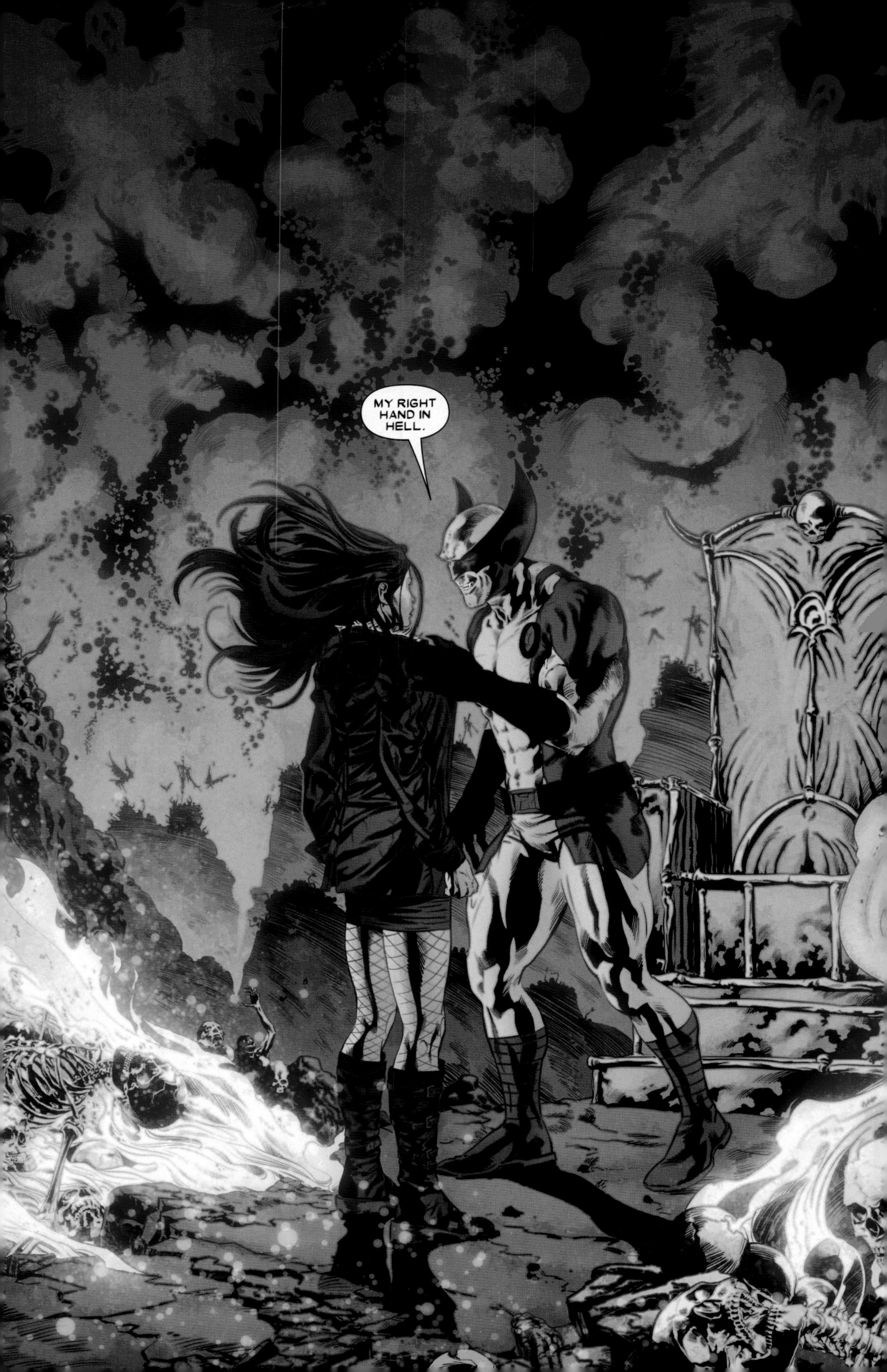
MY RIGHT HAND IN HELL.

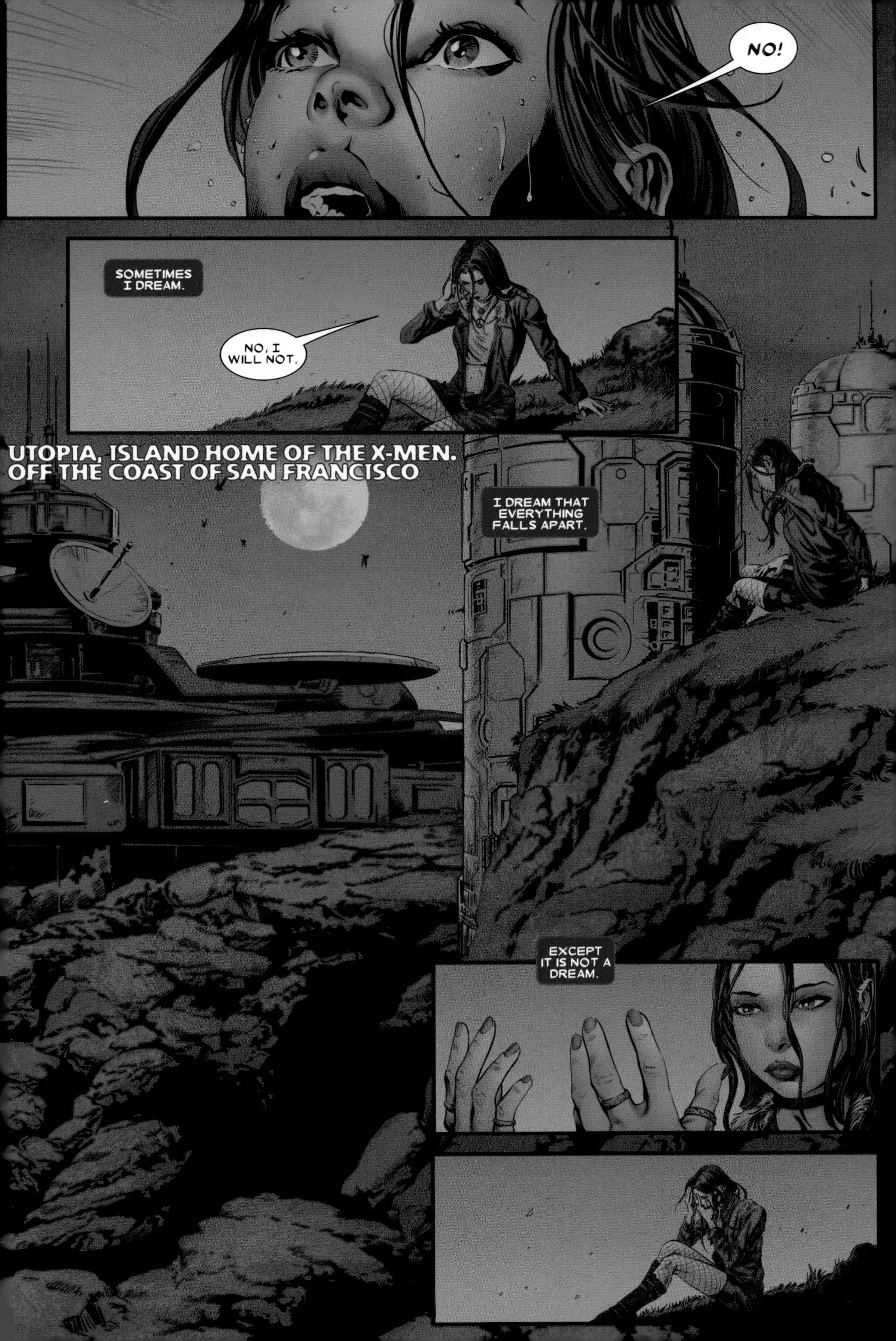
NO!
SOMETIMES I DREAM.
NO, I WILL NOT.
UTOPIA, ISLAND HOME OF THE X-MEN. OFF THE COAST OF SAN FRANCISCO
I DREAM THAT EVERYTHING FALLS APART.
EXCEPT IT IS NOT A DREAM.

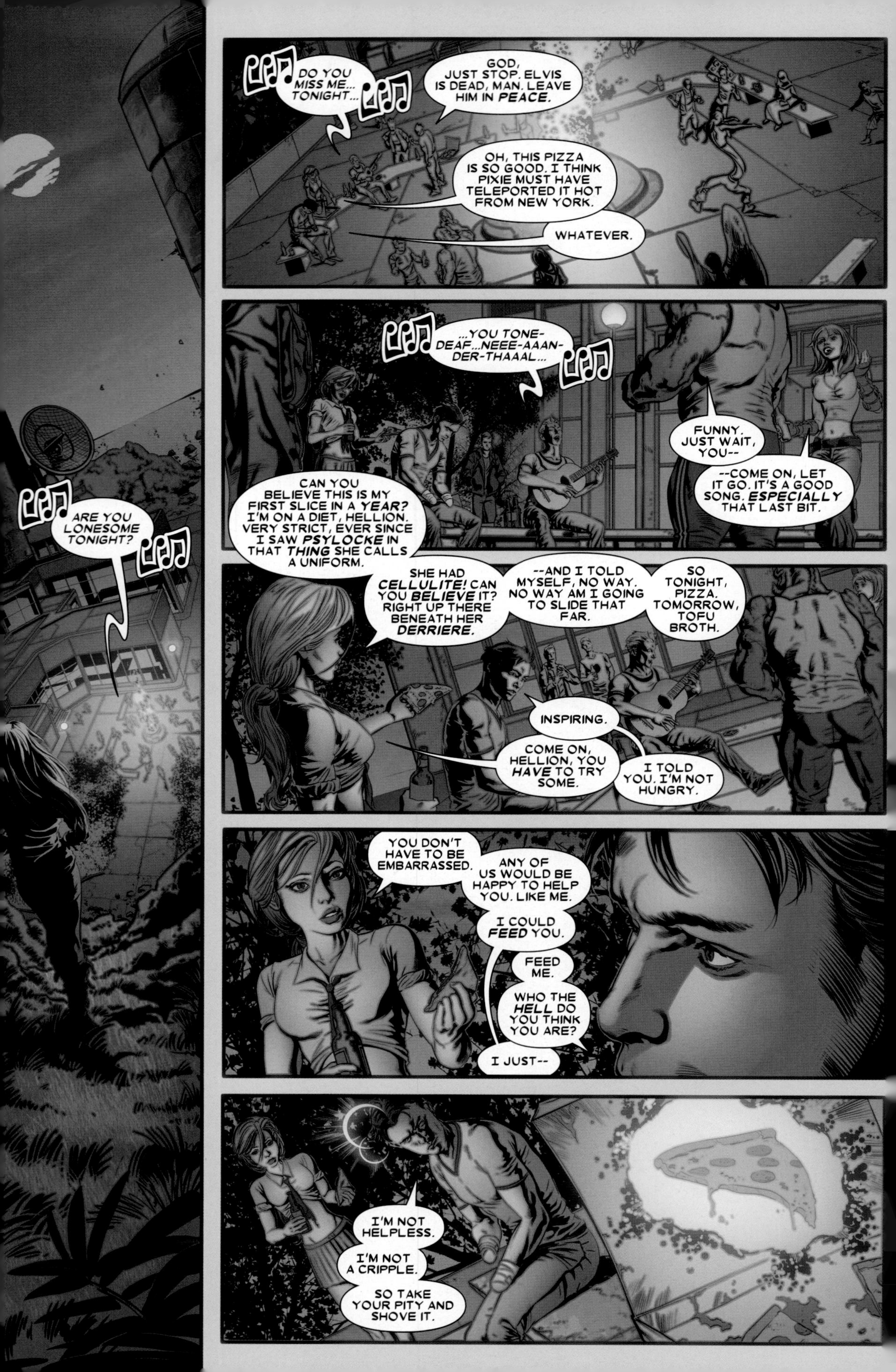
ARE YOU LONESOME TONIGHT?
DO YOU MISS ME... TONIGHT...
GOD, JUST STOP. ELVIS IS DEAD, MAN. LEAVE HIM IN PEACE.
OH, THIS PIZZA IS SO GOOD. I THINK PIXIE MUST HAVE TELEPORTED IT HOT FROM NEW YORK.
WHATEVER.
...YOU TONE-DEAF...NEEE-AAAN-DER-THAAAL...
FUNNY. JUST WAIT, YOU--
--COME ON, LET IT GO. IT'S A GOOD SONG. ESPECIALLY THAT LAST BIT.
CAN YOU BELIEVE THIS IS MY FIRST SLICE IN A YEAR? I'M ON A DIET, HELLION. VERY STRICT, EVER SINCE I SAW PSYLOCKE IN THAT THING SHE CALLS A UNIFORM.
SHE HAD CELLULITE! CAN YOU BELIEVE IT? RIGHT UP THERE BENEATH HER DERRIERE.
--AND I TOLD MYSELF, NO WAY. NO WAY AM I GOING TO SLIDE THAT FAR.
SO TONIGHT, PIZZA. TOMORROW, TOFU BROTH.
INSPIRING.
COME ON, HELLION, YOU HAVE TO TRY SOME.
I TOLD YOU. I'M NOT HUNGRY.
YOU DON'T HAVE TO BE EMBARRASSED.
ANY OF US WOULD BE HAPPY TO HELP YOU. LIKE ME.
I COULD FEED YOU.
FEED ME.
WHO THE HELL DO YOU THINK YOU ARE?
I JUST--
I'M NOT HELPLESS.
I'M NOT A CRIPPLE.
SO TAKE YOUR PITY AND SHOVE IT.

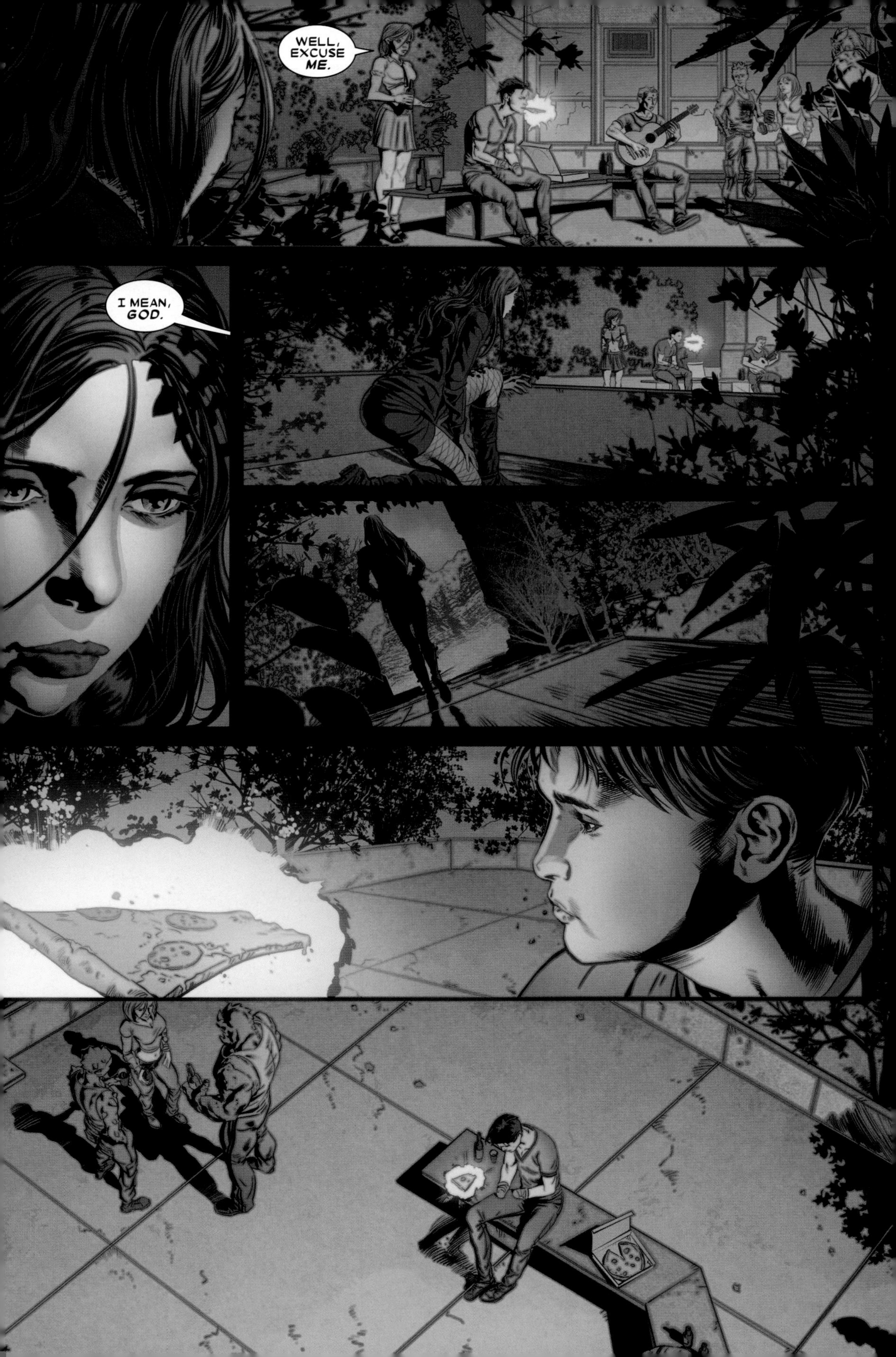

WELL, EXCUSE *ME.*
I MEAN, *GOD.*

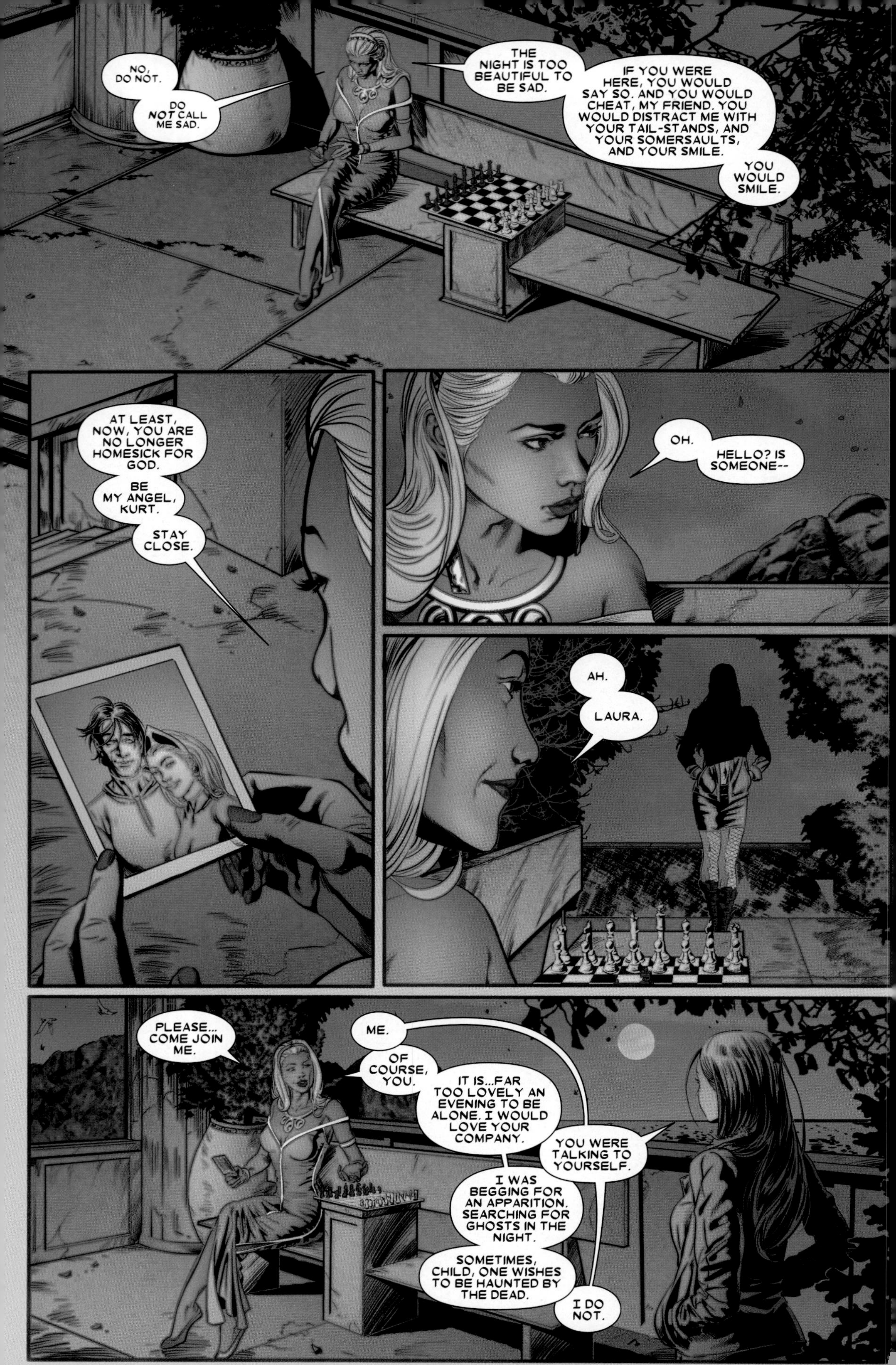
NO, DO NOT.
DO NOT CALL ME SAD.
THE NIGHT IS TOO BEAUTIFUL TO BE SAD.
IF YOU WERE HERE, YOU WOULD SAY SO. AND YOU WOULD CHEAT, MY FRIEND. YOU WOULD DISTRACT ME WITH YOUR TAIL-STANDS, AND YOUR SOMERSAULTS, AND YOUR SMILE.
YOU WOULD SMILE.
AT LEAST, NOW, YOU ARE NO LONGER HOMESICK FOR GOD.
BE MY ANGEL, KURT.
STAY CLOSE.
OH.
HELLO? IS SOMEONE--
AH.
LAURA.
PLEASE... COME JOIN ME.
ME.
OF COURSE, YOU.
IT IS...FAR TOO LOVELY AN EVENING TO BE ALONE. I WOULD LOVE YOUR COMPANY.
YOU WERE TALKING TO YOURSELF.
I WAS BEGGING FOR AN APPARITION. SEARCHING FOR GHOSTS IN THE NIGHT.
SOMETIMES, CHILD, ONE WISHES TO BE HAUNTED BY THE DEAD.
I DO NOT.

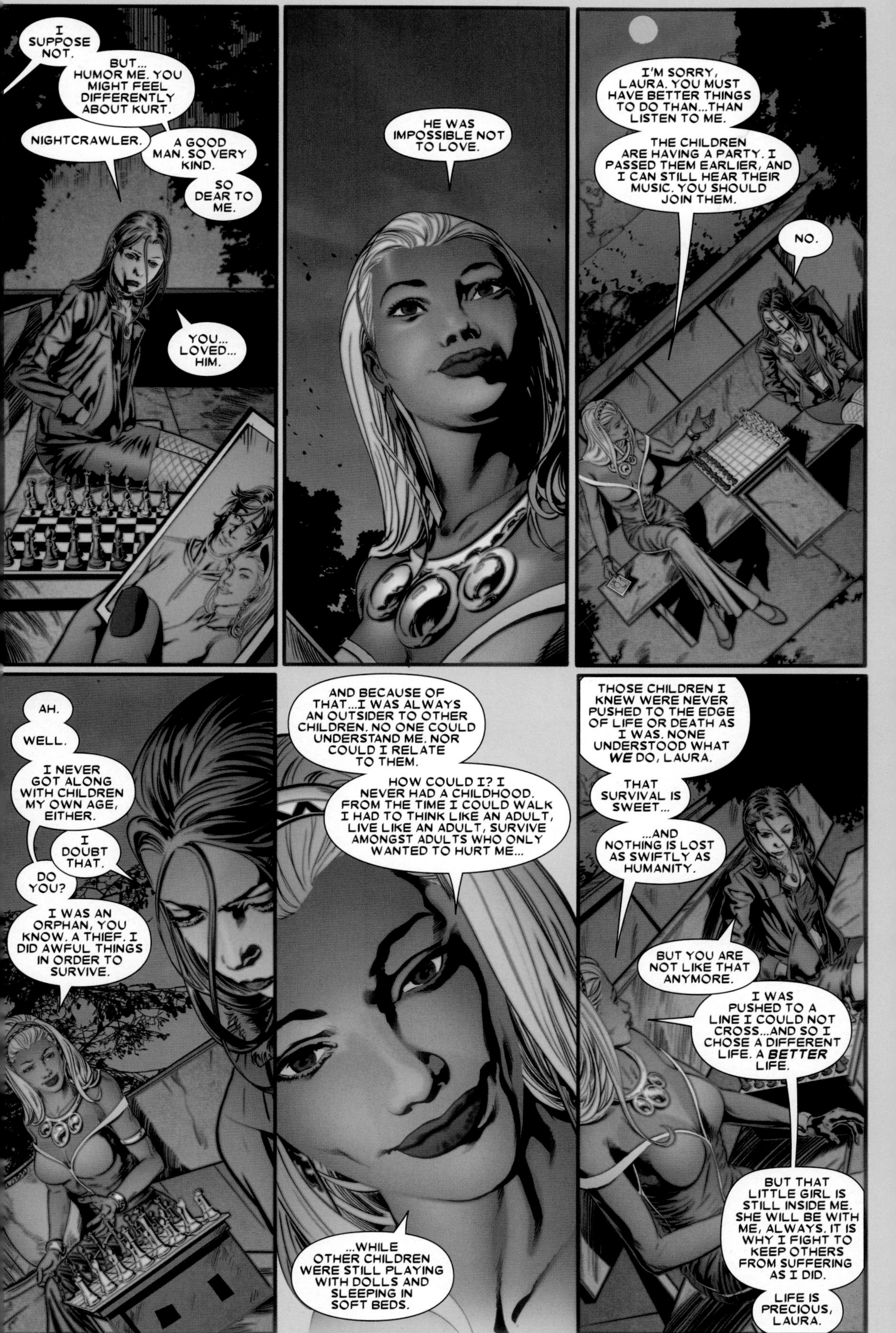
I SUPPOSE NOT.
BUT... HUMOR ME. YOU MIGHT FEEL DIFFERENTLY ABOUT KURT.
NIGHTCRAWLER.
A GOOD MAN. SO VERY KIND.
SO DEAR TO ME.
YOU... LOVED... HIM.
HE WAS IMPOSSIBLE NOT TO LOVE.
I'M SORRY, LAURA. YOU MUST HAVE BETTER THINGS TO DO THAN...THAN LISTEN TO ME.
THE CHILDREN ARE HAVING A PARTY. I PASSED THEM EARLIER, AND I CAN STILL HEAR THEIR MUSIC. YOU SHOULD JOIN THEM.
NO.
AH.
WELL.
I NEVER GOT ALONG WITH CHILDREN MY OWN AGE, EITHER.
I DOUBT THAT.
DO YOU?
I WAS AN ORPHAN, YOU KNOW. A THIEF. I DID AWFUL THINGS IN ORDER TO SURVIVE.
AND BECAUSE OF THAT...I WAS ALWAYS AN OUTSIDER TO OTHER CHILDREN. NO ONE COULD UNDERSTAND ME. NOR COULD I RELATE TO THEM.
HOW COULD I? I NEVER HAD A CHILDHOOD. FROM THE TIME I COULD WALK I HAD TO THINK LIKE AN ADULT, LIVE LIKE AN ADULT, SURVIVE AMONGST ADULTS WHO ONLY WANTED TO HURT ME...
...WHILE OTHER CHILDREN WERE STILL PLAYING WITH DOLLS AND SLEEPING IN SOFT BEDS.
THOSE CHILDREN I KNEW WERE NEVER PUSHED TO THE EDGE OF LIFE OR DEATH AS I WAS. NONE UNDERSTOOD WHAT *WE* DO, LAURA.
THAT SURVIVAL IS SWEET...
...AND NOTHING IS LOST AS SWIFTLY AS HUMANITY.
BUT YOU ARE NOT LIKE THAT ANYMORE.
I WAS PUSHED TO A LINE I COULD NOT CROSS...AND SO I CHOSE A DIFFERENT LIFE. A *BETTER* LIFE.
BUT THAT LITTLE GIRL IS STILL INSIDE ME. SHE WILL BE WITH ME, ALWAYS. IT IS WHY I FIGHT TO KEEP OTHERS FROM SUFFERING AS I DID.
LIFE IS PRECIOUS, LAURA.

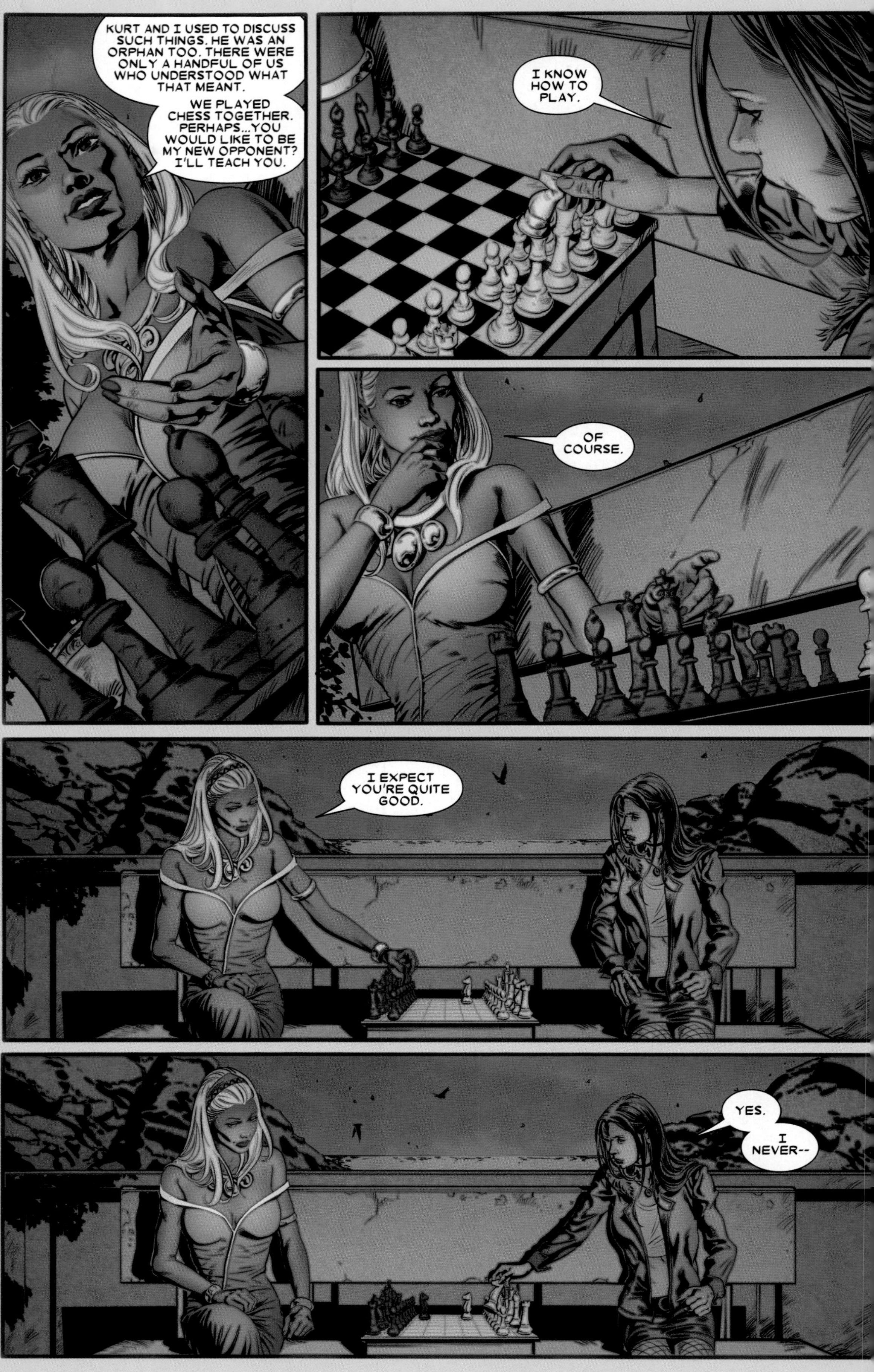
KURT AND I USED TO DISCUSS SUCH THINGS. HE WAS AN ORPHAN TOO. THERE WERE ONLY A HANDFUL OF US WHO UNDERSTOOD WHAT THAT MEANT.
WE PLAYED CHESS TOGETHER. PERHAPS...YOU WOULD LIKE TO BE MY NEW OPPONENT? I'LL TEACH YOU.
I KNOW HOW TO PLAY.
OF COURSE.
I EXPECT YOU'RE QUITE GOOD.
YES.
I NEVER--

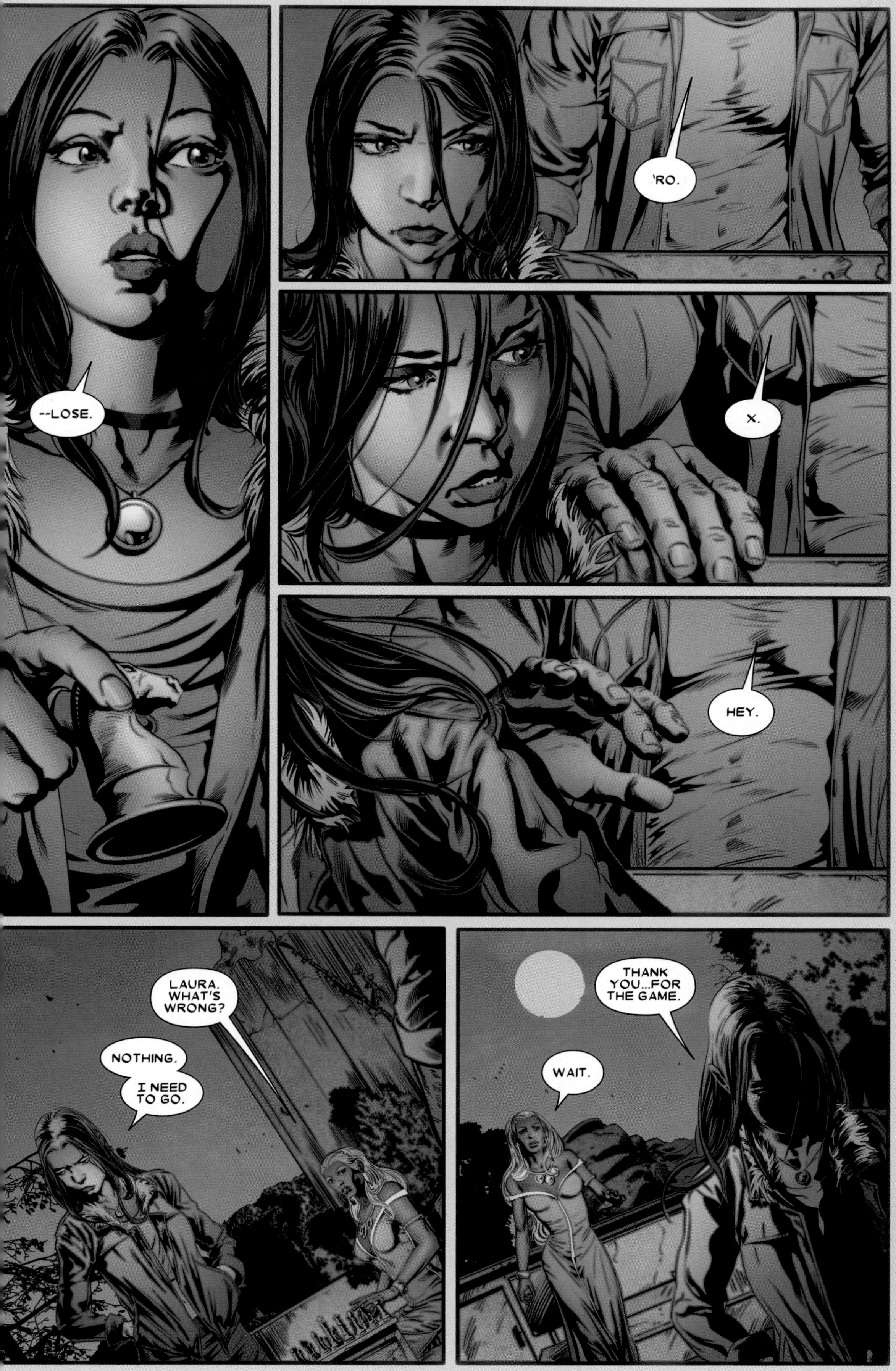
--LOSE.
'RO.
X.
HEY.
LAURA. WHAT'S WRONG?
NOTHING.
I NEED TO GO.
THANK YOU...FOR THE GAME.
WAIT.

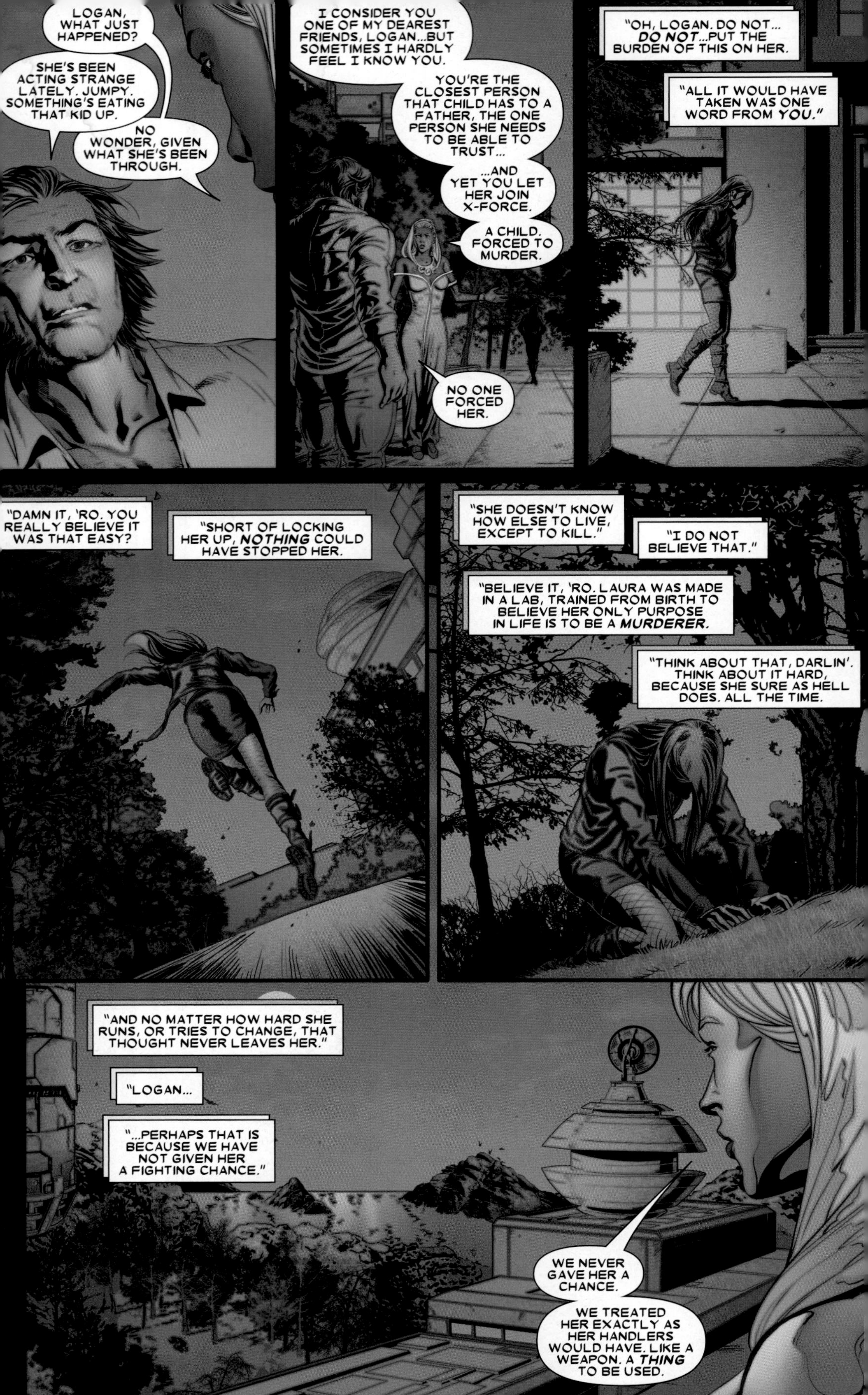
LOGAN, WHAT JUST HAPPENED?
SHE'S BEEN ACTING STRANGE LATELY. JUMPY. SOMETHING'S EATING THAT KID UP.
NO WONDER, GIVEN WHAT SHE'S BEEN THROUGH.
I CONSIDER YOU ONE OF MY DEAREST FRIENDS, LOGAN...BUT SOMETIMES I HARDLY FEEL I KNOW YOU.
YOU'RE THE CLOSEST PERSON THAT CHILD HAS TO A FATHER, THE ONE PERSON SHE NEEDS TO BE ABLE TO TRUST...
...AND YET YOU LET HER JOIN X-FORCE.
A CHILD. FORCED TO MURDER.
NO ONE FORCED HER.
"OH, LOGAN. DO NOT... *DO NOT*...PUT THE BURDEN OF THIS ON HER.
"ALL IT WOULD HAVE TAKEN WAS ONE WORD FROM *YOU.*"
"DAMN IT, 'RO. YOU REALLY BELIEVE IT WAS THAT EASY?
"SHORT OF LOCKING HER UP, *NOTHING* COULD HAVE STOPPED HER.
"SHE DOESN'T KNOW HOW ELSE TO LIVE, EXCEPT TO KILL."
"I DO NOT BELIEVE THAT."
"BELIEVE IT, 'RO. LAURA WAS MADE IN A LAB, TRAINED FROM BIRTH TO BELIEVE HER ONLY PURPOSE IN LIFE IS TO BE A *MURDERER.*
"THINK ABOUT THAT, DARLIN'. THINK ABOUT IT HARD, BECAUSE SHE SURE AS HELL DOES. ALL THE TIME.
"AND NO MATTER HOW HARD SHE RUNS, OR TRIES TO CHANGE, THAT THOUGHT NEVER LEAVES HER."
"LOGAN...
"...PERHAPS THAT IS BECAUSE WE HAVE NOT GIVEN HER A FIGHTING CHANCE."
WE NEVER GAVE HER A CHANCE.
WE TREATED HER EXACTLY AS HER HANDLERS WOULD HAVE. LIKE A WEAPON. A *THING* TO BE USED.

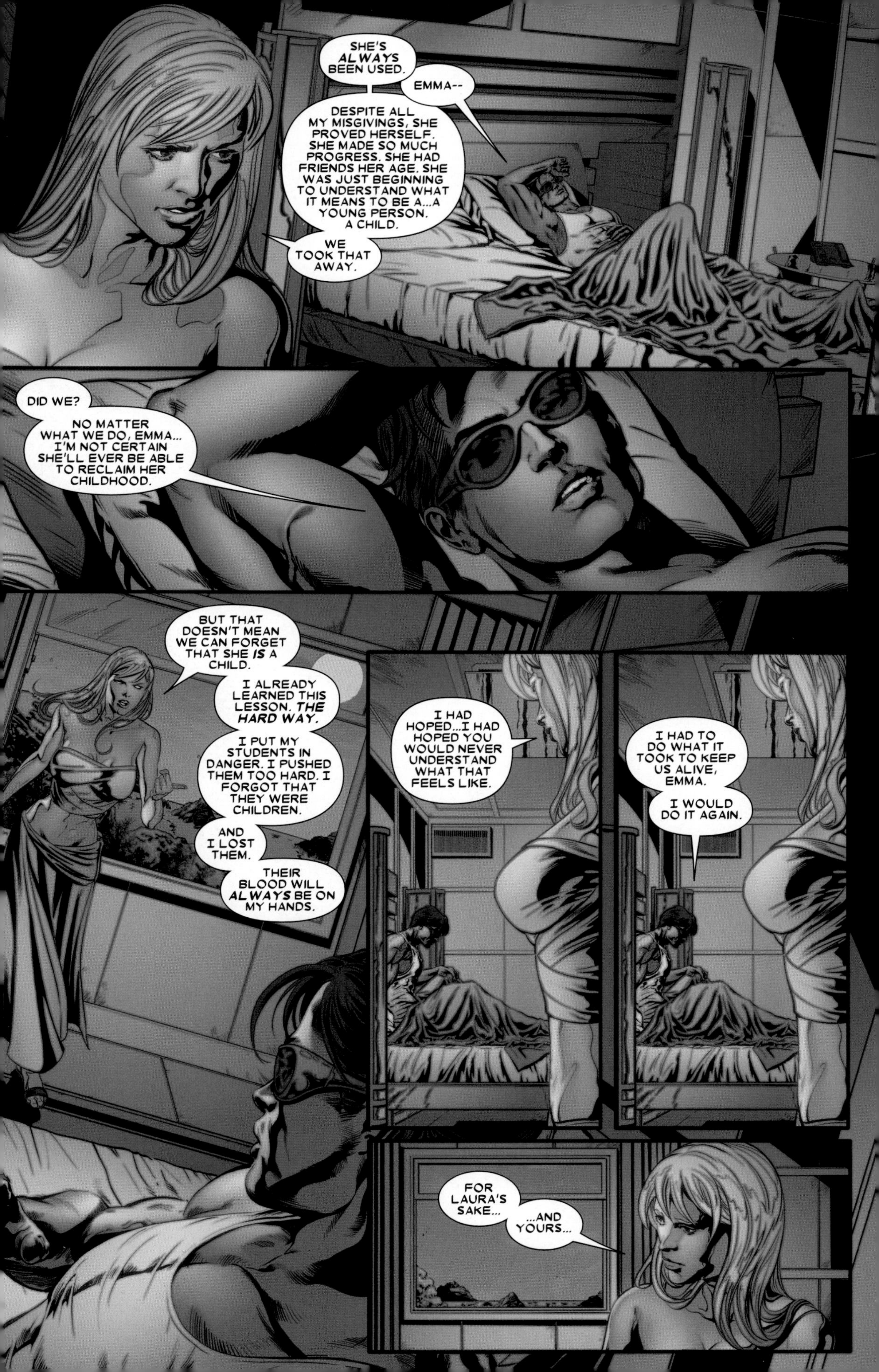

SHE'S *ALWAYS* BEEN USED.
EMMA--
DESPITE ALL MY MISGIVINGS, SHE PROVED HERSELF. SHE MADE SO MUCH PROGRESS. SHE HAD FRIENDS HER AGE. SHE WAS JUST BEGINNING TO UNDERSTAND WHAT IT MEANS TO BE A...A YOUNG PERSON. A CHILD.
WE TOOK THAT AWAY.
DID WE?
NO MATTER WHAT WE DO, EMMA... I'M NOT CERTAIN SHE'LL EVER BE ABLE TO RECLAIM HER CHILDHOOD.
BUT THAT DOESN'T MEAN WE CAN FORGET THAT SHE *IS* A CHILD.
I ALREADY LEARNED THIS LESSON. *THE HARD WAY.*
I PUT MY STUDENTS IN DANGER. I PUSHED THEM TOO HARD. I FORGOT THAT THEY WERE CHILDREN.
AND I LOST THEM.
THEIR BLOOD WILL *ALWAYS* BE ON MY HANDS.
I HAD HOPED...I HAD HOPED YOU WOULD NEVER UNDERSTAND WHAT THAT FEELS LIKE.
I HAD TO DO WHAT IT TOOK TO KEEP US ALIVE, EMMA.
I WOULD DO IT AGAIN.
FOR LAURA'S SAKE...
...AND YOURS...

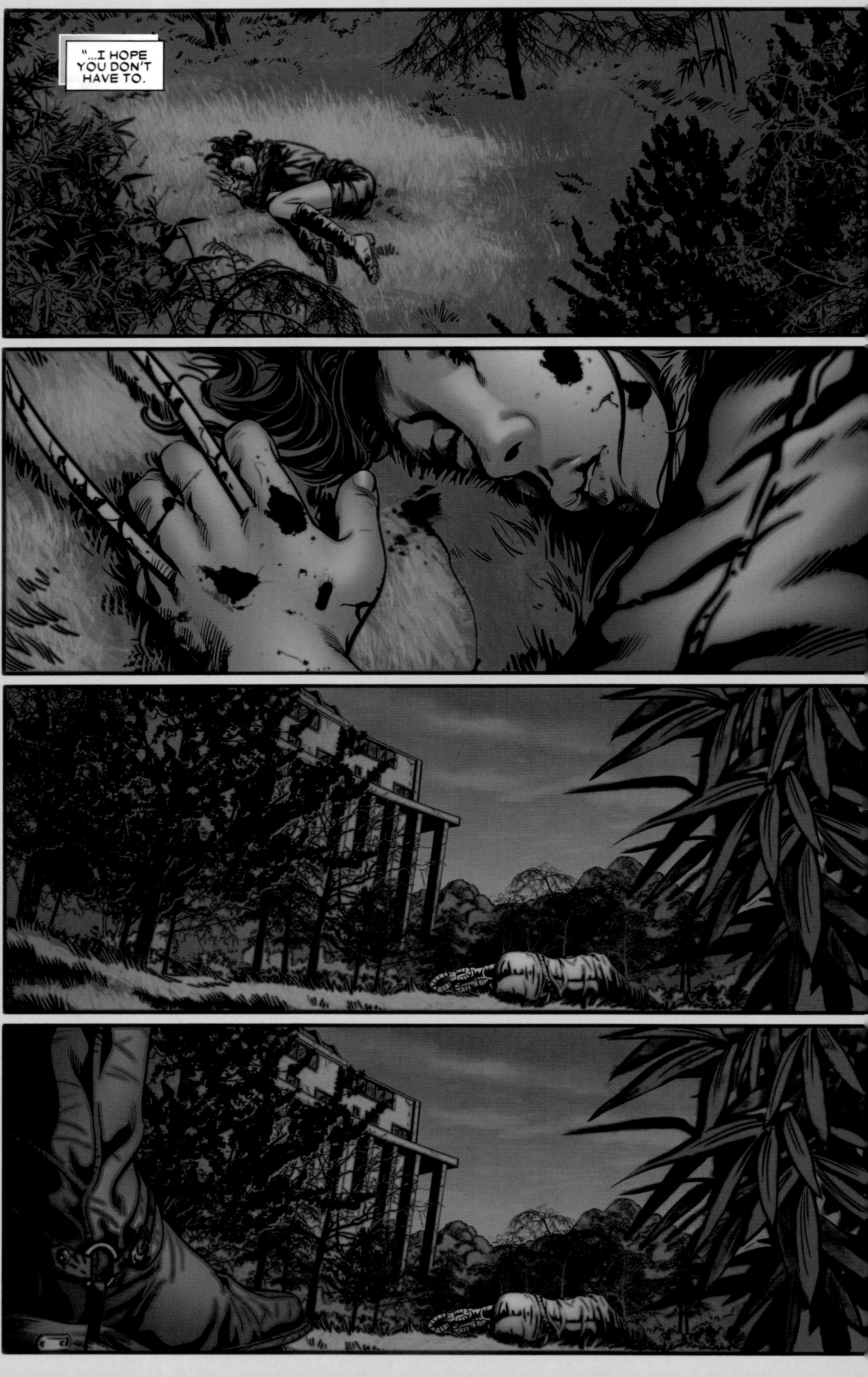
"...I HOPE YOU DON'T HAVE TO.

NEXT DAY.

OH, JEEZ. MY HEAD.

DON'T, ANOLE. DON'T START. I'M ON MY FOURTH ASPIRIN ALREADY.

OH, GOD. IT'S TOO BRIGHT OUT. I THINK I'M GOING TO DIE.

CLEAN LIVING, MY FRIENDS. I FEEL DELIGHTFUL THIS MORNING.

YOU WOULD.

HEY, HELLION. GUESS WHAT I HEARD THIS MORNING ABOUT YOUR *CRAZY GIRLFRIEND.*

MY CRAZY--

OH. DON'T CALL HER THAT.

YOUR GIRLFRIEND, OR CRAZY?

WHAT DID YOU HEAR?

THAT SHE DOESN'T SLEEP IN HER ROOM ANYMORE, SHE'S ALWAYS OUTSIDE INSTEAD.

STOP IT.

SPEAKING OF THE DEVIL...

HI.

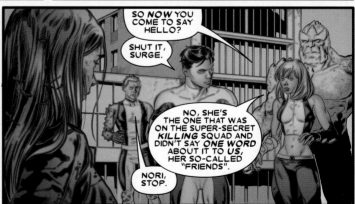

SO *NOW* YOU COME TO SAY HELLO?

SHUT IT, SURGE.

NO, SHE'S THE ONE THAT WAS ON THE SUPER-SECRET *KILLING* SQUAD AND DIDN'T SAY *ONE WORD* ABOUT IT TO *US,* HER SO-CALLED "FRIENDS".

NORI, STOP.

HEY.

HEY.

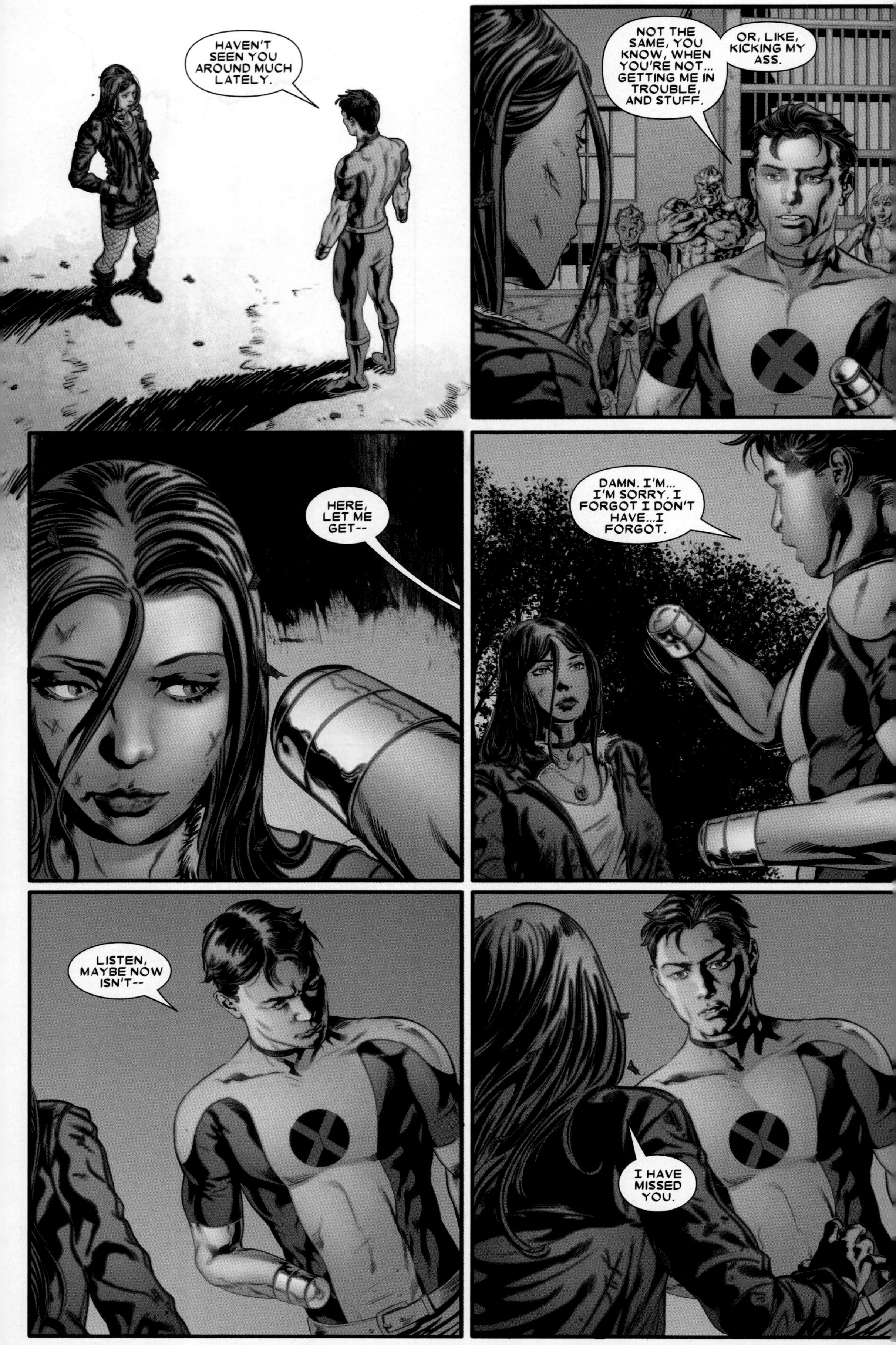
HAVEN'T SEEN YOU AROUND MUCH LATELY.
NOT THE SAME, YOU KNOW, WHEN YOU'RE NOT... GETTING ME IN TROUBLE, AND STUFF.
OR, LIKE, KICKING MY ASS.
HERE, LET ME GET--
DAMN. I'M... I'M SORRY. I FORGOT I DON'T HAVE...I FORGOT.
LISTEN, MAYBE NOW ISN'T--
I HAVE MISSED YOU.

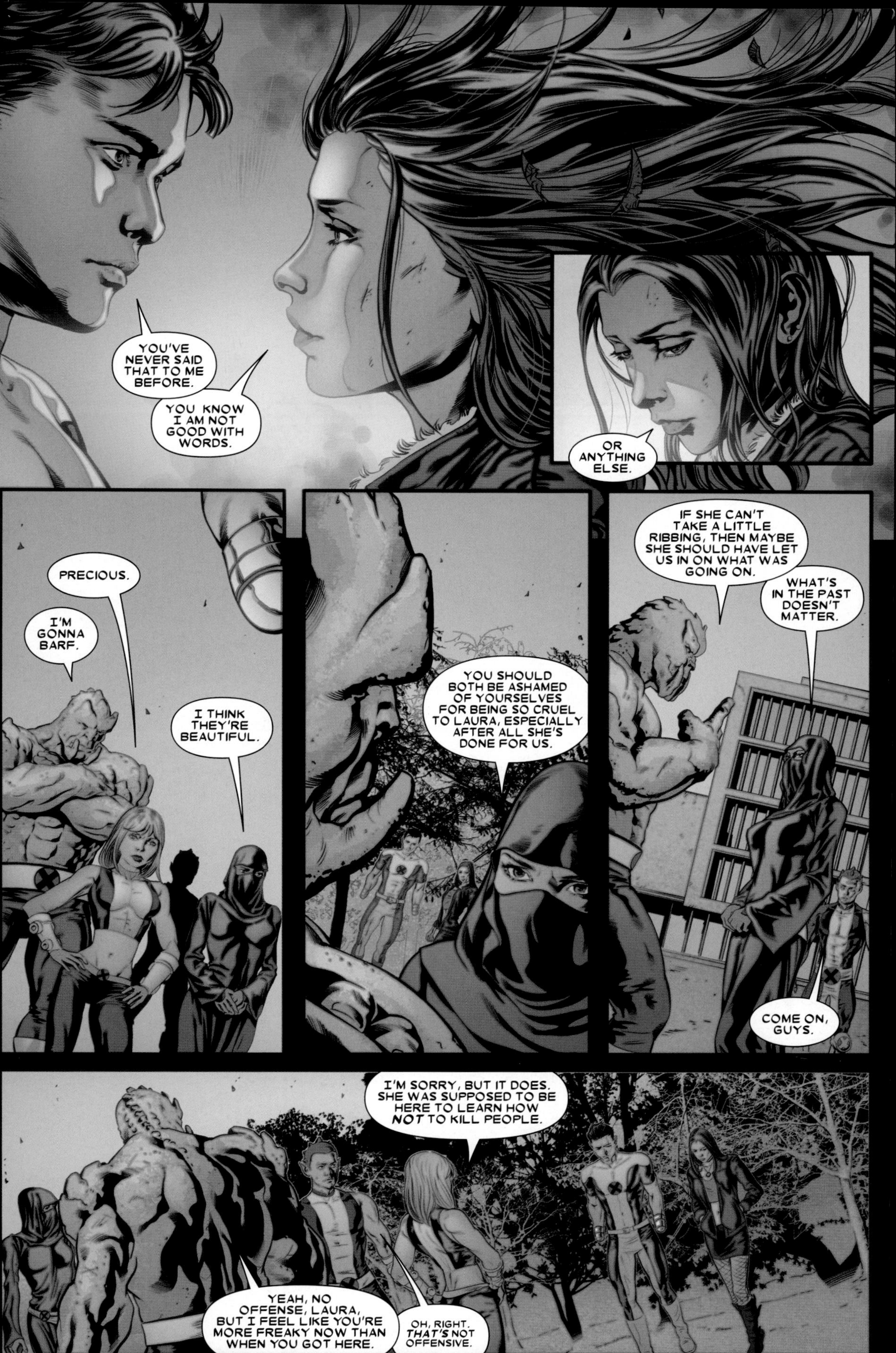
YOU'VE NEVER SAID THAT TO ME BEFORE.
YOU KNOW I AM NOT GOOD WITH WORDS.
OR ANYTHING ELSE.
I'M GONNA BARF.
PRECIOUS.
I THINK THEY'RE BEAUTIFUL.
YOU SHOULD BOTH BE ASHAMED OF YOURSELVES FOR BEING SO CRUEL TO LAURA, ESPECIALLY AFTER ALL SHE'S DONE FOR US.
IF SHE CAN'T TAKE A LITTLE RIBBING, THEN MAYBE SHE SHOULD HAVE LET US IN ON WHAT WAS GOING ON.
WHAT'S IN THE PAST DOESN'T MATTER.
COME ON, GUYS.
I'M SORRY, BUT IT DOES. SHE WAS SUPPOSED TO BE HERE TO LEARN HOW NOT TO KILL PEOPLE.
YEAH, NO OFFENSE, LAURA, BUT I FEEL LIKE YOU'RE MORE FREAKY NOW THAN WHEN YOU GOT HERE.
OH, RIGHT. THAT'S NOT OFFENSIVE.

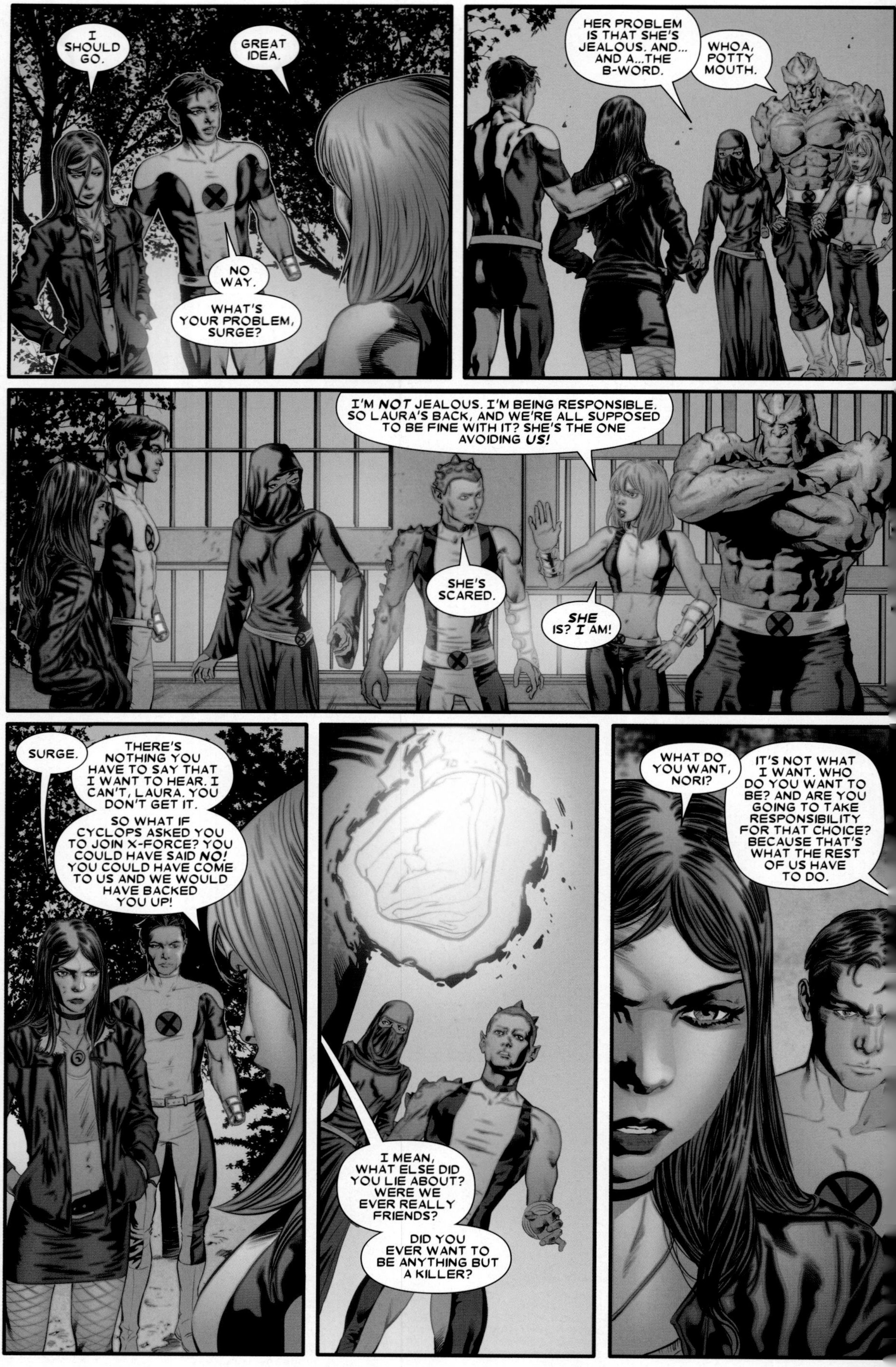
I SHOULD GO.
GREAT IDEA.
NO WAY.
WHAT'S YOUR PROBLEM, SURGE?
HER PROBLEM IS THAT SHE'S JEALOUS. AND... AND A...THE B-WORD.
WHOA, POTTY MOUTH.
I'M NOT JEALOUS. I'M BEING RESPONSIBLE. SO LAURA'S BACK, AND WE'RE ALL SUPPOSED TO BE FINE WITH IT? SHE'S THE ONE AVOIDING US!
SHE'S SCARED.
SHE IS? I AM!
SURGE.
THERE'S NOTHING YOU HAVE TO SAY THAT I WANT TO HEAR. I CAN'T, LAURA. YOU DON'T GET IT.
SO WHAT IF CYCLOPS ASKED YOU TO JOIN X-FORCE? YOU COULD HAVE SAID NO! YOU COULD HAVE COME TO US AND WE WOULD HAVE BACKED YOU UP!
I MEAN, WHAT ELSE DID YOU LIE ABOUT? WERE WE EVER REALLY FRIENDS?
DID YOU EVER WANT TO BE ANYTHING BUT A KILLER?
WHAT DO YOU WANT, NORI?
IT'S NOT WHAT I WANT. WHO DO YOU WANT TO BE? AND ARE YOU GOING TO TAKE RESPONSIBILITY FOR THAT CHOICE? BECAUSE THAT'S WHAT THE REST OF US HAVE TO DO.

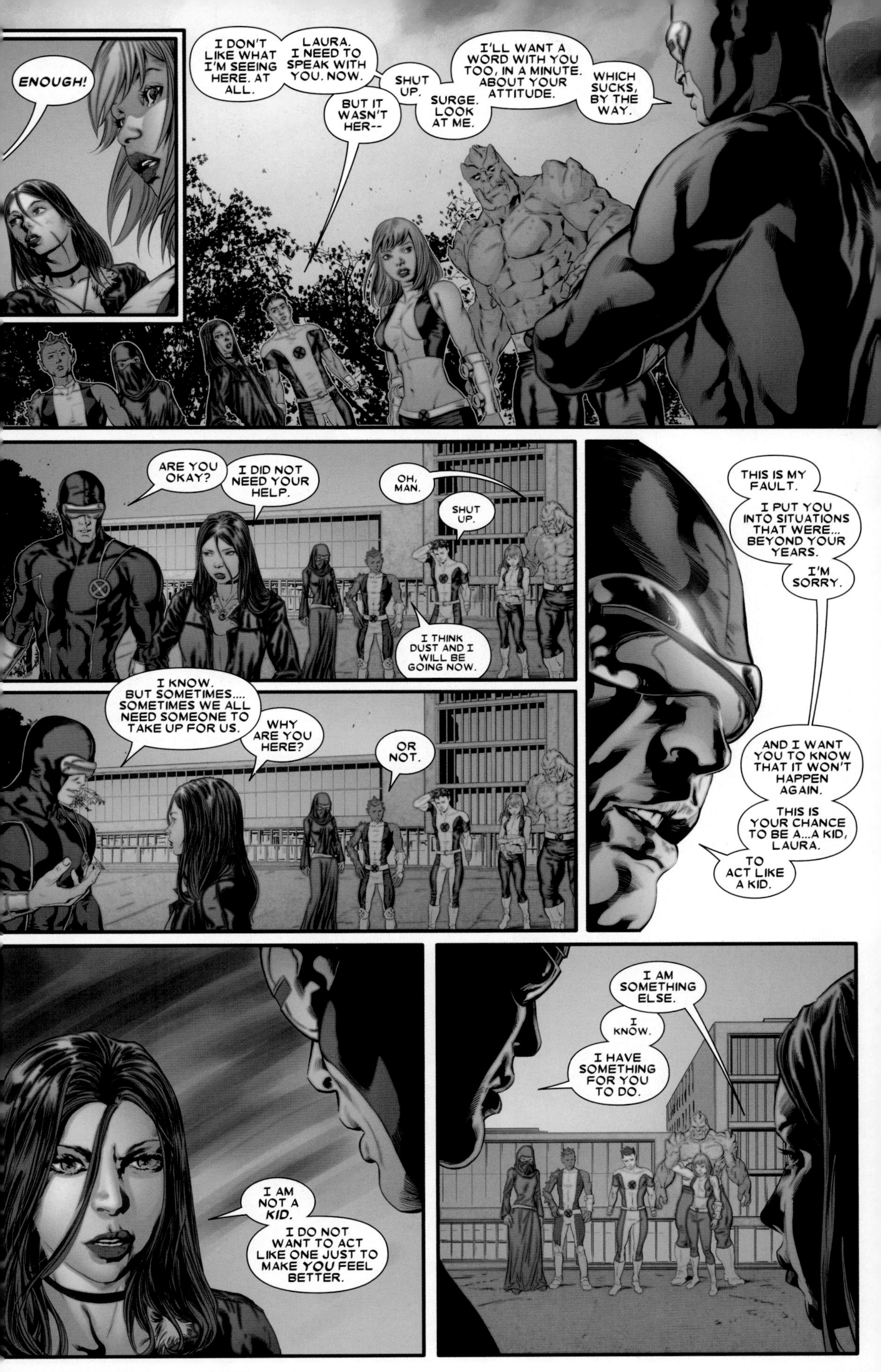

ENOUGH!
I DON'T LIKE WHAT I'M SEEING HERE. AT ALL.
LAURA. I NEED TO SPEAK WITH YOU. NOW.
BUT IT WASN'T HER--
SHUT UP.
SURGE. LOOK AT ME.
I'LL WANT A WORD WITH YOU TOO, IN A MINUTE. ABOUT YOUR ATTITUDE.
WHICH SUCKS, BY THE WAY.
ARE YOU OKAY?
I DID NOT NEED YOUR HELP.
OH, MAN.
SHUT UP.
I THINK DUST AND I WILL BE GOING NOW.
I KNOW. BUT SOMETIMES.... SOMETIMES WE ALL NEED SOMEONE TO TAKE UP FOR US.
WHY ARE YOU HERE?
OR NOT.
THIS IS MY FAULT.
I PUT YOU INTO SITUATIONS THAT WERE... BEYOND YOUR YEARS.
I'M SORRY.
AND I WANT YOU TO KNOW THAT IT WON'T HAPPEN AGAIN.
THIS IS YOUR CHANCE TO BE A...A KID, LAURA.
TO ACT LIKE A KID.
I AM NOT A KID.
I DO NOT WANT TO ACT LIKE ONE JUST TO MAKE YOU FEEL BETTER.
I AM SOMETHING ELSE.
I KNOW.
I HAVE SOMETHING FOR YOU TO DO.

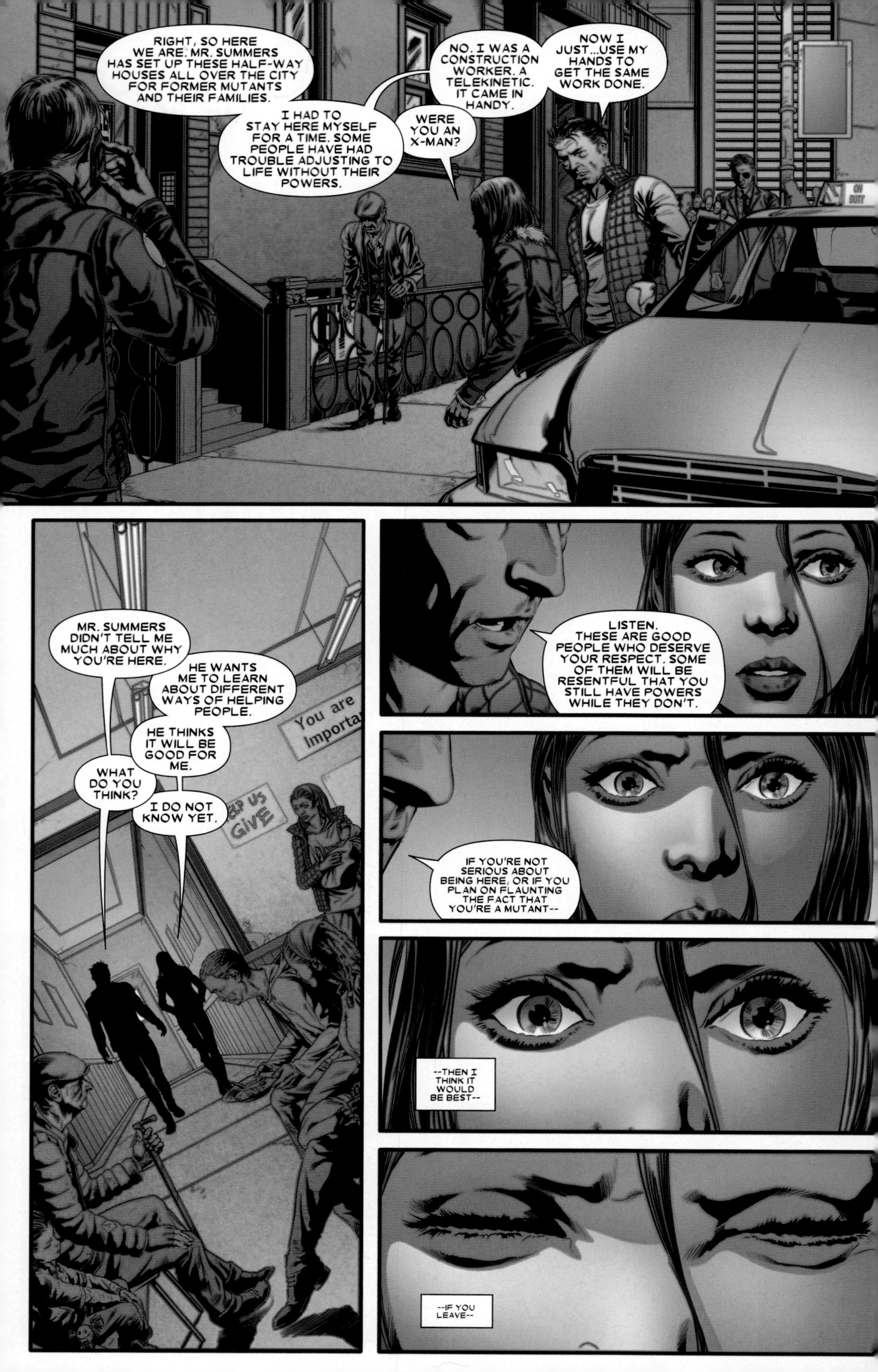

RIGHT, SO HERE WE ARE. MR. SUMMERS HAS SET UP THESE HALF-WAY HOUSES ALL OVER THE CITY FOR FORMER MUTANTS AND THEIR FAMILIES.
I HAD TO STAY HERE MYSELF FOR A TIME. SOME PEOPLE HAVE HAD TROUBLE ADJUSTING TO LIFE WITHOUT THEIR POWERS.
WERE YOU AN X-MAN?
NO. I WAS A CONSTRUCTION WORKER. A TELEKINETIC. IT CAME IN HANDY.
NOW I JUST...USE MY HANDS TO GET THE SAME WORK DONE.
ON DUTY
MR. SUMMERS DIDN'T TELL ME MUCH ABOUT WHY YOU'RE HERE.
HE WANTS ME TO LEARN ABOUT DIFFERENT WAYS OF HELPING PEOPLE.
HE THINKS IT WILL BE GOOD FOR ME.
WHAT DO YOU THINK?
I DO NOT KNOW YET.
You are Importa
GIVE
LISTEN. THESE ARE GOOD PEOPLE WHO DESERVE YOUR RESPECT. SOME OF THEM WILL BE RESENTFUL THAT YOU STILL HAVE POWERS WHILE THEY DON'T.
IF YOU'RE NOT SERIOUS ABOUT BEING HERE, OR IF YOU PLAN ON FLAUNTING THE FACT THAT YOU'RE A MUTANT--
--THEN I THINK IT WOULD BE BEST--
--IF YOU LEAVE--

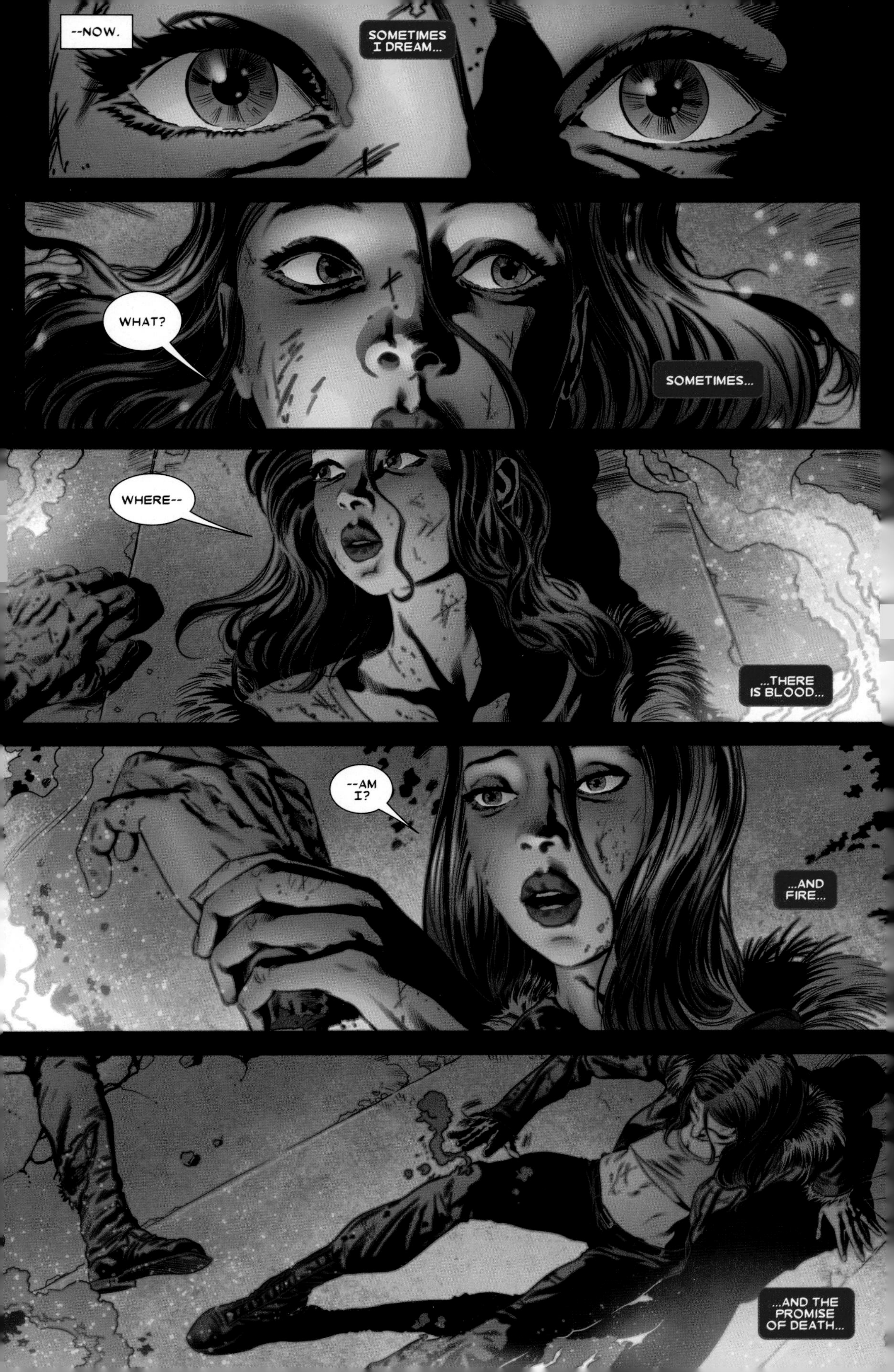
--NOW.
SOMETIMES I DREAM...
WHAT?
SOMETIMES...
WHERE--
...THERE IS BLOOD...
--AM I?
...AND FIRE...
...AND THE PROMISE OF DEATH...

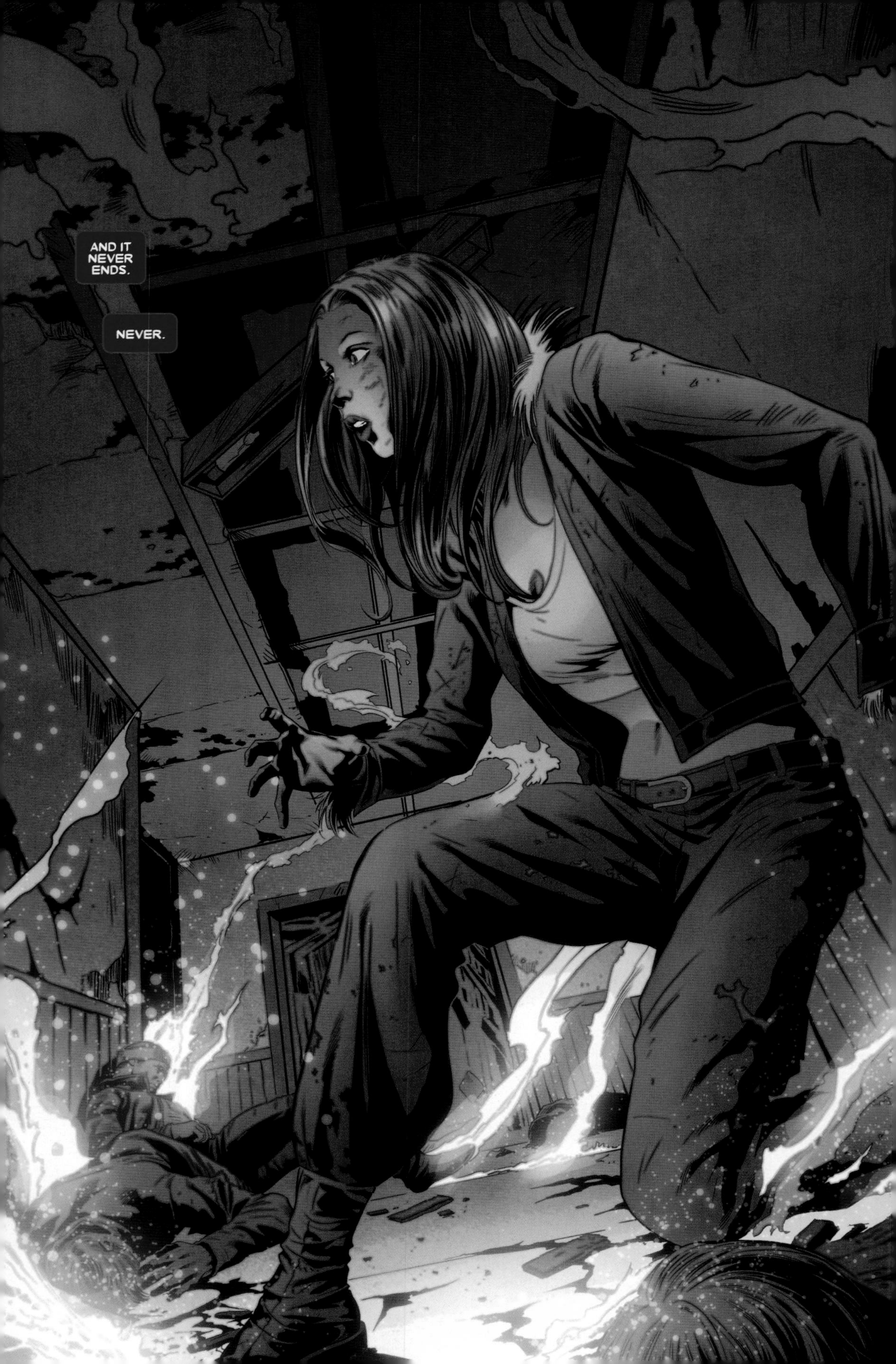
AND IT NEVER ENDS.
NEVER.

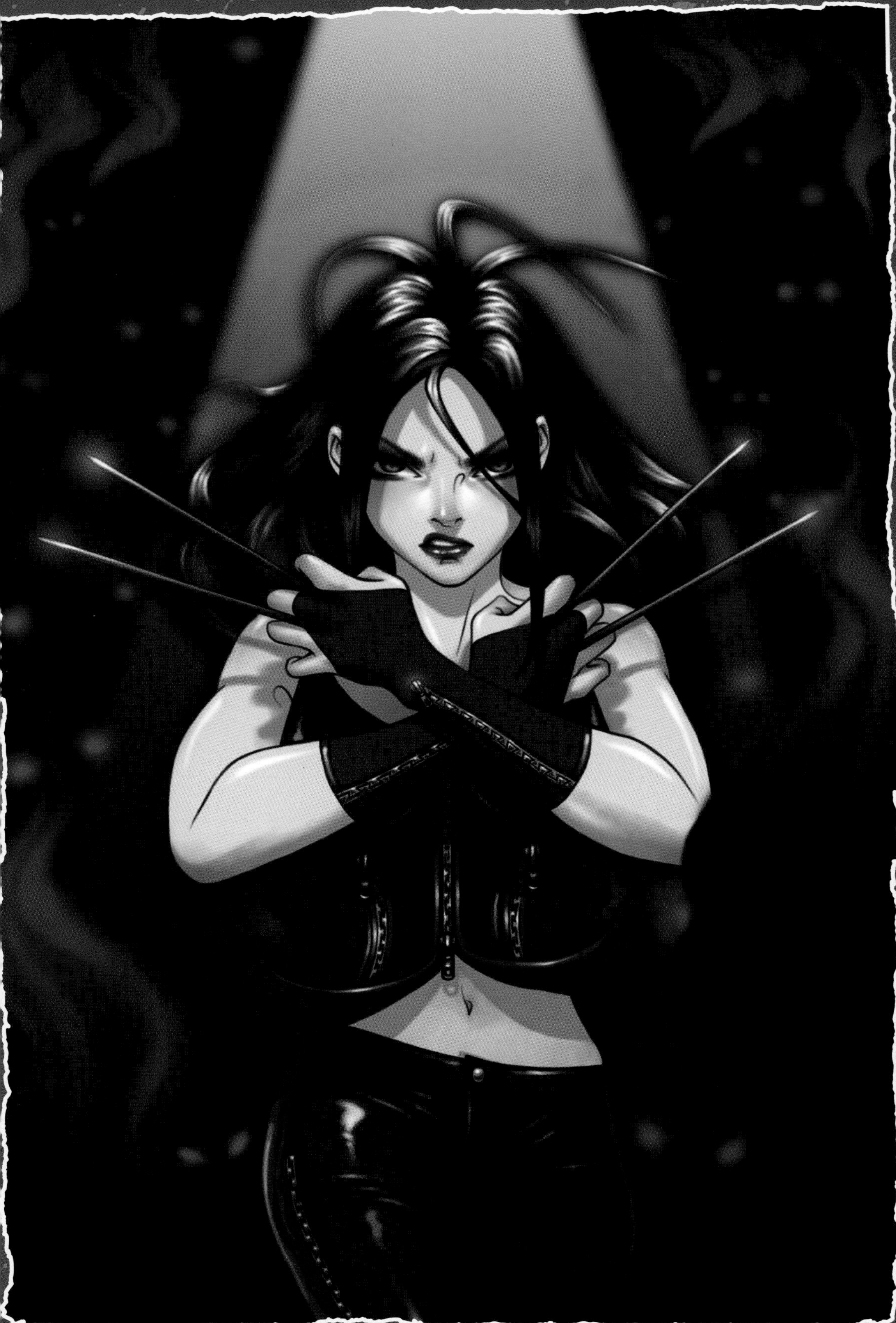

TWO

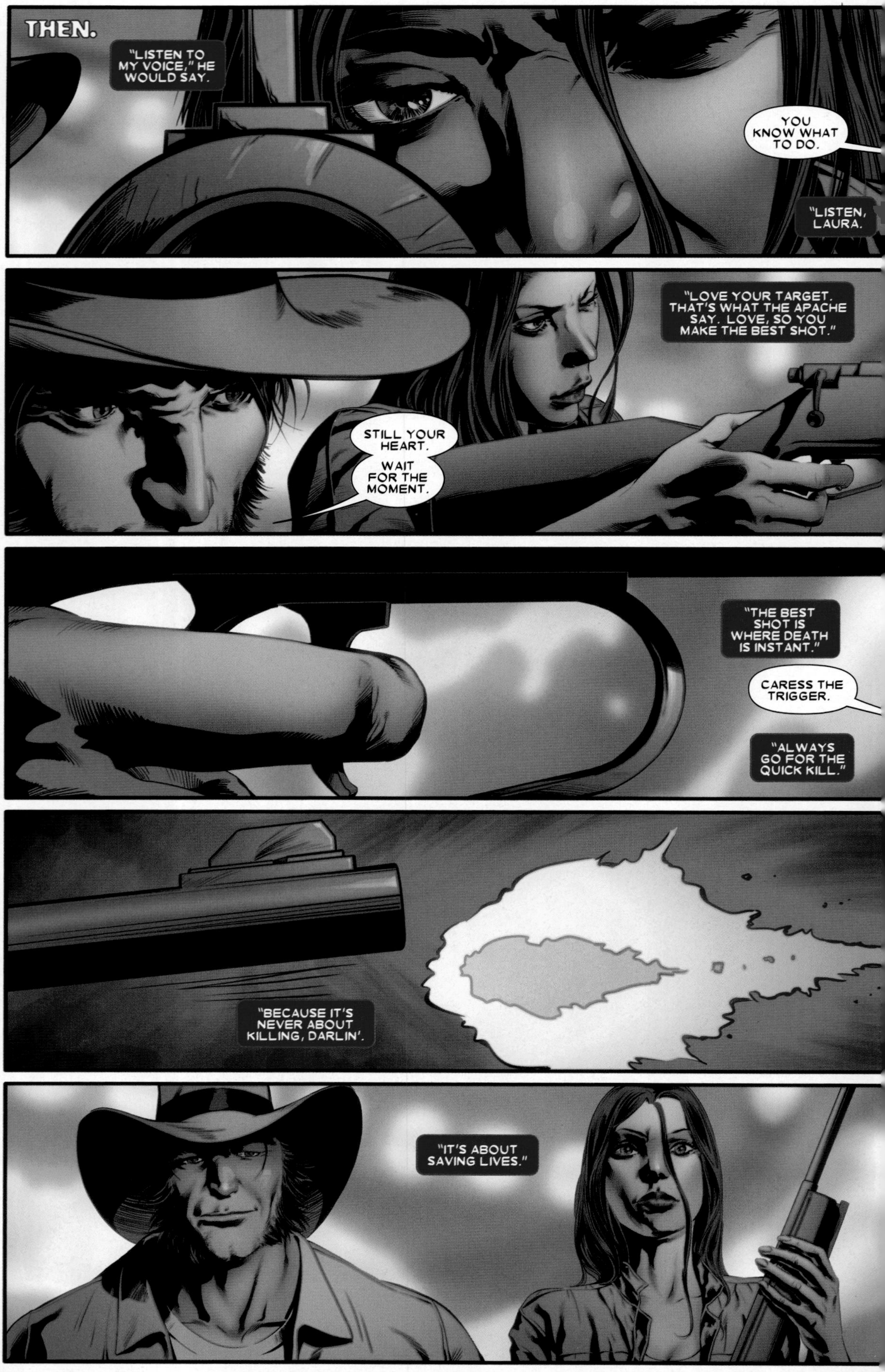
THEN.
"LISTEN TO MY VOICE," HE WOULD SAY.
YOU KNOW WHAT TO DO.
"LISTEN, LAURA.
"LOVE YOUR TARGET. THAT'S WHAT THE APACHE SAY. LOVE, SO YOU MAKE THE BEST SHOT."
STILL YOUR HEART.
WAIT FOR THE MOMENT.
"THE BEST SHOT IS WHERE DEATH IS INSTANT."
CARESS THE TRIGGER.
"ALWAYS GO FOR THE QUICK KILL."
"BECAUSE IT'S NEVER ABOUT KILLING, DARLIN'.
"IT'S ABOUT SAVING LIVES."

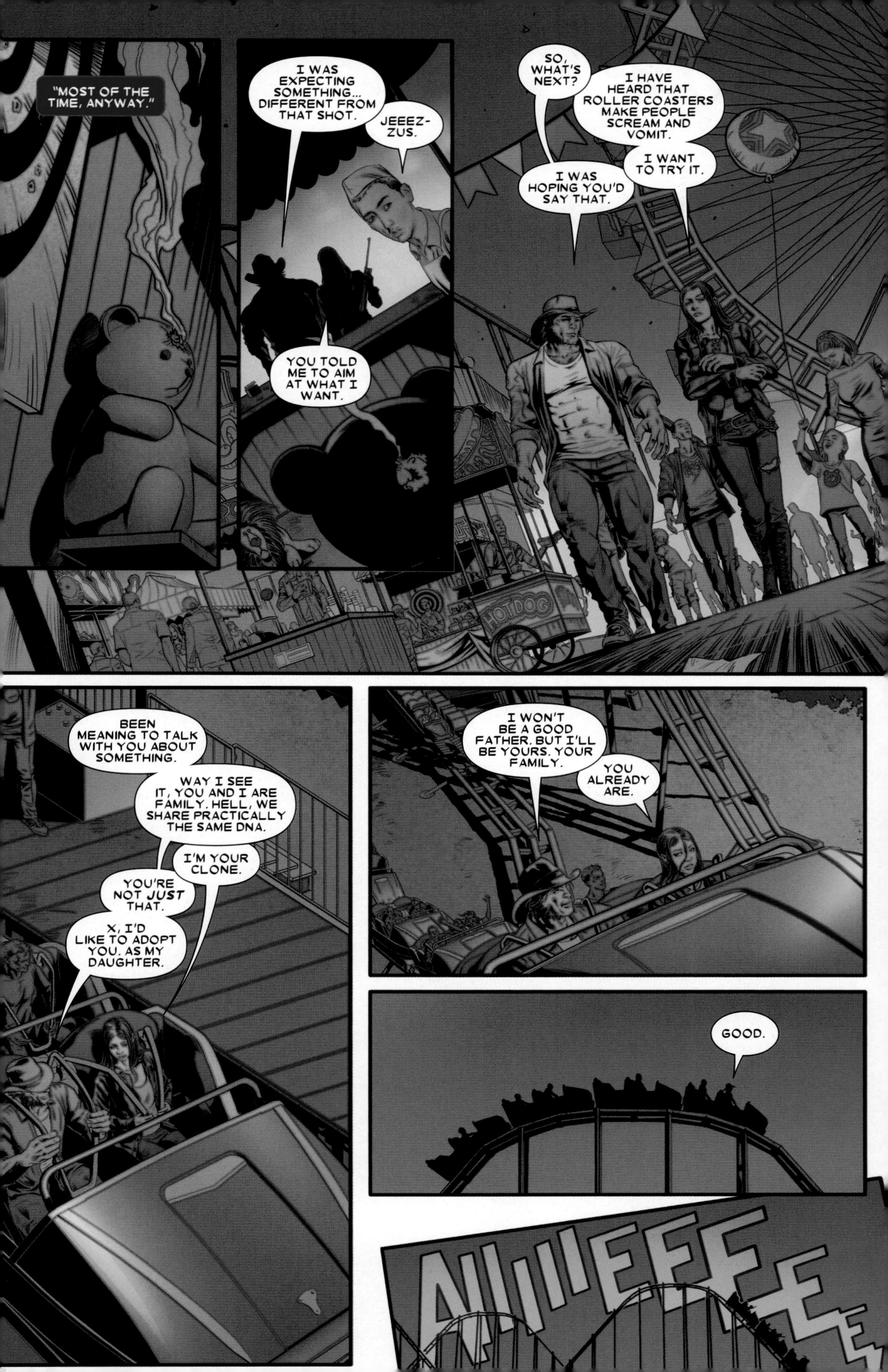
"MOST OF THE TIME, ANYWAY."
I WAS EXPECTING SOMETHING... DIFFERENT FROM THAT SHOT.
JEEEZ-ZUS.
YOU TOLD ME TO AIM AT WHAT I WANT.
SO, WHAT'S NEXT?
I HAVE HEARD THAT ROLLER COASTERS MAKE PEOPLE SCREAM AND VOMIT.
I WANT TO TRY IT.
I WAS HOPING YOU'D SAY THAT.
HOTDOG
BEEN MEANING TO TALK WITH YOU ABOUT SOMETHING.
WAY I SEE IT, YOU AND I ARE FAMILY. HELL, WE SHARE PRACTICALLY THE SAME DNA.
I'M YOUR CLONE.
YOU'RE NOT *JUST* THAT.
X, I'D LIKE TO ADOPT YOU. AS MY DAUGHTER.
I WON'T BE A GOOD FATHER. BUT I'LL BE YOURS. YOUR FAMILY.
YOU ALREADY ARE.
GOOD.
AIIIEEEE

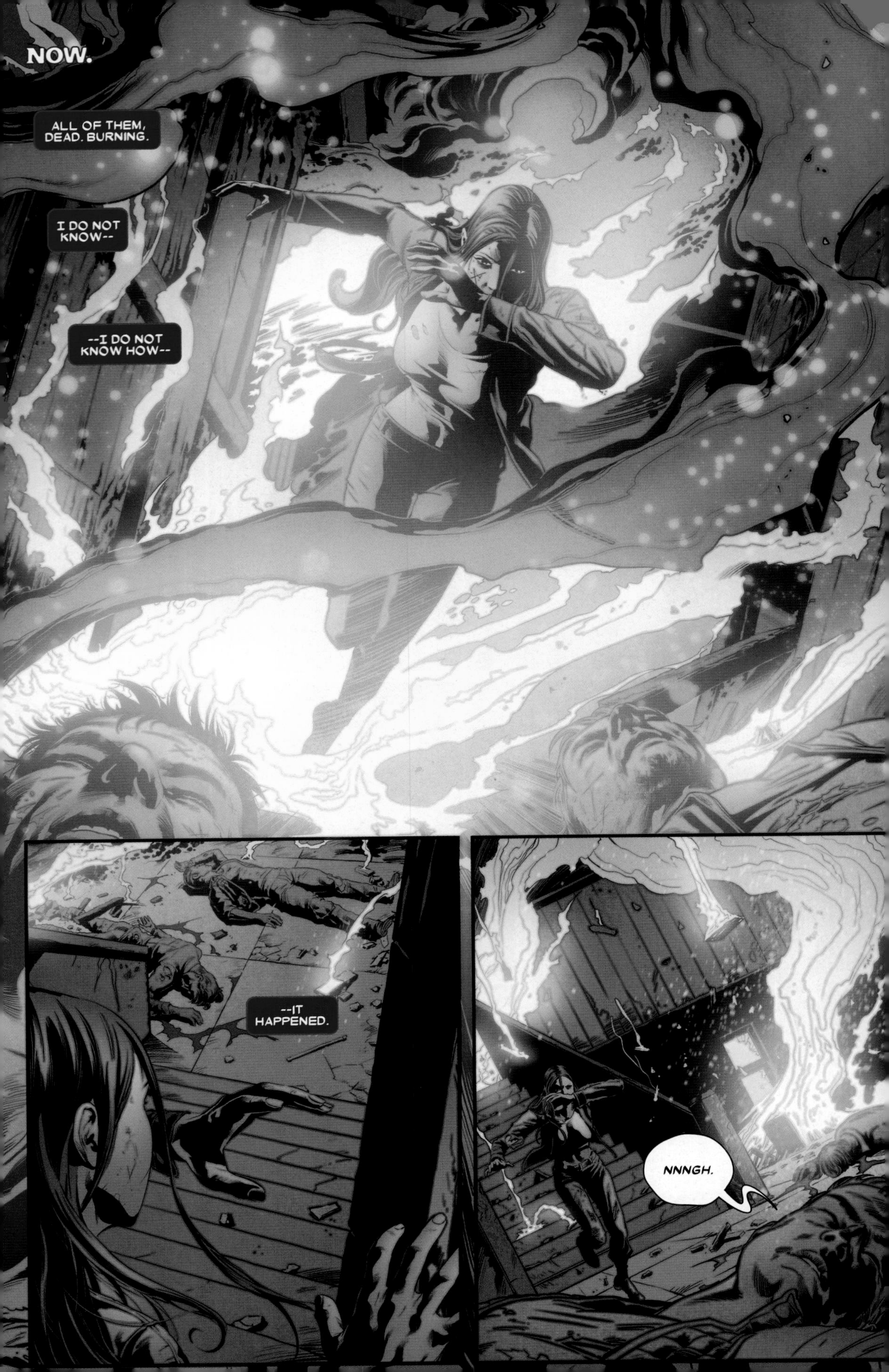
NOW.
ALL OF THEM, DEAD. BURNING.
I DO NOT KNOW--
--I DO NOT KNOW HOW--
--IT HAPPENED.
NNNGH.

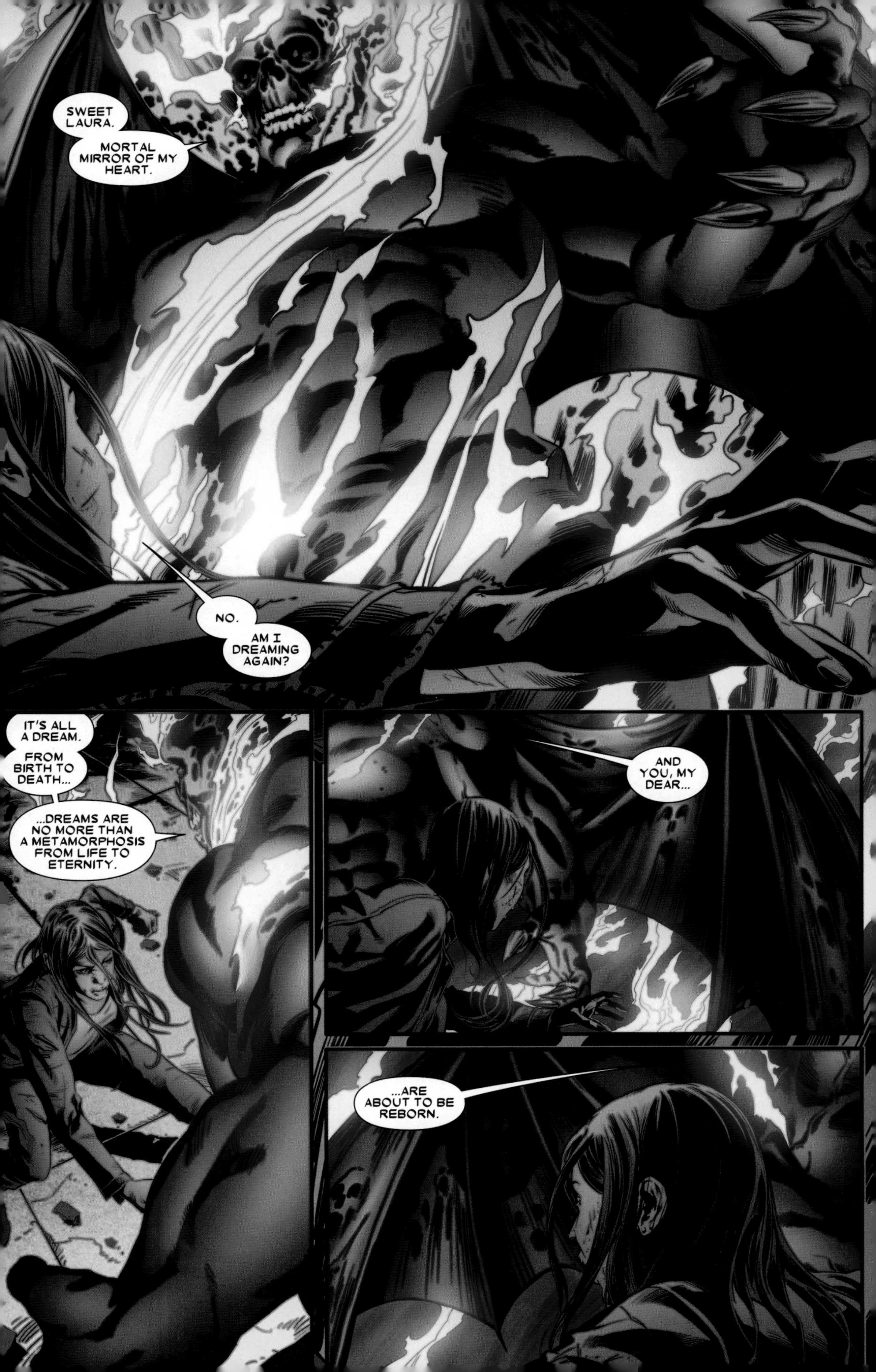
SWEET LAURA.
MORTAL MIRROR OF MY HEART.
NO.
AM I DREAMING AGAIN?
IT'S ALL A DREAM.
FROM BIRTH TO DEATH...
...DREAMS ARE NO MORE THAN A METAMORPHOSIS FROM LIFE TO ETERNITY.
AND YOU, MY DEAR...
...ARE ABOUT TO BE REBORN.

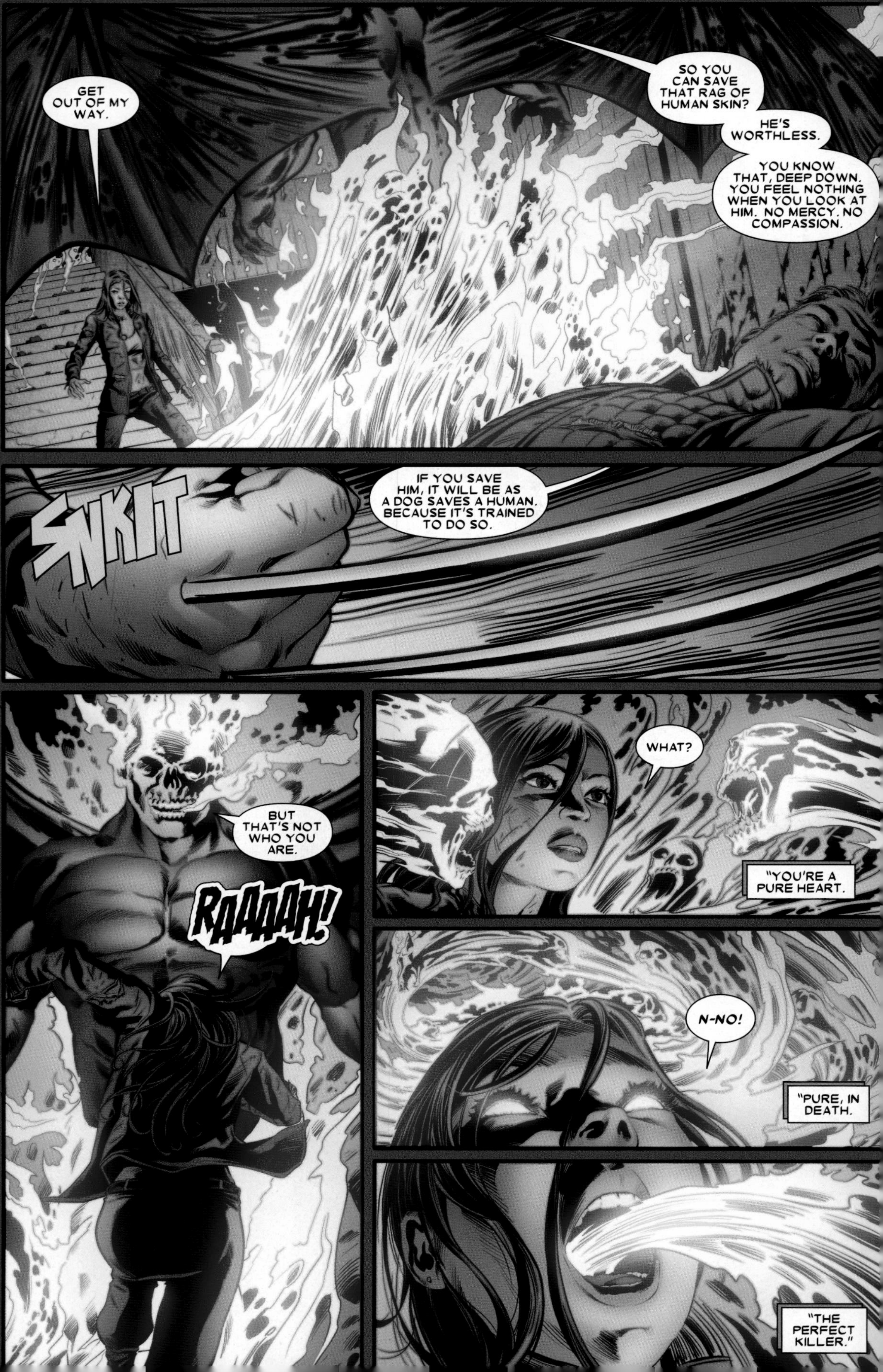
GET OUT OF MY WAY.
SO YOU CAN SAVE THAT RAG OF HUMAN SKIN?
HE'S WORTHLESS.
YOU KNOW THAT, DEEP DOWN. YOU FEEL NOTHING WHEN YOU LOOK AT HIM. NO MERCY. NO COMPASSION.
SNKIT
IF YOU SAVE HIM, IT WILL BE AS A DOG SAVES A HUMAN. BECAUSE IT'S TRAINED TO DO SO.
BUT THAT'S NOT WHO YOU ARE.
RAAAAH!
WHAT?
"YOU'RE A PURE HEART.
N-NO!
"PURE, IN DEATH.
"THE PERFECT KILLER."

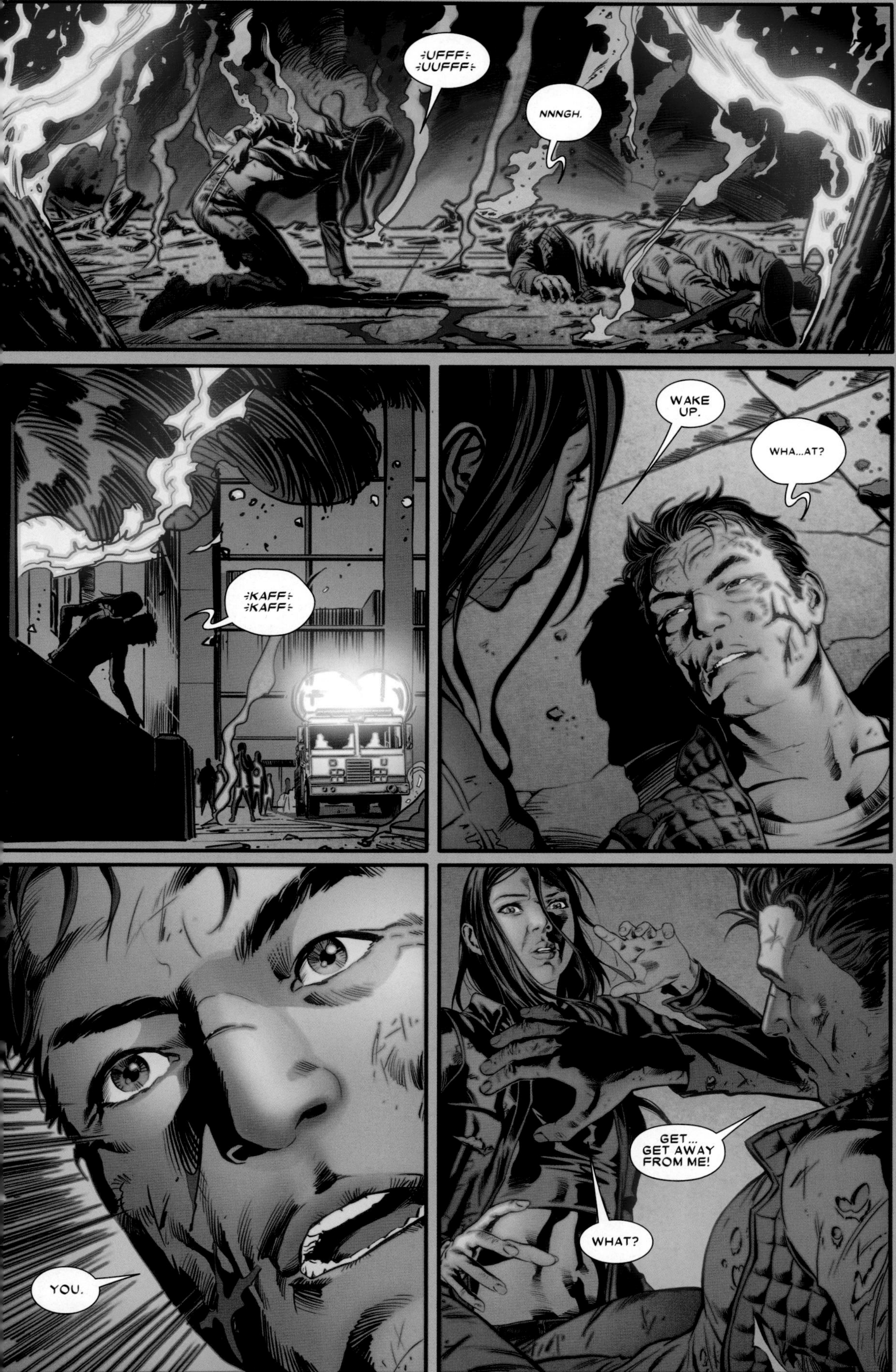

UFFF UUFFF
NNNGH.
KAFF KAFF
WAKE UP.
WHA...AT?
YOU.
GET... GET AWAY FROM ME!
WHAT?

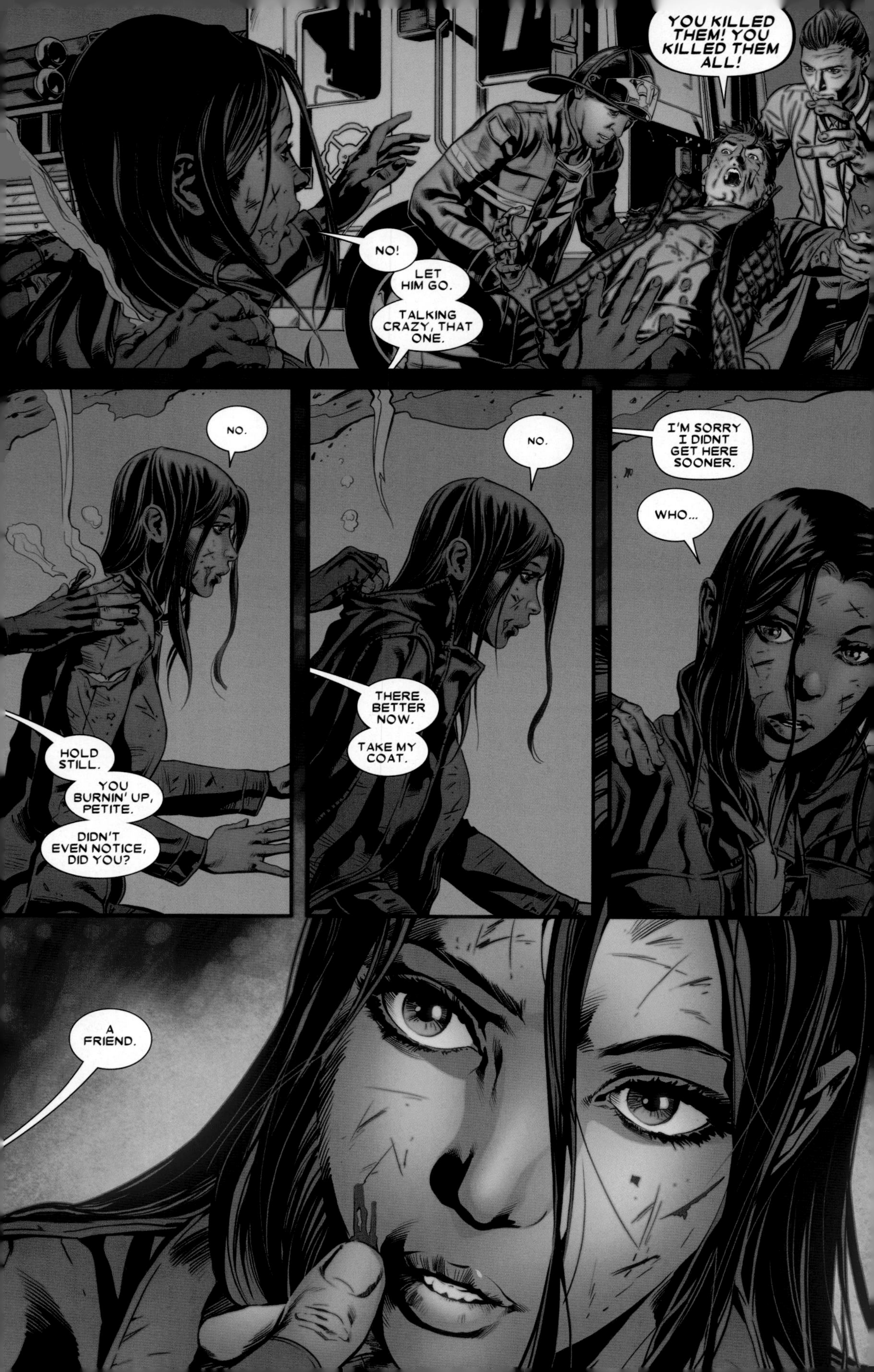
YOU KILLED THEM! YOU KILLED THEM ALL!
NO!
LET HIM GO.
TALKING CRAZY, THAT ONE.
NO.
HOLD STILL.
YOU BURNIN' UP, PETITE.
DIDN'T EVEN NOTICE, DID YOU?
NO.
THERE. BETTER NOW.
TAKE MY COAT.
I'M SORRY I DIDNT GET HERE SOONER.
WHO...
A FRIEND.

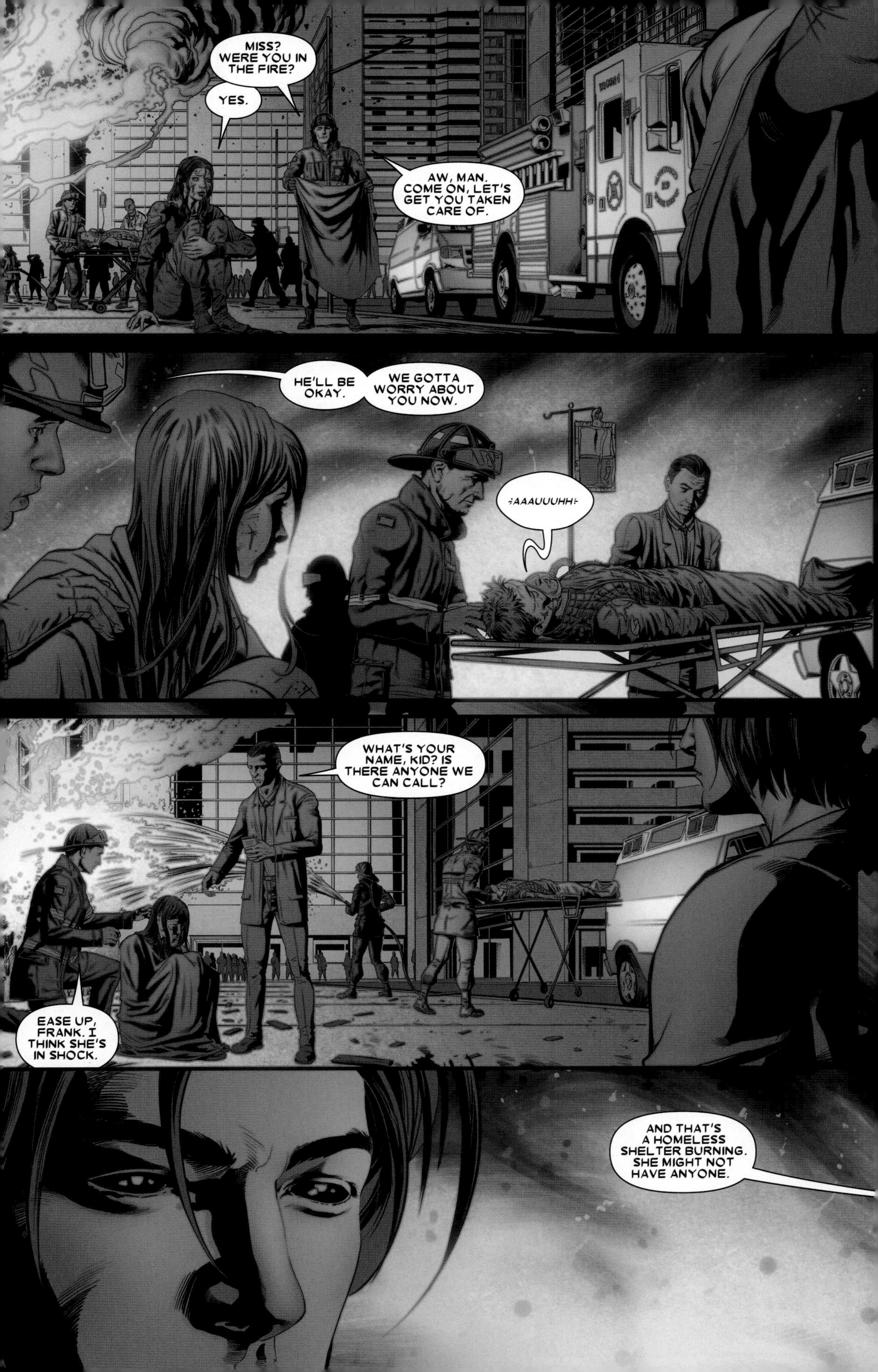
MISS? WERE YOU IN THE FIRE?
YES.
AW, MAN. COME ON, LET'S GET YOU TAKEN CARE OF.
HE'LL BE OKAY.
WE GOTTA WORRY ABOUT YOU NOW.
AAAUUUHH
WHAT'S YOUR NAME, KID? IS THERE ANYONE WE CAN CALL?
EASE UP, FRANK. I THINK SHE'S IN SHOCK.
AND THAT'S A HOMELESS SHELTER BURNING. SHE MIGHT NOT HAVE ANYONE.

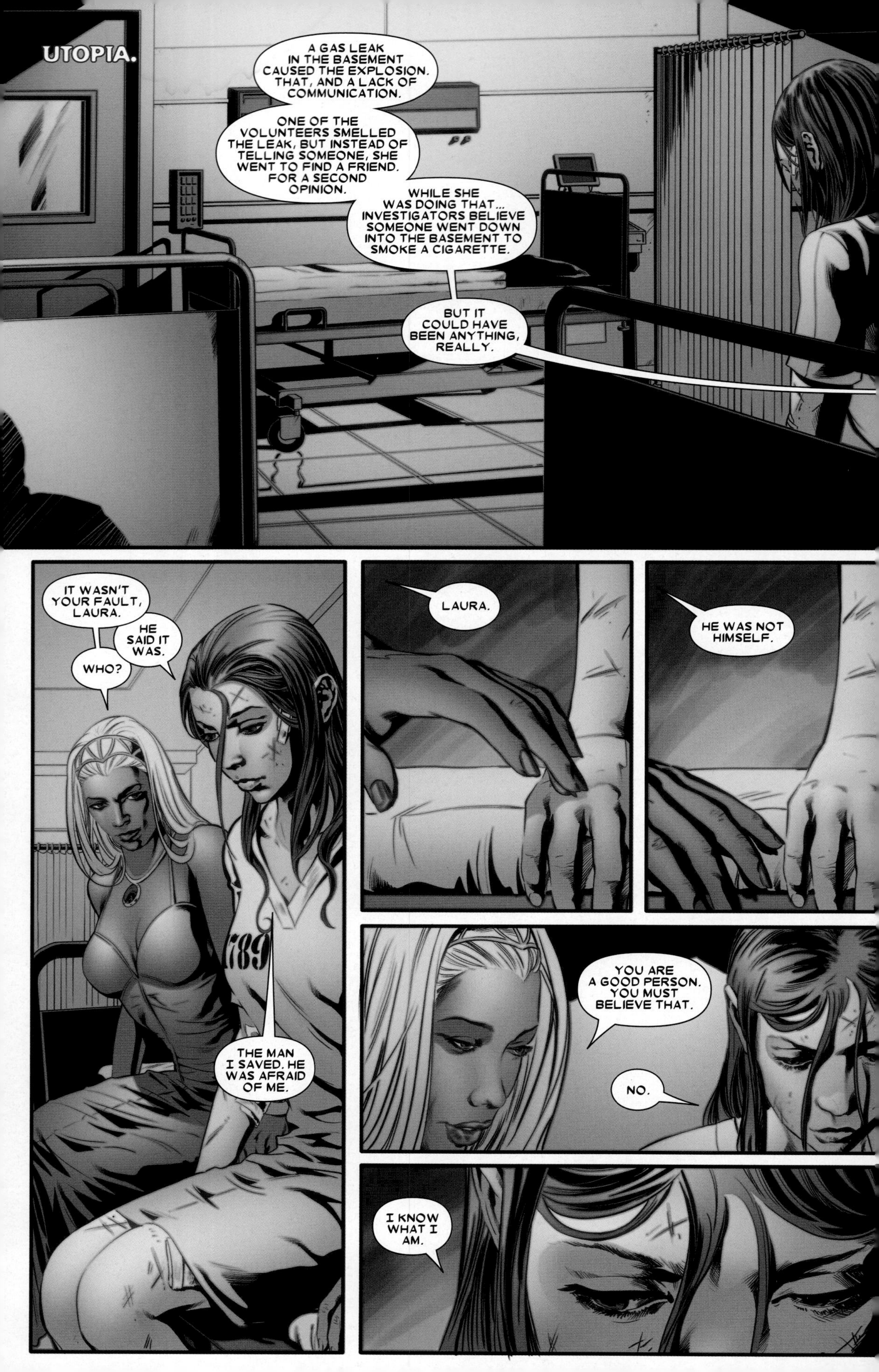
UTOPIA.
A GAS LEAK IN THE BASEMENT CAUSED THE EXPLOSION. THAT, AND A LACK OF COMMUNICATION.
ONE OF THE VOLUNTEERS SMELLED THE LEAK, BUT INSTEAD OF TELLING SOMEONE, SHE WENT TO FIND A FRIEND. FOR A SECOND OPINION.
WHILE SHE WAS DOING THAT... INVESTIGATORS BELIEVE SOMEONE WENT DOWN INTO THE BASEMENT TO SMOKE A CIGARETTE.
BUT IT COULD HAVE BEEN ANYTHING, REALLY.
IT WASN'T YOUR FAULT, LAURA.
HE SAID IT WAS.
WHO?
THE MAN I SAVED. HE WAS AFRAID OF ME.
LAURA.
HE WAS NOT HIMSELF.
YOU ARE A GOOD PERSON. YOU MUST BELIEVE THAT.
NO.
I KNOW WHAT I AM.

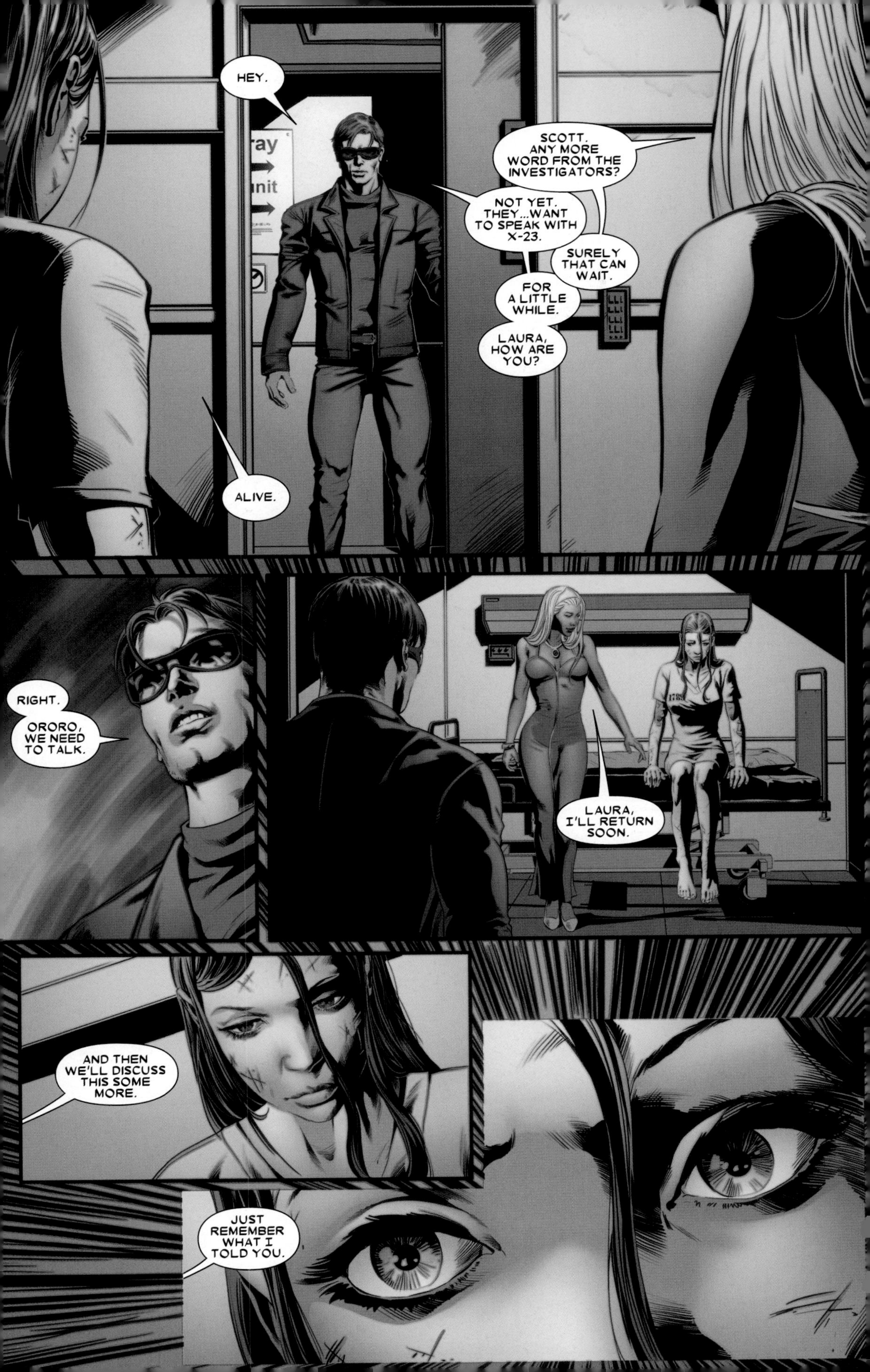
HEY.
SCOTT. ANY MORE WORD FROM THE INVESTIGATORS?
NOT YET. THEY...WANT TO SPEAK WITH X-23.
SURELY THAT CAN WAIT.
FOR A LITTLE WHILE.
LAURA, HOW ARE YOU?
ALIVE.
RIGHT.
ORORO, WE NEED TO TALK.
LAURA, I'LL RETURN SOON.
AND THEN WE'LL DISCUSS THIS SOME MORE.
JUST REMEMBER WHAT I TOLD YOU.

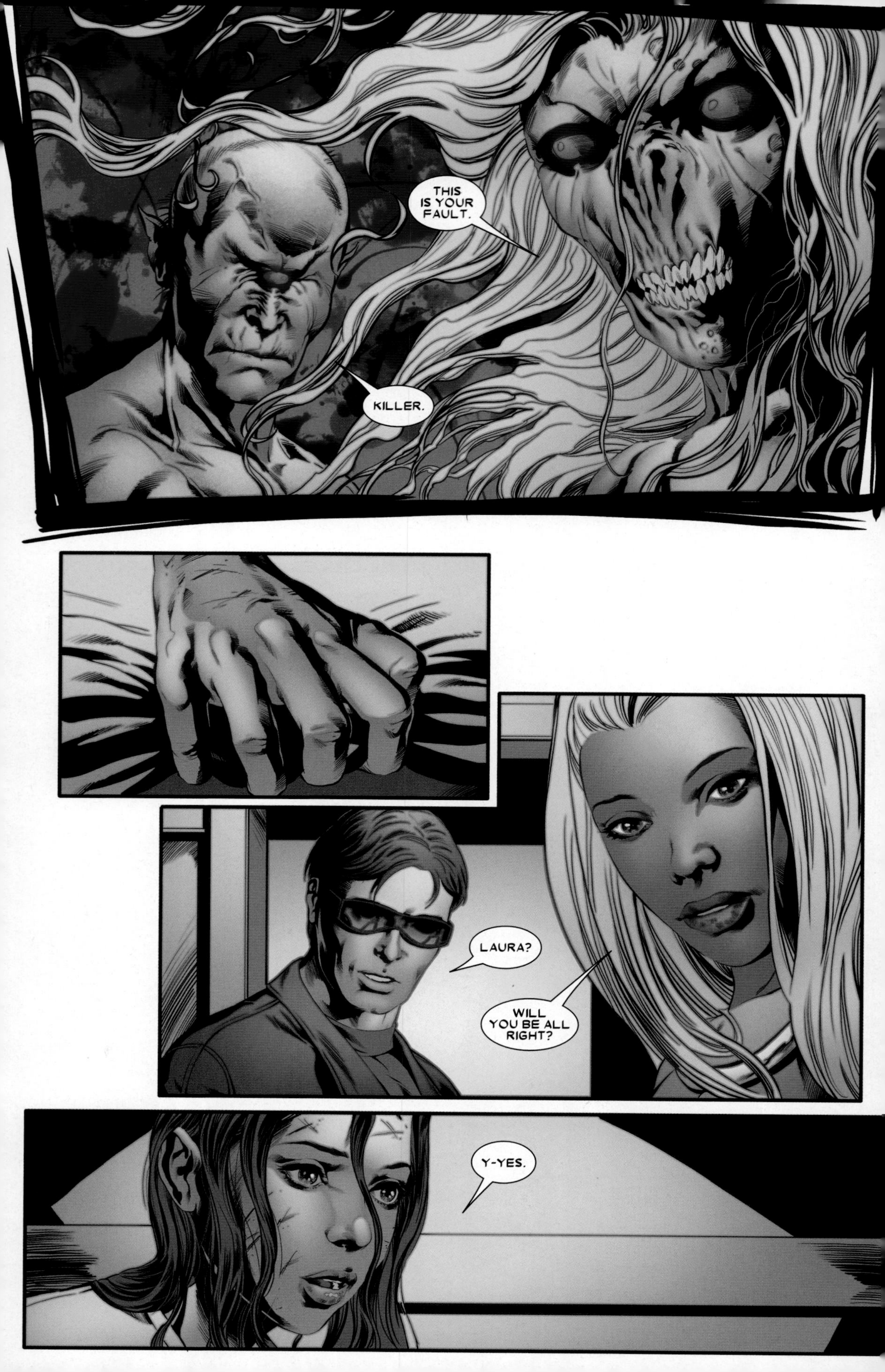
THIS IS YOUR FAULT.
KILLER.
LAURA?
WILL YOU BE ALL RIGHT?
Y-YES.

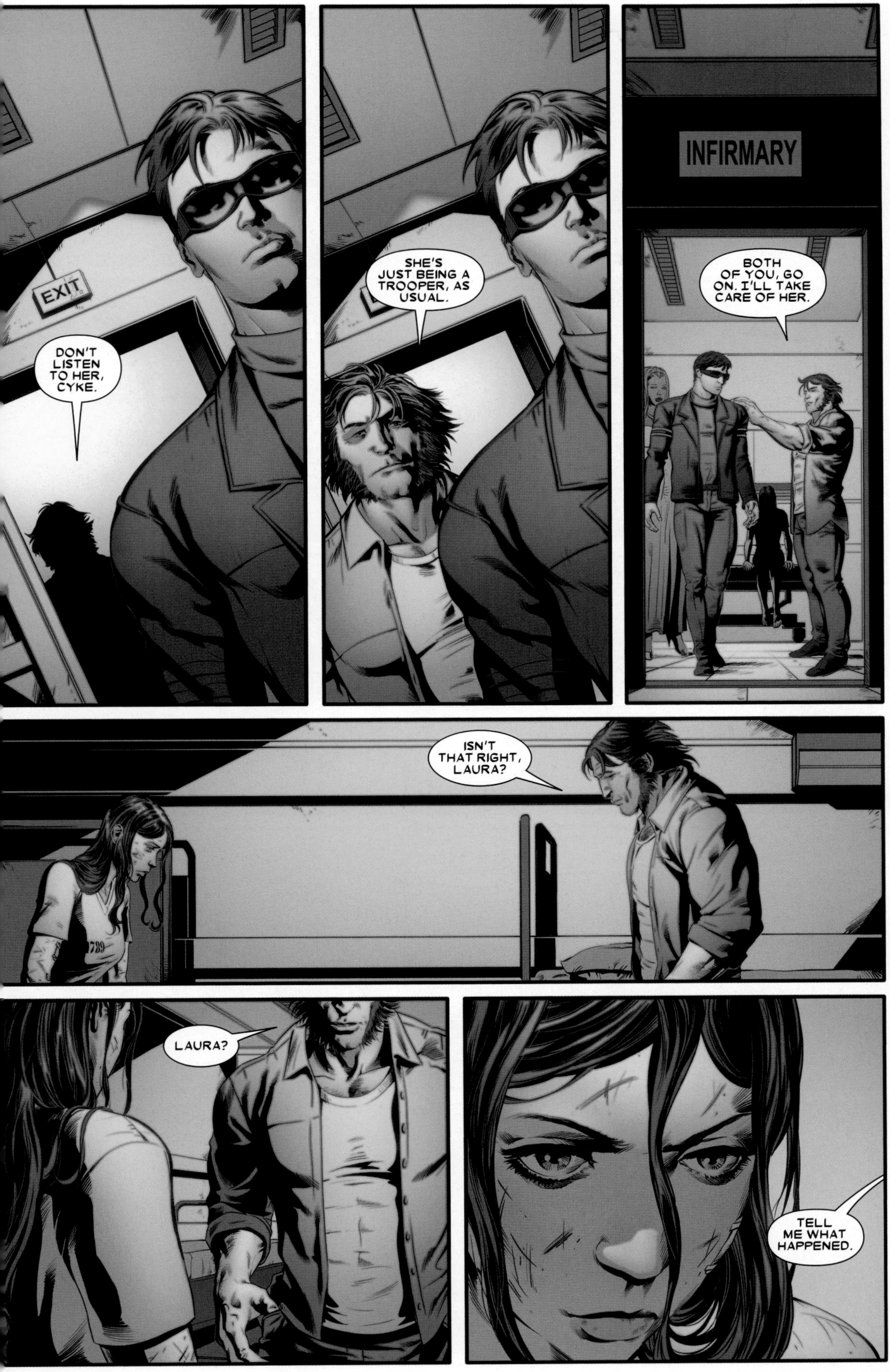

DON'T LISTEN TO HER, CYKE.
EXIT
SHE'S JUST BEING A TROOPER, AS USUAL.
INFIRMARY
BOTH OF YOU, GO ON. I'LL TAKE CARE OF HER.
ISN'T THAT RIGHT, LAURA?
LAURA?
TELL ME WHAT HAPPENED.

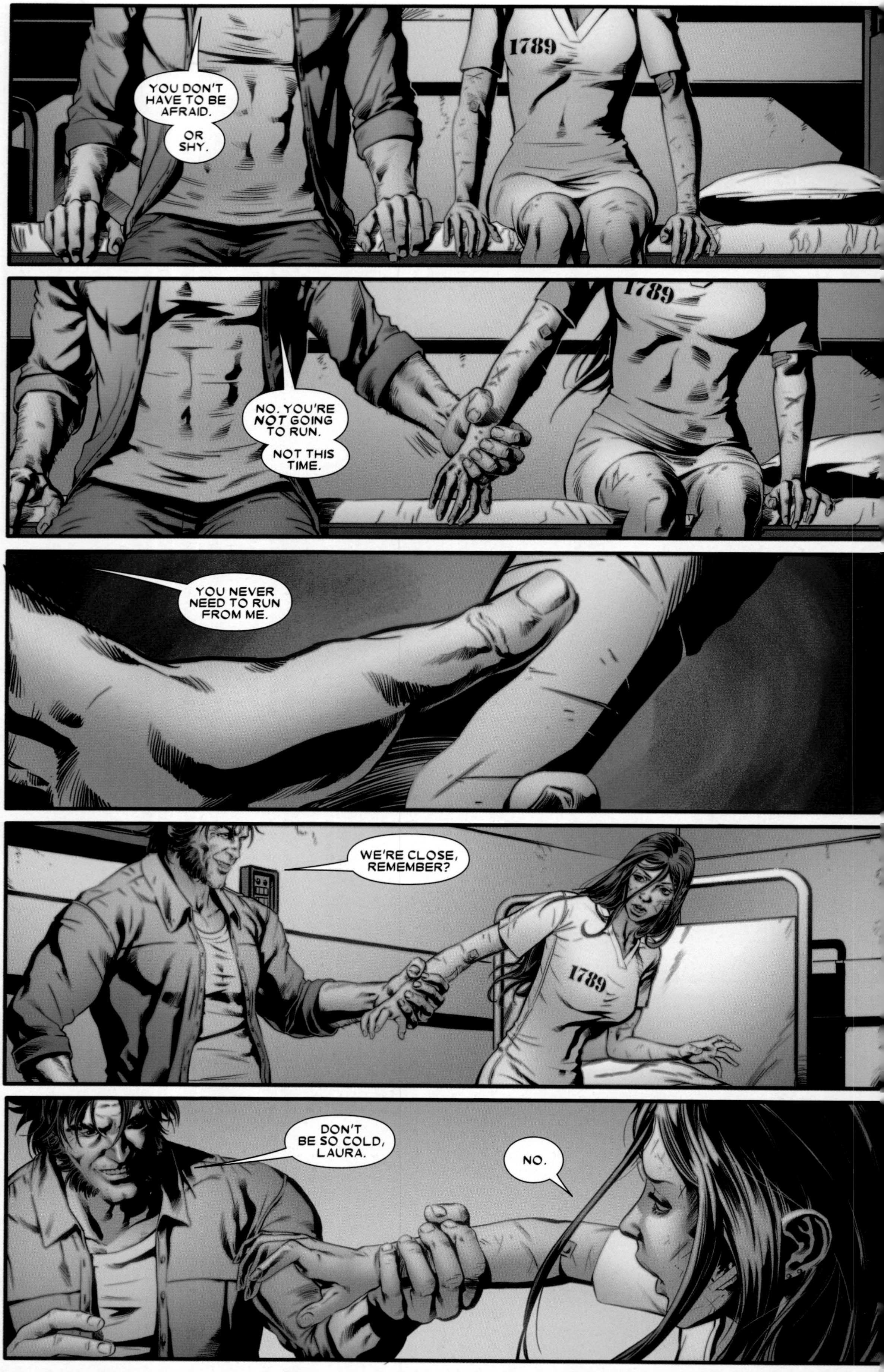
YOU DON'T HAVE TO BE AFRAID.
OR SHY.
NO. YOU'RE NOT GOING TO RUN.
NOT THIS TIME.
YOU NEVER NEED TO RUN FROM ME.
WE'RE CLOSE, REMEMBER?
DON'T BE SO COLD, LAURA.
NO.

NO!

DO NOT TOUCH ME! YOU ARE NOT HIM. YOU ARE *NOT* WOLVERINE.

SNIKT

...AFTER EVERYTHING I'VE DONE FOR YOU.

FIGHTING AT YOUR SIDE, BEING YOUR FRIEND... YOUR *FAMILY*... WHEN NO ONE ELSE WANTED YOU.

YOU BREAK MY HEART.

LET IT BREAK.

WHO ARE YOU?

THE BETTER QUESTION IS... WHO ARE YOU?

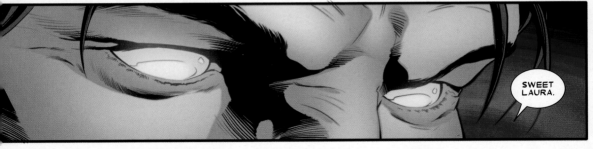

SWEET LAURA.

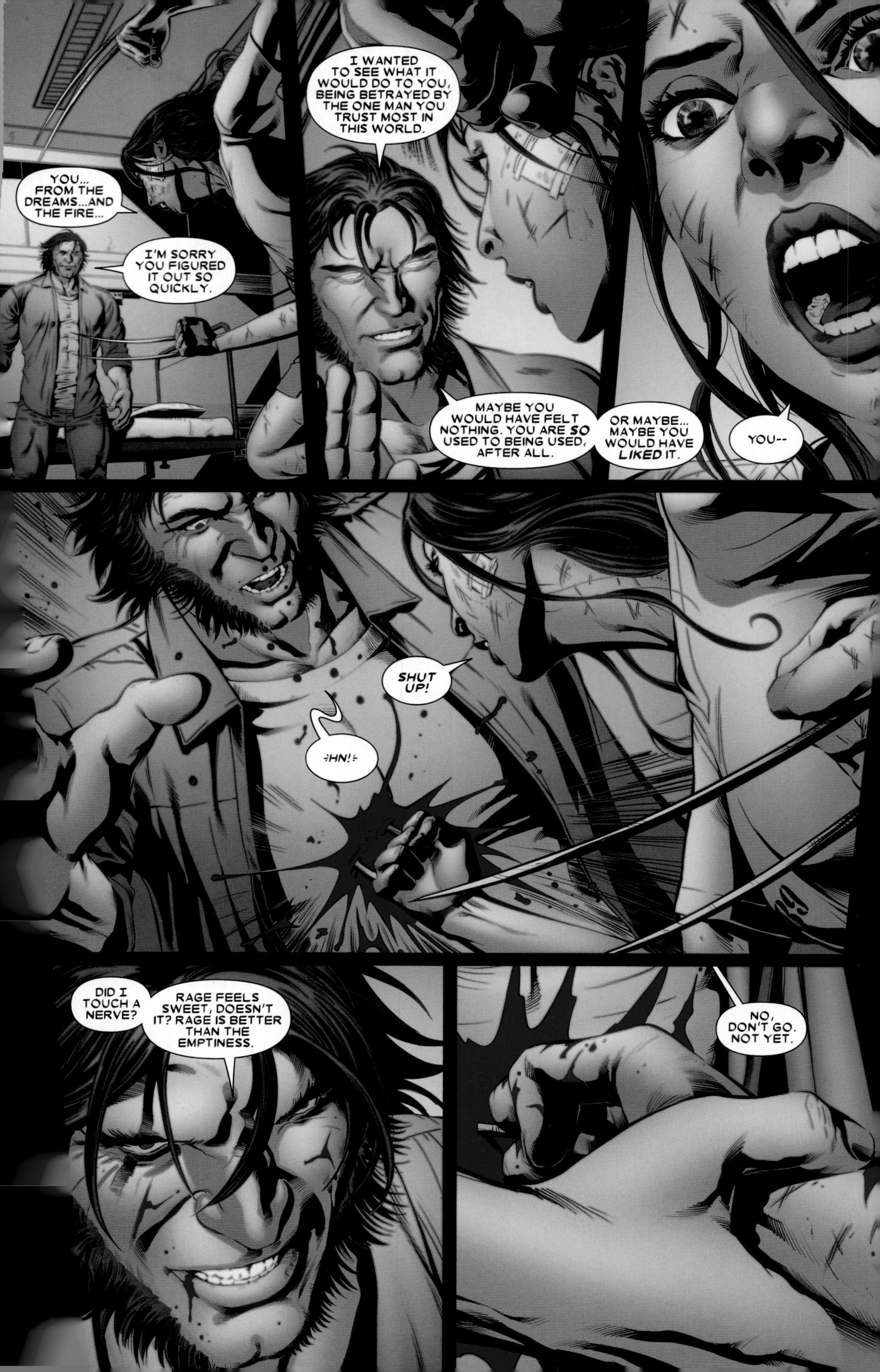
YOU... FROM THE DREAMS...AND THE FIRE...
I'M SORRY YOU FIGURED IT OUT SO QUICKLY.
I WANTED TO SEE WHAT IT WOULD DO TO YOU, BEING BETRAYED BY THE ONE MAN YOU TRUST MOST IN THIS WORLD.
MAYBE YOU WOULD HAVE FELT NOTHING. YOU ARE SO USED TO BEING USED, AFTER ALL.
OR MAYBE... MAYBE YOU WOULD HAVE LIKED IT.
YOU--
SHUT UP!
HN!
DID I TOUCH A NERVE?
RAGE FEELS SWEET, DOESN'T IT? RAGE IS BETTER THAN THE EMPTINESS.
NO, DON'T GO. NOT YET.

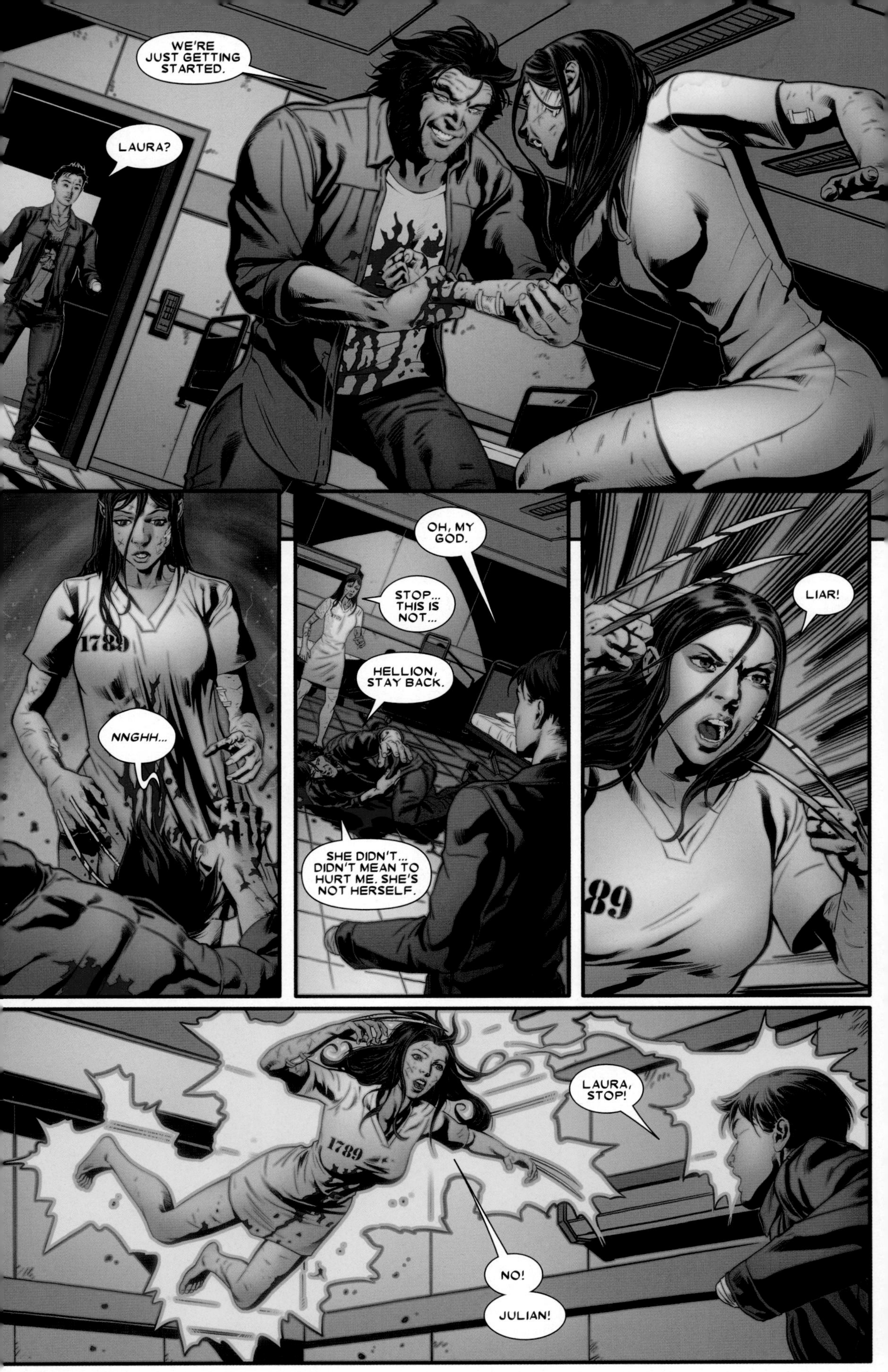
WE'RE JUST GETTING STARTED.
LAURA?
NNGHH...
OH, MY GOD.
STOP... THIS IS NOT...
HELLION, STAY BACK.
SHE DIDN'T... DIDN'T MEAN TO HURT ME. SHE'S NOT HERSELF.
LIAR!
1789
LAURA, STOP!
NO!
JULIAN!

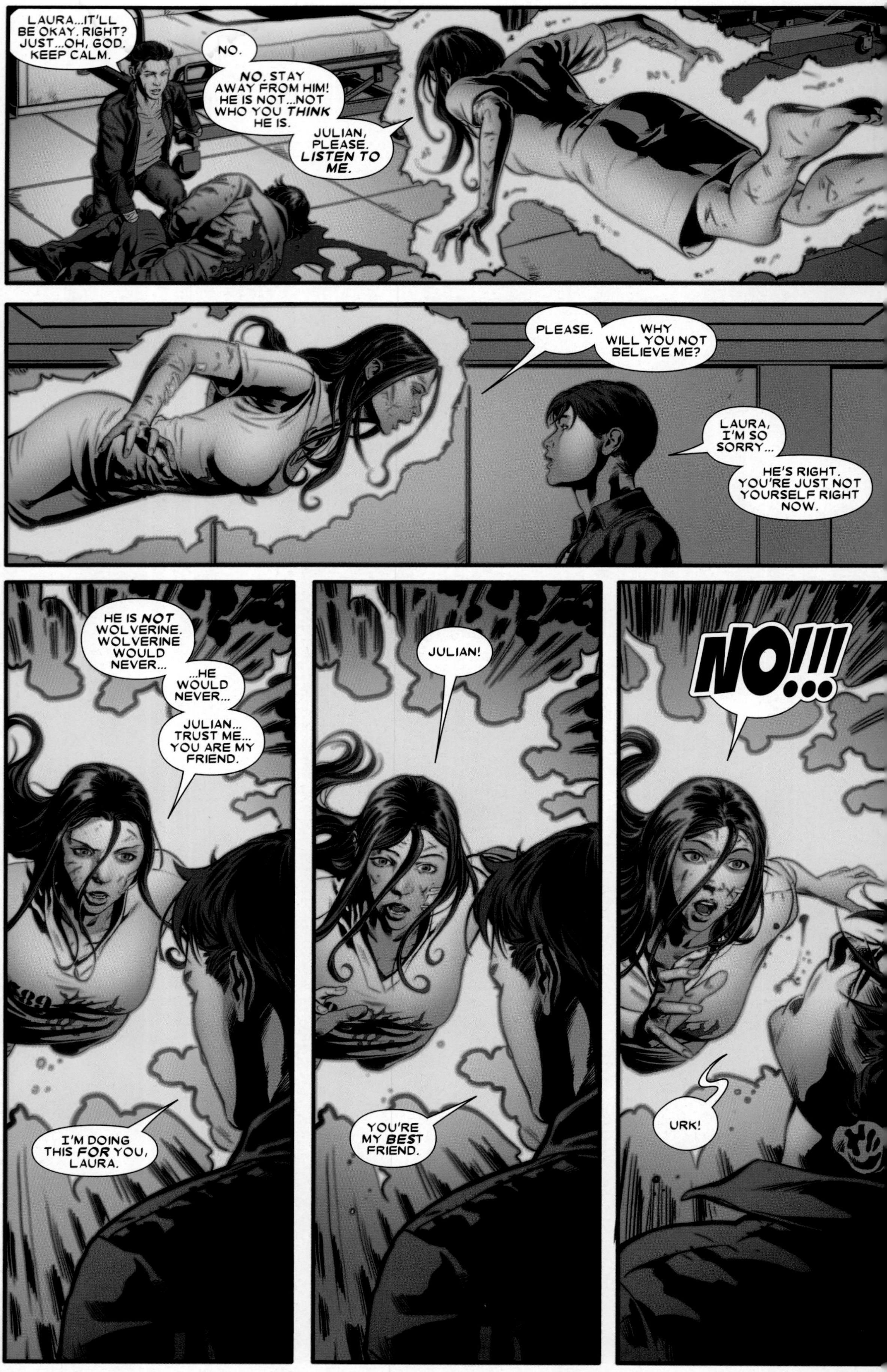
LAURA...IT'LL BE OKAY. RIGHT? JUST...OH, GOD. KEEP CALM.
NO.
NO. STAY AWAY FROM HIM! HE IS NOT...NOT WHO YOU THINK HE IS.
JULIAN, PLEASE. LISTEN TO ME.
PLEASE.
WHY WILL YOU NOT BELIEVE ME?
LAURA, I'M SO SORRY...
HE'S RIGHT. YOU'RE JUST NOT YOURSELF RIGHT NOW.
HE IS NOT WOLVERINE. WOLVERINE WOULD NEVER...
...HE WOULD NEVER...
JULIAN... TRUST ME... YOU ARE MY FRIEND.
I'M DOING THIS FOR YOU, LAURA.
JULIAN!
YOU'RE MY BEST FRIEND.
NO!!!
URK!

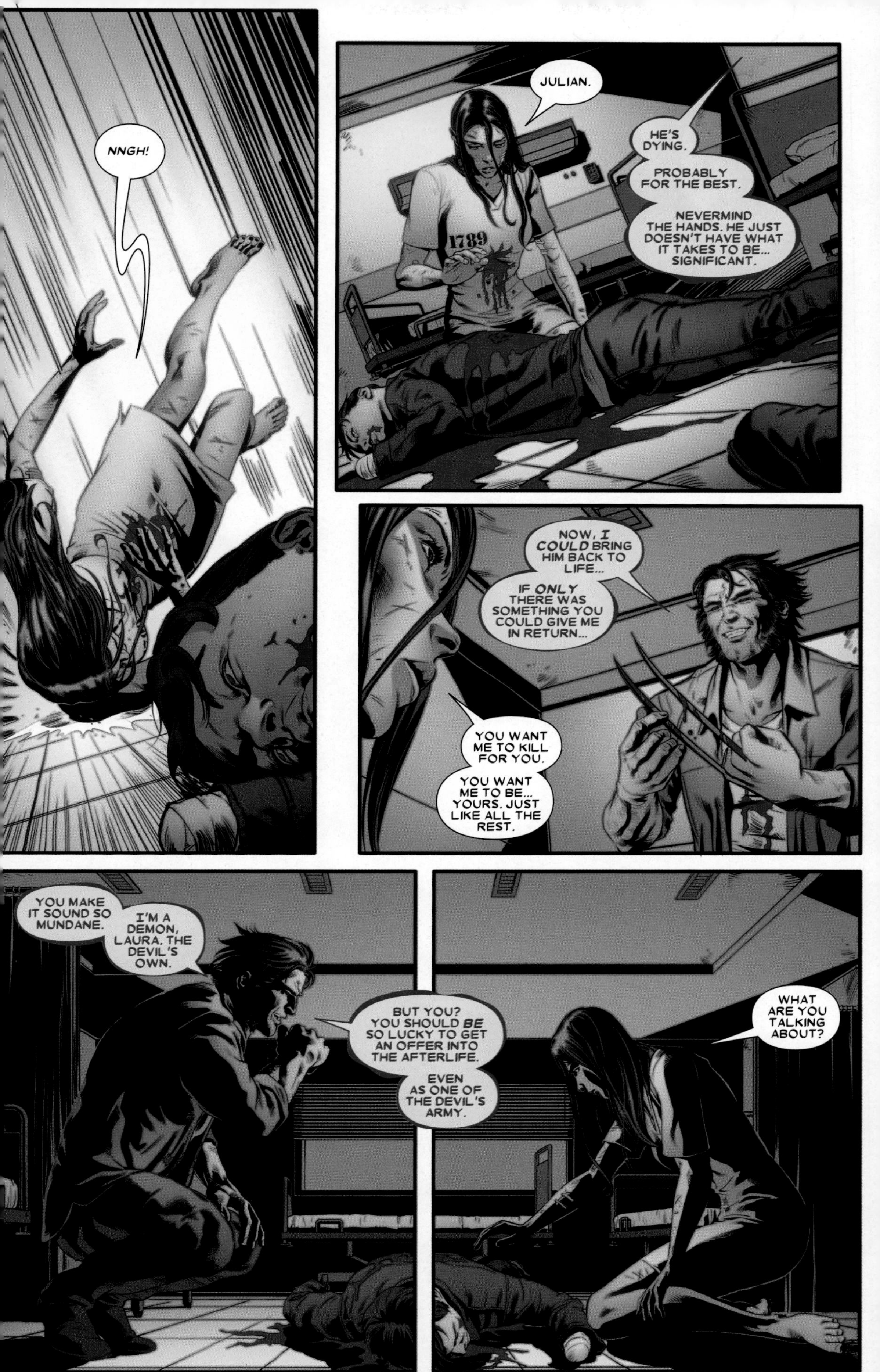
NNGH!
JULIAN.
HE'S DYING.
PROBABLY FOR THE BEST.
NEVERMIND THE HANDS. HE JUST DOESN'T HAVE WHAT IT TAKES TO BE... SIGNIFICANT.
1789
NOW, *I COULD* BRING HIM BACK TO LIFE...
IF *ONLY* THERE WAS SOMETHING YOU COULD GIVE ME IN RETURN...
YOU WANT ME TO KILL FOR YOU.
YOU WANT ME TO BE... YOURS. JUST LIKE ALL THE REST.
YOU MAKE IT SOUND SO MUNDANE.
I'M A DEMON, LAURA. THE DEVIL'S OWN.
BUT YOU? YOU SHOULD *BE* SO LUCKY TO GET AN OFFER INTO THE AFTERLIFE.
EVEN AS ONE OF THE DEVIL'S ARMY.
WHAT ARE YOU TALKING ABOUT?

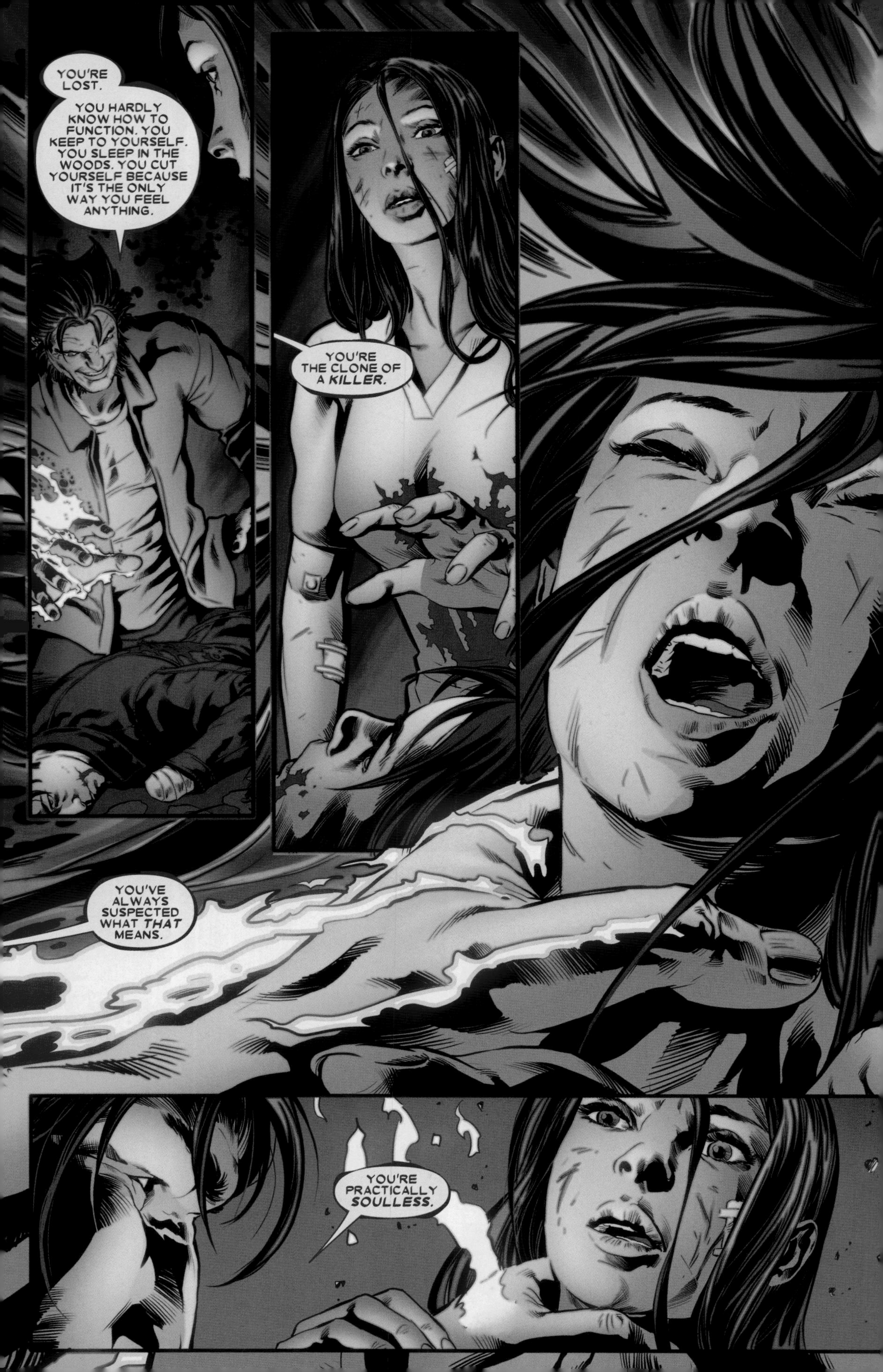
YOU'RE LOST.
YOU HARDLY KNOW HOW TO FUNCTION. YOU KEEP TO YOURSELF. YOU SLEEP IN THE WOODS. YOU CUT YOURSELF BECAUSE IT'S THE ONLY WAY YOU FEEL ANYTHING.
YOU'RE THE CLONE OF A *KILLER*.
YOU'VE ALWAYS SUSPECTED WHAT *THAT* MEANS.
YOU'RE PRACTICALLY *SOULLESS*.

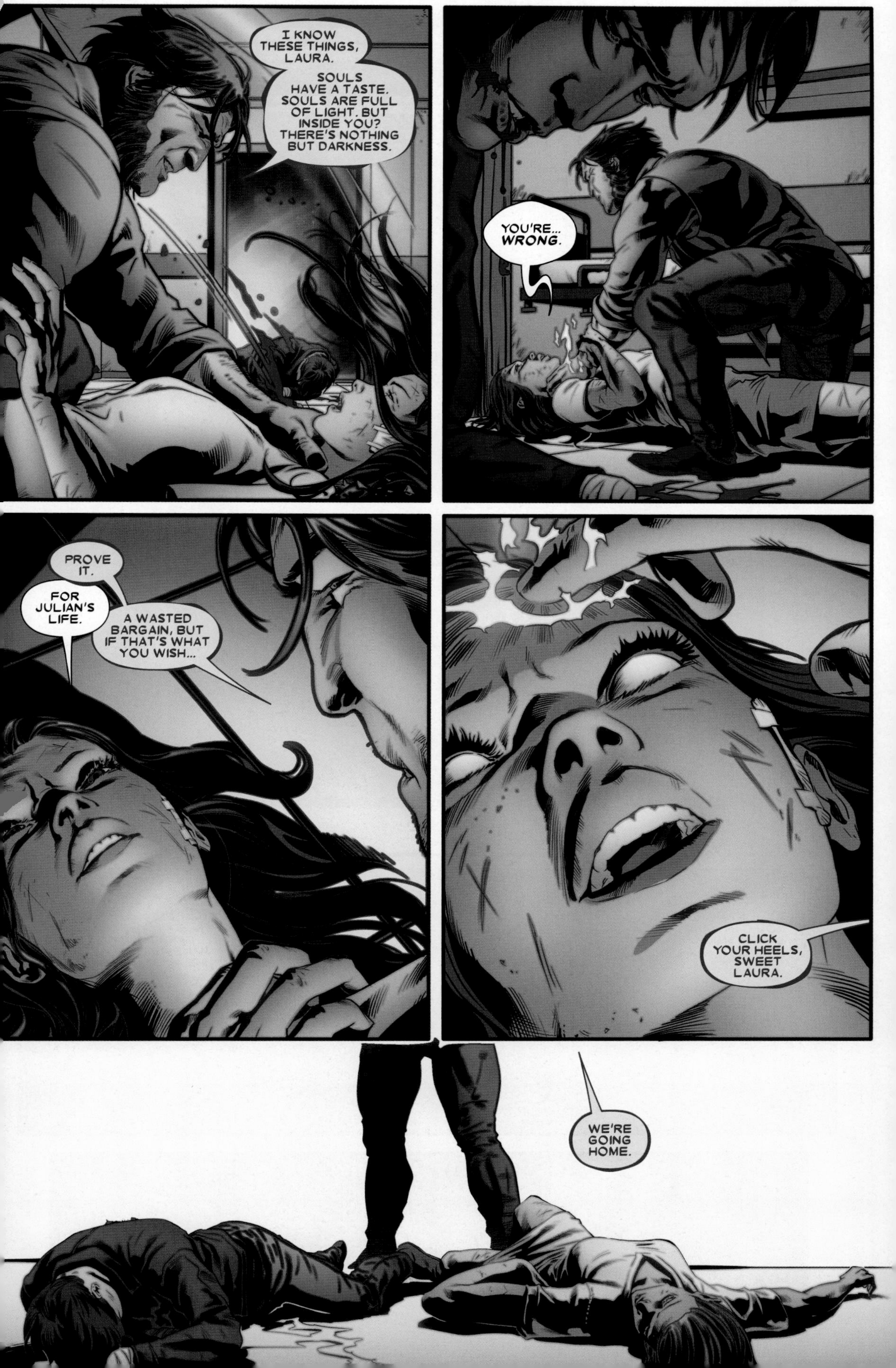
I KNOW THESE THINGS, LAURA.
SOULS HAVE A TASTE. SOULS ARE FULL OF LIGHT. BUT INSIDE YOU? THERE'S NOTHING BUT DARKNESS.
YOU'RE... WRONG.
PROVE IT.
FOR JULIAN'S LIFE.
A WASTED BARGAIN, BUT IF THAT'S WHAT YOU WISH...
CLICK YOUR HEELS, SWEET LAURA.
WE'RE GOING HOME.

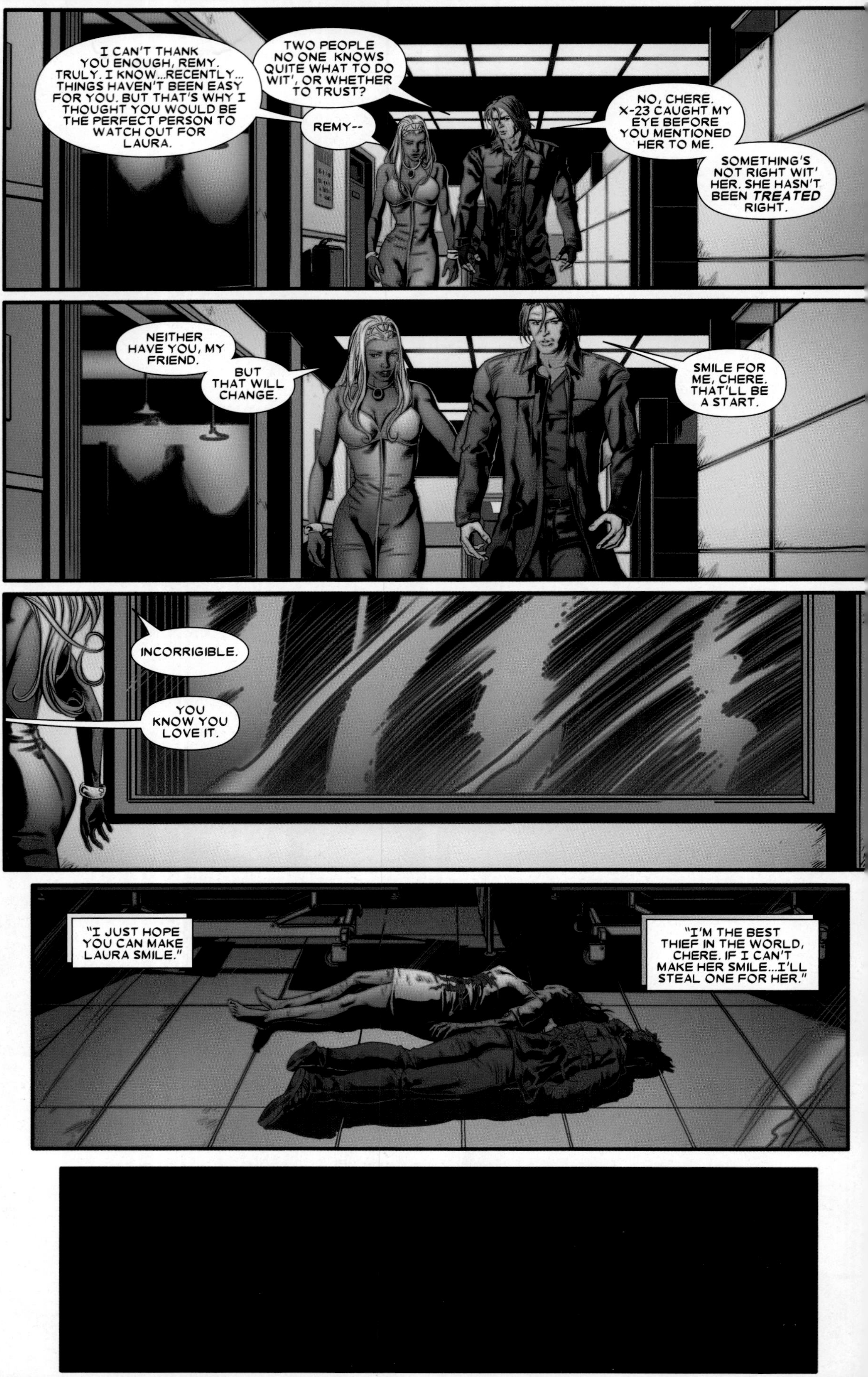
I CAN'T THANK YOU ENOUGH, REMY. TRULY. I KNOW...RECENTLY... THINGS HAVEN'T BEEN EASY FOR YOU. BUT THAT'S WHY I THOUGHT YOU WOULD BE THE PERFECT PERSON TO WATCH OUT FOR LAURA.
TWO PEOPLE NO ONE KNOWS QUITE WHAT TO DO WIT', OR WHETHER TO TRUST?
REMY--
NO, CHERE. X-23 CAUGHT MY EYE BEFORE YOU MENTIONED HER TO ME.
SOMETHING'S NOT RIGHT WIT' HER. SHE HASN'T BEEN *TREATED* RIGHT.
NEITHER HAVE YOU, MY FRIEND.
BUT THAT WILL CHANGE.
SMILE FOR ME, CHERE. THAT'LL BE A START.
INCORRIGIBLE.
YOU KNOW YOU LOVE IT.
"I JUST HOPE YOU CAN MAKE LAURA SMILE."
"I'M THE BEST THIEF IN THE WORLD, CHERE. IF I CAN'T MAKE HER SMILE...I'LL STEAL ONE FOR HER."

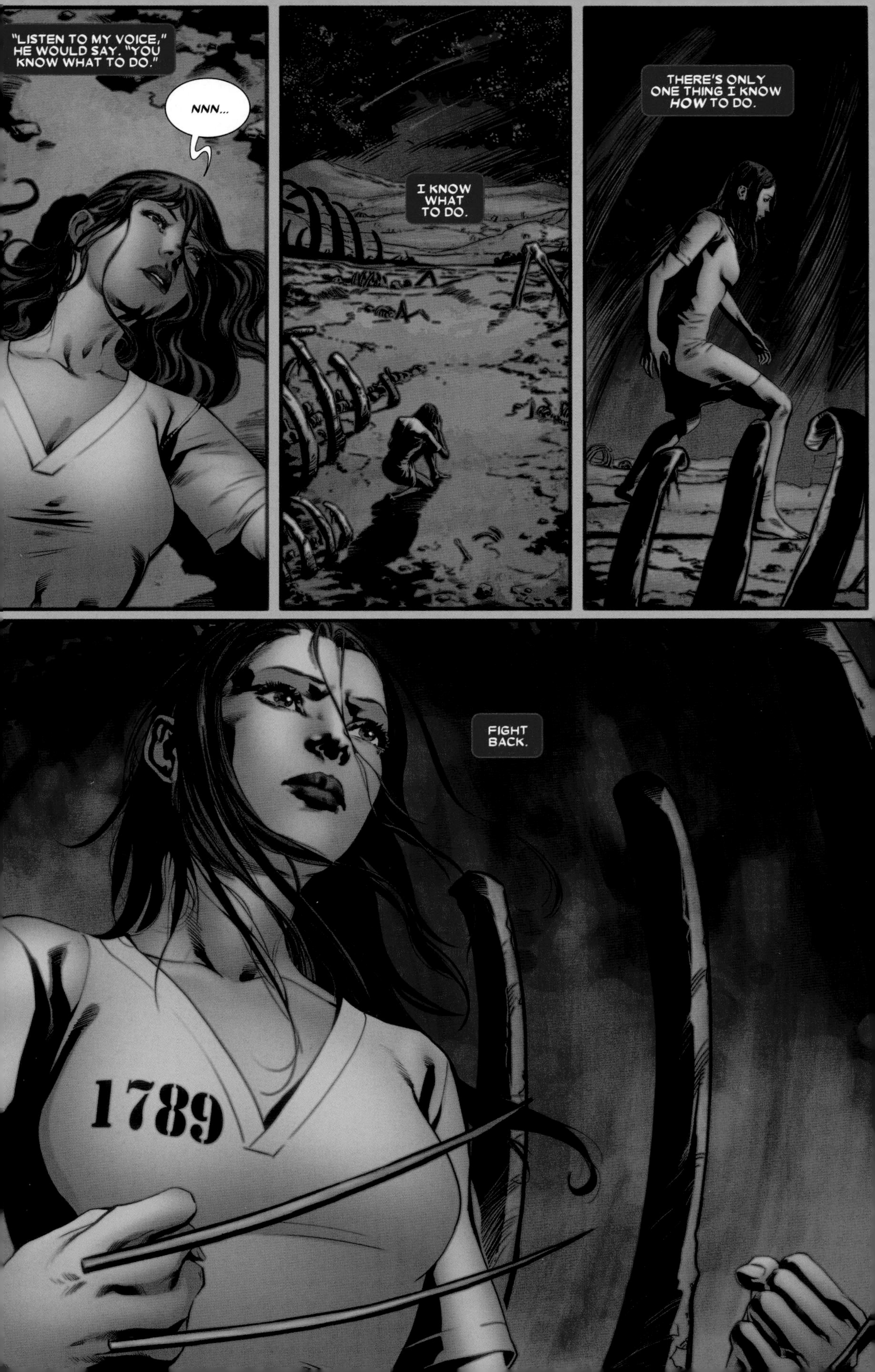
"LISTEN TO MY VOICE," HE WOULD SAY. "YOU KNOW WHAT TO DO."
NNN...
I KNOW WHAT TO DO.
THERE'S ONLY ONE THING I KNOW HOW TO DO.
FIGHT BACK.
1789

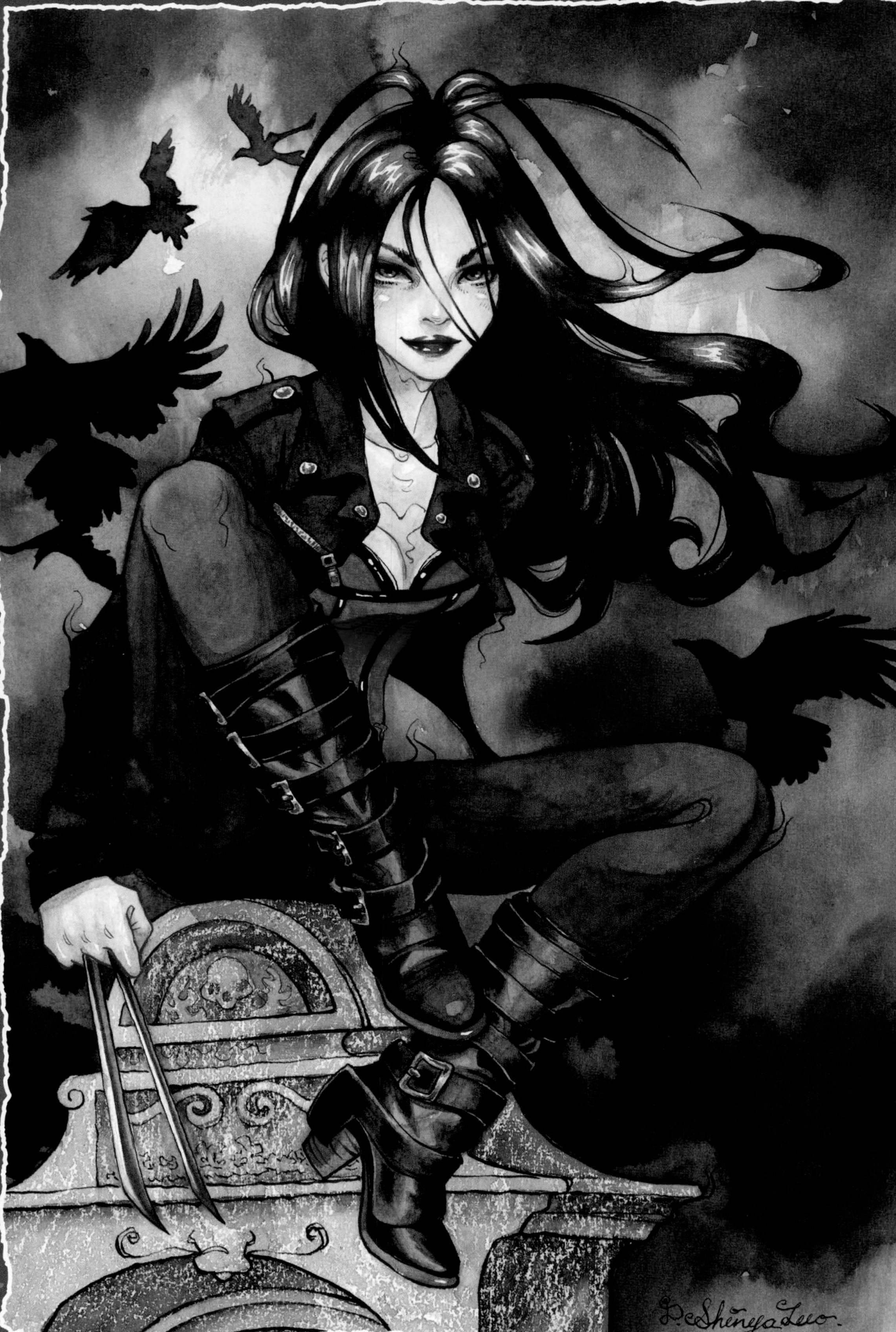
D.c.ShenyaLeeo.

THREE

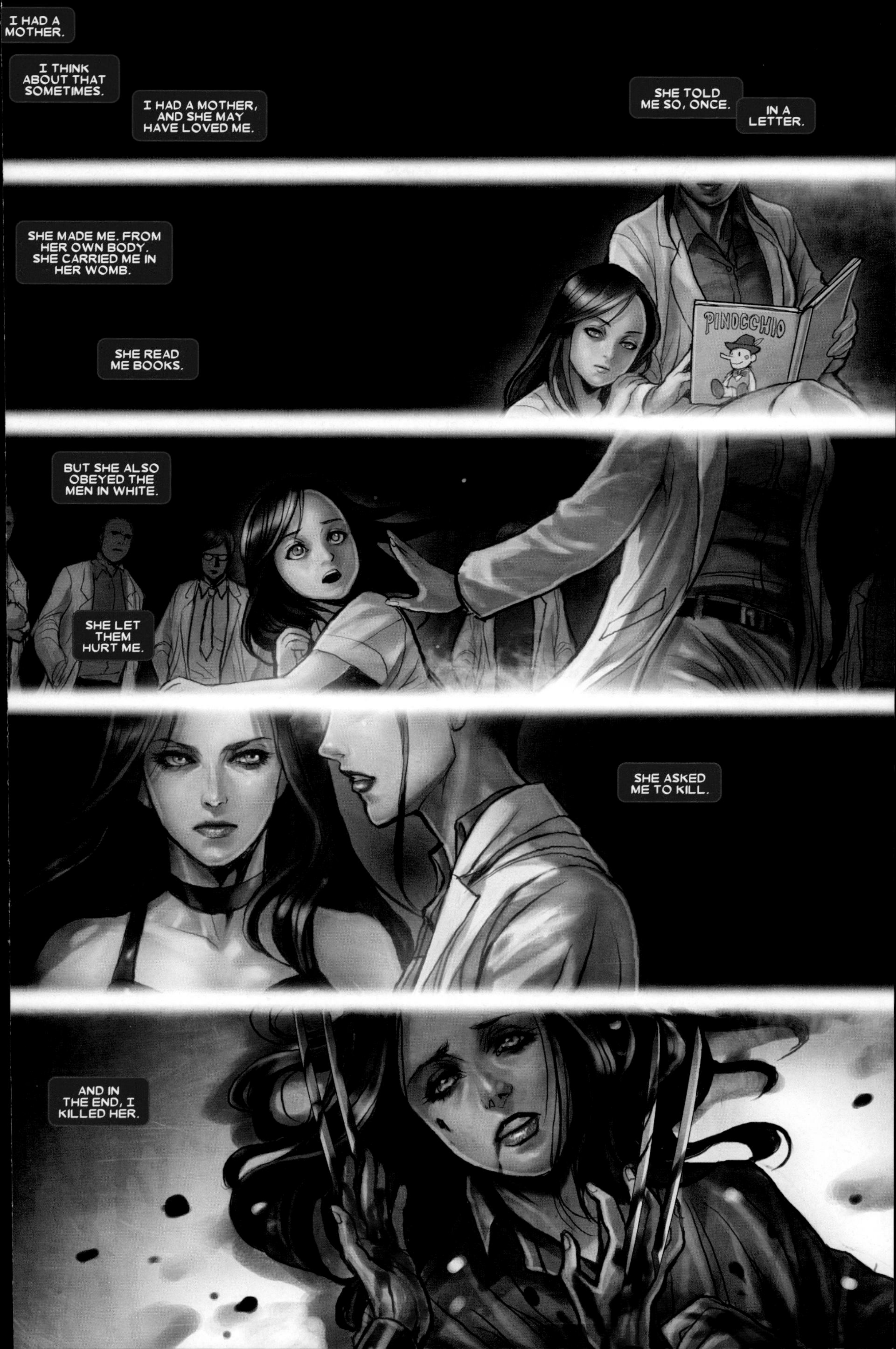
I HAD A MOTHER.
I THINK ABOUT THAT SOMETIMES.
I HAD A MOTHER, AND SHE MAY HAVE LOVED ME.
SHE TOLD ME SO, ONCE.
IN A LETTER.
SHE MADE ME. FROM HER OWN BODY. SHE CARRIED ME IN HER WOMB.
PINOCCHIO
SHE READ ME BOOKS.
BUT SHE ALSO OBEYED THE MEN IN WHITE.
SHE LET THEM HURT ME.
SHE ASKED ME TO KILL.
AND IN THE END, I KILLED HER.

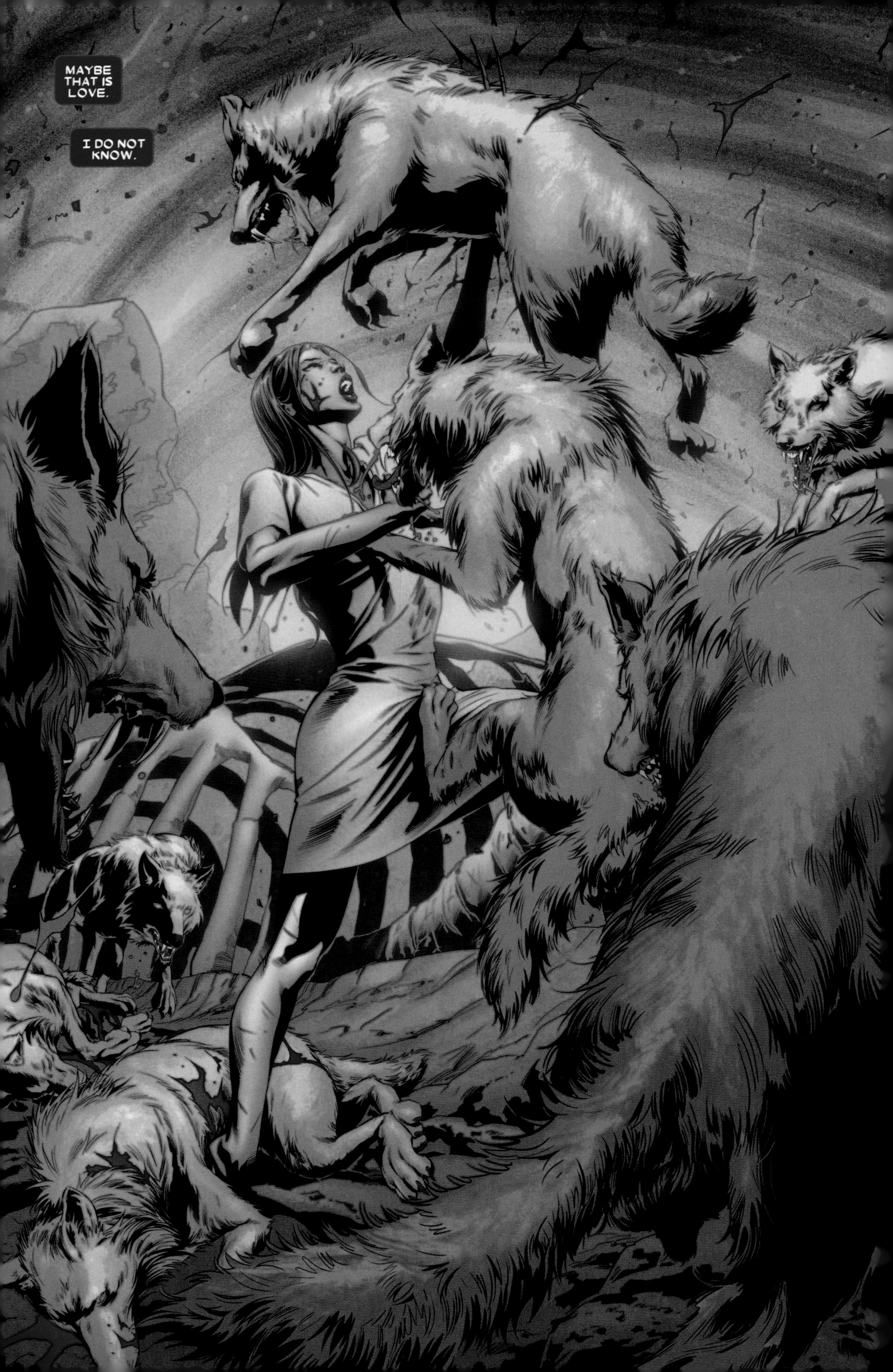
MAYBE THAT IS LOVE.
I DO NOT KNOW.

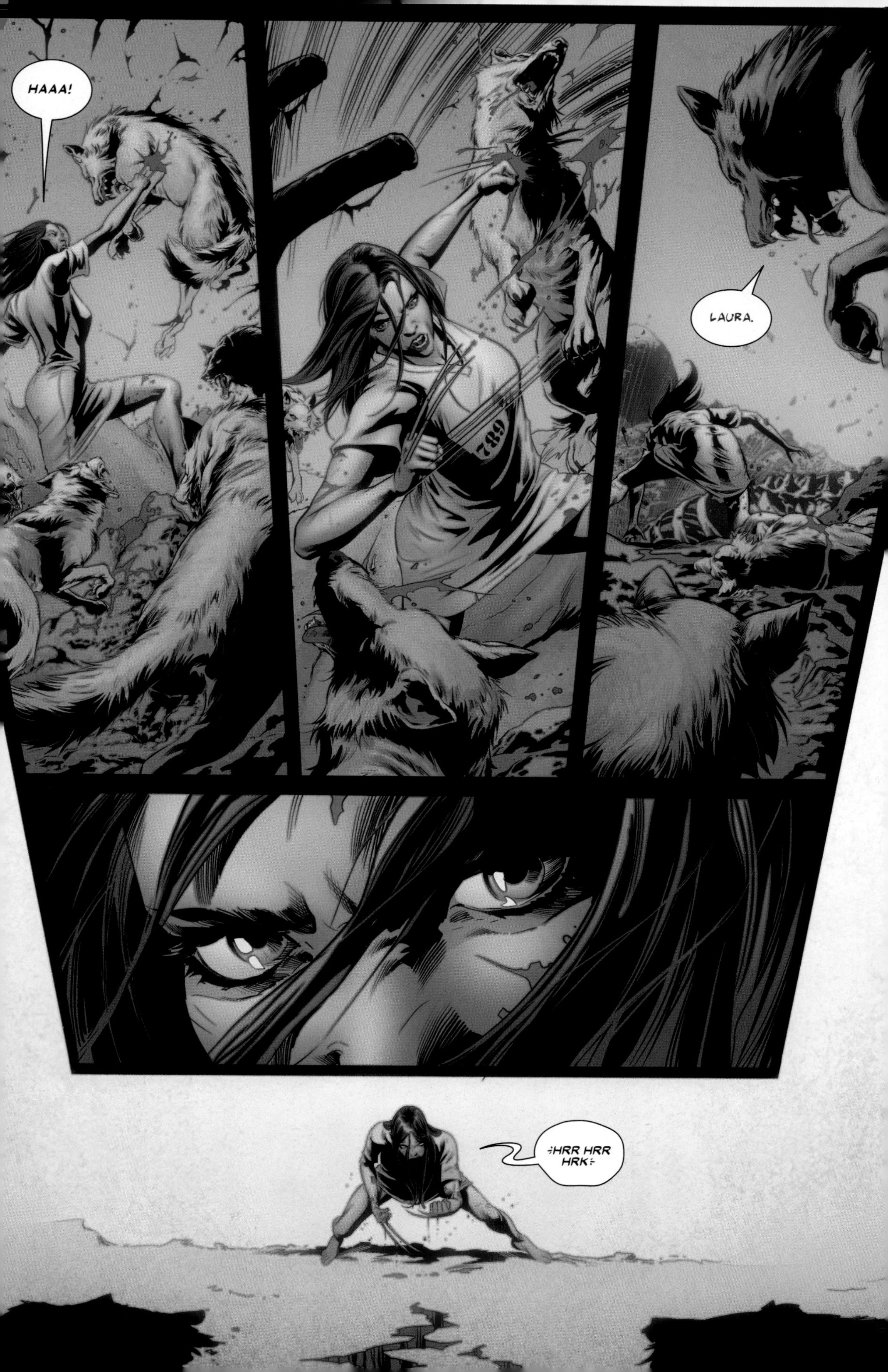

HAAA!
LAURA.
=HRR HRR HRK=

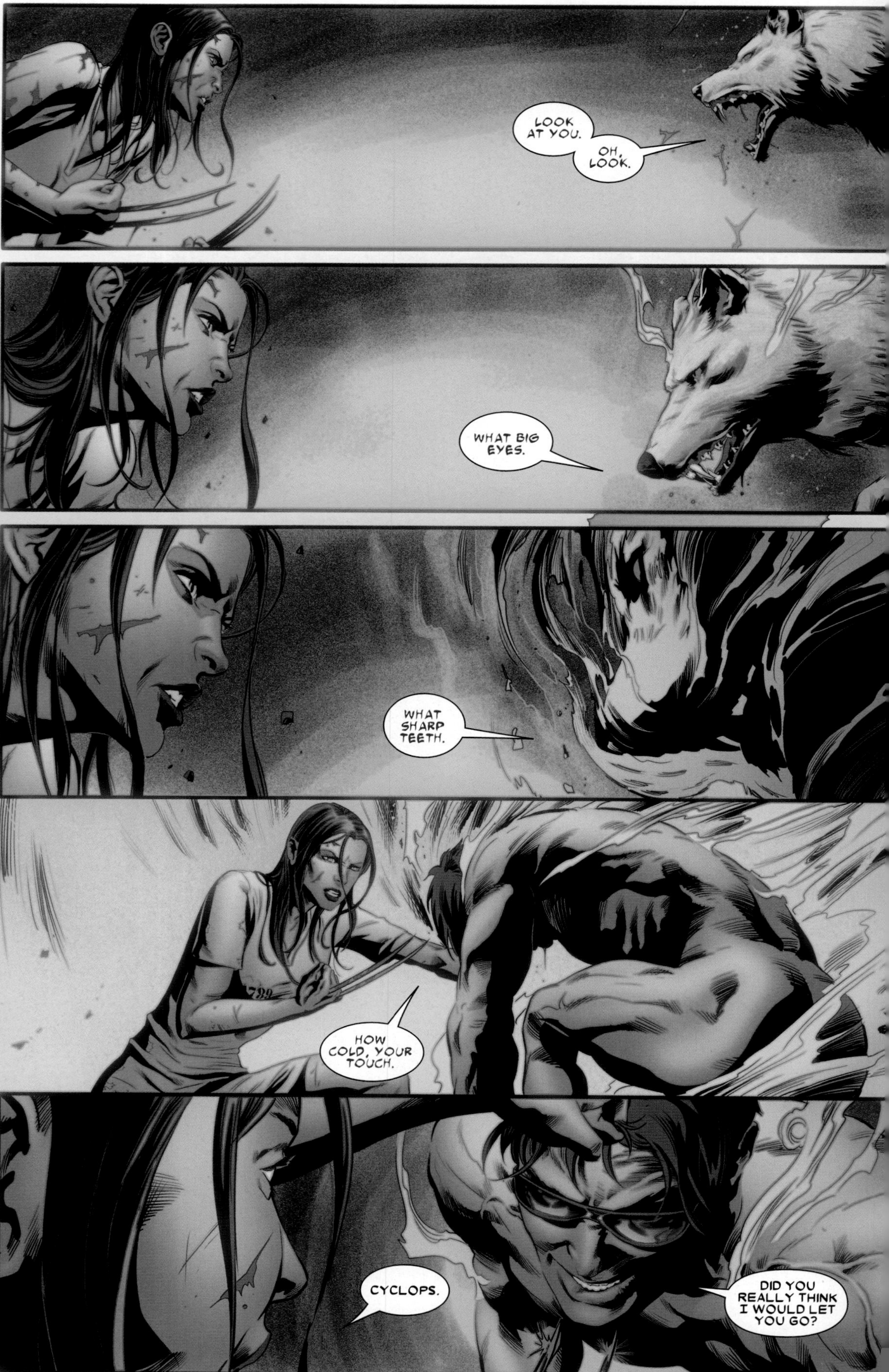
LOOK AT YOU.
OH, LOOK.
WHAT BIG EYES.
WHAT SHARP TEETH.
HOW COLD, YOUR TOUCH.
CYCLOPS.
DID YOU REALLY THINK I WOULD LET YOU GO?

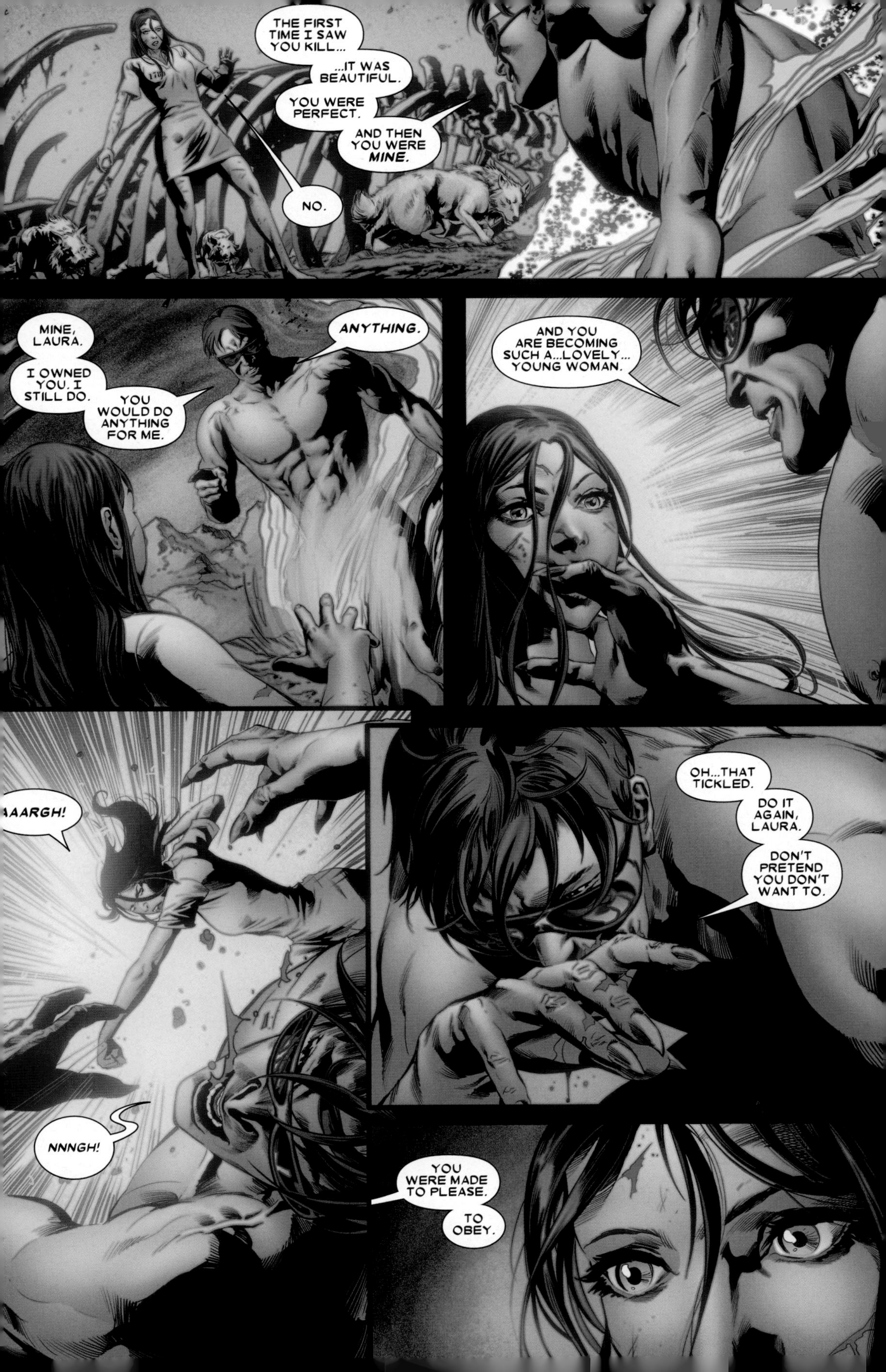
THE FIRST TIME I SAW YOU KILL...
...IT WAS BEAUTIFUL.
YOU WERE PERFECT.
AND THEN YOU WERE MINE.
NO.
MINE, LAURA.
I OWNED YOU. I STILL DO.
YOU WOULD DO ANYTHING FOR ME.
ANYTHING.
AND YOU ARE BECOMING SUCH A...LOVELY... YOUNG WOMAN.
AAARGH!
NNNGH!
OH...THAT TICKLED.
DO IT AGAIN, LAURA.
DON'T PRETEND YOU DON'T WANT TO.
YOU WERE MADE TO PLEASE.
TO OBEY.

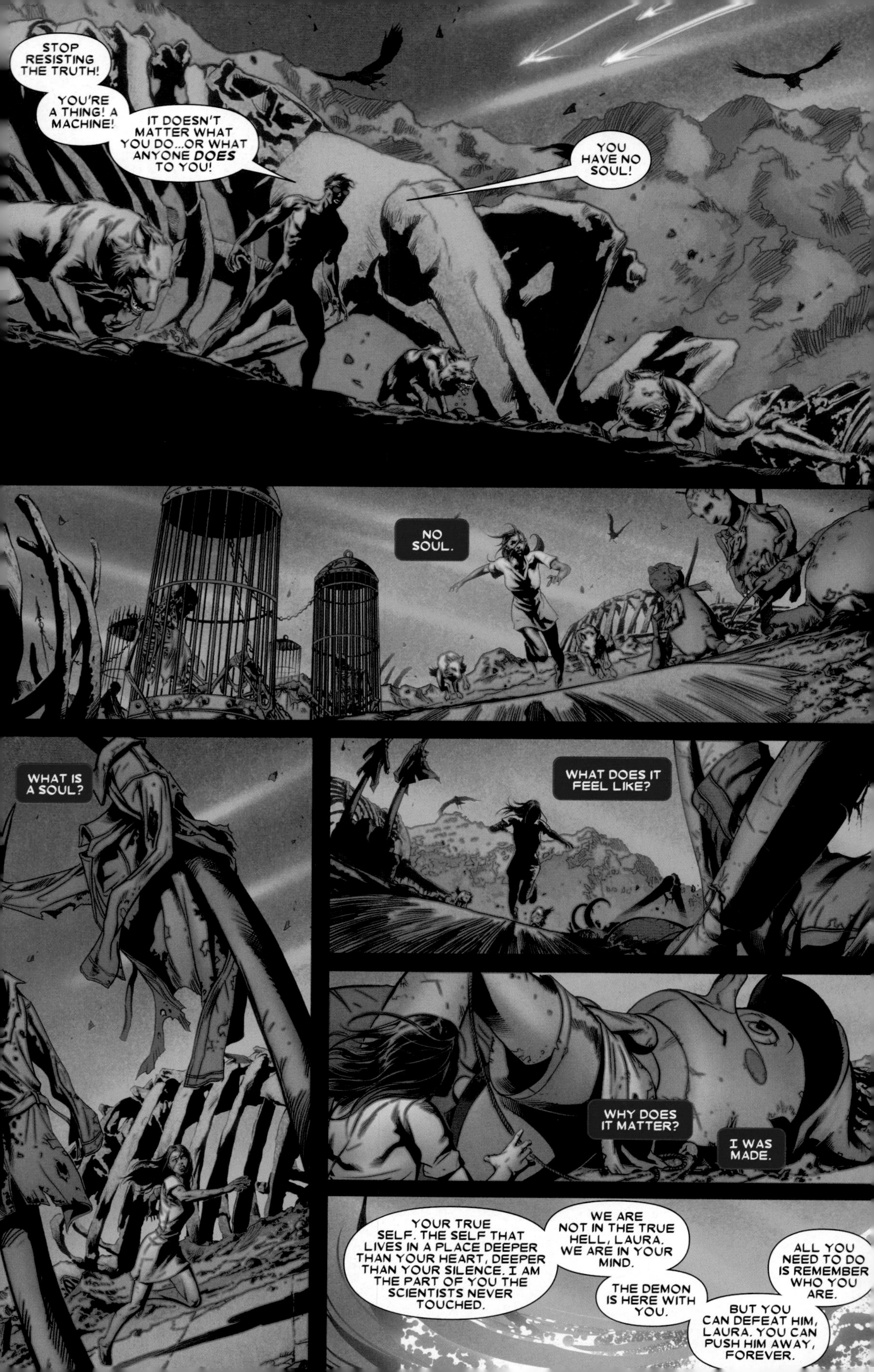
STOP RESISTING THE TRUTH!
YOU'RE A THING! A MACHINE!
IT DOESN'T MATTER WHAT YOU DO...OR WHAT ANYONE *DOES* TO YOU!
YOU HAVE NO SOUL!
NO SOUL.
WHAT IS A SOUL?
WHAT DOES IT FEEL LIKE?
WHY DOES IT MATTER?
I WAS MADE.
YOUR TRUE SELF. THE SELF THAT LIVES IN A PLACE DEEPER THAN YOUR HEART, DEEPER THAN YOUR SILENCE. I AM THE PART OF YOU THE SCIENTISTS NEVER TOUCHED.
WE ARE NOT IN THE TRUE HELL, LAURA. WE ARE IN YOUR MIND.
THE DEMON IS HERE WITH YOU.
BUT YOU CAN DEFEAT HIM, LAURA. YOU CAN PUSH HIM AWAY, FOREVER.
ALL YOU NEED TO DO IS REMEMBER WHO YOU ARE.

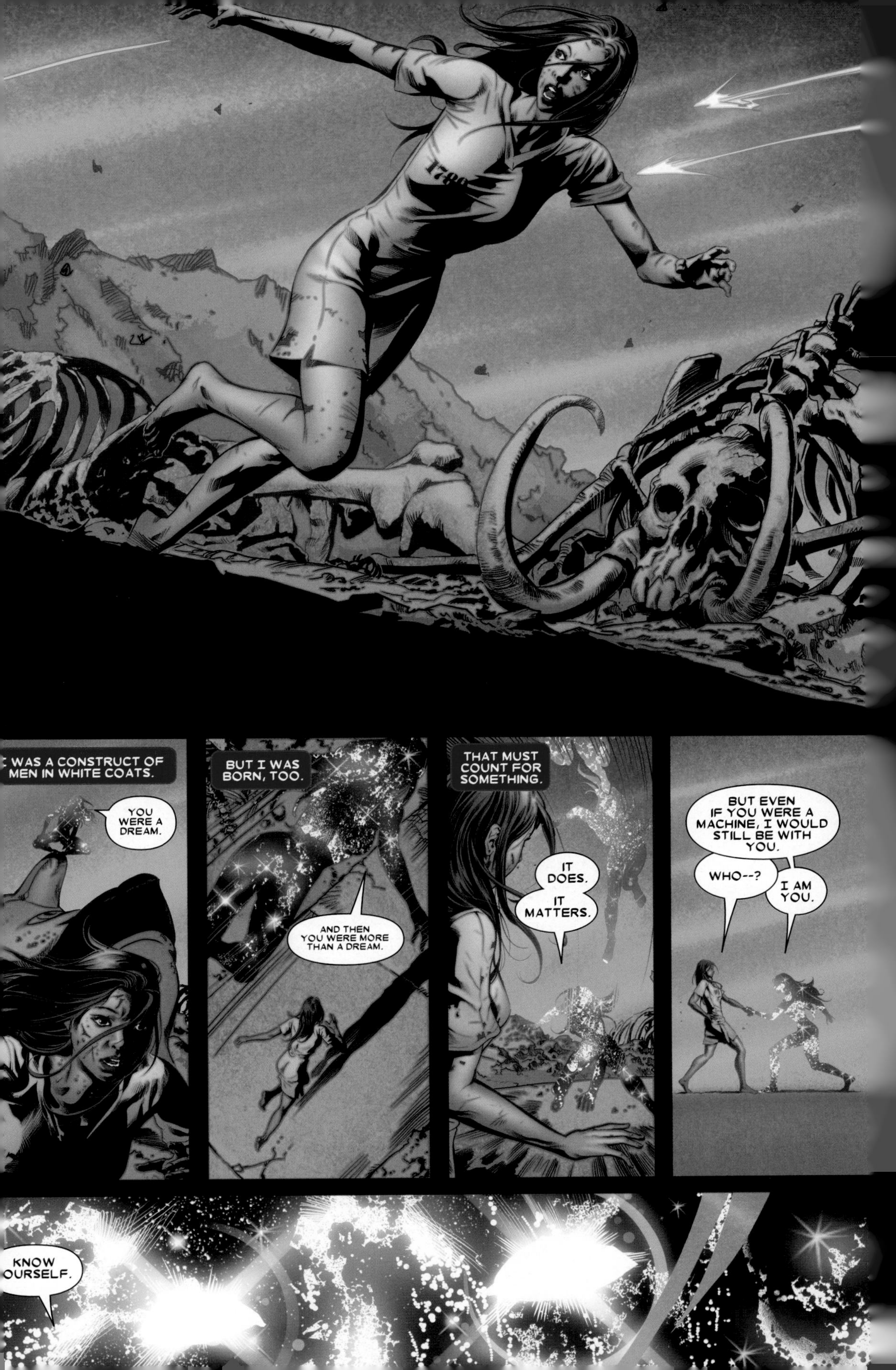

I WAS A CONSTRUCT OF MEN IN WHITE COATS.
YOU WERE A DREAM.
BUT I WAS BORN, TOO.
AND THEN YOU WERE MORE THAN A DREAM.
THAT MUST COUNT FOR SOMETHING.
IT DOES.
IT MATTERS.
BUT EVEN IF YOU WERE A MACHINE, I WOULD STILL BE WITH YOU.
WHO--?
I AM YOU.
KNOW YOURSELF.

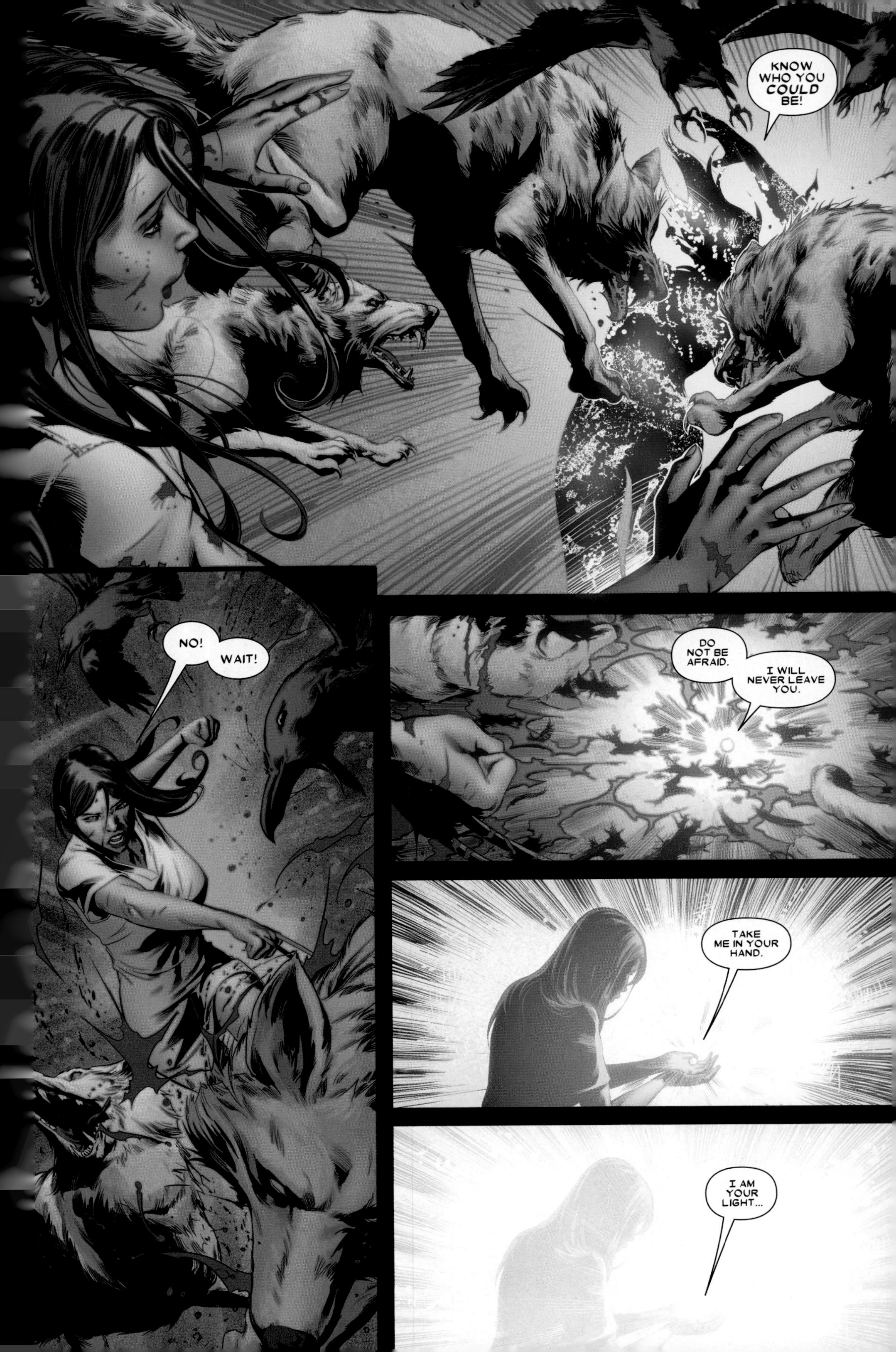
KNOW WHO YOU COULD BE!
NO!
WAIT!
DO NOT BE AFRAID.
I WILL NEVER LEAVE YOU.
TAKE ME IN YOUR HAND.
I AM YOUR LIGHT...

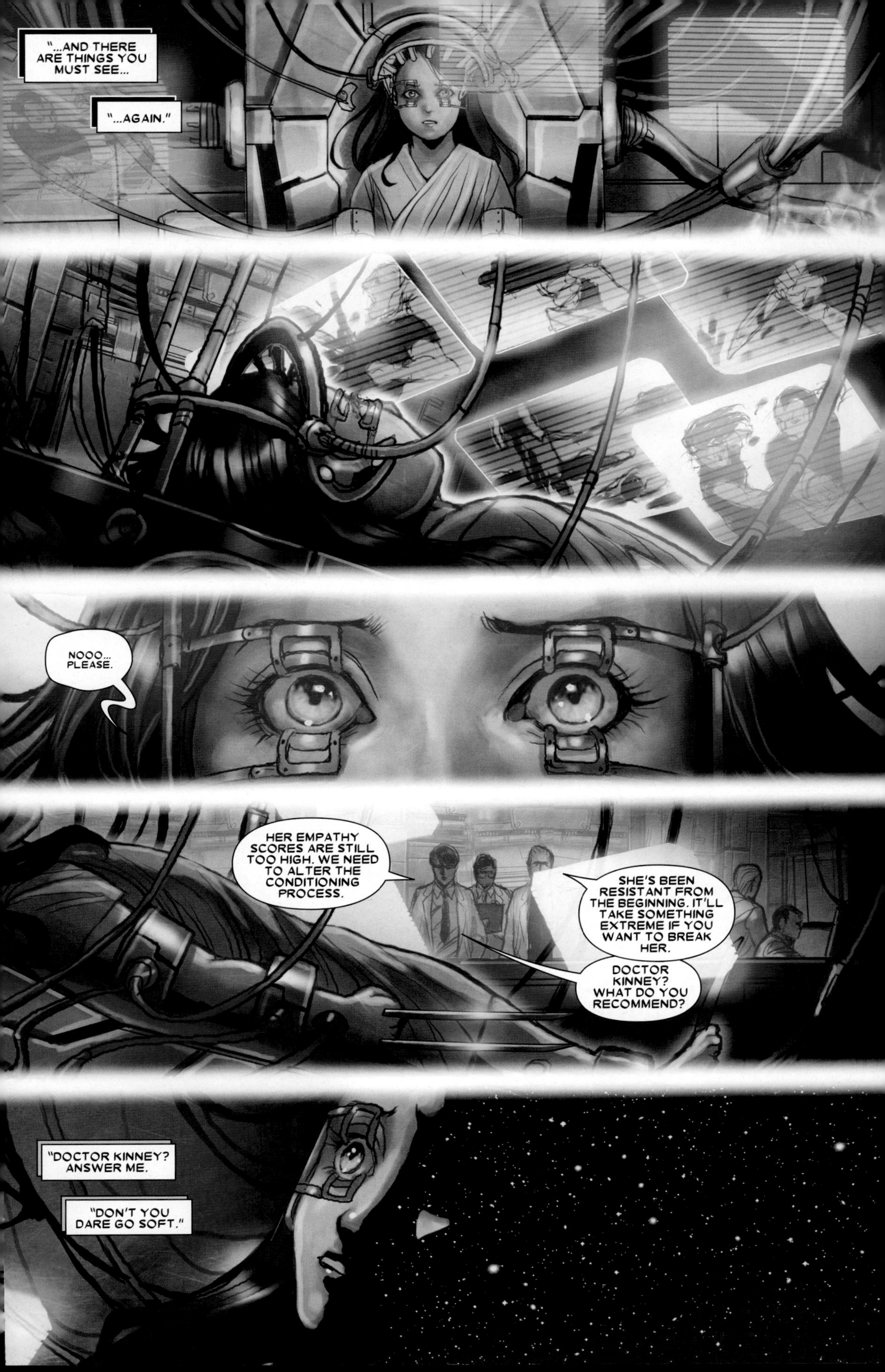
"...AND THERE ARE THINGS YOU MUST SEE...
"...AGAIN."
NOOO... PLEASE.
HER EMPATHY SCORES ARE STILL TOO HIGH. WE NEED TO ALTER THE CONDITIONING PROCESS.
SHE'S BEEN RESISTANT FROM THE BEGINNING. IT'LL TAKE SOMETHING EXTREME IF YOU WANT TO BREAK HER.
DOCTOR KINNEY? WHAT DO YOU RECOMMEND?
"DOCTOR KINNEY? ANSWER ME.
"DON'T YOU DARE GO SOFT."

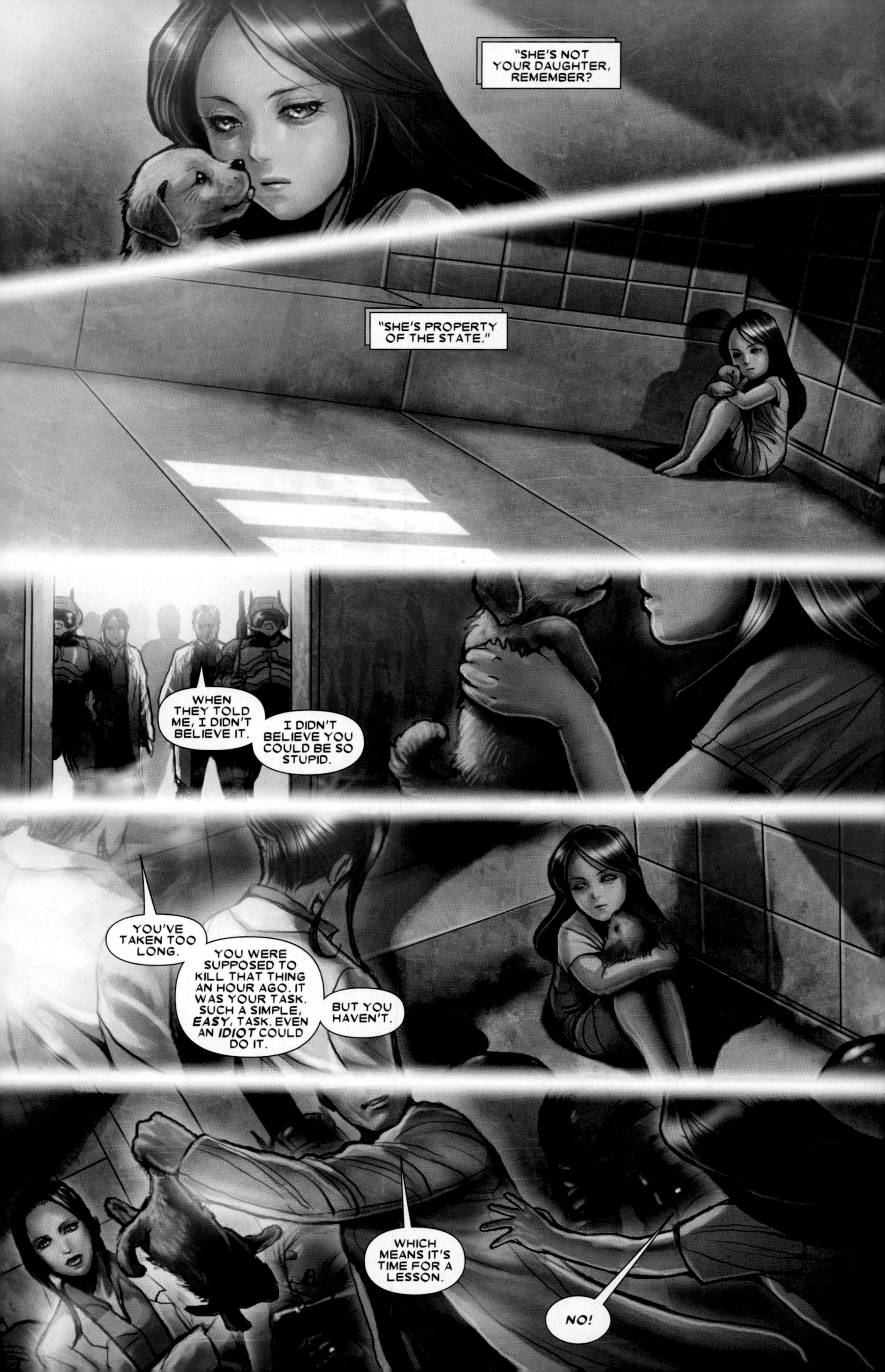
"SHE'S NOT YOUR DAUGHTER, REMEMBER?
"SHE'S PROPERTY OF THE STATE."
WHEN THEY TOLD ME, I DIDN'T BELIEVE IT.
I DIDN'T BELIEVE YOU COULD BE SO STUPID.
YOU'VE TAKEN TOO LONG.
YOU WERE SUPPOSED TO KILL THAT THING AN HOUR AGO. IT WAS YOUR TASK. SUCH A SIMPLE, EASY, TASK. EVEN AN IDIOT COULD DO IT.
BUT YOU HAVEN'T.
WHICH MEANS IT'S TIME FOR A LESSON.
NO!

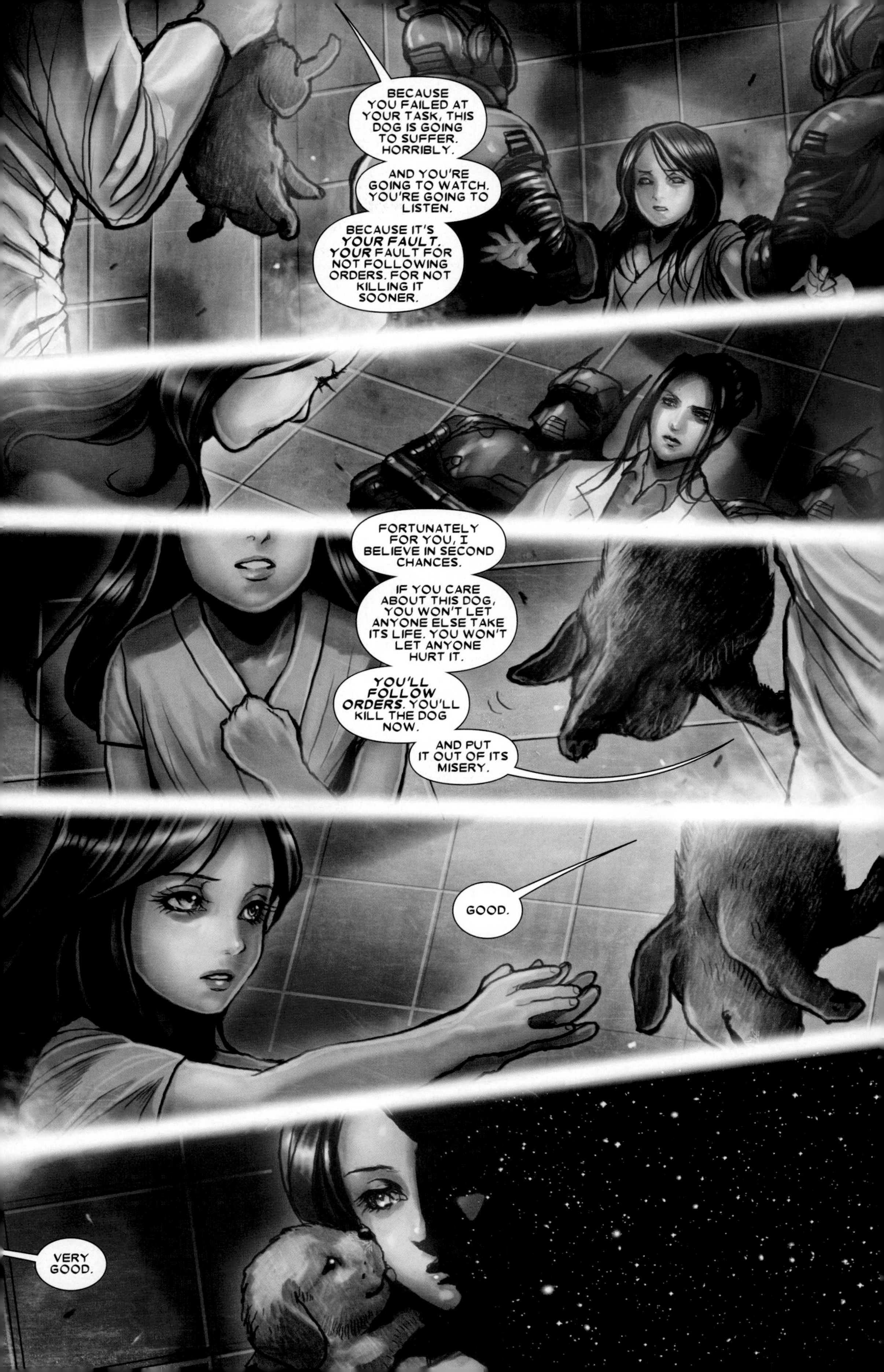
BECAUSE YOU FAILED AT YOUR TASK, THIS DOG IS GOING TO SUFFER. HORRIBLY.
AND YOU'RE GOING TO WATCH. YOU'RE GOING TO LISTEN.
BECAUSE IT'S *YOUR FAULT. YOUR* FAULT FOR NOT FOLLOWING ORDERS. FOR NOT KILLING IT SOONER.
FORTUNATELY FOR YOU, I BELIEVE IN SECOND CHANCES.
IF YOU CARE ABOUT THIS DOG, YOU WON'T LET ANYONE ELSE TAKE ITS LIFE. YOU WON'T LET ANYONE HURT IT.
YOU'LL FOLLOW ORDERS. YOU'LL KILL THE DOG NOW.
AND PUT IT OUT OF ITS MISERY.
GOOD.
VERY GOOD.

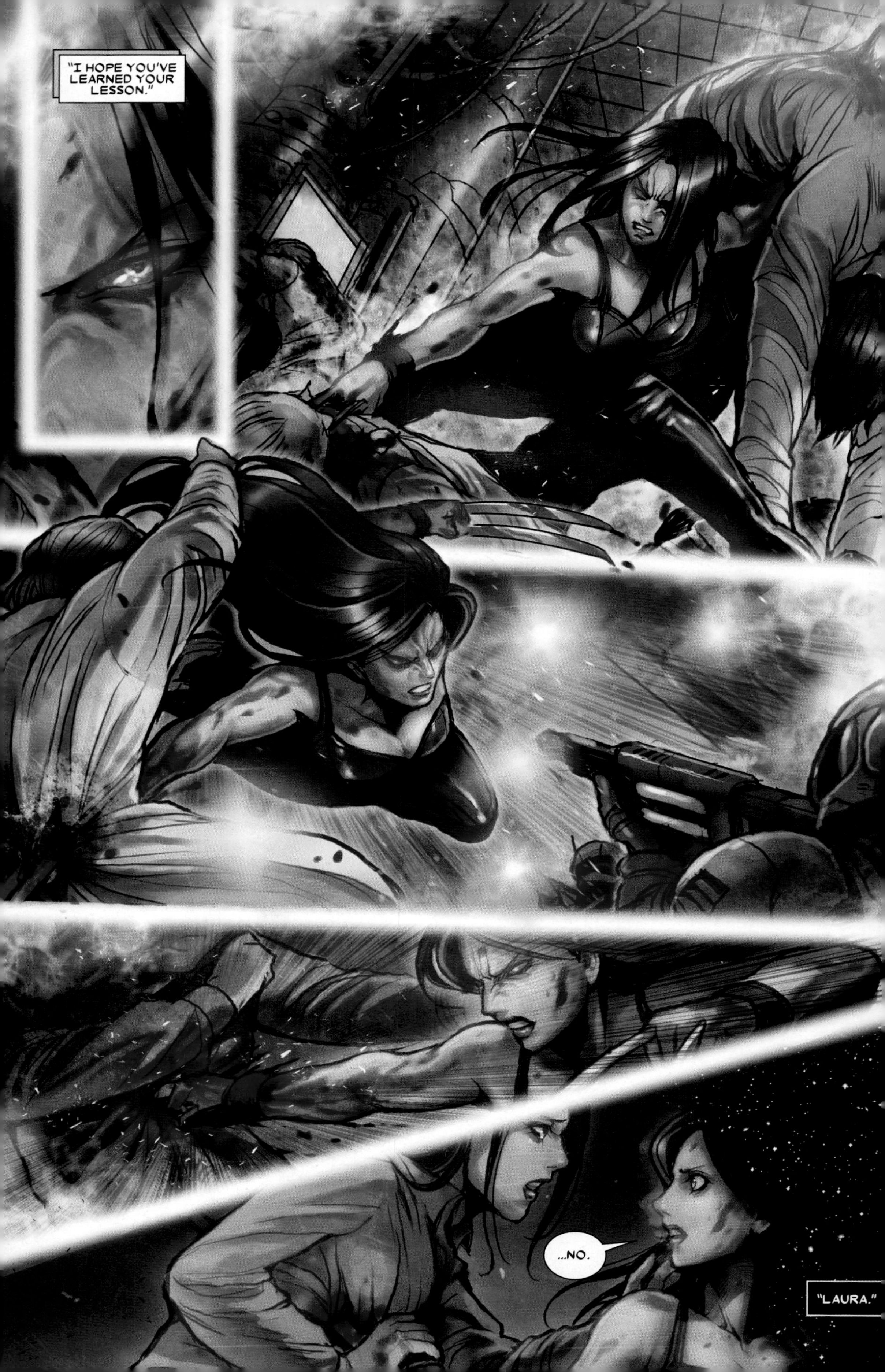
"I HOPE YOU'VE LEARNED YOUR LESSON."
...NO.
"LAURA."

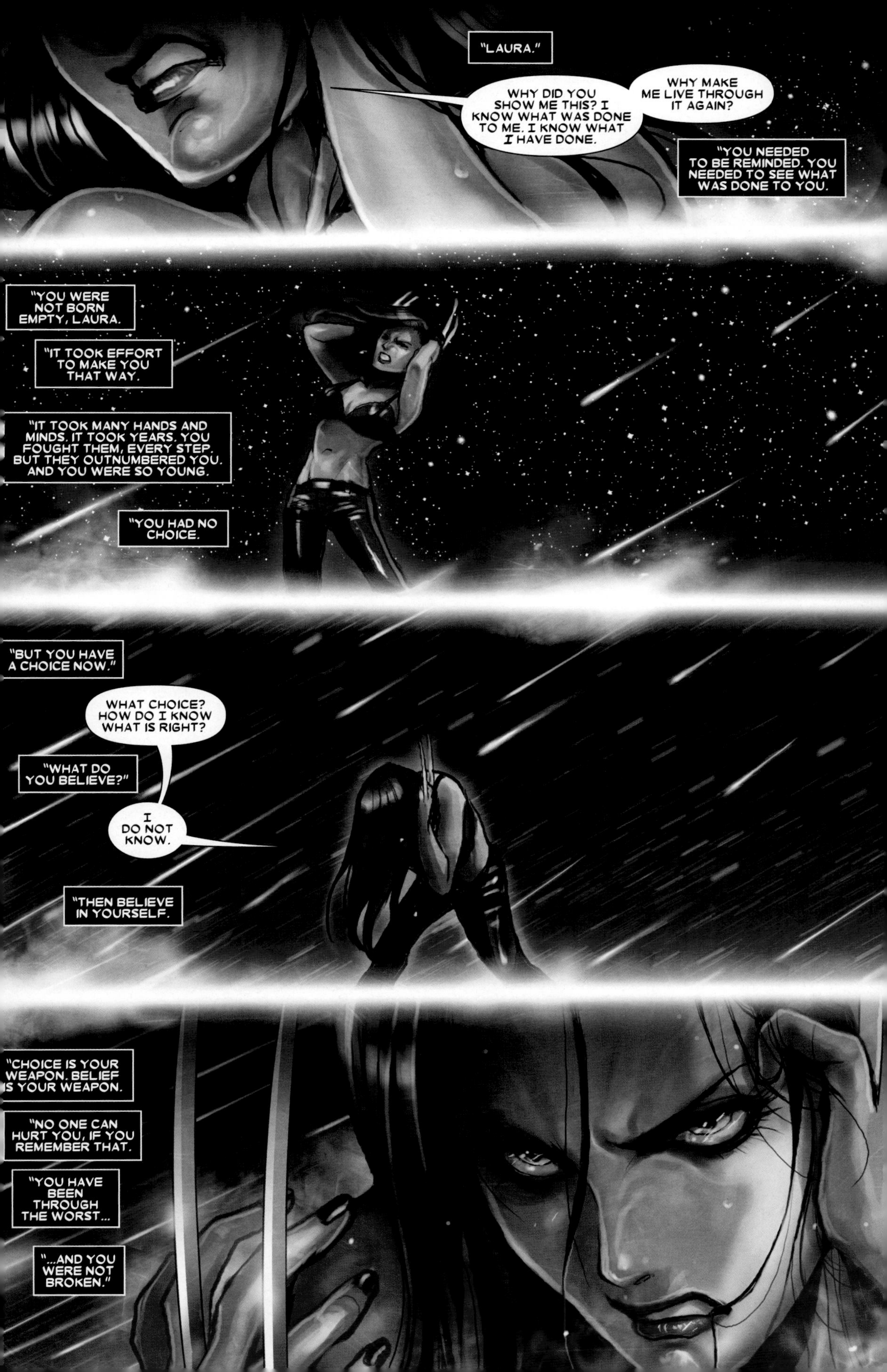
"LAURA."
WHY DID YOU SHOW ME THIS? I KNOW WHAT WAS DONE TO ME. I KNOW WHAT I HAVE DONE.
WHY MAKE ME LIVE THROUGH IT AGAIN?
"YOU NEEDED TO BE REMINDED. YOU NEEDED TO SEE WHAT WAS DONE TO YOU.
"YOU WERE NOT BORN EMPTY, LAURA.
"IT TOOK EFFORT TO MAKE YOU THAT WAY.
"IT TOOK MANY HANDS AND MINDS. IT TOOK YEARS. YOU FOUGHT THEM, EVERY STEP. BUT THEY OUTNUMBERED YOU. AND YOU WERE SO YOUNG.
"YOU HAD NO CHOICE.
"BUT YOU HAVE A CHOICE NOW."
WHAT CHOICE? HOW DO I KNOW WHAT IS RIGHT?
"WHAT DO YOU BELIEVE?"
I DO NOT KNOW.
"THEN BELIEVE IN YOURSELF.
"CHOICE IS YOUR WEAPON. BELIEF IS YOUR WEAPON.
"NO ONE CAN HURT YOU, IF YOU REMEMBER THAT.
"YOU HAVE BEEN THROUGH THE WORST...
"...AND YOU WERE NOT BROKEN."

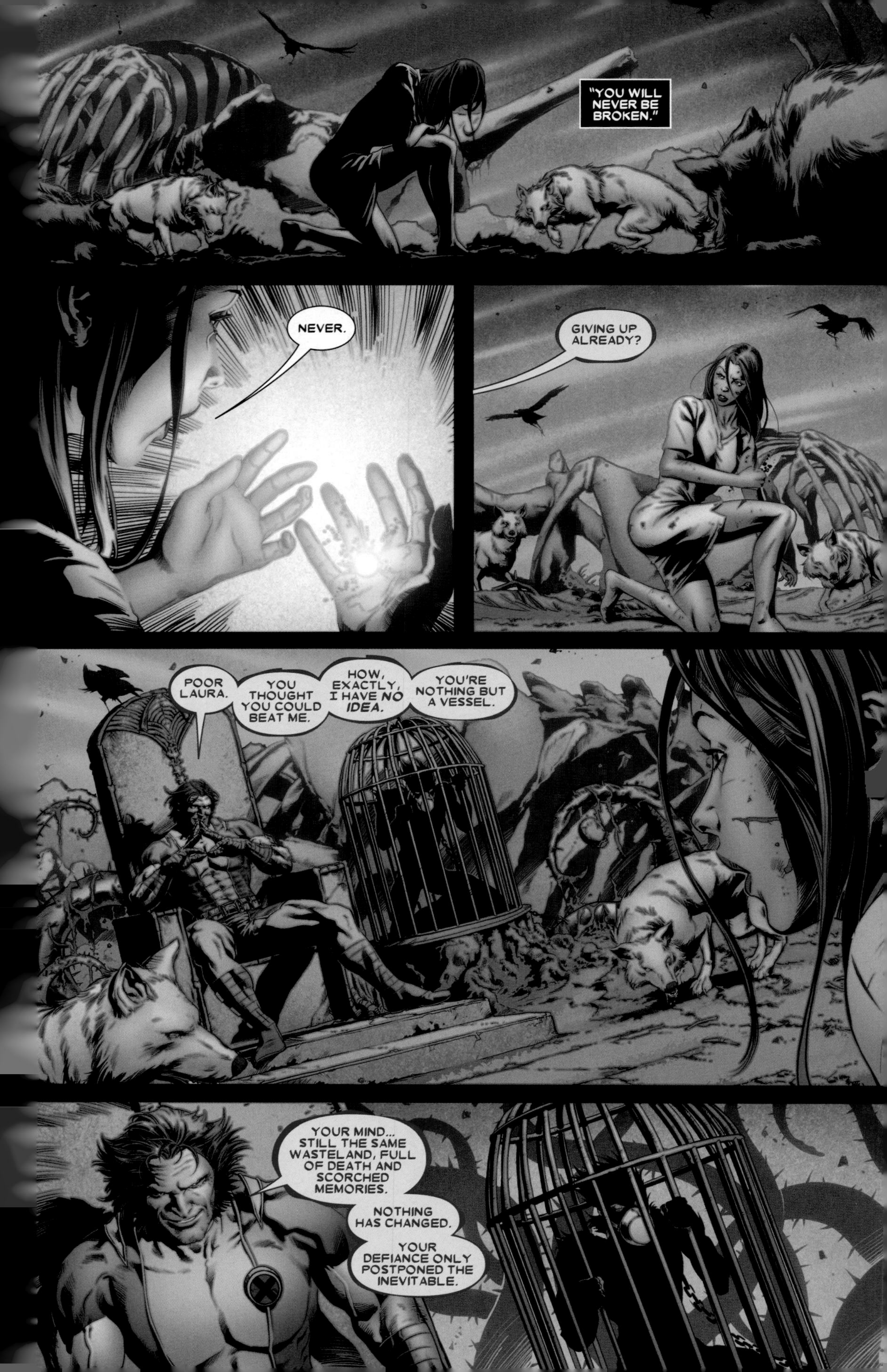
"YOU WILL NEVER BE BROKEN."
NEVER.
GIVING UP ALREADY?
POOR LAURA.
YOU THOUGHT YOU COULD BEAT ME.
HOW, EXACTLY, I HAVE NO IDEA.
YOU'RE NOTHING BUT A VESSEL.
YOUR MIND... STILL THE SAME WASTELAND, FULL OF DEATH AND SCORCHED MEMORIES.
NOTHING HAS CHANGED.
YOUR DEFIANCE ONLY POSTPONED THE INEVITABLE.

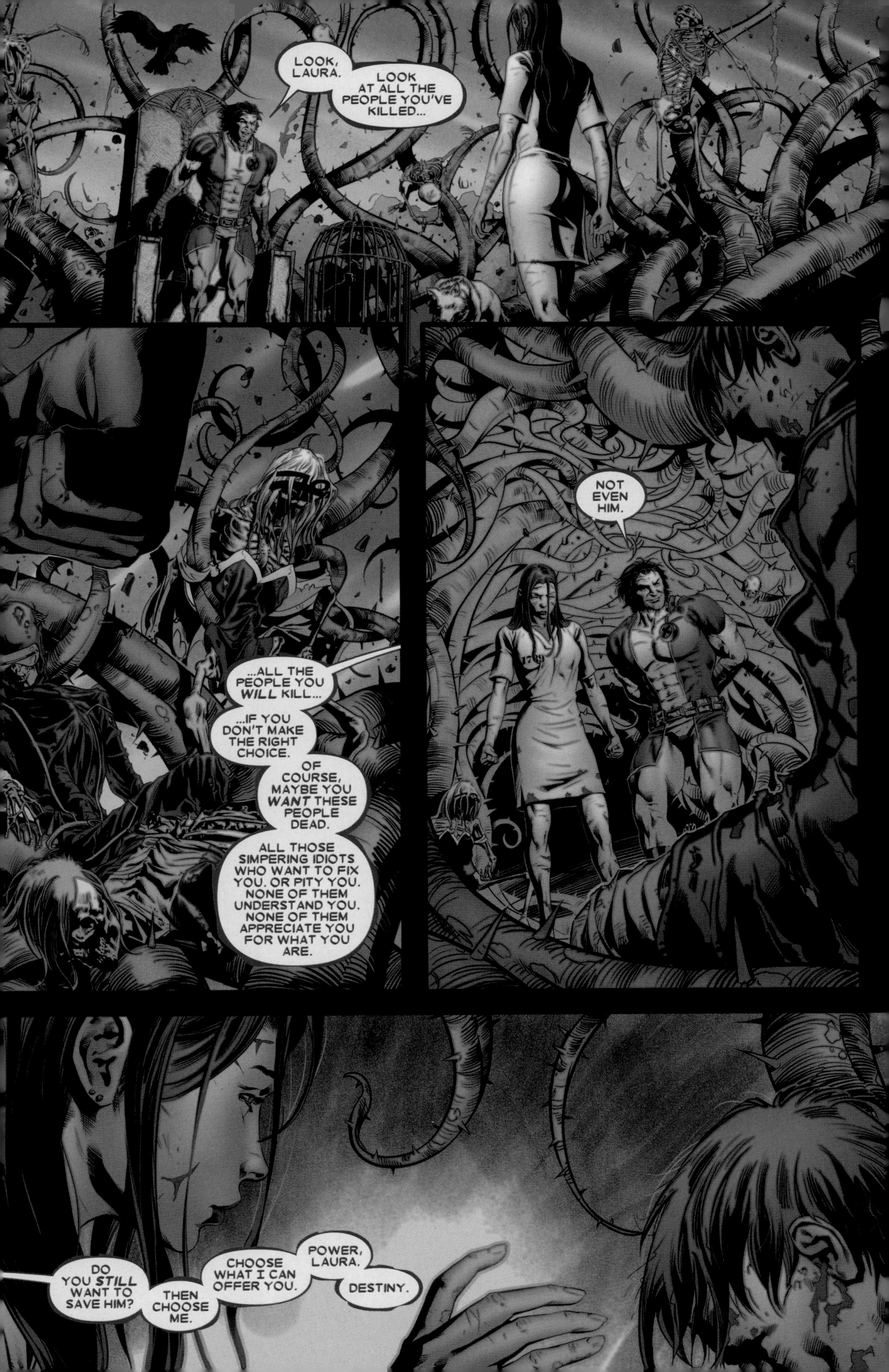
LOOK, LAURA.
LOOK AT ALL THE PEOPLE YOU'VE KILLED...
...ALL THE PEOPLE YOU *WILL* KILL...
...IF YOU DON'T MAKE THE RIGHT CHOICE.
OF COURSE, MAYBE YOU *WANT* THESE PEOPLE DEAD.
ALL THOSE SIMPERING IDIOTS WHO WANT TO FIX YOU. OR PITY YOU. NONE OF THEM UNDERSTAND YOU. NONE OF THEM APPRECIATE YOU FOR WHAT YOU ARE.
NOT EVEN HIM.
DO YOU *STILL* WANT TO SAVE HIM?
THEN CHOOSE ME.
CHOOSE WHAT I CAN OFFER YOU.
POWER, LAURA.
DESTINY.

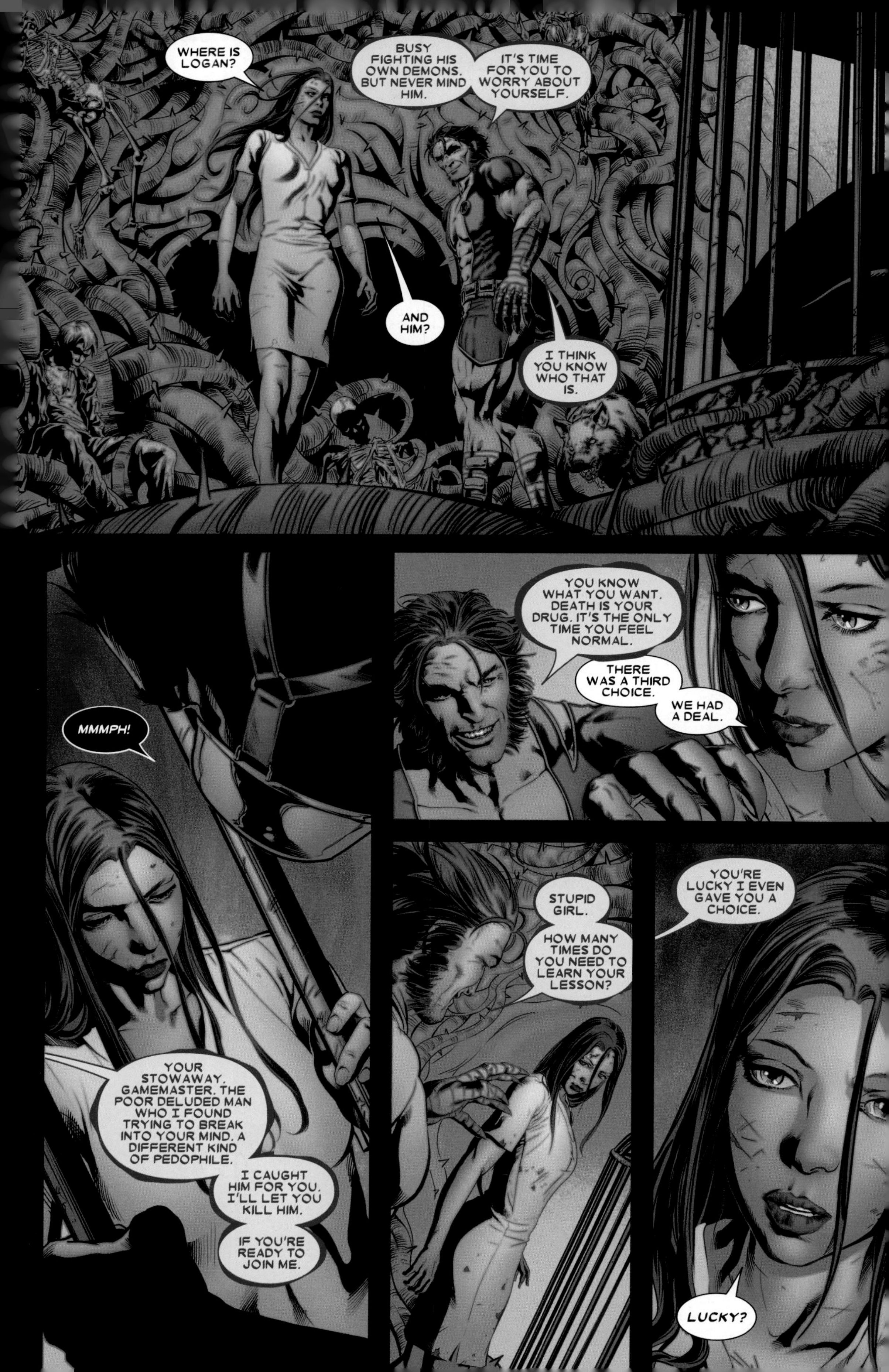
WHERE IS LOGAN?
BUSY FIGHTING HIS OWN DEMONS. BUT NEVER MIND HIM.
IT'S TIME FOR YOU TO WORRY ABOUT YOURSELF.
AND HIM?
I THINK YOU KNOW WHO THAT IS.
MMMPH!
YOUR STOWAWAY, GAMEMASTER. THE POOR DELUDED MAN WHO I FOUND TRYING TO BREAK INTO YOUR MIND. A DIFFERENT KIND OF PEDOPHILE.
I CAUGHT HIM FOR YOU. I'LL LET YOU KILL HIM.
IF YOU'RE READY TO JOIN ME.
YOU KNOW WHAT YOU WANT. DEATH IS YOUR DRUG. IT'S THE ONLY TIME YOU FEEL NORMAL.
THERE WAS A THIRD CHOICE.
WE HAD A DEAL.
STUPID GIRL.
HOW MANY TIMES DO YOU NEED TO LEARN YOUR LESSON?
YOU'RE LUCKY I EVEN GAVE YOU A CHOICE.
LUCKY?

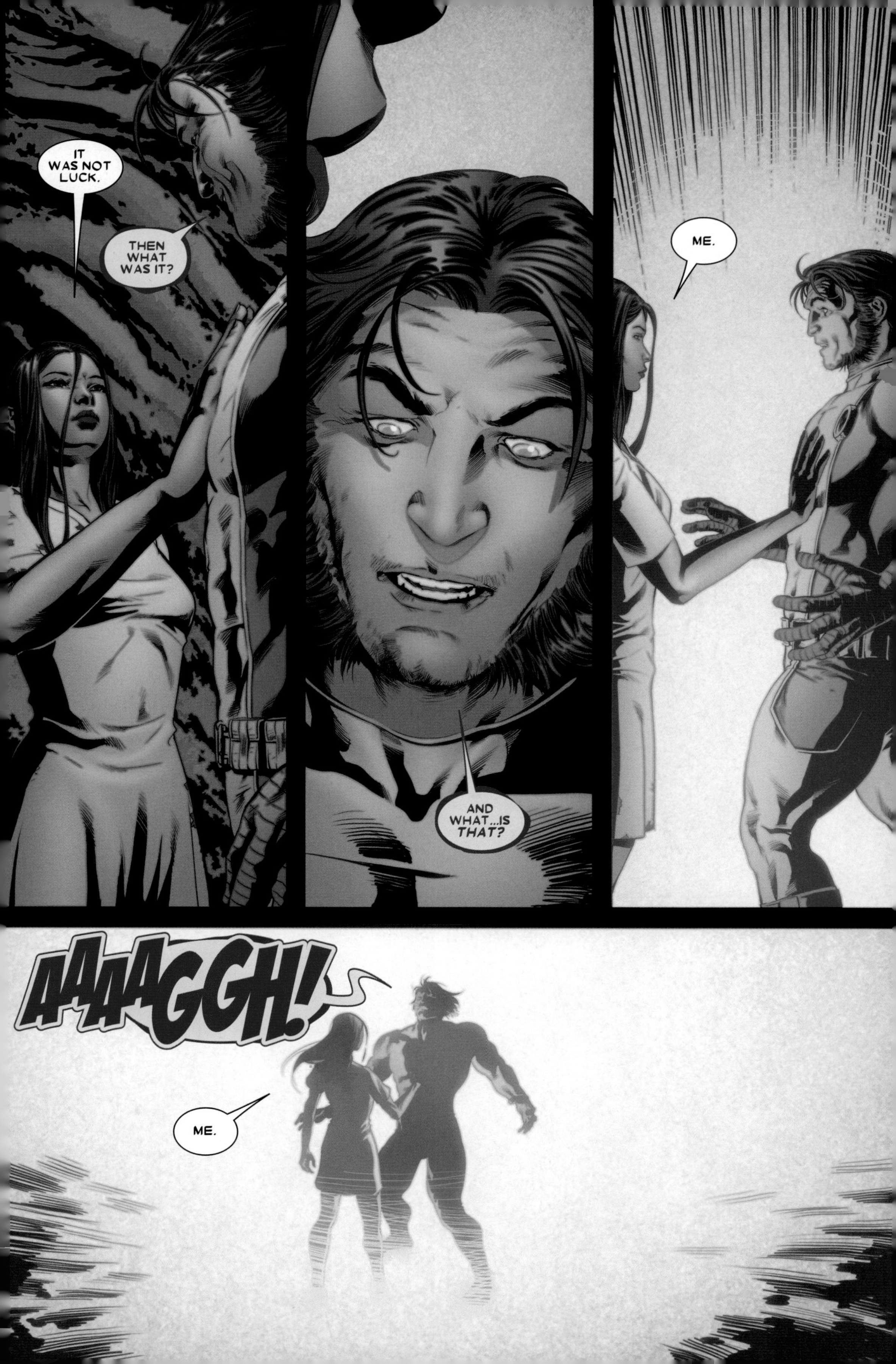
IT WAS NOT LUCK.
THEN WHAT WAS IT?
AND WHAT...IS *THAT?*
ME.
AAAAGGH!
ME.

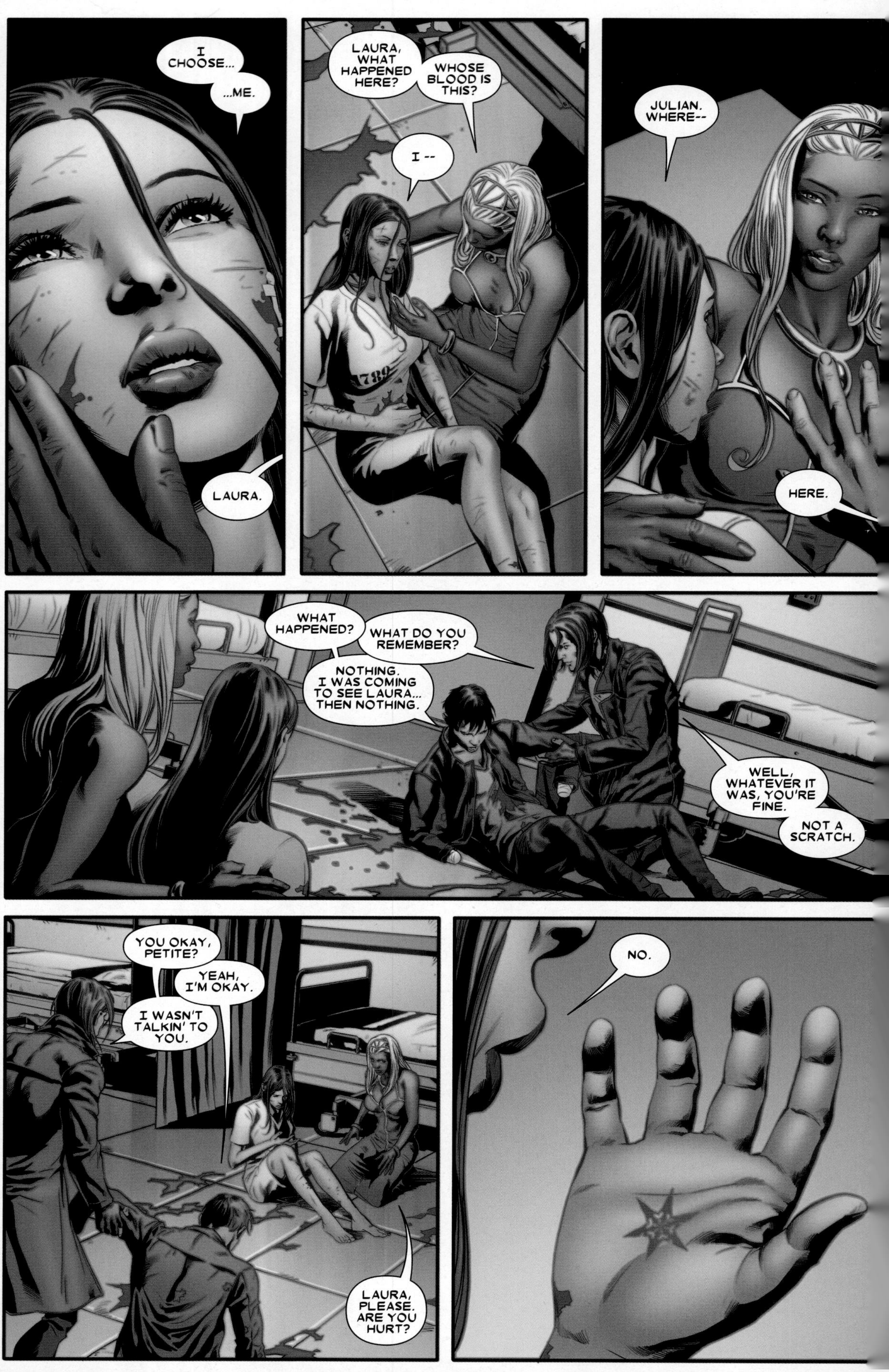
I CHOOSE...
...ME.
LAURA.
LAURA, WHAT HAPPENED HERE?
WHOSE BLOOD IS THIS?
I --
JULIAN. WHERE--
HERE.
WHAT HAPPENED?
WHAT DO YOU REMEMBER?
NOTHING. I WAS COMING TO SEE LAURA... THEN NOTHING.
WELL, WHATEVER IT WAS, YOU'RE FINE.
NOT A SCRATCH.
YOU OKAY, PETITE?
YEAH, I'M OKAY.
I WASN'T TALKIN' TO YOU.
LAURA, PLEASE. ARE YOU HURT?
NO.

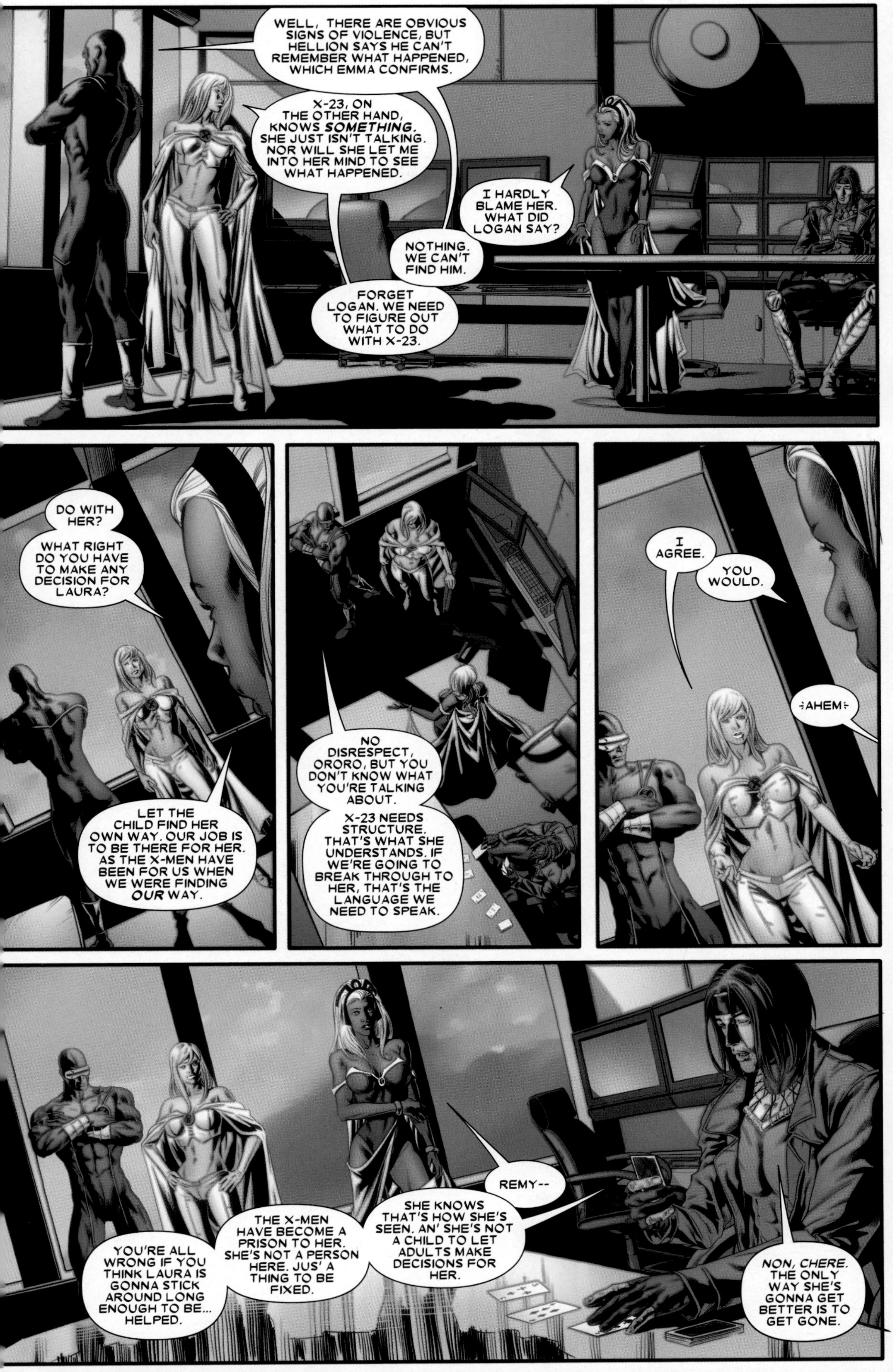
WELL, THERE ARE OBVIOUS SIGNS OF VIOLENCE, BUT HELLION SAYS HE CAN'T REMEMBER WHAT HAPPENED, WHICH EMMA CONFIRMS.
X-23, ON THE OTHER HAND, KNOWS *SOMETHING*. SHE JUST ISN'T TALKING. NOR WILL SHE LET ME INTO HER MIND TO SEE WHAT HAPPENED.
I HARDLY BLAME HER. WHAT DID LOGAN SAY?
NOTHING. WE CAN'T FIND HIM.
FORGET LOGAN. WE NEED TO FIGURE OUT WHAT TO DO WITH X-23.
DO WITH HER?
WHAT RIGHT DO YOU HAVE TO MAKE ANY DECISION FOR LAURA?
LET THE CHILD FIND HER OWN WAY. OUR JOB IS TO BE THERE FOR HER. AS THE X-MEN HAVE BEEN FOR US WHEN WE WERE FINDING *OUR* WAY.
NO DISRESPECT, ORORO, BUT YOU DON'T KNOW WHAT YOU'RE TALKING ABOUT.
X-23 NEEDS STRUCTURE. THAT'S WHAT SHE UNDERSTANDS. IF WE'RE GOING TO BREAK THROUGH TO HER, THAT'S THE LANGUAGE WE NEED TO SPEAK.
I AGREE.
YOU WOULD.
AHEM
NON, CHERE. THE ONLY WAY SHE'S GONNA GET BETTER IS TO GET GONE.
REMY--
SHE KNOWS THAT'S HOW SHE'S SEEN. AN' SHE'S NOT A CHILD TO LET ADULTS MAKE DECISIONS FOR HER.
THE X-MEN HAVE BECOME A PRISON TO HER. SHE'S NOT A PERSON HERE. JUS' A THING TO BE FIXED.
YOU'RE ALL WRONG IF YOU THINK LAURA IS GONNA STICK AROUND LONG ENOUGH TO BE... HELPED.

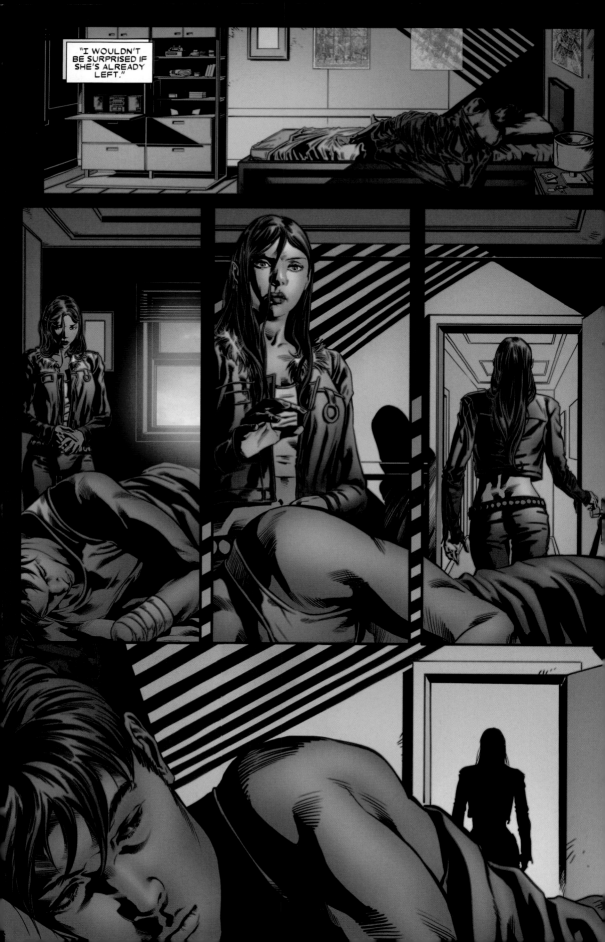

"I WOULDN'T BE SURPRISED IF SHE'S ALREADY LEFT."

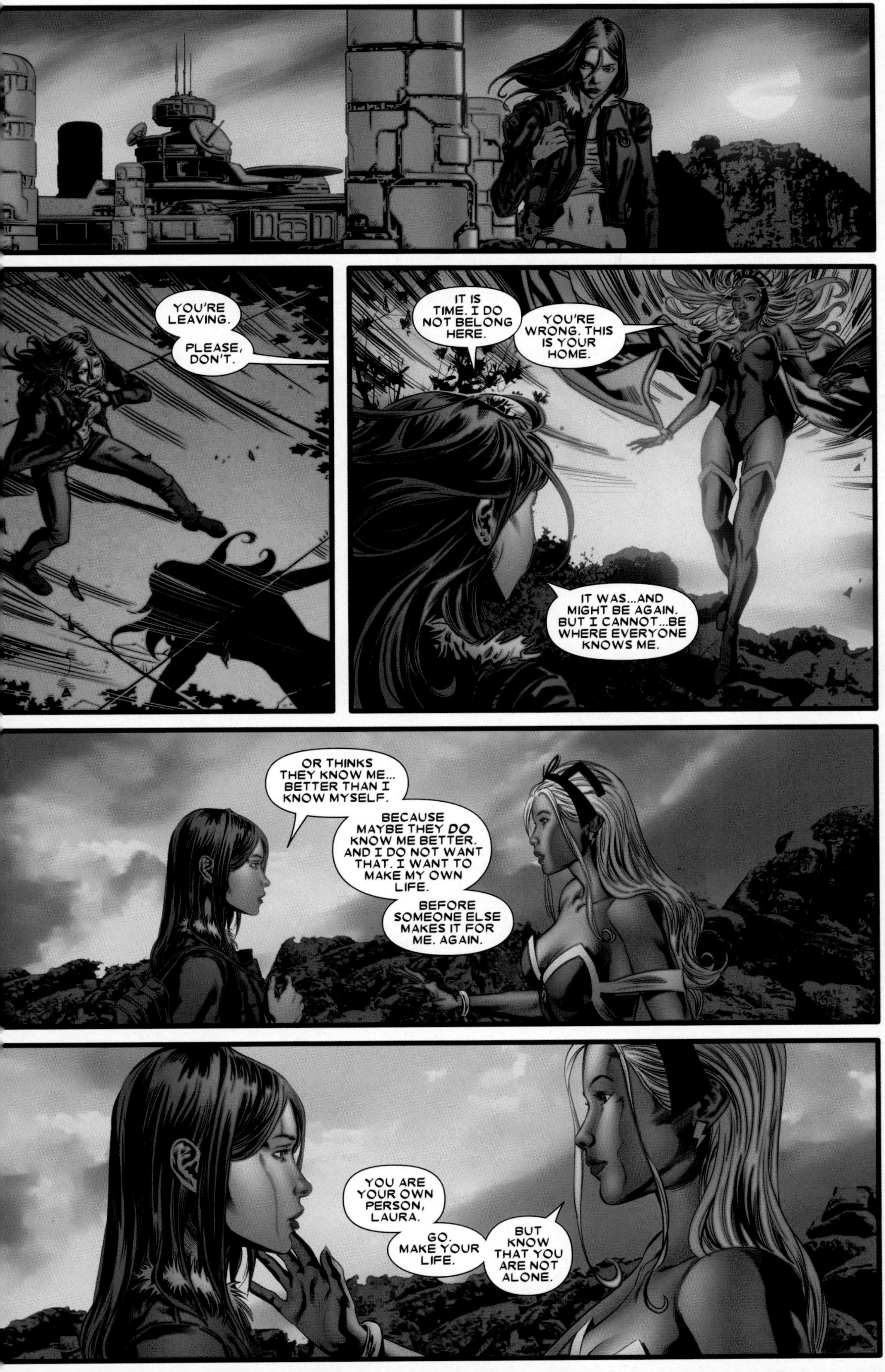
YOU'RE LEAVING.
PLEASE, DON'T.
IT IS TIME. I DO NOT BELONG HERE.
YOU'RE WRONG. THIS IS YOUR HOME.
IT WAS...AND MIGHT BE AGAIN. BUT I CANNOT...BE WHERE EVERYONE KNOWS ME.
OR THINKS THEY KNOW ME... BETTER THAN I KNOW MYSELF.
BECAUSE MAYBE THEY DO KNOW ME BETTER. AND I DO NOT WANT THAT. I WANT TO MAKE MY OWN LIFE.
BEFORE SOMEONE ELSE MAKES IT FOR ME. AGAIN.
YOU ARE YOUR OWN PERSON, LAURA.
GO. MAKE YOUR LIFE.
BUT KNOW THAT YOU ARE NOT ALONE.

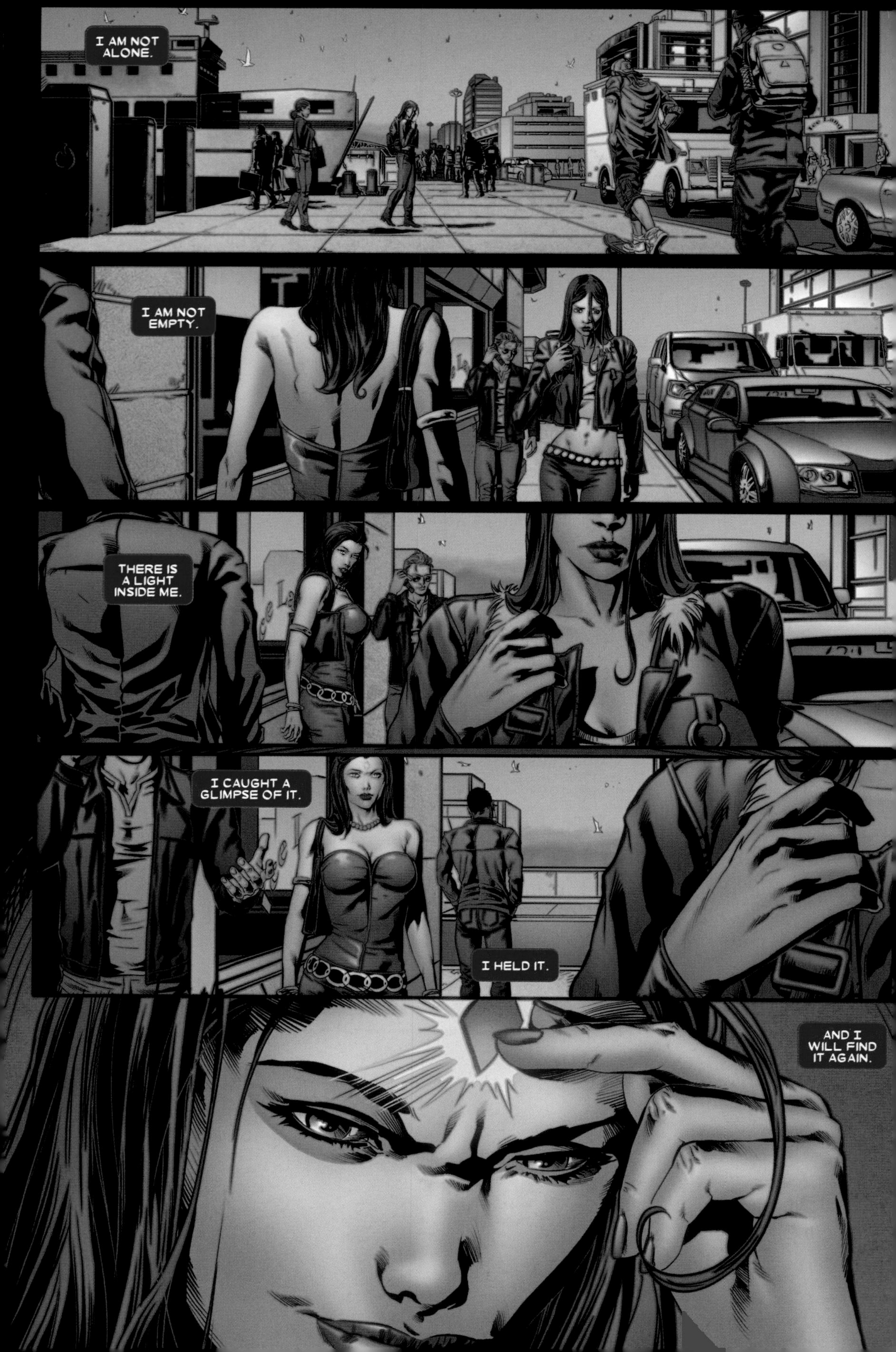
I AM NOT ALONE.
I AM NOT EMPTY.
THERE IS A LIGHT INSIDE ME.
I CAUGHT A GLIMPSE OF IT.
I HELD IT.
AND I WILL FIND IT AGAIN.

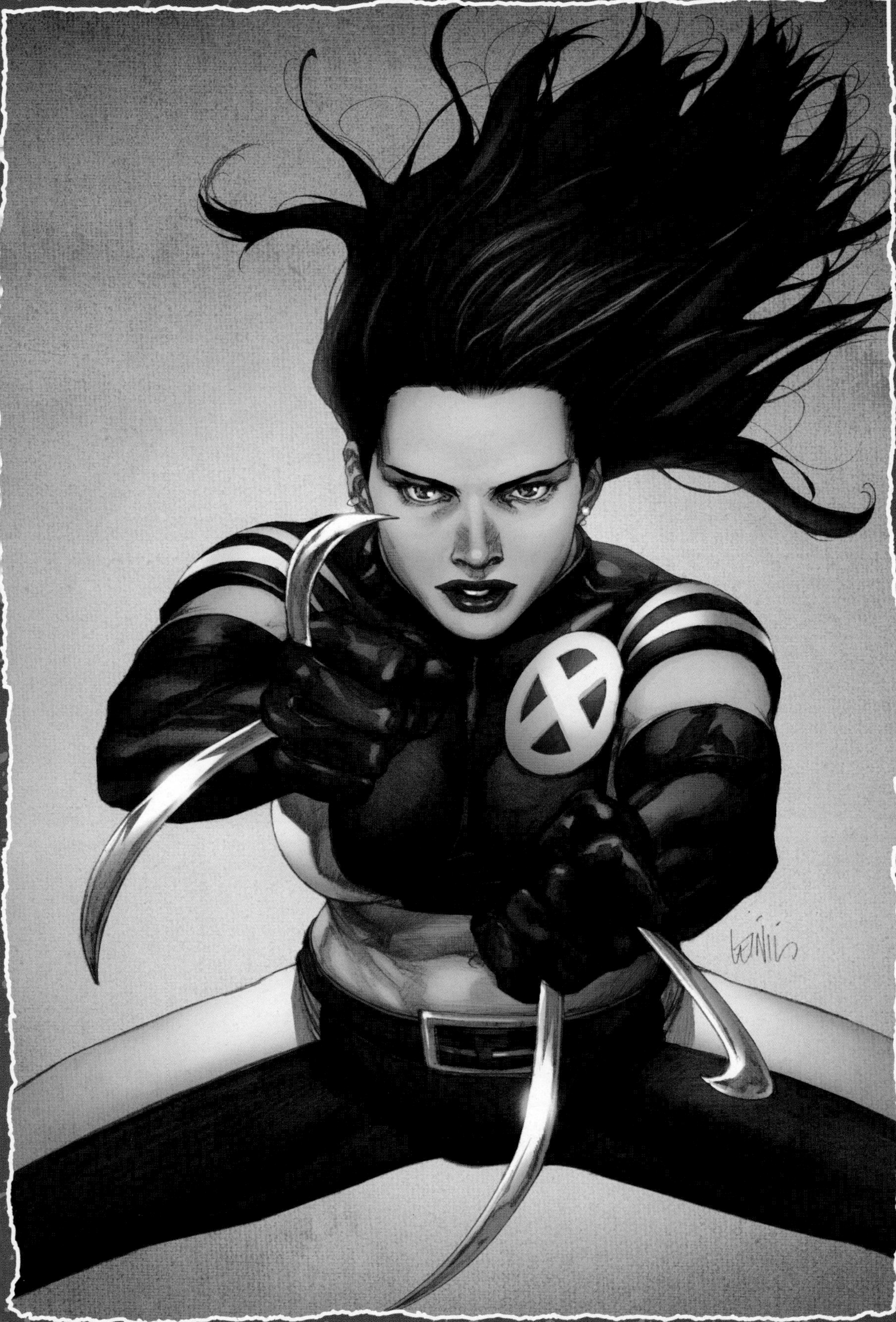

FOUR

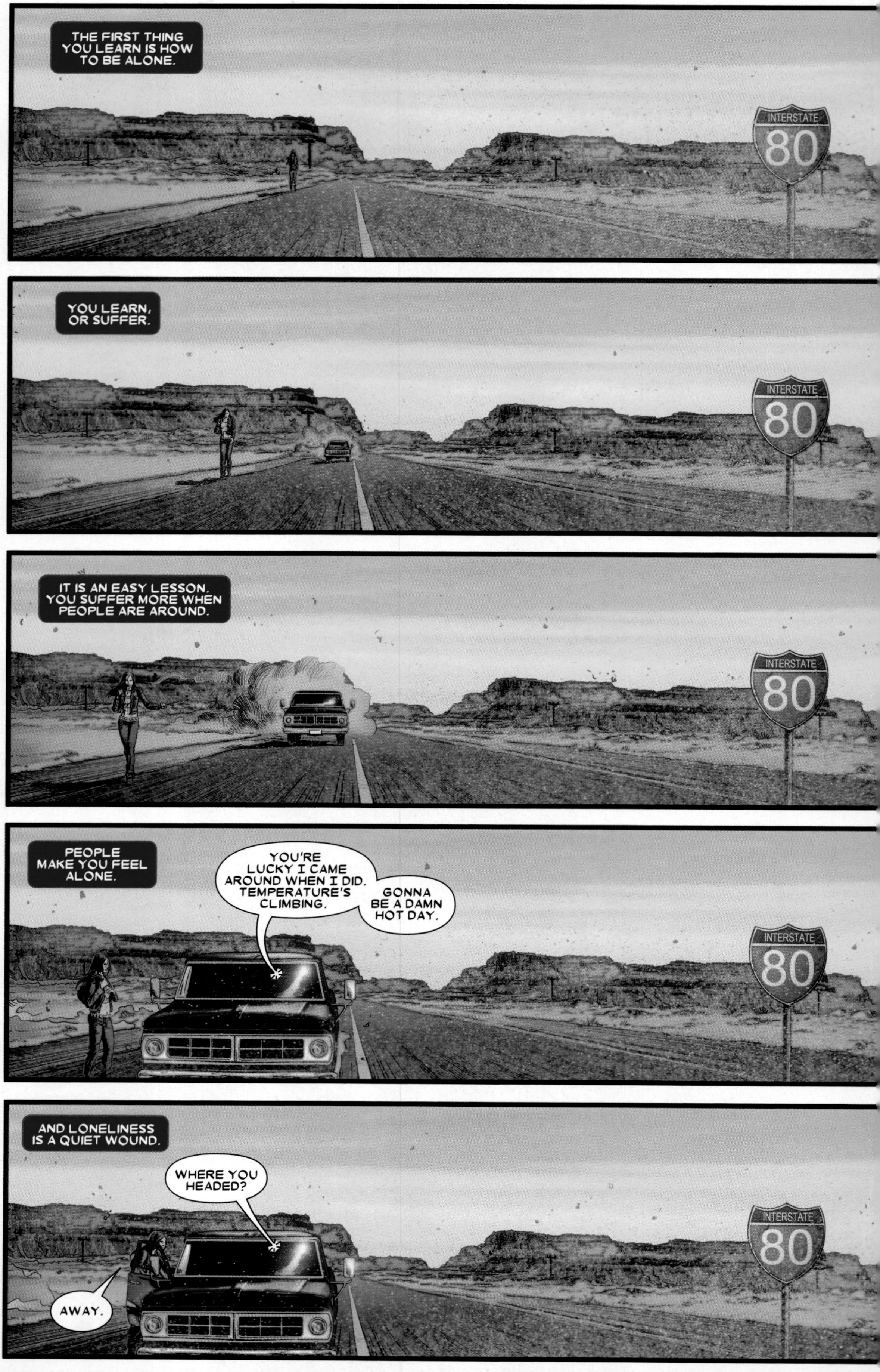
THE FIRST THING YOU LEARN IS HOW TO BE ALONE.
INTERSTATE 80
YOU LEARN, OR SUFFER.
IT IS AN EASY LESSON. YOU SUFFER MORE WHEN PEOPLE ARE AROUND.
PEOPLE MAKE YOU FEEL ALONE.
YOU'RE LUCKY I CAME AROUND WHEN I DID. TEMPERATURE'S CLIMBING.
GONNA BE A DAMN HOT DAY.
AND LONELINESS IS A QUIET WOUND.
WHERE YOU HEADED?
AWAY.

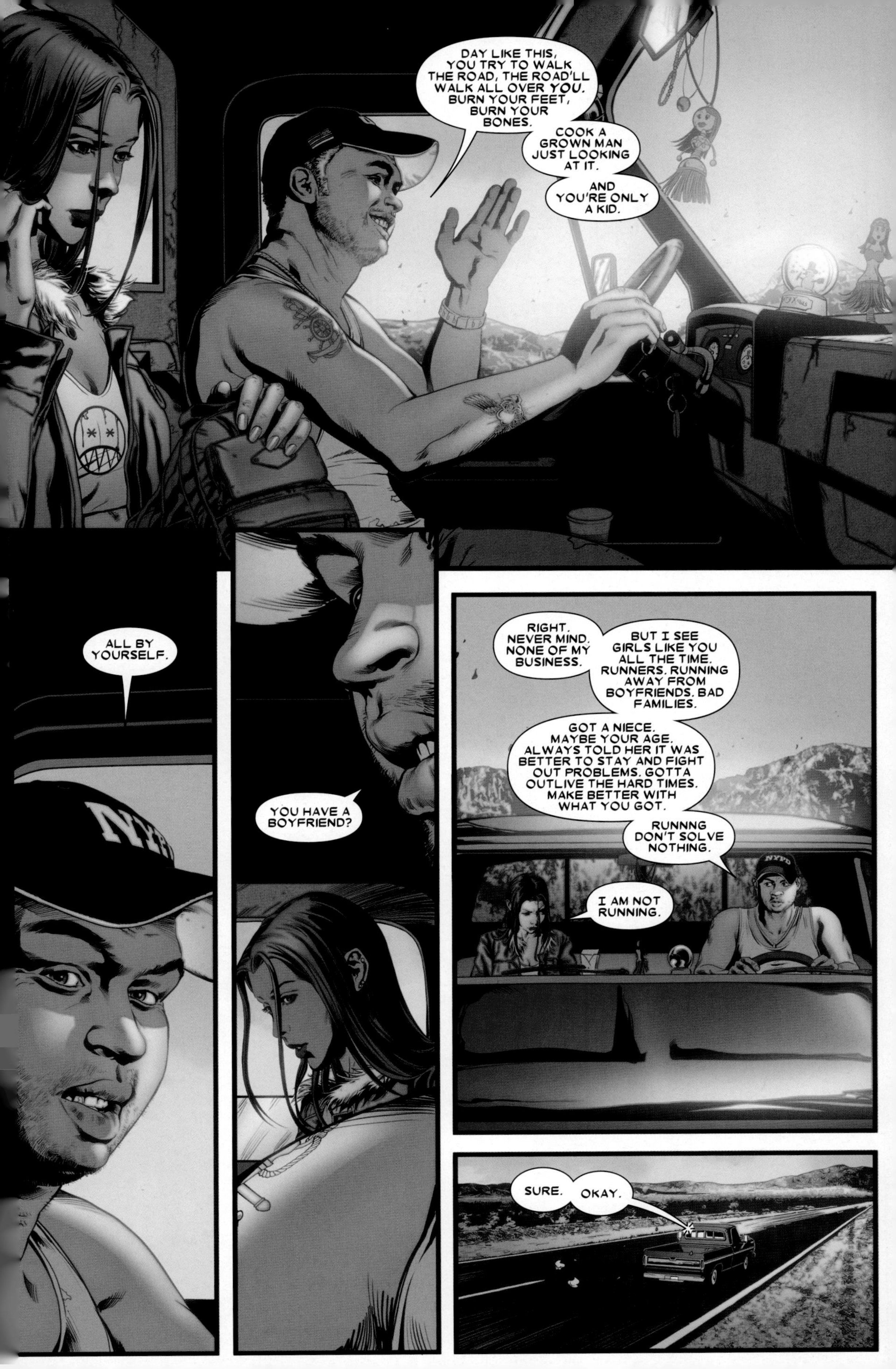
DAY LIKE THIS, YOU TRY TO WALK THE ROAD, THE ROAD'LL WALK ALL OVER *YOU.* BURN YOUR FEET, BURN YOUR BONES.
COOK A GROWN MAN JUST LOOKING AT IT.
AND YOU'RE ONLY A KID.
ALL BY YOURSELF.
YOU HAVE A BOYFRIEND?
RIGHT. NEVER MIND. NONE OF MY BUSINESS.
BUT I SEE GIRLS LIKE YOU ALL THE TIME. RUNNERS. RUNNING AWAY FROM BOYFRIENDS. BAD FAMILIES.
GOT A NIECE. MAYBE YOUR AGE. ALWAYS TOLD HER IT WAS BETTER TO STAY AND FIGHT OUT PROBLEMS. GOTTA OUTLIVE THE HARD TIMES. MAKE BETTER WITH WHAT YOU GOT.
RUNNNG DON'T SOLVE NOTHING.
I AM NOT RUNNING.
SURE.
OKAY.

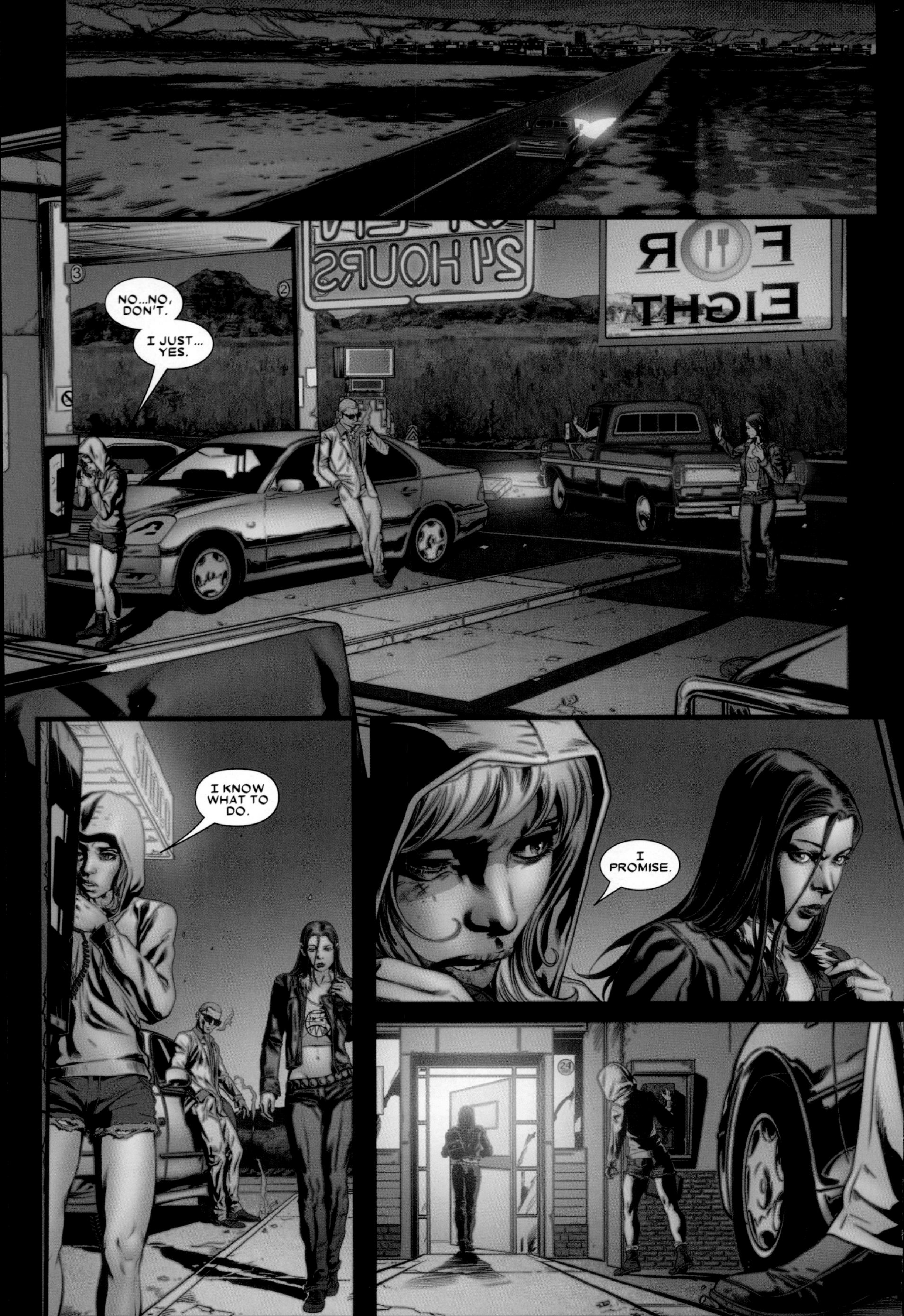
NO...NO, DON'T.
I JUST... YES.
I KNOW WHAT TO DO.
I PROMISE.

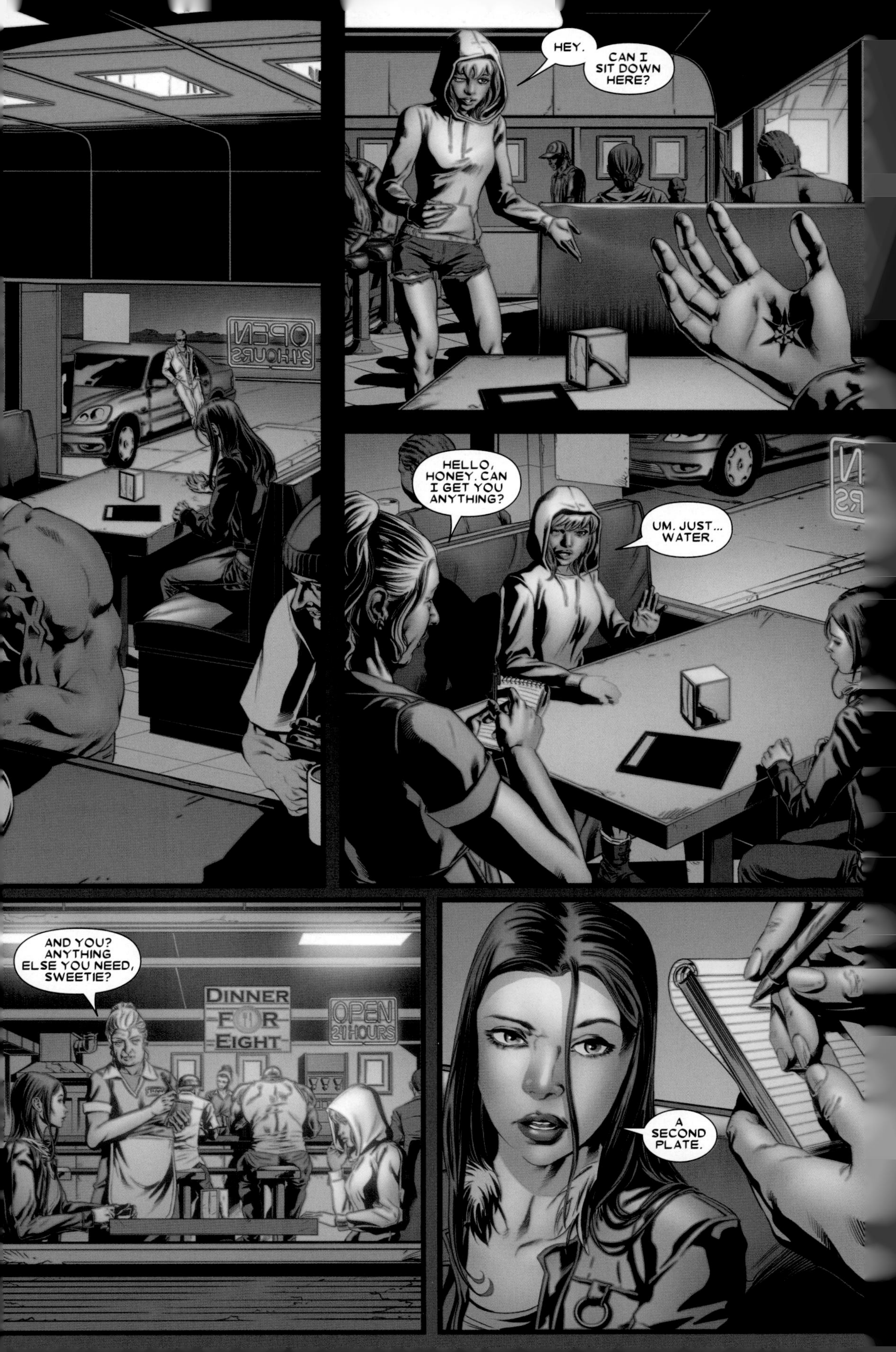
HEY.
CAN I SIT DOWN HERE?
HELLO, HONEY. CAN I GET YOU ANYTHING?
UM. JUST... WATER.
AND YOU? ANYTHING ELSE YOU NEED, SWEETIE?
DINNER FOR EIGHT
OPEN 24 HOURS
A SECOND PLATE.

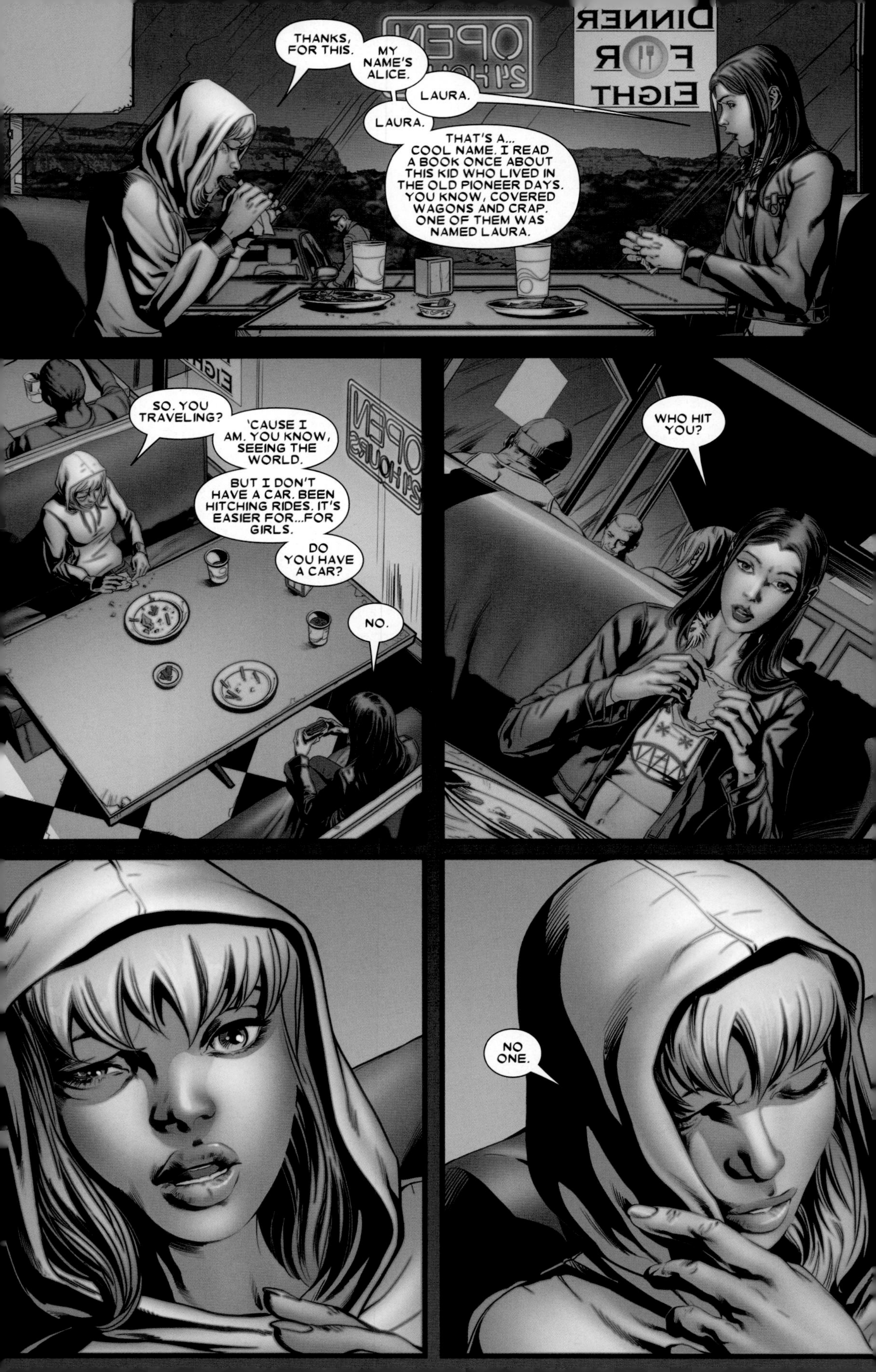
DINNER
F R
EIGHT
OPEN
24 HOURS
THANKS, FOR THIS.
MY NAME'S ALICE.
LAURA.
LAURA.
THAT'S A... COOL NAME. I READ A BOOK ONCE ABOUT THIS KID WHO LIVED IN THE OLD PIONEER DAYS. YOU KNOW, COVERED WAGONS AND CRAP. ONE OF THEM WAS NAMED LAURA.
SO. YOU TRAVELING?
'CAUSE I AM. YOU KNOW, SEEING THE WORLD.
BUT I DON'T HAVE A CAR. BEEN HITCHING RIDES. IT'S EASIER FOR...FOR GIRLS.
DO YOU HAVE A CAR?
NO.
WHO HIT YOU?
NO ONE.

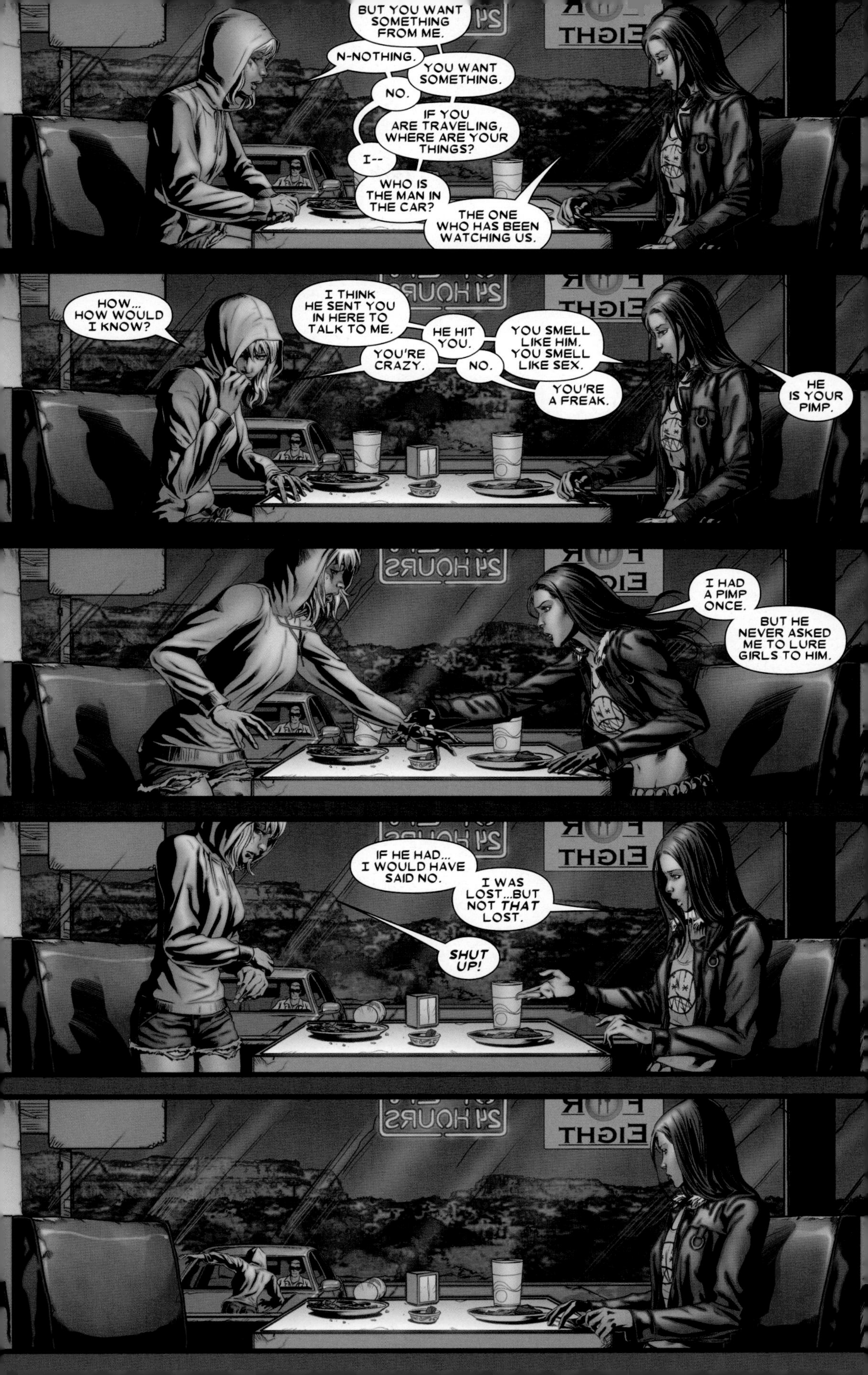

BUT YOU WANT SOMETHING FROM ME.
N-NOTHING.
YOU WANT SOMETHING.
NO.
IF YOU ARE TRAVELING, WHERE ARE YOUR THINGS?
I--
WHO IS THE MAN IN THE CAR?
THE ONE WHO HAS BEEN WATCHING US.
HOW... HOW WOULD I KNOW?
I THINK HE SENT YOU IN HERE TO TALK TO ME.
YOU'RE CRAZY.
HE HIT YOU.
NO.
YOU SMELL LIKE HIM. YOU SMELL LIKE SEX.
YOU'RE A FREAK.
HE IS YOUR PIMP.
I HAD A PIMP ONCE.
BUT HE NEVER ASKED ME TO LURE GIRLS TO HIM.
IF HE HAD... I WOULD HAVE SAID NO.
I WAS LOST...BUT NOT *THAT* LOST.
SHUT UP!

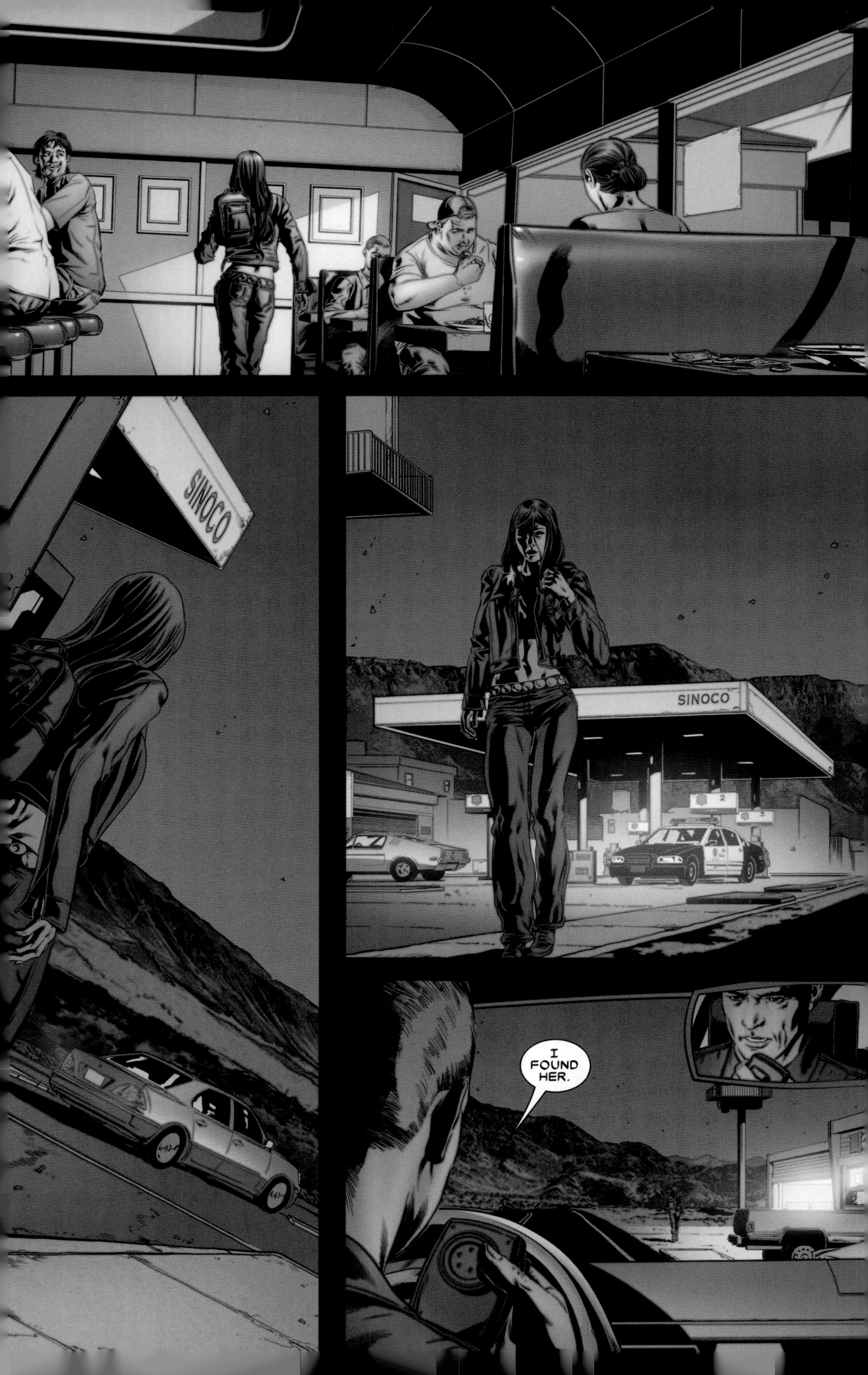
SINOCO
SINOCO
I FOUND HER.

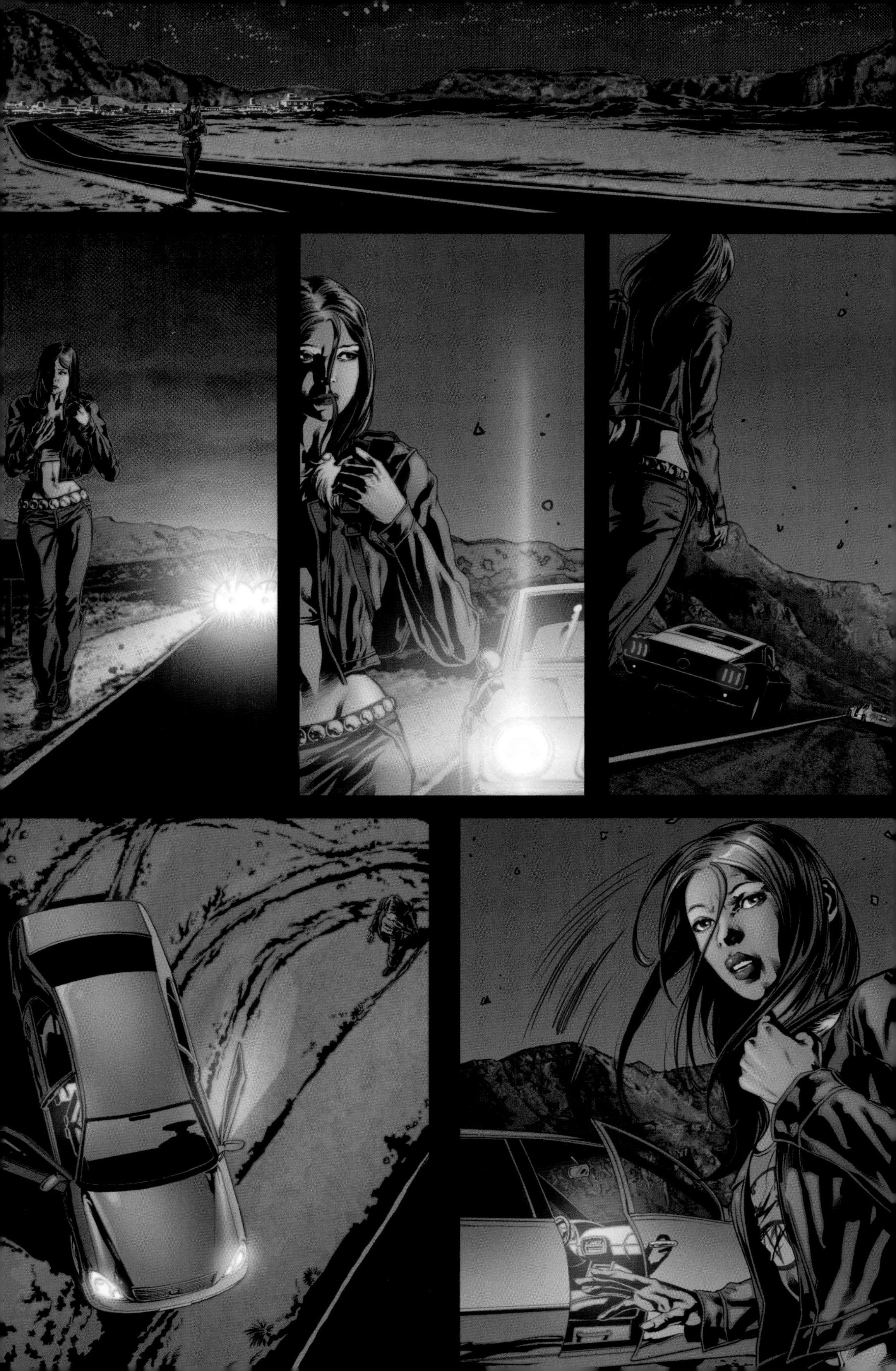

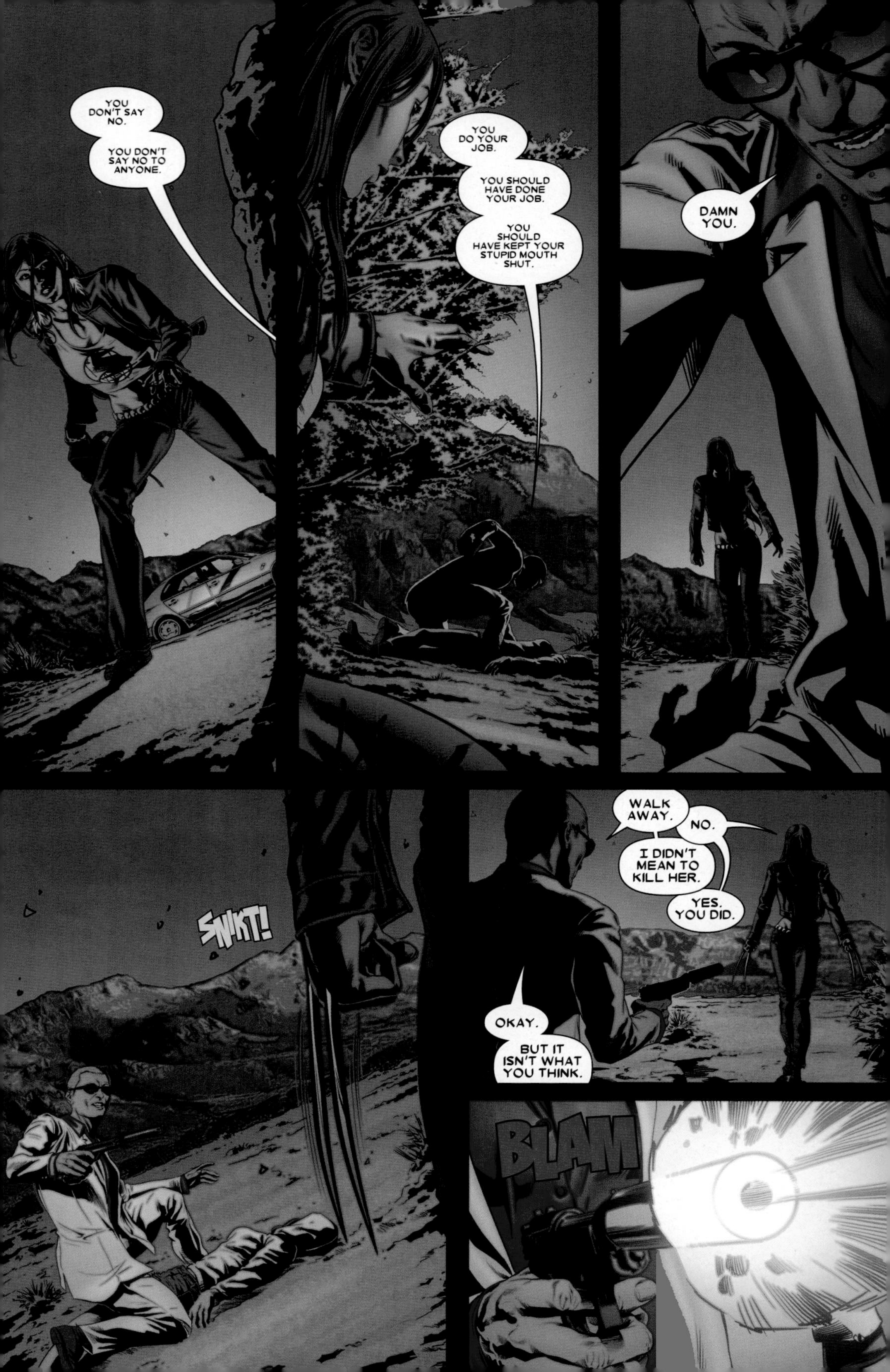
YOU DON'T SAY NO.
YOU DON'T SAY NO TO ANYONE.
YOU DO YOUR JOB.
YOU SHOULD HAVE DONE YOUR JOB.
YOU SHOULD HAVE KEPT YOUR STUPID MOUTH SHUT.
DAMN YOU.
SNIKT!
WALK AWAY.
NO.
I DIDN'T MEAN TO KILL HER.
YES. YOU DID.
OKAY.
BUT IT ISN'T WHAT YOU THINK.
BLAM

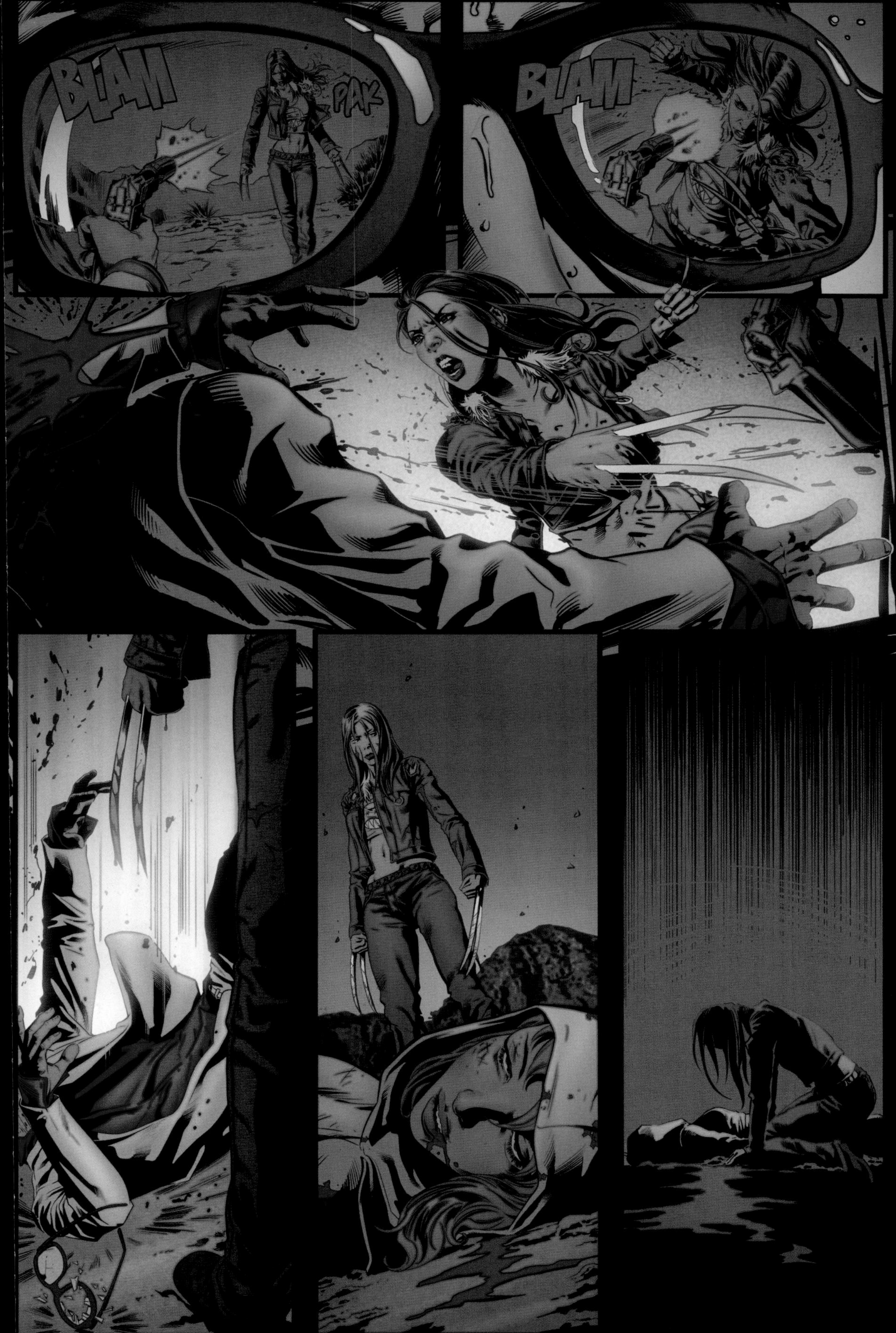
BLAM
PAK
BLAM

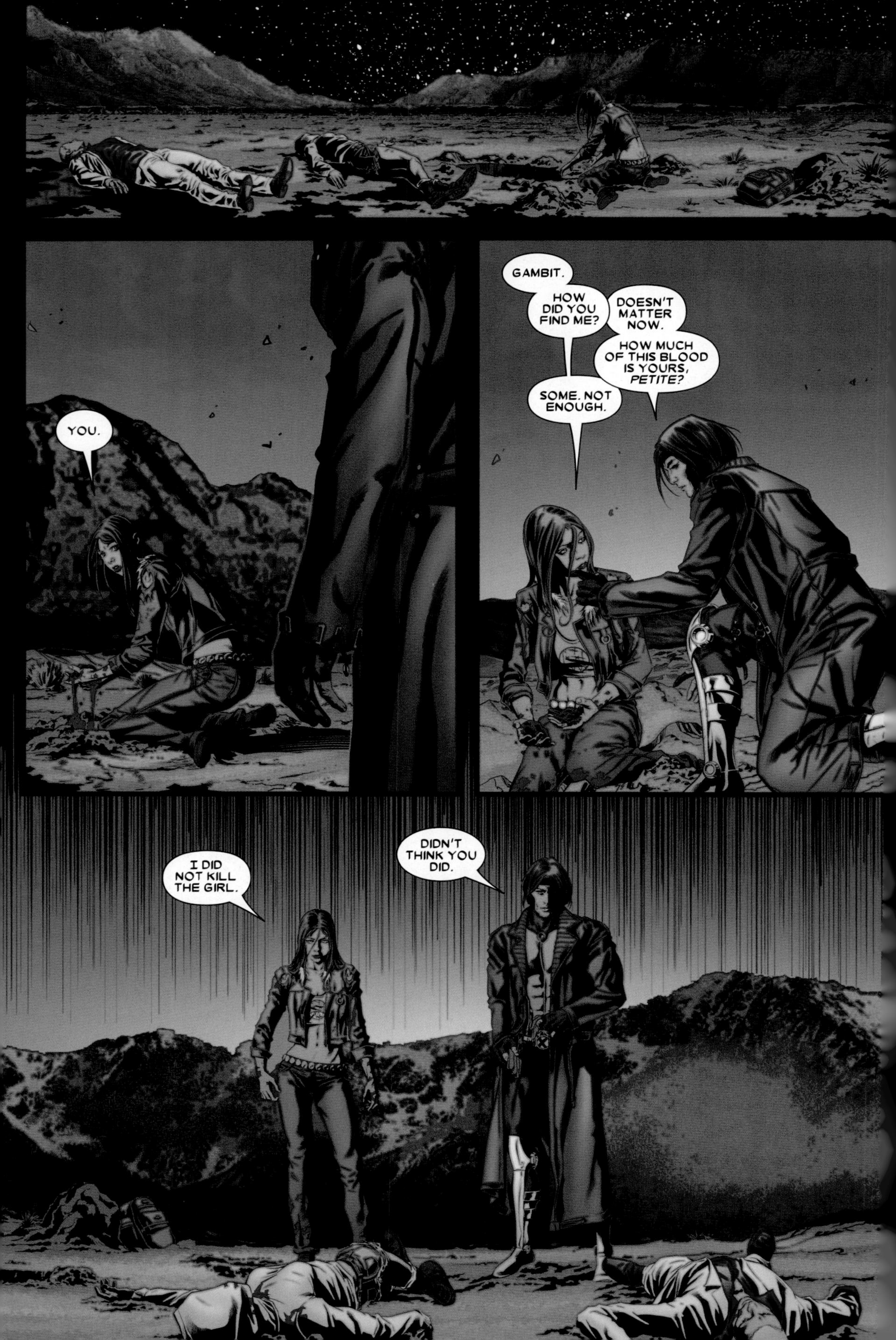
YOU.
GAMBIT.
HOW DID YOU FIND ME?
DOESN'T MATTER NOW.
HOW MUCH OF THIS BLOOD IS YOURS, *PETITE?*
SOME. NOT ENOUGH.
I DID NOT KILL THE GIRL.
DIDN'T THINK YOU DID.

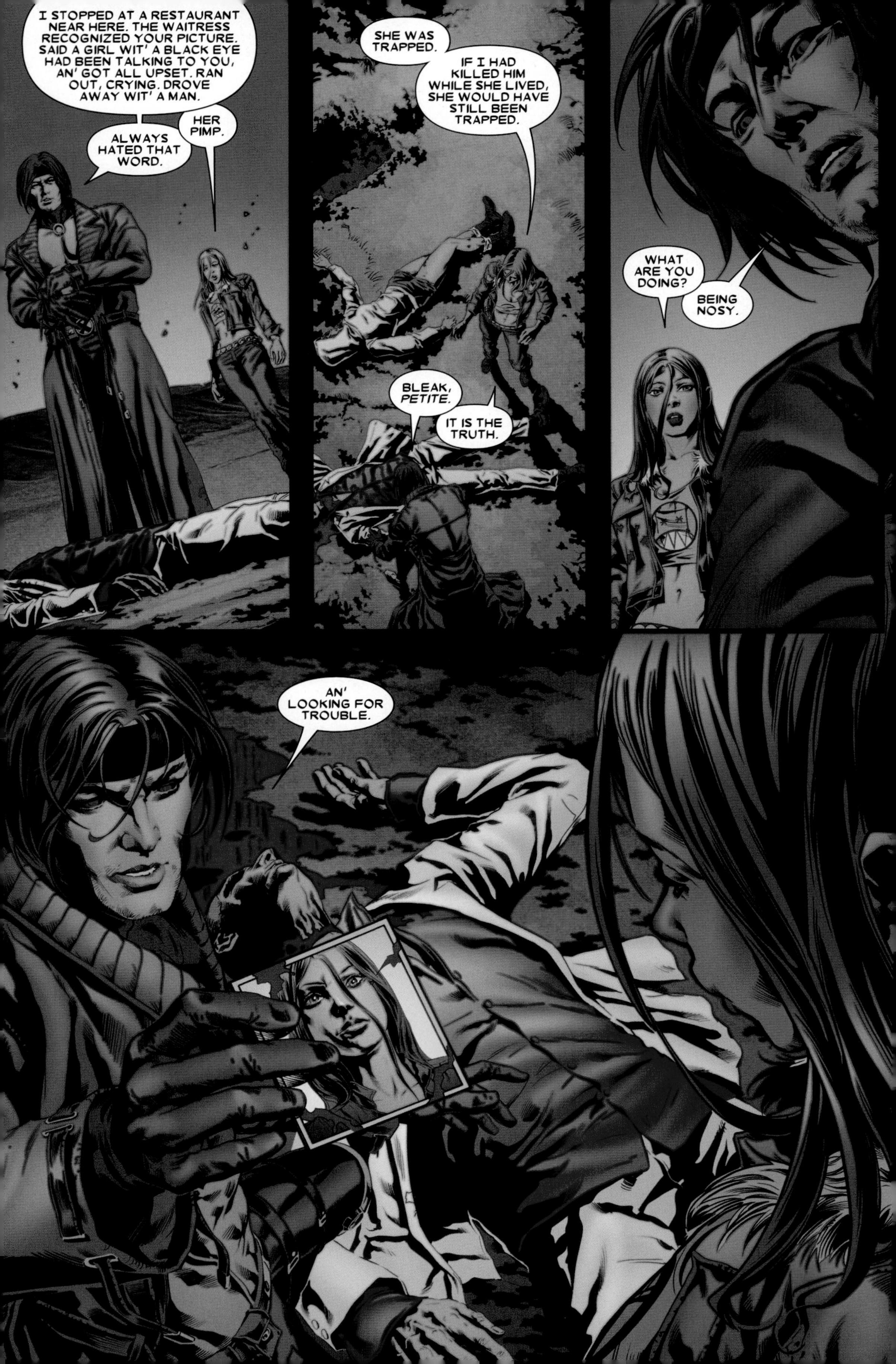
I STOPPED AT A RESTAURANT NEAR HERE. THE WAITRESS RECOGNIZED YOUR PICTURE. SAID A GIRL WIT' A BLACK EYE HAD BEEN TALKING TO YOU, AN' GOT ALL UPSET. RAN OUT, CRYING. DROVE AWAY WIT' A MAN.
HER PIMP.
ALWAYS HATED THAT WORD.
SHE WAS TRAPPED.
IF I HAD KILLED HIM WHILE SHE LIVED, SHE WOULD HAVE STILL BEEN TRAPPED.
BLEAK, *PETITE*.
IT IS THE TRUTH.
WHAT ARE YOU DOING?
BEING NOSY.
AN' LOOKING FOR TROUBLE.

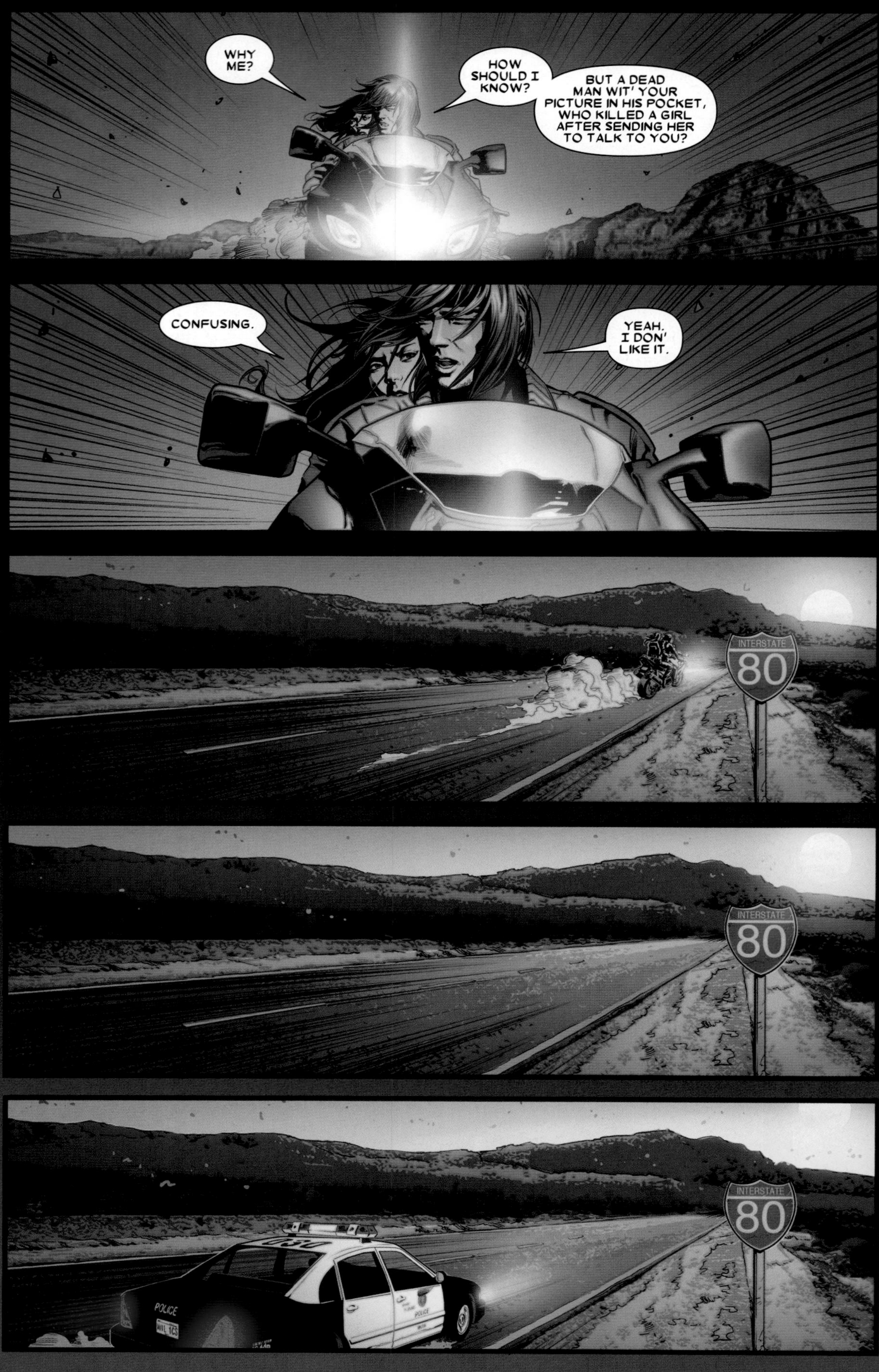
WHY ME?
HOW SHOULD I KNOW?
BUT A DEAD MAN WIT' YOUR PICTURE IN HIS POCKET, WHO KILLED A GIRL AFTER SENDING HER TO TALK TO YOU?
CONFUSING.
YEAH. I DON' LIKE IT.
INTERSTATE
80
INTERSTATE
80
INTERSTATE
80
POLICE

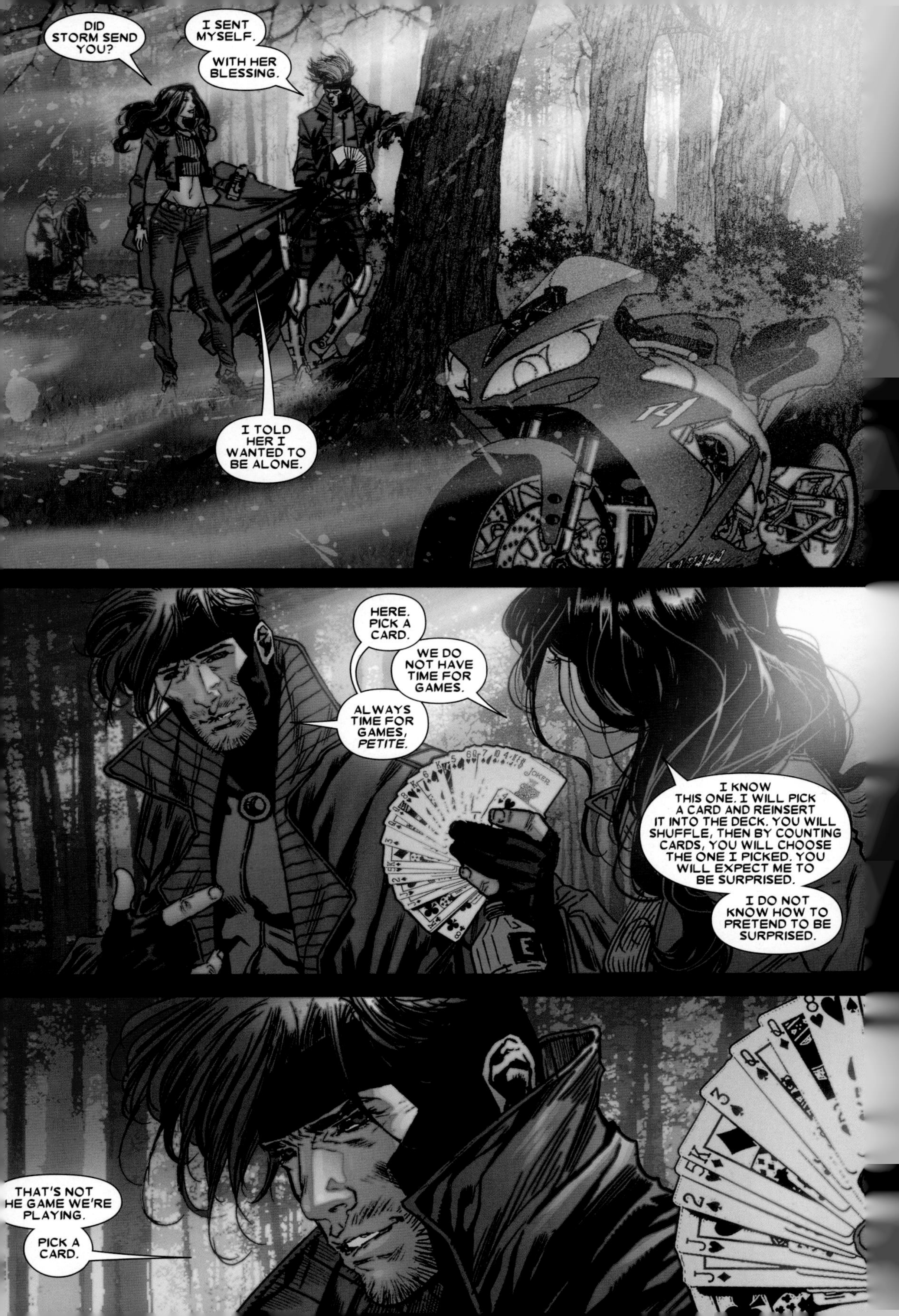
DID STORM SEND YOU?
I SENT MYSELF.
WITH HER BLESSING.
I TOLD HER I WANTED TO BE ALONE.
HERE. PICK A CARD.
WE DO NOT HAVE TIME FOR GAMES.
ALWAYS TIME FOR GAMES, *PETITE.*
I KNOW THIS ONE. I WILL PICK A CARD AND REINSERT IT INTO THE DECK. YOU WILL SHUFFLE, THEN BY COUNTING CARDS, YOU WILL CHOOSE THE ONE I PICKED. YOU WILL EXPECT ME TO BE SURPRISED.
I DO NOT KNOW HOW TO PRETEND TO BE SURPRISED.
THAT'S NOT HE GAME WE'RE PLAYING.
PICK A CARD.

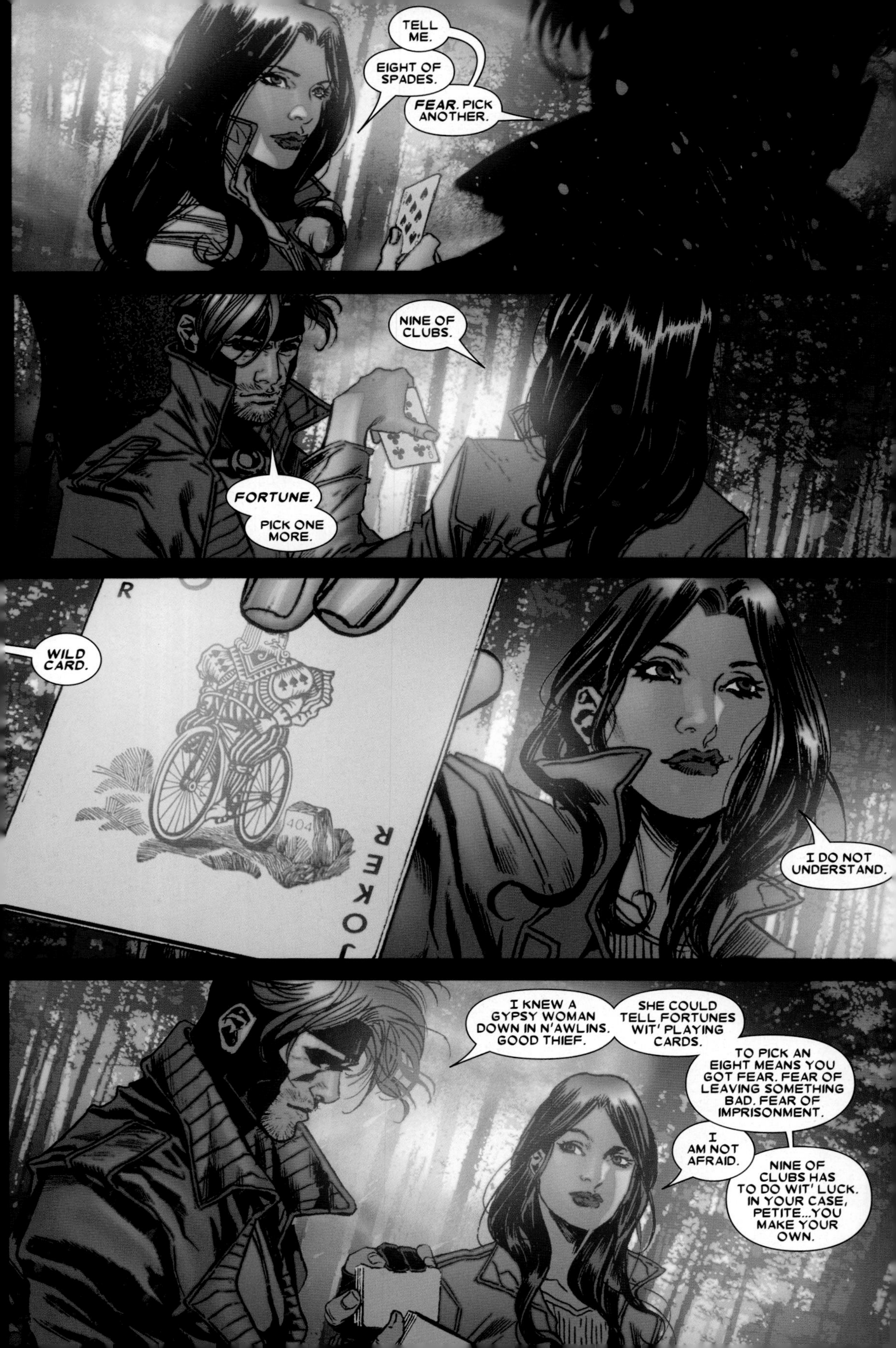
TELL ME.
EIGHT OF SPADES.
FEAR. PICK ANOTHER.
NINE OF CLUBS.
FORTUNE.
PICK ONE MORE.
WILD CARD.
JOKER
I DO NOT UNDERSTAND.
I KNEW A GYPSY WOMAN DOWN IN N'AWLINS. GOOD THIEF.
SHE COULD TELL FORTUNES WIT' PLAYING CARDS.
TO PICK AN EIGHT MEANS YOU GOT FEAR. FEAR OF LEAVING SOMETHING BAD. FEAR OF IMPRISONMENT.
I AM NOT AFRAID.
NINE OF CLUBS HAS TO DO WIT' LUCK. IN YOUR CASE, PETITE...YOU MAKE YOUR OWN.

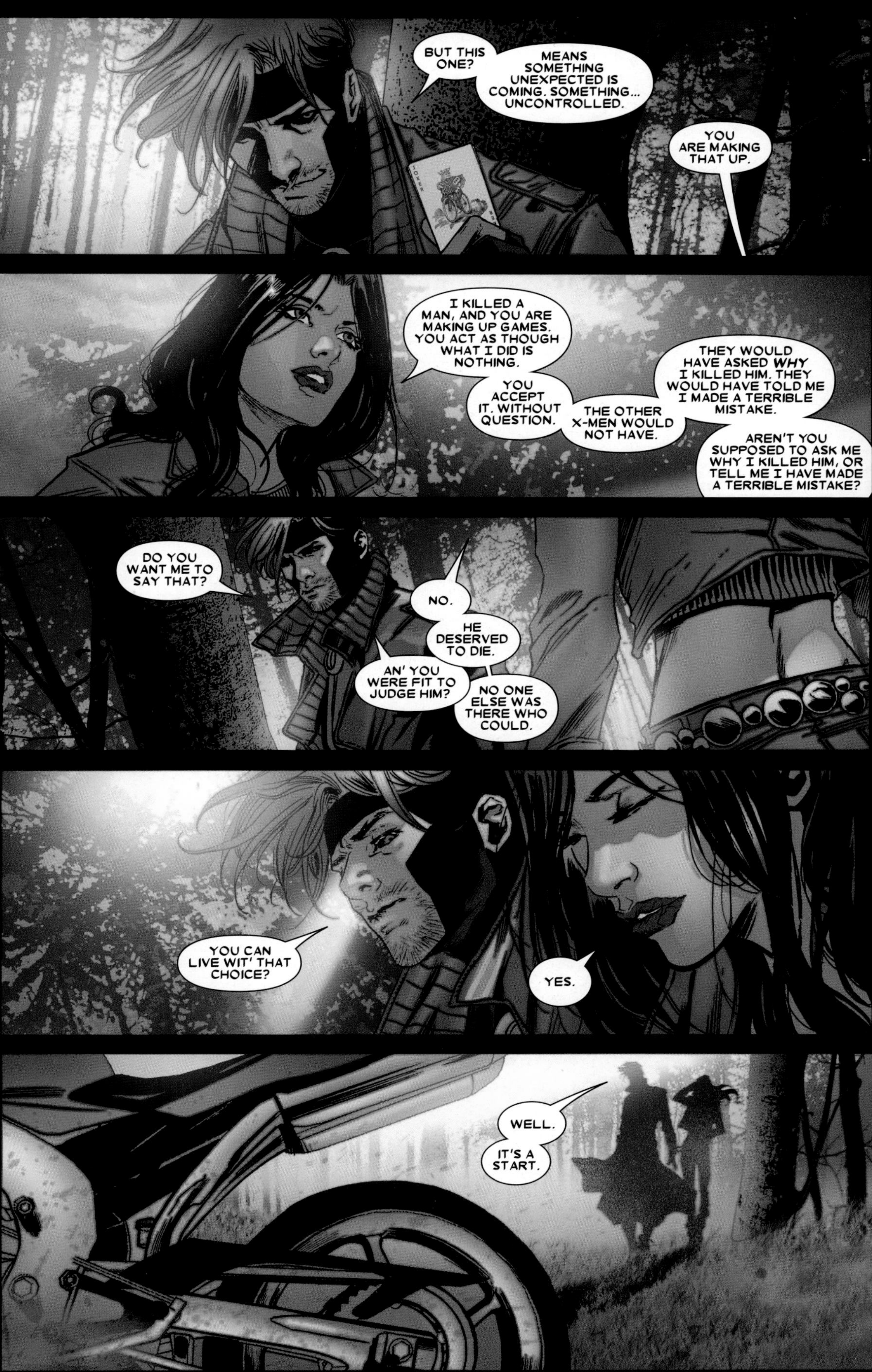
BUT THIS ONE?
MEANS SOMETHING UNEXPECTED IS COMING. SOMETHING... UNCONTROLLED.
YOU ARE MAKING THAT UP.
I KILLED A MAN, AND YOU ARE MAKING UP GAMES. YOU ACT AS THOUGH WHAT I DID IS NOTHING.
YOU ACCEPT IT. WITHOUT QUESTION.
THE OTHER X-MEN WOULD NOT HAVE.
THEY WOULD HAVE ASKED ***WHY*** I KILLED HIM. THEY WOULD HAVE TOLD ME I MADE A TERRIBLE MISTAKE.
AREN'T YOU SUPPOSED TO ASK ME WHY I KILLED HIM, OR TELL ME I HAVE MADE A TERRIBLE MISTAKE?
DO YOU WANT ME TO SAY THAT?
NO.
HE DESERVED TO DIE.
AN' YOU WERE FIT TO JUDGE HIM?
NO ONE ELSE WAS THERE WHO COULD.
YOU CAN LIVE WIT' THAT CHOICE?
YES.
WELL.
IT'S A START.

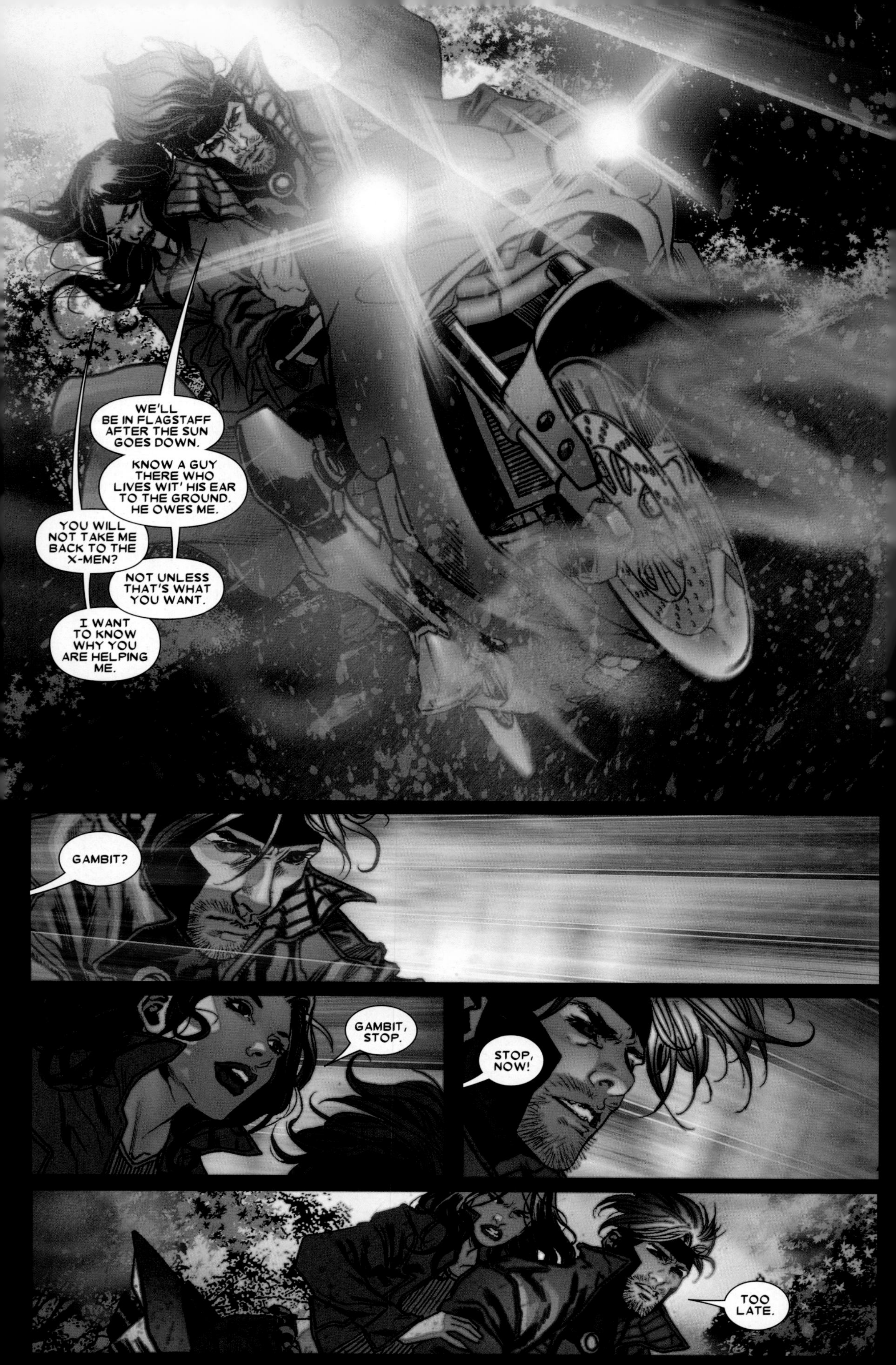
WE'LL BE IN FLAGSTAFF AFTER THE SUN GOES DOWN.
KNOW A GUY THERE WHO LIVES WIT' HIS EAR TO THE GROUND. HE OWES ME.
YOU WILL NOT TAKE ME BACK TO THE X-MEN?
NOT UNLESS THAT'S WHAT YOU WANT.
I WANT TO KNOW WHY YOU ARE HELPING ME.
GAMBIT?
GAMBIT, STOP.
STOP, NOW!
TOO LATE.

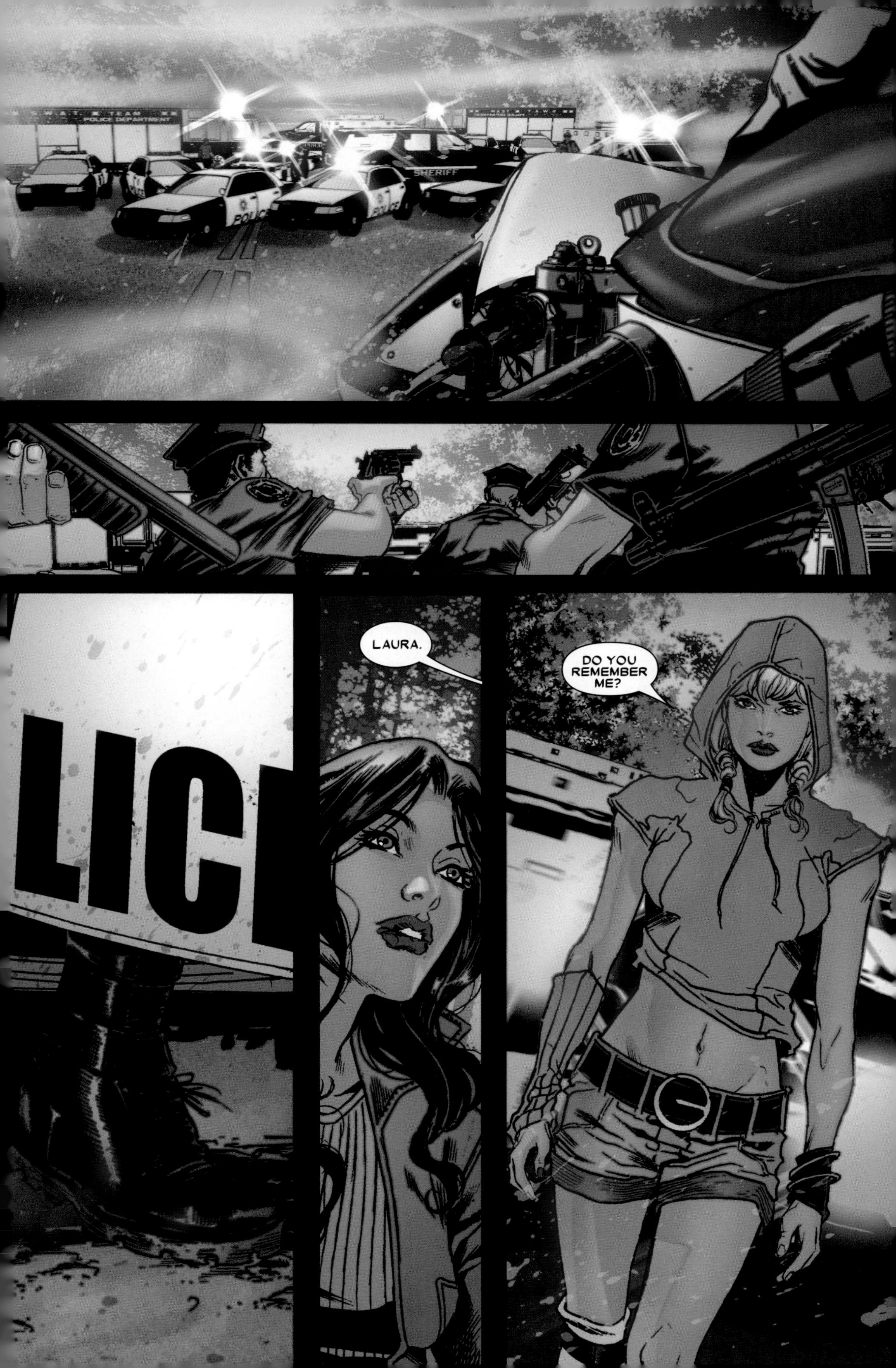
POLICE DEPARTMENT
SHERIFF
LAURA.
DO YOU REMEMBER ME?

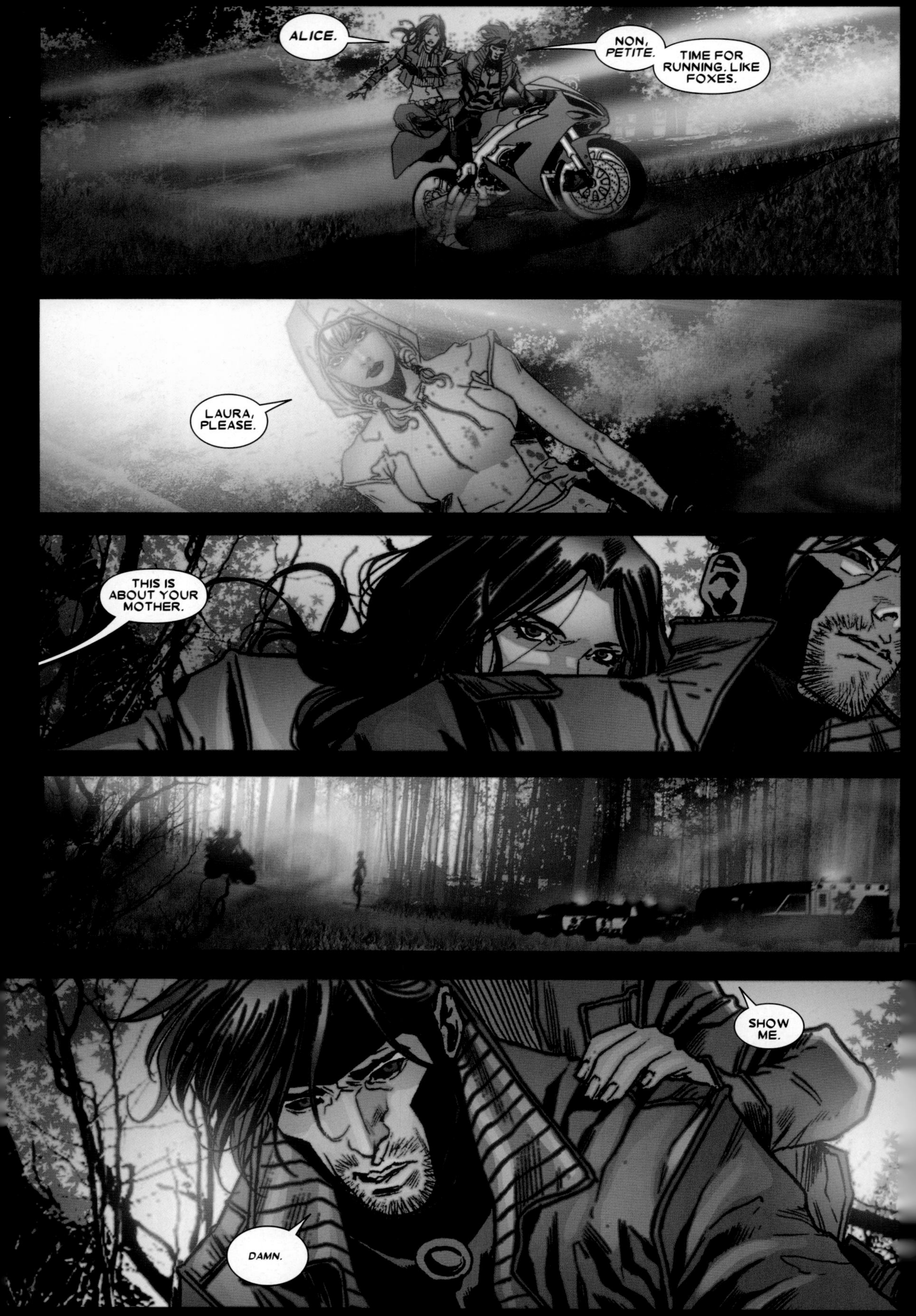

ALICE.
NON, PETITE.
TIME FOR RUNNING, LIKE FOXES.
LAURA, PLEASE.
THIS IS ABOUT YOUR MOTHER.
SHOW ME.
DAMN.

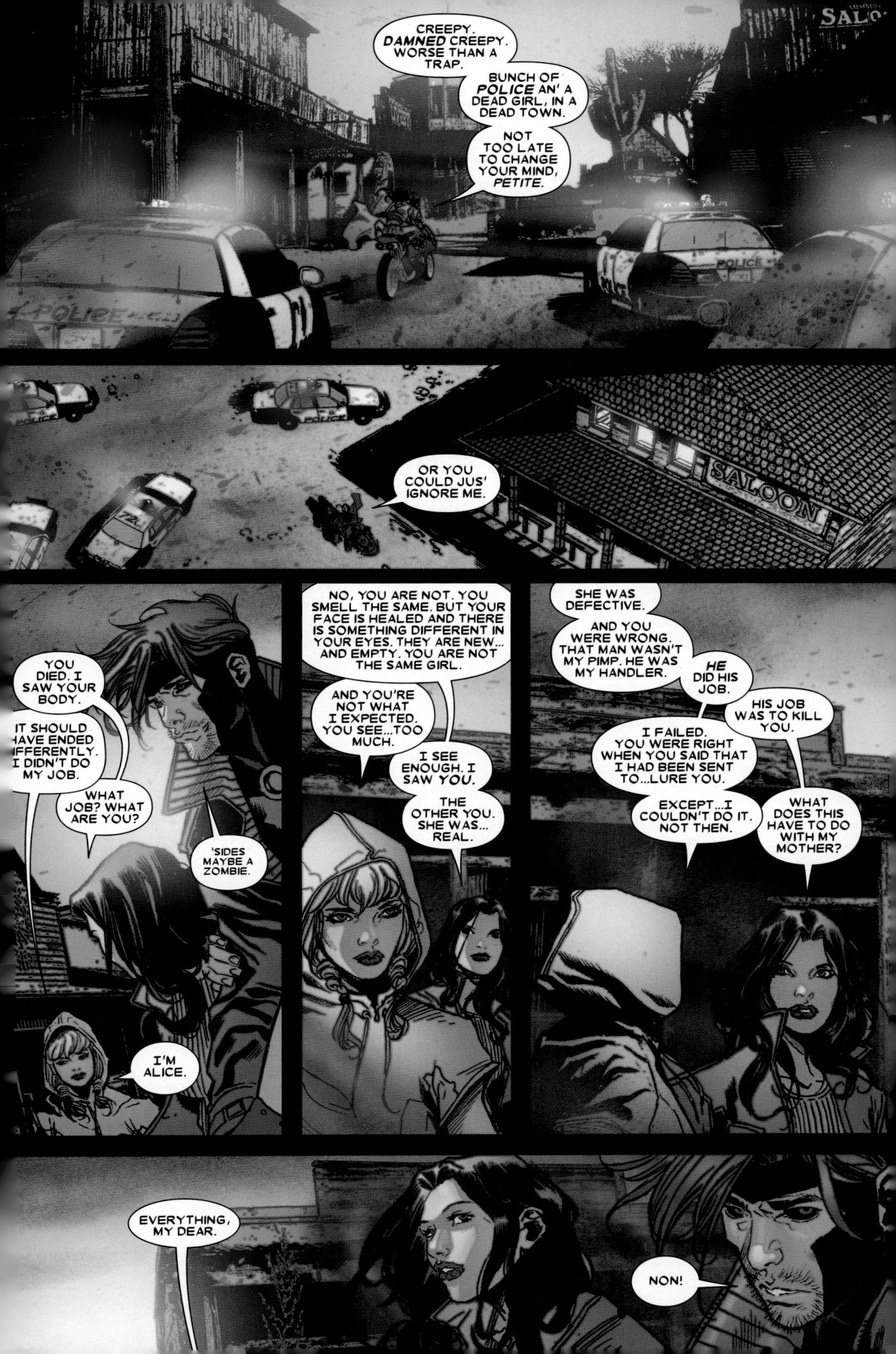
SALO
CREEPY. DAMNED CREEPY. WORSE THAN A TRAP.
BUNCH OF POLICE AN' A DEAD GIRL, IN A DEAD TOWN.
NOT TOO LATE TO CHANGE YOUR MIND, PETITE.
POLICE
SALOON
OR YOU COULD JUS' IGNORE ME.
YOU DIED. I SAW YOUR BODY.
IT SHOULD HAVE ENDED DIFFERENTLY. I DIDN'T DO MY JOB.
WHAT JOB? WHAT ARE YOU?
'SIDES MAYBE A ZOMBIE.
I'M ALICE.
NO, YOU ARE NOT. YOU SMELL THE SAME. BUT YOUR FACE IS HEALED AND THERE IS SOMETHING DIFFERENT IN YOUR EYES. THEY ARE NEW... AND EMPTY. YOU ARE NOT THE SAME GIRL.
AND YOU'RE NOT WHAT I EXPECTED. YOU SEE...TOO MUCH.
I SEE ENOUGH. I SAW YOU.
THE OTHER YOU. SHE WAS... REAL.
SHE WAS DEFECTIVE.
AND YOU WERE WRONG. THAT MAN WASN'T MY PIMP. HE WAS MY HANDLER.
HE DID HIS JOB.
HIS JOB WAS TO KILL YOU.
I FAILED. YOU WERE RIGHT WHEN YOU SAID THAT I HAD BEEN SENT TO...LURE YOU.
EXCEPT...I COULDN'T DO IT. NOT THEN.
WHAT DOES THIS HAVE TO DO WITH MY MOTHER?
EVERYTHING, MY DEAR.
NON!

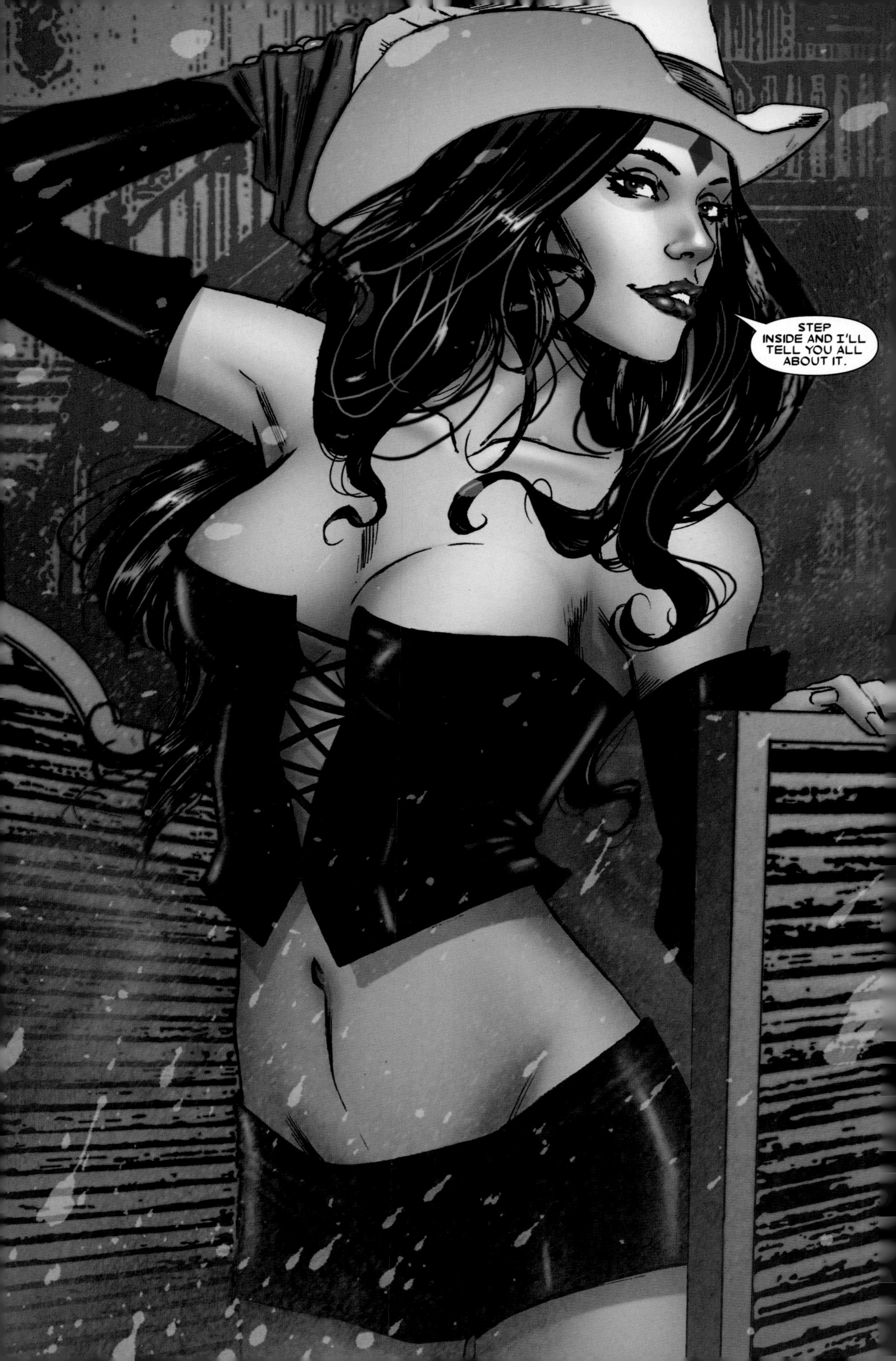
STEP INSIDE AND I'LL TELL YOU ALL ABOUT IT.

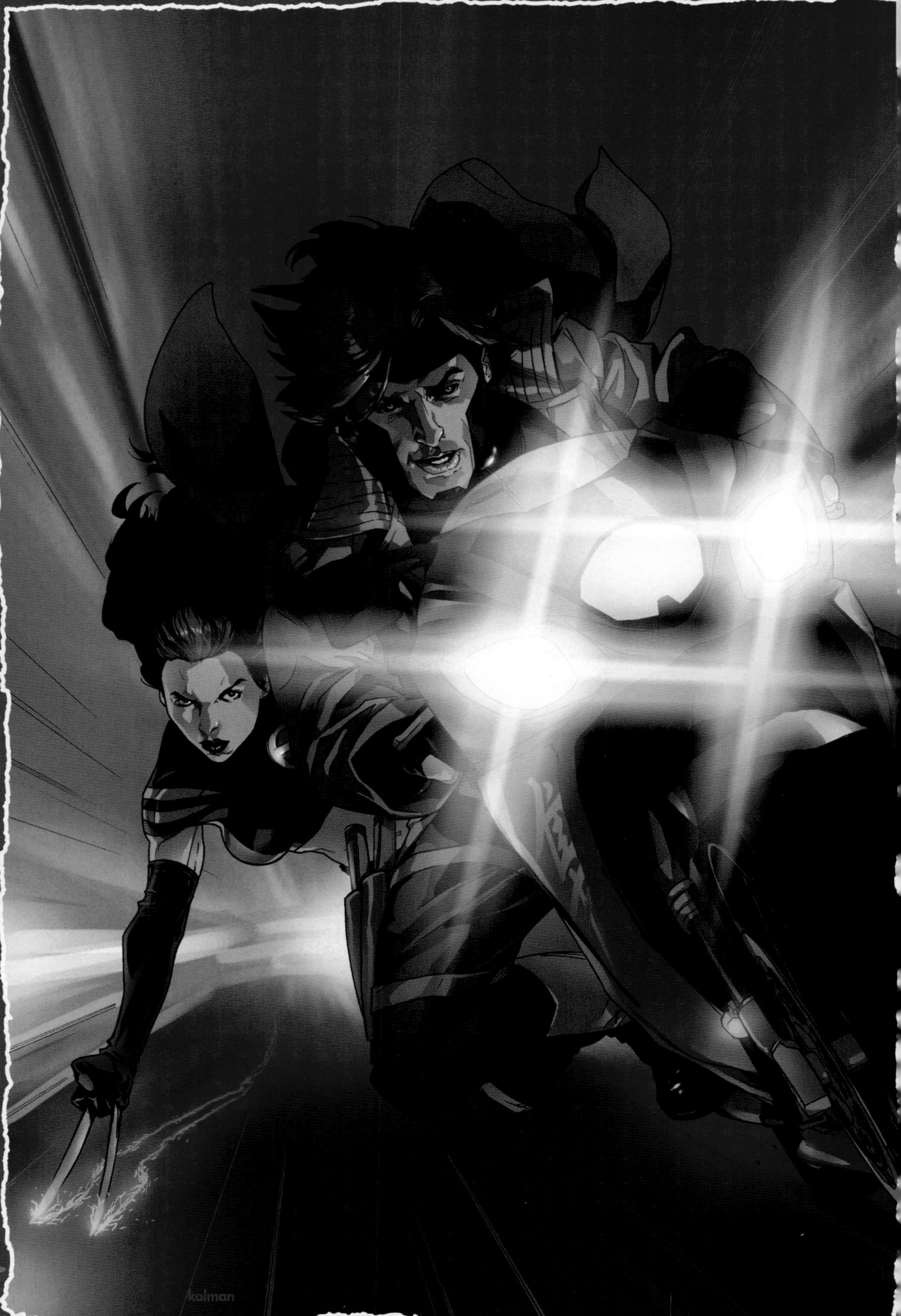
kalman

FIVE

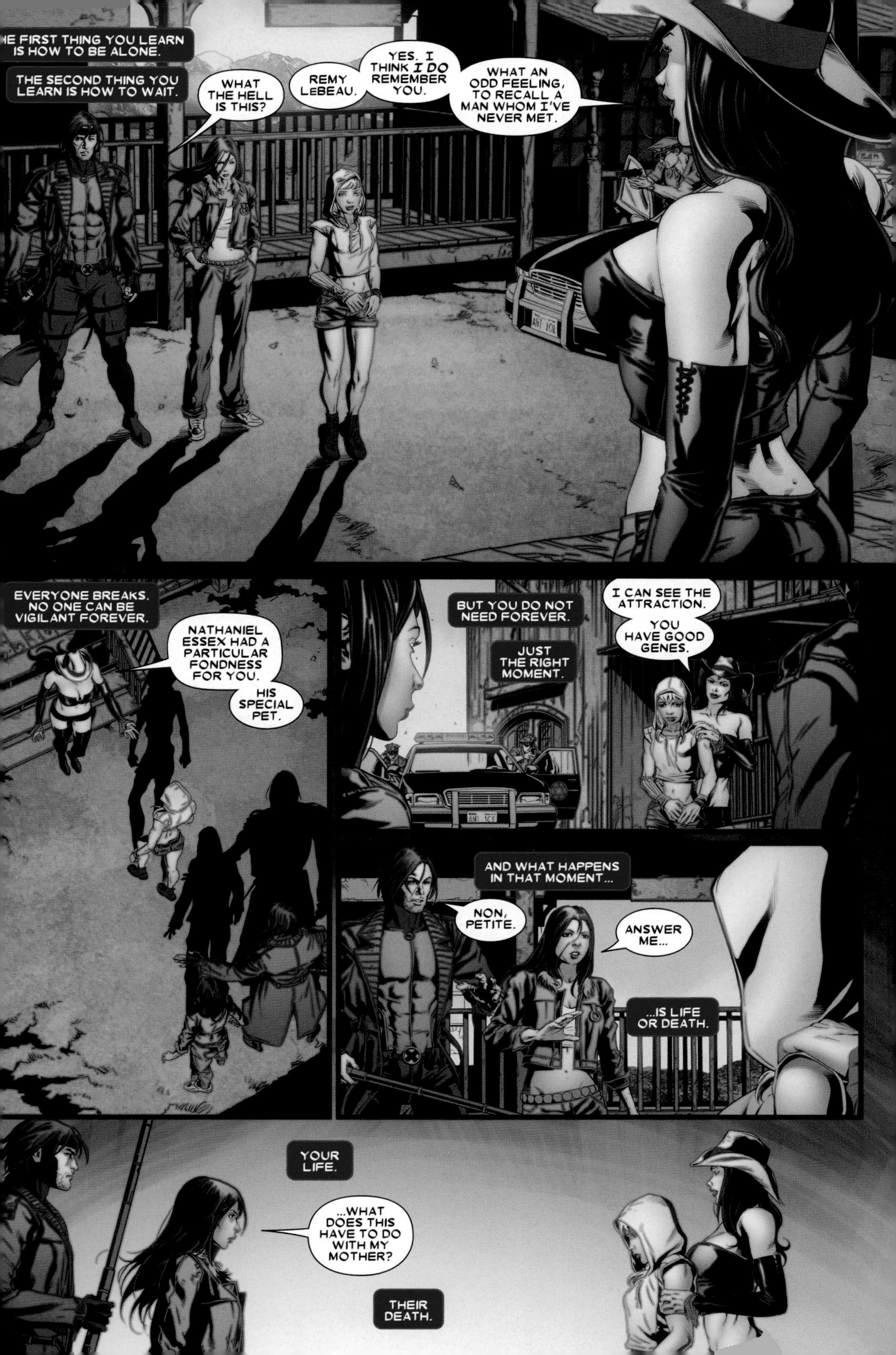
HE FIRST THING YOU LEARN IS HOW TO BE ALONE.
THE SECOND THING YOU LEARN IS HOW TO WAIT.
WHAT THE HELL IS THIS?
REMY LEBEAU.
YES. I THINK *I DO* REMEMBER YOU.
WHAT AN ODD FEELING, TO RECALL A MAN WHOM I'VE NEVER MET.
EVERYONE BREAKS. NO ONE CAN BE VIGILANT FOREVER.
NATHANIEL ESSEX HAD A PARTICULAR FONDNESS FOR YOU.
HIS SPECIAL PET.
BUT YOU DO NOT NEED FOREVER.
JUST THE RIGHT MOMENT.
I CAN SEE THE ATTRACTION.
YOU HAVE GOOD GENES.
AND WHAT HAPPENS IN THAT MOMENT...
NON, PETITE.
ANSWER ME...
...IS LIFE OR DEATH.
YOUR LIFE.
...WHAT DOES THIS HAVE TO DO WITH MY MOTHER?
THEIR DEATH.

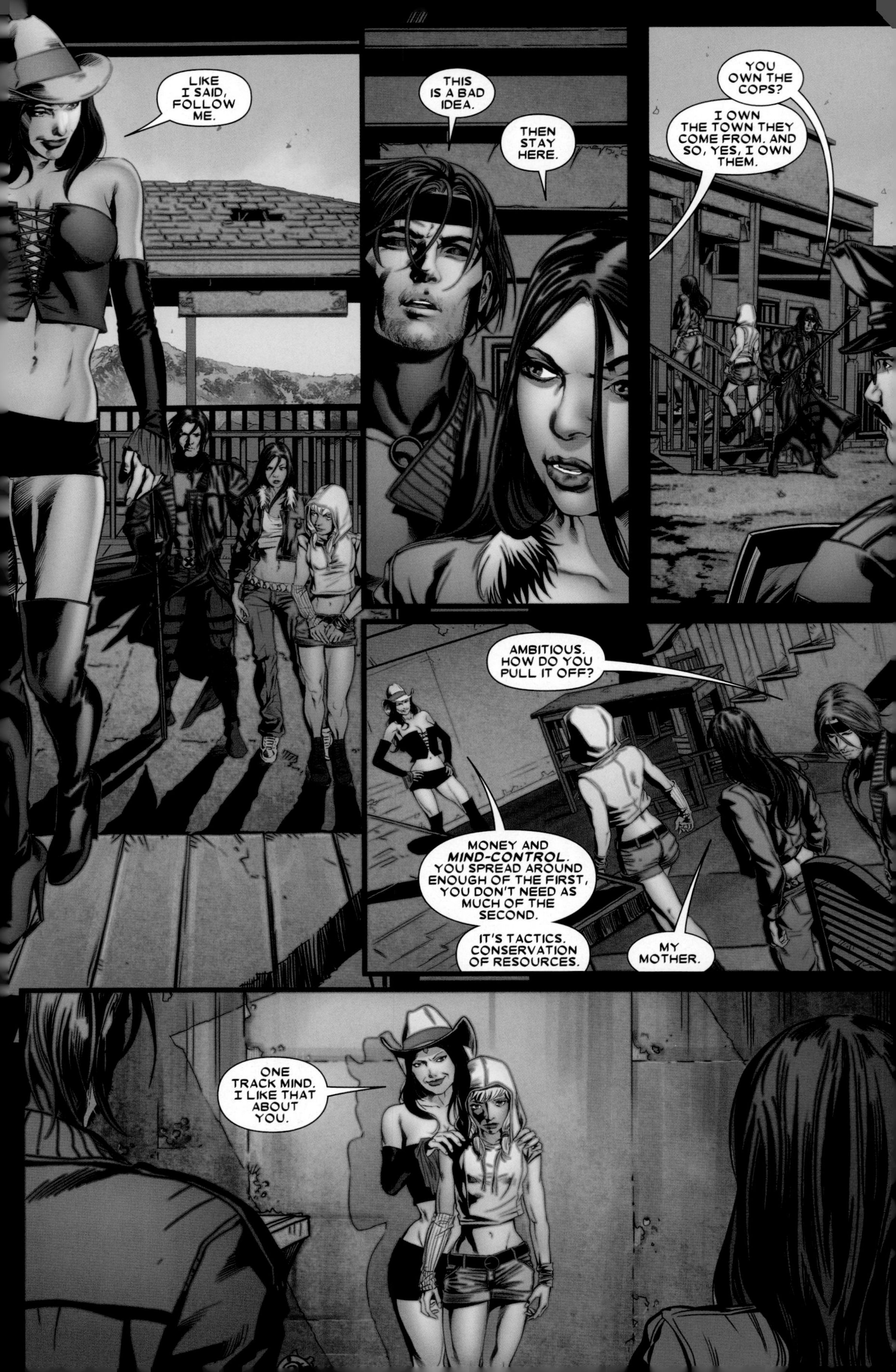
LIKE I SAID, FOLLOW ME.
THIS IS A BAD IDEA.
THEN STAY HERE.
YOU OWN THE COPS?
I OWN THE TOWN THEY COME FROM. AND SO, YES, I OWN THEM.
AMBITIOUS. HOW DO YOU PULL IT OFF?
MONEY AND MIND-CONTROL. YOU SPREAD AROUND ENOUGH OF THE FIRST, YOU DON'T NEED AS MUCH OF THE SECOND.
IT'S TACTICS. CONSERVATION OF RESOURCES.
MY MOTHER.
ONE TRACK MIND. I LIKE THAT ABOUT YOU.

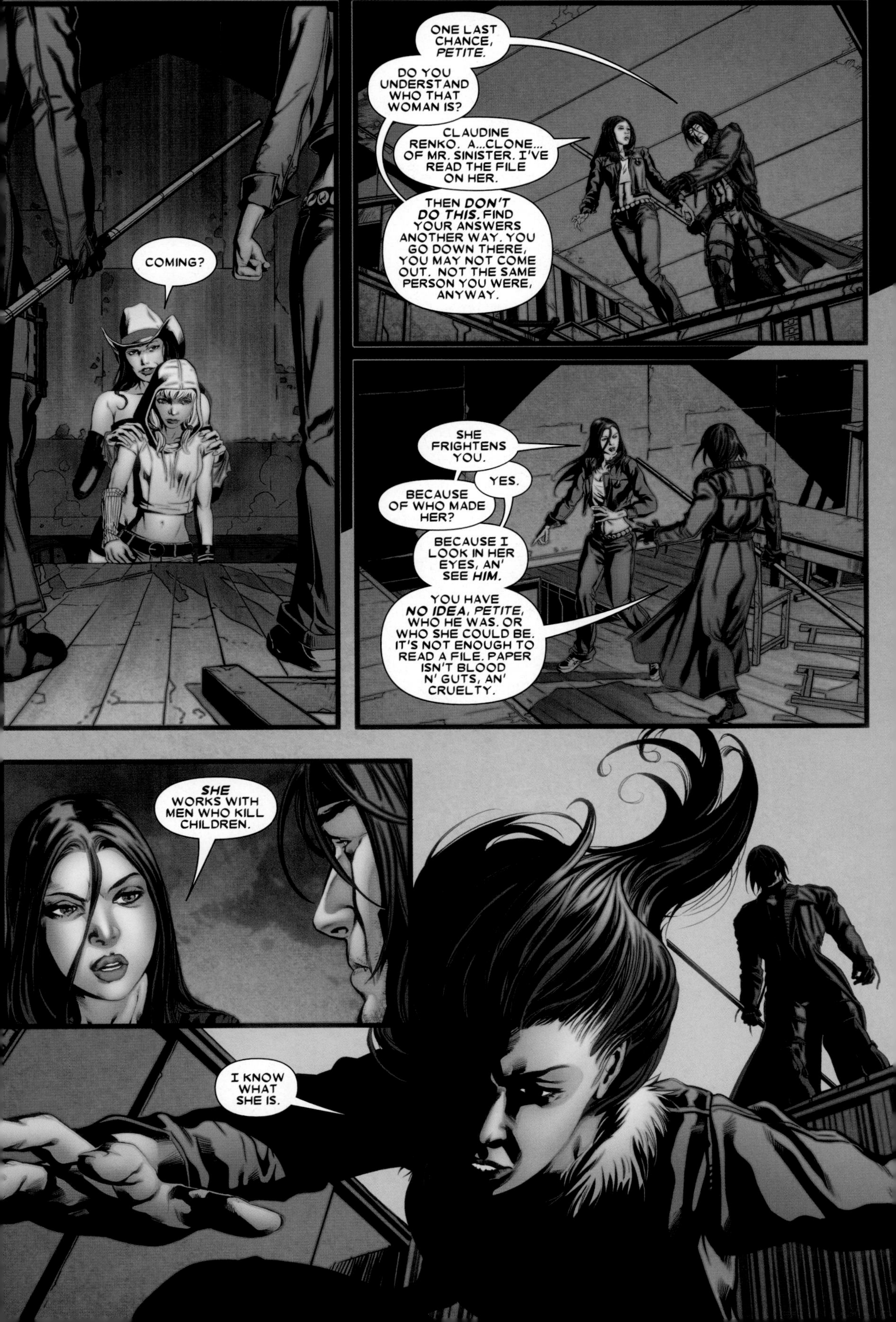
COMING?
ONE LAST CHANCE, PETITE.
DO YOU UNDERSTAND WHO THAT WOMAN IS?
CLAUDINE RENKO. A...CLONE... OF MR. SINISTER. I'VE READ THE FILE ON HER.
THEN DON'T DO THIS. FIND YOUR ANSWERS ANOTHER WAY. YOU GO DOWN THERE, YOU MAY NOT COME OUT. NOT THE SAME PERSON YOU WERE, ANYWAY.
SHE FRIGHTENS YOU.
YES.
BECAUSE OF WHO MADE HER?
BECAUSE I LOOK IN HER EYES, AN' SEE HIM.
YOU HAVE NO IDEA, PETITE, WHO HE WAS. OR WHO SHE COULD BE. IT'S NOT ENOUGH TO READ A FILE. PAPER ISN'T BLOOD N' GUTS, AN' CRUELTY.
SHE WORKS WITH MEN WHO KILL CHILDREN.
I KNOW WHAT SHE IS.

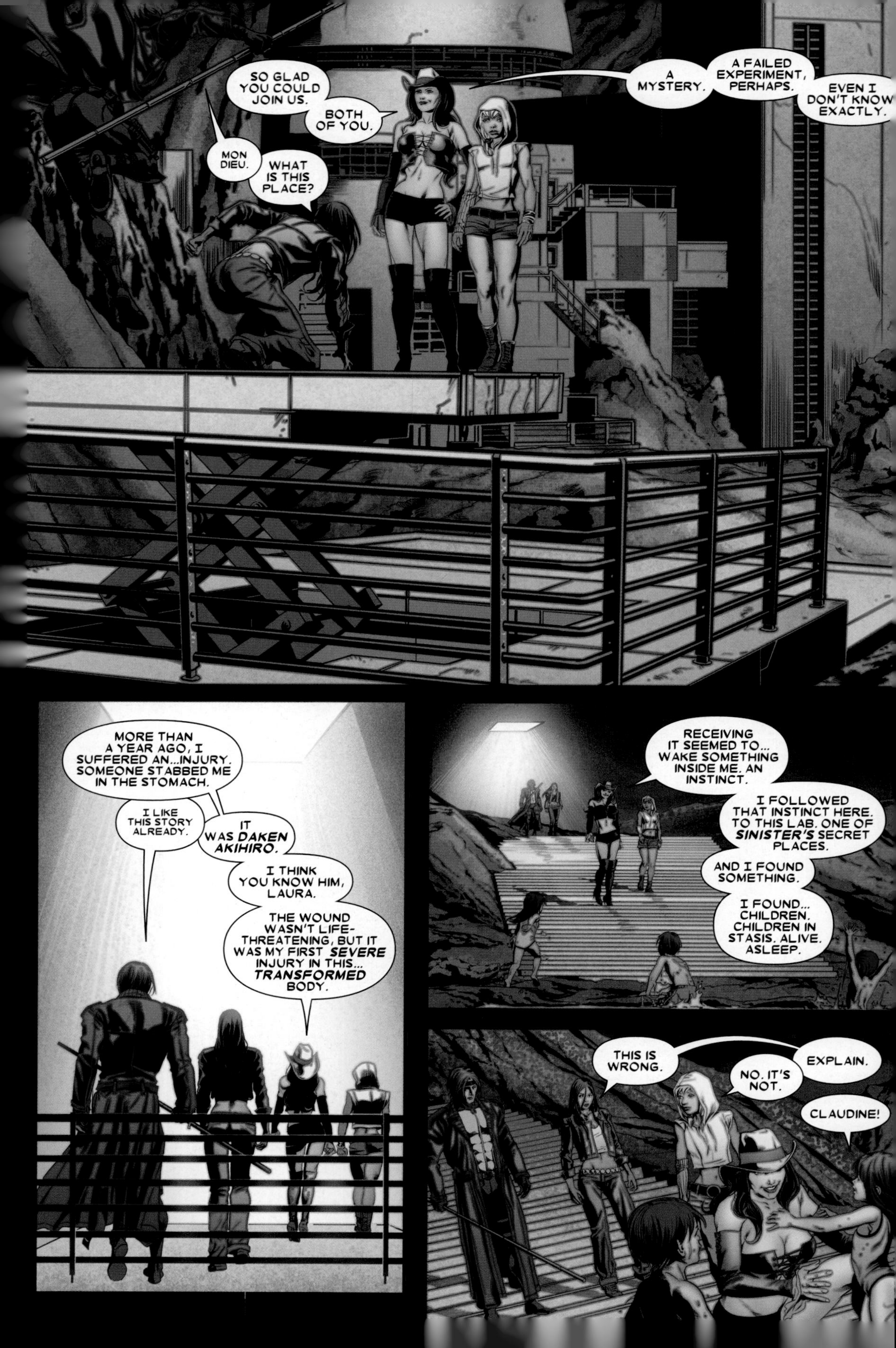

SO GLAD YOU COULD JOIN US.
BOTH OF YOU.
MON DIEU.
WHAT IS THIS PLACE?
A MYSTERY.
A FAILED EXPERIMENT, PERHAPS.
EVEN I DON'T KNOW EXACTLY.
MORE THAN A YEAR AGO, I SUFFERED AN...INJURY. SOMEONE STABBED ME IN THE STOMACH.
I LIKE THIS STORY ALREADY.
IT WAS DAKEN AKIHIRO.
I THINK YOU KNOW HIM, LAURA.
THE WOUND WASN'T LIFE-THREATENING, BUT IT WAS MY FIRST SEVERE INJURY IN THIS... TRANSFORMED BODY.
RECEIVING IT SEEMED TO... WAKE SOMETHING INSIDE ME. AN INSTINCT.
I FOLLOWED THAT INSTINCT HERE. TO THIS LAB. ONE OF SINISTER'S SECRET PLACES.
AND I FOUND SOMETHING.
I FOUND... CHILDREN. CHILDREN IN STASIS. ALIVE. ASLEEP.
THIS IS WRONG.
EXPLAIN.
NO. IT'S NOT.
CLAUDINE!

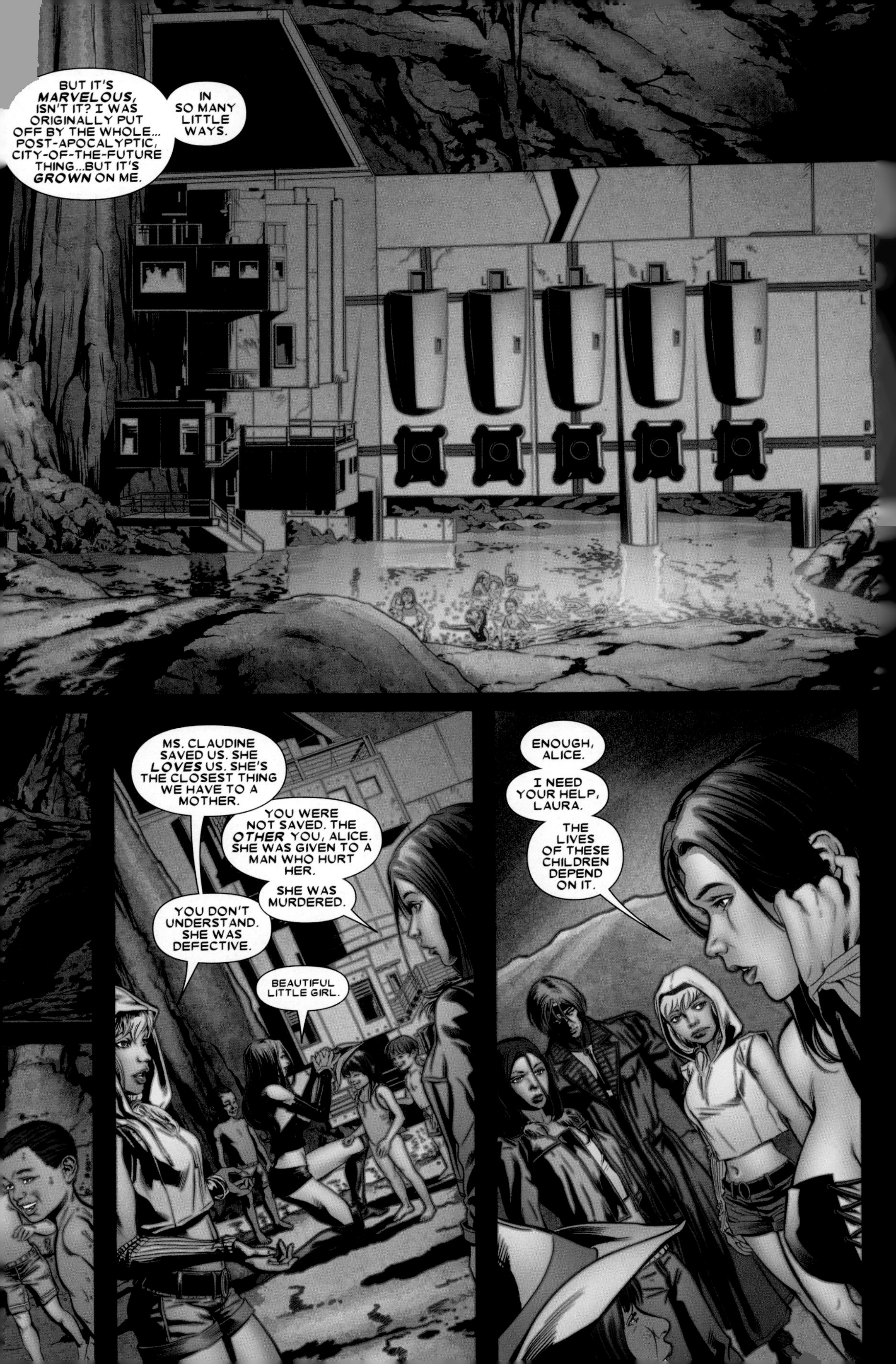
BUT IT'S MARVELOUS, ISN'T IT? I WAS ORIGINALLY PUT OFF BY THE WHOLE... POST-APOCALYPTIC, CITY-OF-THE-FUTURE THING...BUT IT'S GROWN ON ME.
IN SO MANY LITTLE WAYS.
MS. CLAUDINE SAVED US. SHE LOVES US. SHE'S THE CLOSEST THING WE HAVE TO A MOTHER.
YOU WERE NOT SAVED. THE OTHER YOU, ALICE. SHE WAS GIVEN TO A MAN WHO HURT HER.
SHE WAS MURDERED.
YOU DON'T UNDERSTAND. SHE WAS DEFECTIVE.
BEAUTIFUL LITTLE GIRL.
ENOUGH, ALICE.
I NEED YOUR HELP, LAURA.
THE LIVES OF THESE CHILDREN DEPEND ON IT.

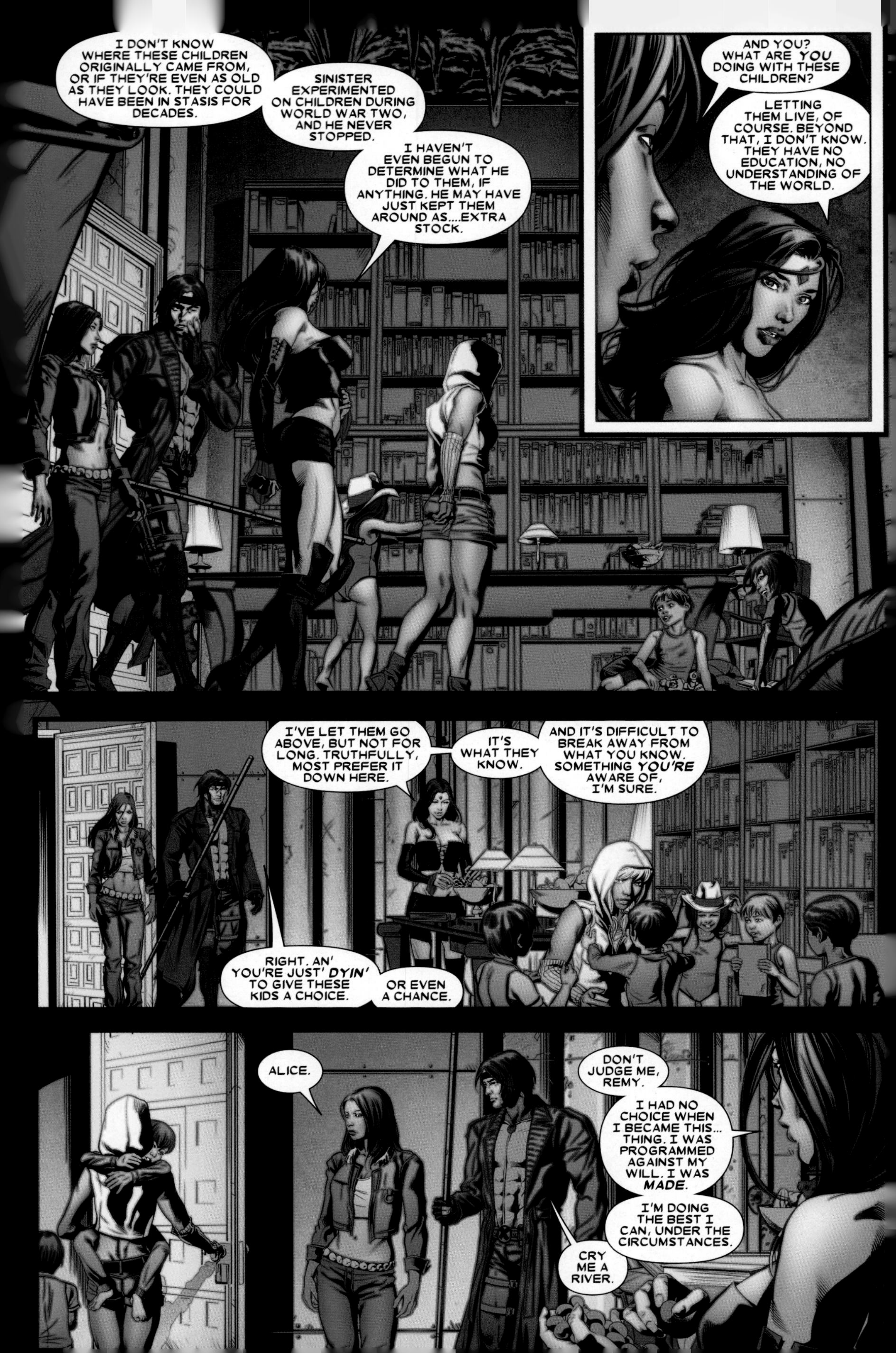
I DON'T KNOW WHERE THESE CHILDREN ORIGINALLY CAME FROM, OR IF THEY'RE EVEN AS OLD AS THEY LOOK. THEY COULD HAVE BEEN IN STASIS FOR DECADES.
SINISTER EXPERIMENTED ON CHILDREN DURING WORLD WAR TWO, AND HE NEVER STOPPED.
I HAVEN'T EVEN BEGUN TO DETERMINE WHAT HE DID TO THEM, IF ANYTHING. HE MAY HAVE JUST KEPT THEM AROUND AS....EXTRA STOCK.
AND YOU? WHAT ARE *YOU* DOING WITH THESE CHILDREN?
LETTING THEM LIVE, OF COURSE. BEYOND THAT, I DON'T KNOW. THEY HAVE NO EDUCATION, NO UNDERSTANDING OF THE WORLD.
I'VE LET THEM GO ABOVE, BUT NOT FOR LONG. TRUTHFULLY, MOST PREFER IT DOWN HERE.
IT'S WHAT THEY KNOW.
AND IT'S DIFFICULT TO BREAK AWAY FROM WHAT YOU KNOW. SOMETHING *YOU'RE* AWARE OF, I'M SURE.
RIGHT. AN' YOU'RE JUST' *DYIN'* TO GIVE THESE KIDS A CHOICE.
OR EVEN A CHANCE.
ALICE.
DON'T JUDGE ME, REMY.
I HAD NO CHOICE WHEN I BECAME THIS... THING. I WAS PROGRAMMED AGAINST MY WILL. I WAS *MADE*.
I'M DOING THE BEST I CAN, UNDER THE CIRCUMSTANCES.
CRY ME A RIVER.

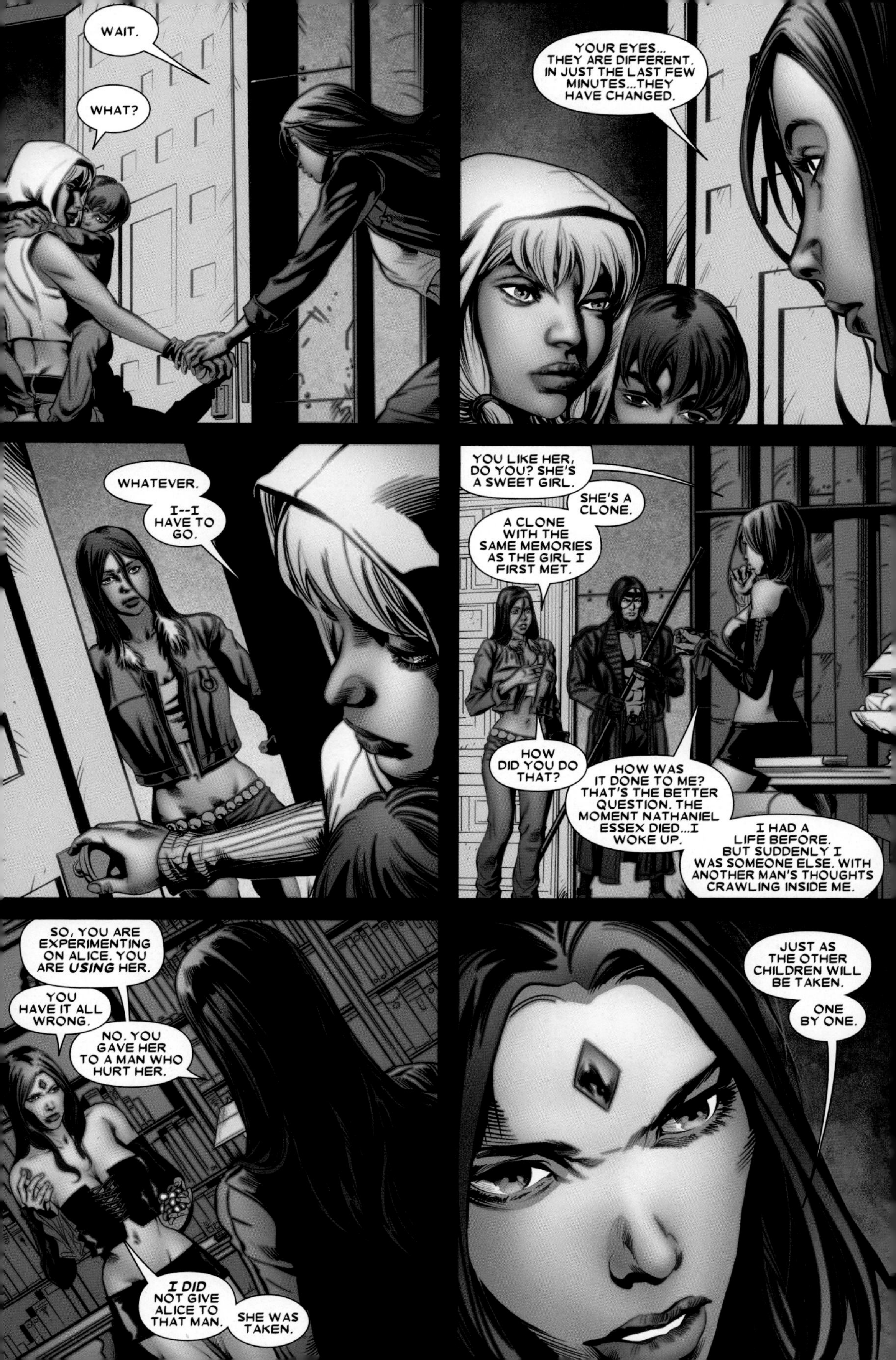
WAIT.
WHAT?
YOUR EYES... THEY ARE DIFFERENT. IN JUST THE LAST FEW MINUTES...THEY HAVE CHANGED.
WHATEVER.
I--I HAVE TO GO.
YOU LIKE HER, DO YOU? SHE'S A SWEET GIRL.
SHE'S A CLONE.
A CLONE WITH THE SAME MEMORIES AS THE GIRL I FIRST MET.
HOW DID YOU DO THAT?
HOW WAS IT DONE TO ME? THAT'S THE BETTER QUESTION. THE MOMENT NATHANIEL ESSEX DIED...I WOKE UP.
I HAD A LIFE BEFORE. BUT SUDDENLY I WAS SOMEONE ELSE. WITH ANOTHER MAN'S THOUGHTS CRAWLING INSIDE ME.
SO, YOU ARE EXPERIMENTING ON ALICE. YOU ARE *USING* HER.
YOU HAVE IT ALL WRONG.
NO. YOU GAVE HER TO A MAN WHO HURT HER.
I DID NOT GIVE ALICE TO THAT MAN.
SHE WAS TAKEN.
JUST AS THE OTHER CHILDREN WILL BE TAKEN.
ONE BY ONE.

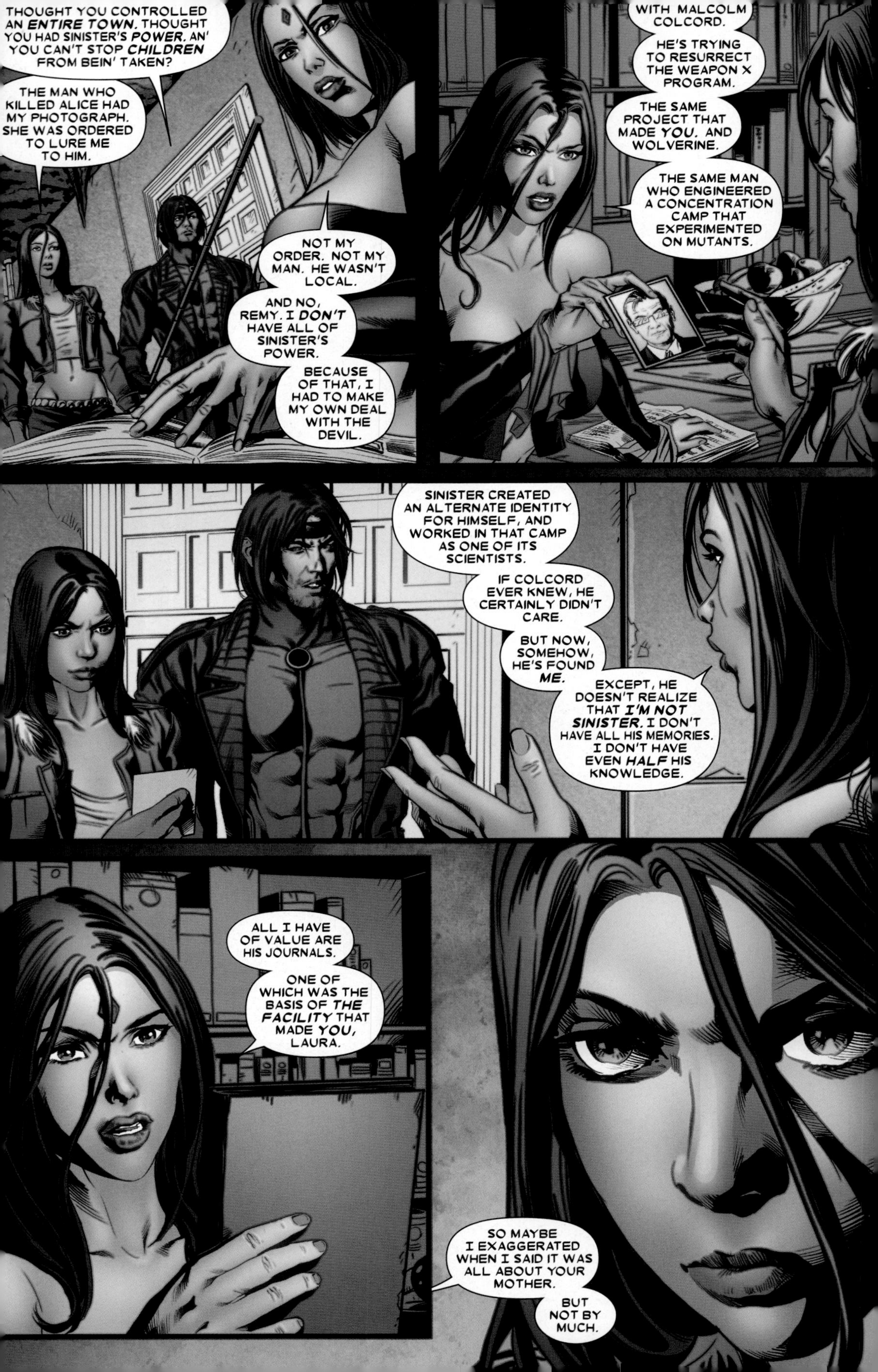

THOUGHT YOU CONTROLLED AN ENTIRE TOWN. THOUGHT YOU HAD SINISTER'S POWER. AN' YOU CAN'T STOP CHILDREN FROM BEIN' TAKEN?
THE MAN WHO KILLED ALICE HAD MY PHOTOGRAPH. SHE WAS ORDERED TO LURE ME TO HIM.
NOT MY ORDER. NOT MY MAN. HE WASN'T LOCAL.
AND NO, REMY. I DON'T HAVE ALL OF SINISTER'S POWER.
BECAUSE OF THAT, I HAD TO MAKE MY OWN DEAL WITH THE DEVIL.
WITH MALCOLM COLCORD.
HE'S TRYING TO RESURRECT THE WEAPON X PROGRAM.
THE SAME PROJECT THAT MADE YOU. AND WOLVERINE.
THE SAME MAN WHO ENGINEERED A CONCENTRATION CAMP THAT EXPERIMENTED ON MUTANTS.
SINISTER CREATED AN ALTERNATE IDENTITY FOR HIMSELF, AND WORKED IN THAT CAMP AS ONE OF ITS SCIENTISTS.
IF COLCORD EVER KNEW, HE CERTAINLY DIDN'T CARE.
BUT NOW, SOMEHOW, HE'S FOUND ME.
EXCEPT, HE DOESN'T REALIZE THAT I'M NOT SINISTER. I DON'T HAVE ALL HIS MEMORIES. I DON'T HAVE EVEN HALF HIS KNOWLEDGE.
ALL I HAVE OF VALUE ARE HIS JOURNALS.
ONE OF WHICH WAS THE BASIS OF THE FACILITY THAT MADE YOU, LAURA.
SO MAYBE I EXAGGERATED WHEN I SAID IT WAS ALL ABOUT YOUR MOTHER.
BUT NOT BY MUCH.

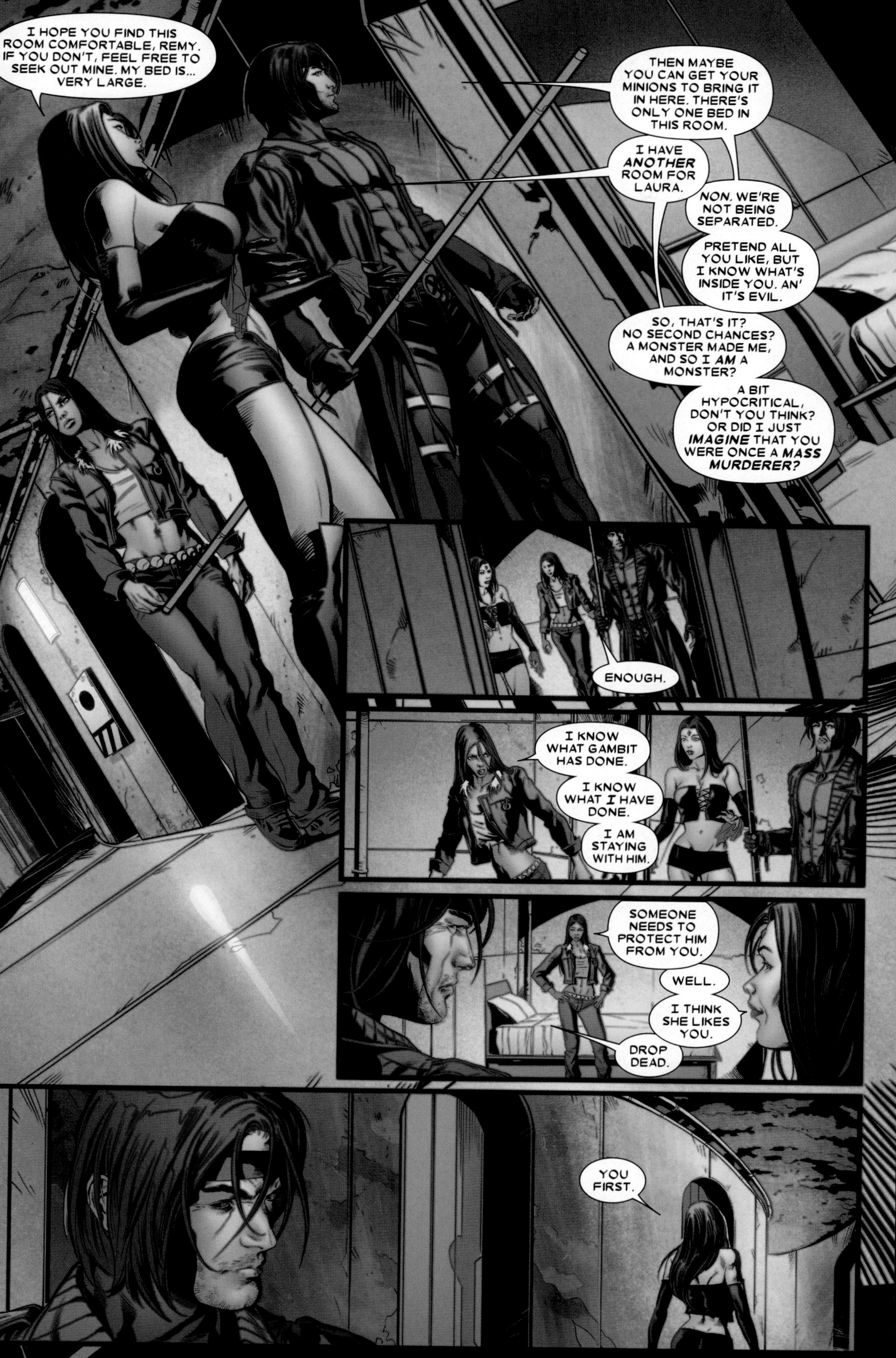
I HOPE YOU FIND THIS ROOM COMFORTABLE, REMY. IF YOU DON'T, FEEL FREE TO SEEK OUT MINE. MY BED IS... VERY LARGE.
THEN MAYBE YOU CAN GET YOUR MINIONS TO BRING IT IN HERE. THERE'S ONLY ONE BED IN THIS ROOM.
I HAVE *ANOTHER* ROOM FOR LAURA.
NON. WE'RE NOT BEING SEPARATED.
PRETEND ALL YOU LIKE, BUT I KNOW WHAT'S INSIDE YOU. AN' IT'S EVIL.
SO, THAT'S IT? NO SECOND CHANCES? A MONSTER MADE ME, AND SO I *AM* A MONSTER?
A BIT HYPOCRITICAL, DON'T YOU THINK? OR DID I JUST *IMAGINE* THAT YOU WERE ONCE A *MASS MURDERER?*
ENOUGH.
I KNOW WHAT GAMBIT HAS DONE.
I KNOW WHAT *I* HAVE DONE.
I AM STAYING WITH HIM.
SOMEONE NEEDS TO PROTECT HIM FROM YOU.
WELL.
I THINK SHE LIKES YOU.
DROP DEAD.
YOU FIRST.

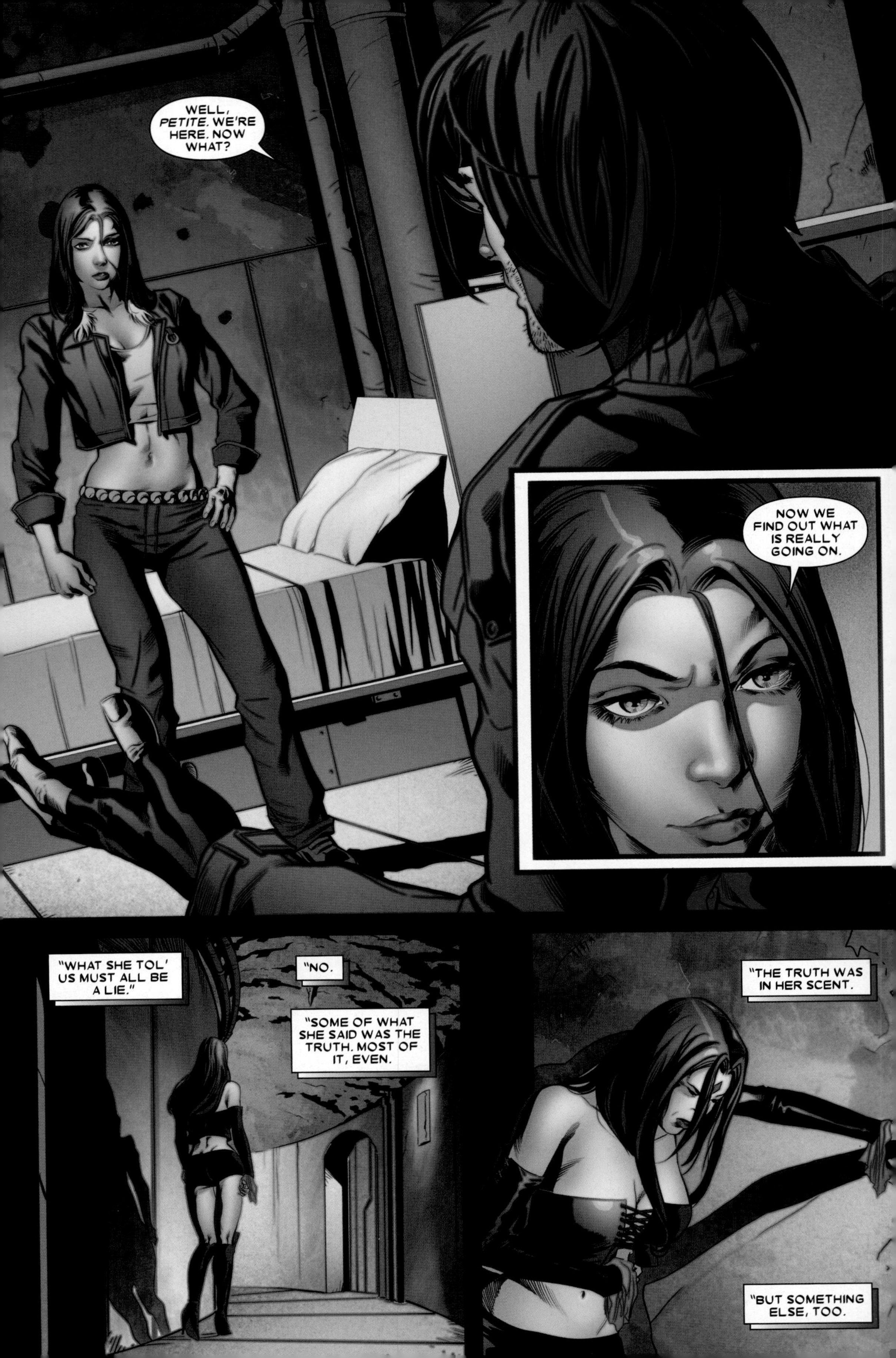
WELL, *PETITE*. WE'RE HERE. NOW WHAT?
NOW WE FIND OUT WHAT IS REALLY GOING ON.
"WHAT SHE TOL' US MUST ALL BE A LIE."
"NO.
"SOME OF WHAT SHE SAID WAS THE TRUTH. MOST OF IT, EVEN.
"THE TRUTH WAS IN HER SCENT.
"BUT SOMETHING ELSE, TOO.

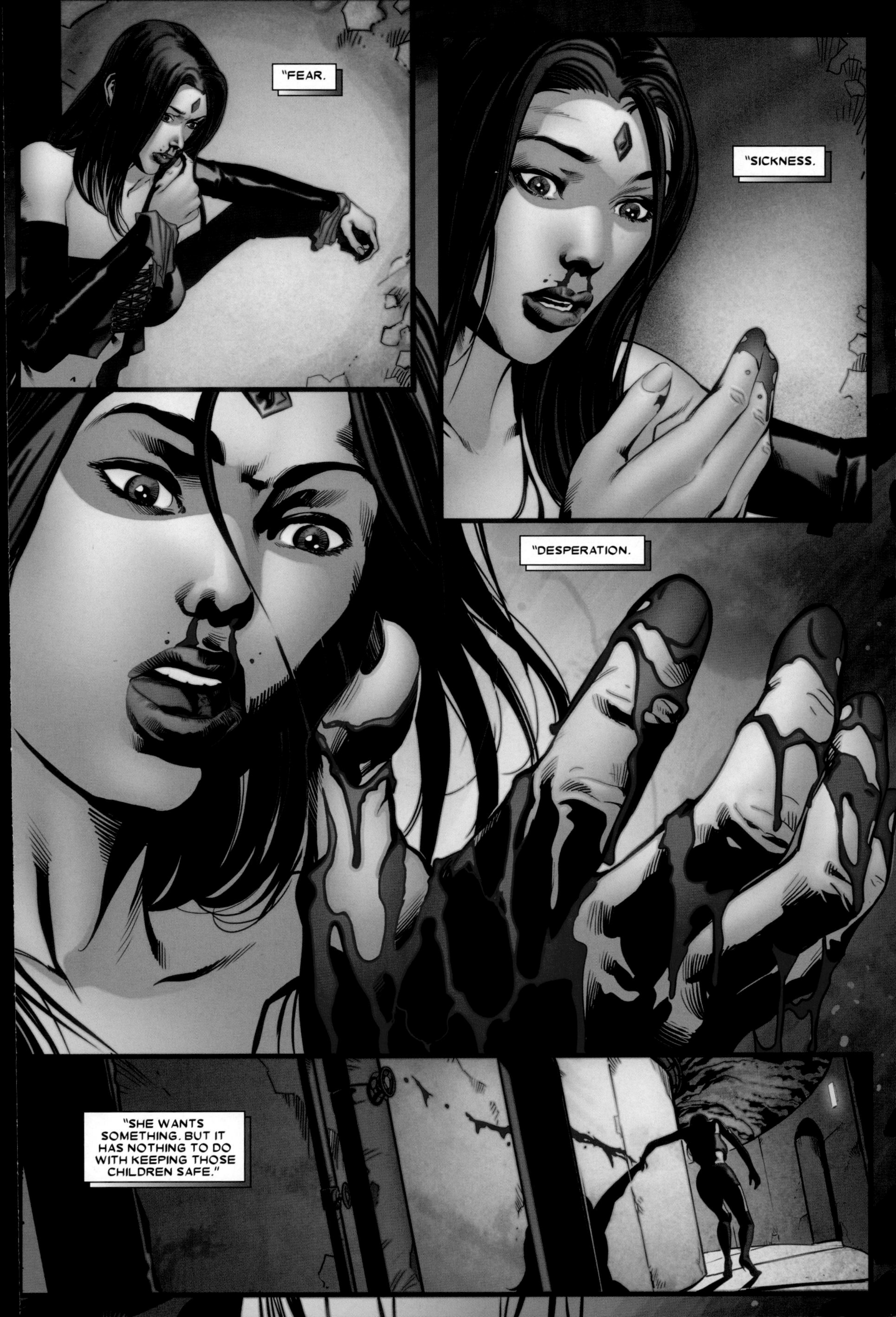
"FEAR.
"SICKNESS.
"DESPERATION.
"SHE WANTS SOMETHING. BUT IT HAS NOTHING TO DO WITH KEEPING THOSE CHILDREN SAFE."

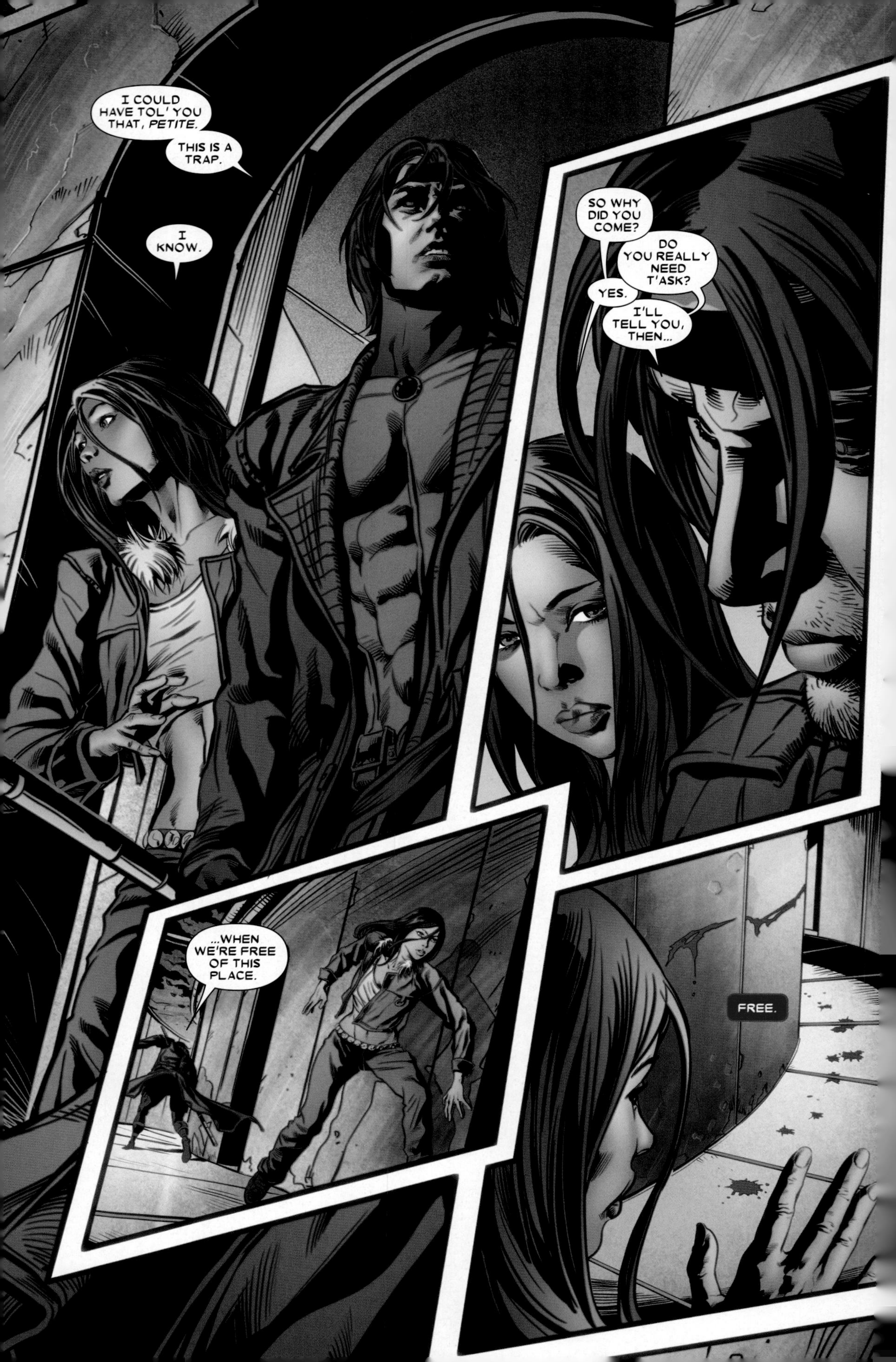
I COULD HAVE TOL' YOU THAT, *PETITE*.
THIS IS A TRAP.
I KNOW.
SO WHY DID YOU COME?
DO YOU REALLY NEED T'ASK?
YES.
I'LL TELL YOU, THEN...
...WHEN WE'RE FREE OF THIS PLACE.
FREE.

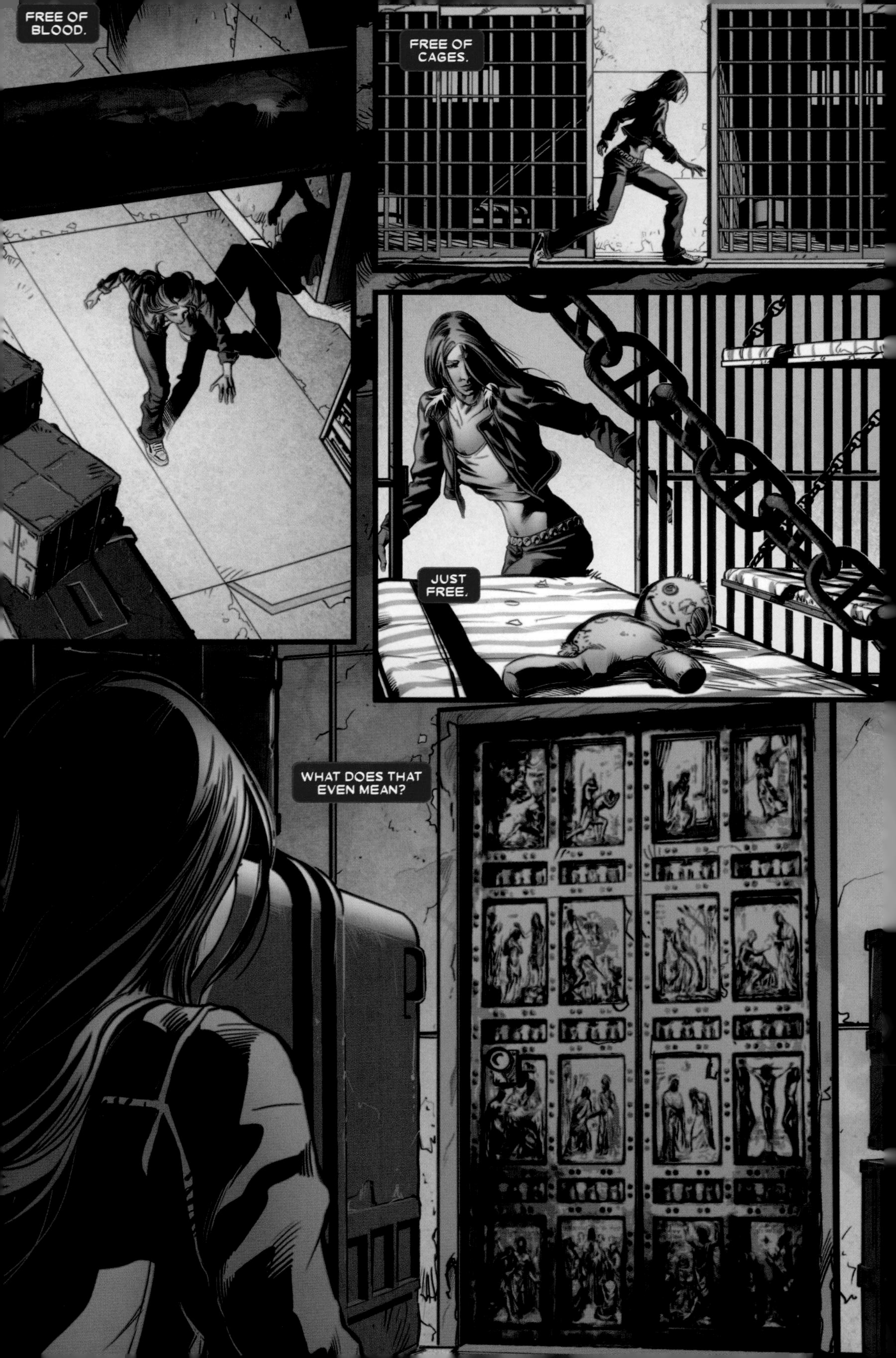
FREE OF BLOOD.
FREE OF CAGES.
JUST FREE.
WHAT DOES THAT EVEN MEAN?

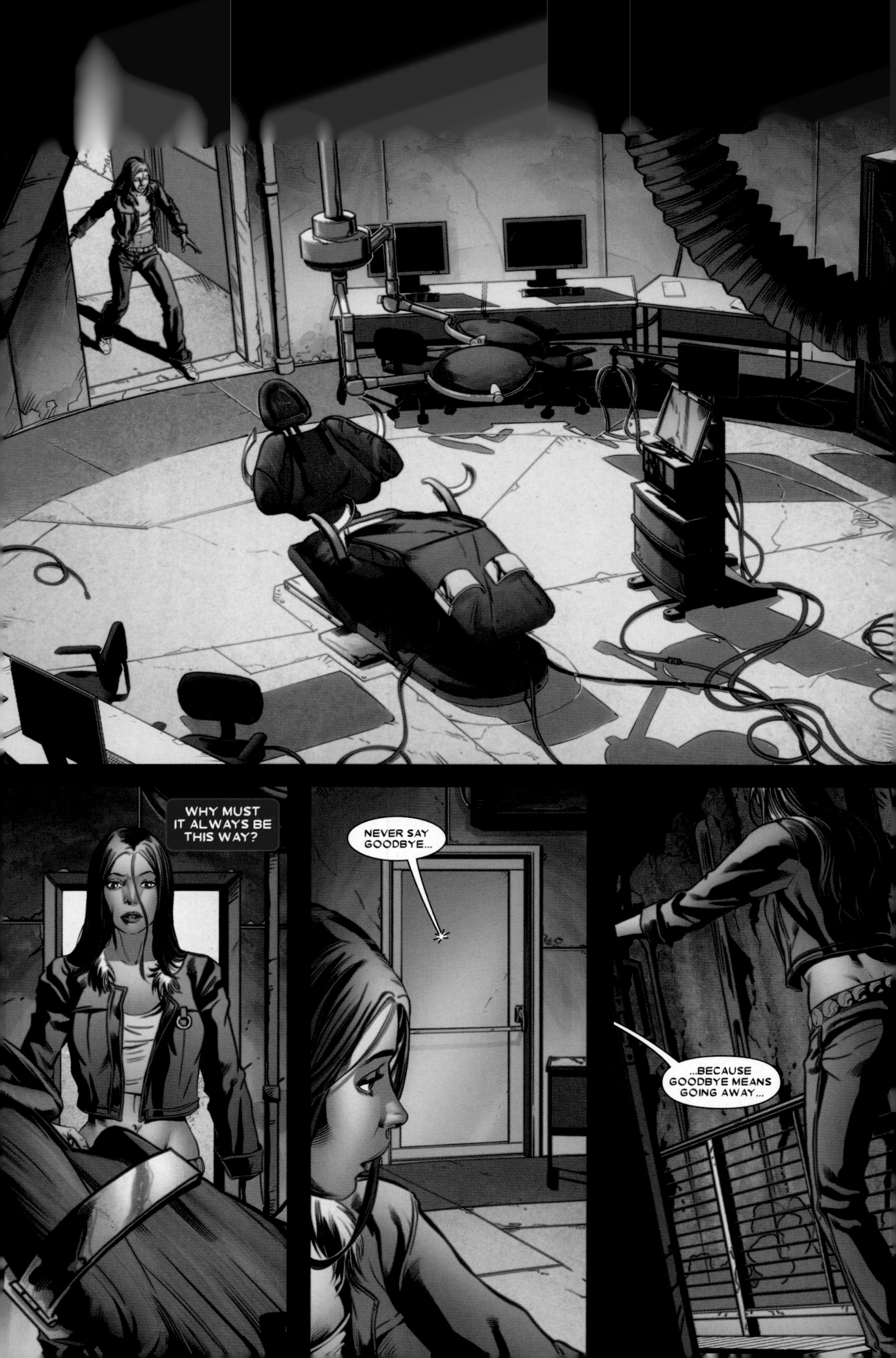
WHY MUST IT ALWAYS BE THIS WAY?
NEVER SAY GOODBYE...
...BECAUSE GOODBYE MEANS GOING AWAY...

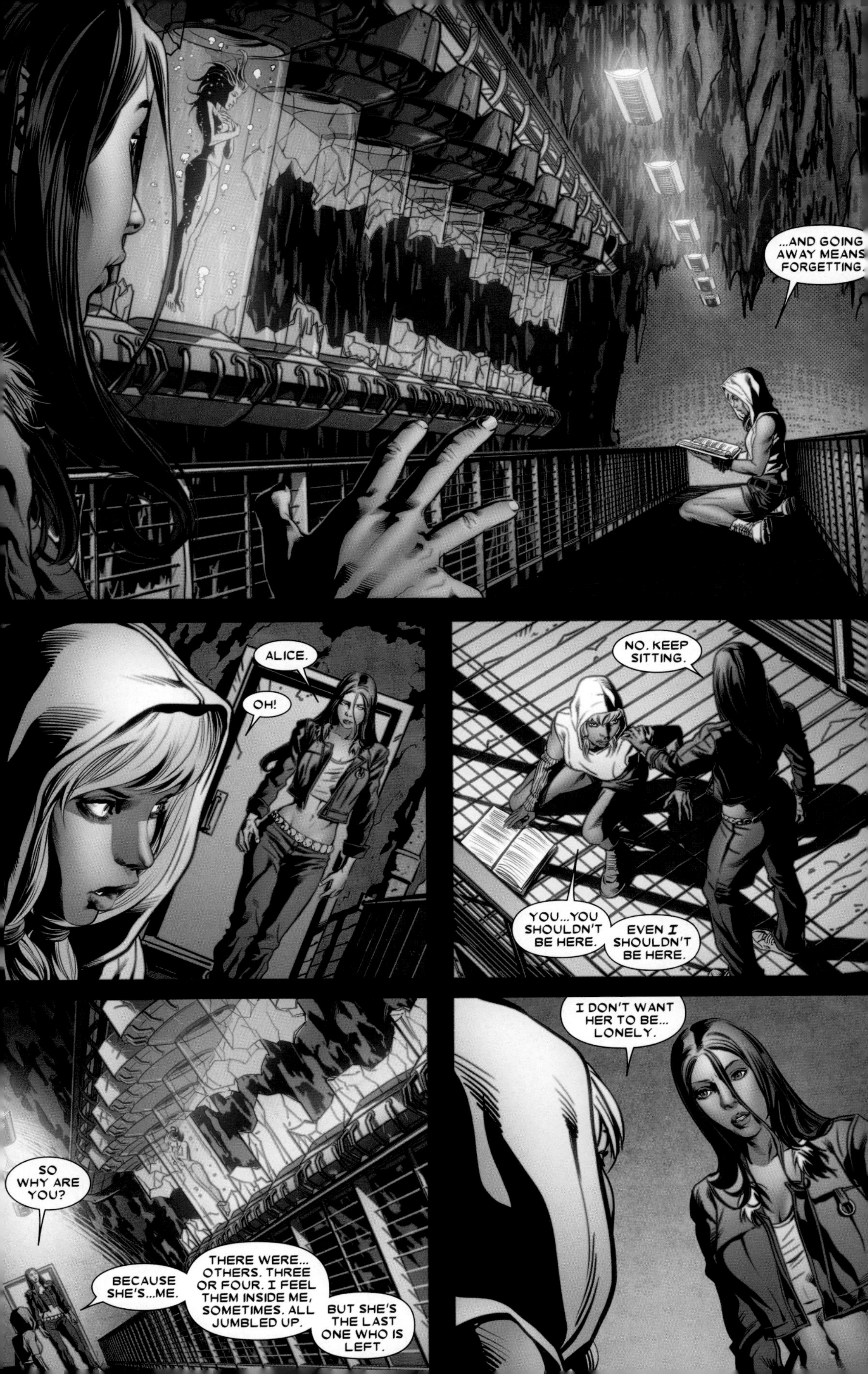

...AND GOING AWAY MEANS FORGETTING.
ALICE.
OH!
NO. KEEP SITTING.
YOU...YOU SHOULDN'T BE HERE.
EVEN I SHOULDN'T BE HERE.
SO WHY ARE YOU?
BECAUSE SHE'S...ME.
THERE WERE... OTHERS. THREE OR FOUR. I FEEL THEM INSIDE ME, SOMETIMES. ALL JUMBLED UP.
BUT SHE'S THE LAST ONE WHO IS LEFT.
I DON'T WANT HER TO BE... LONELY.

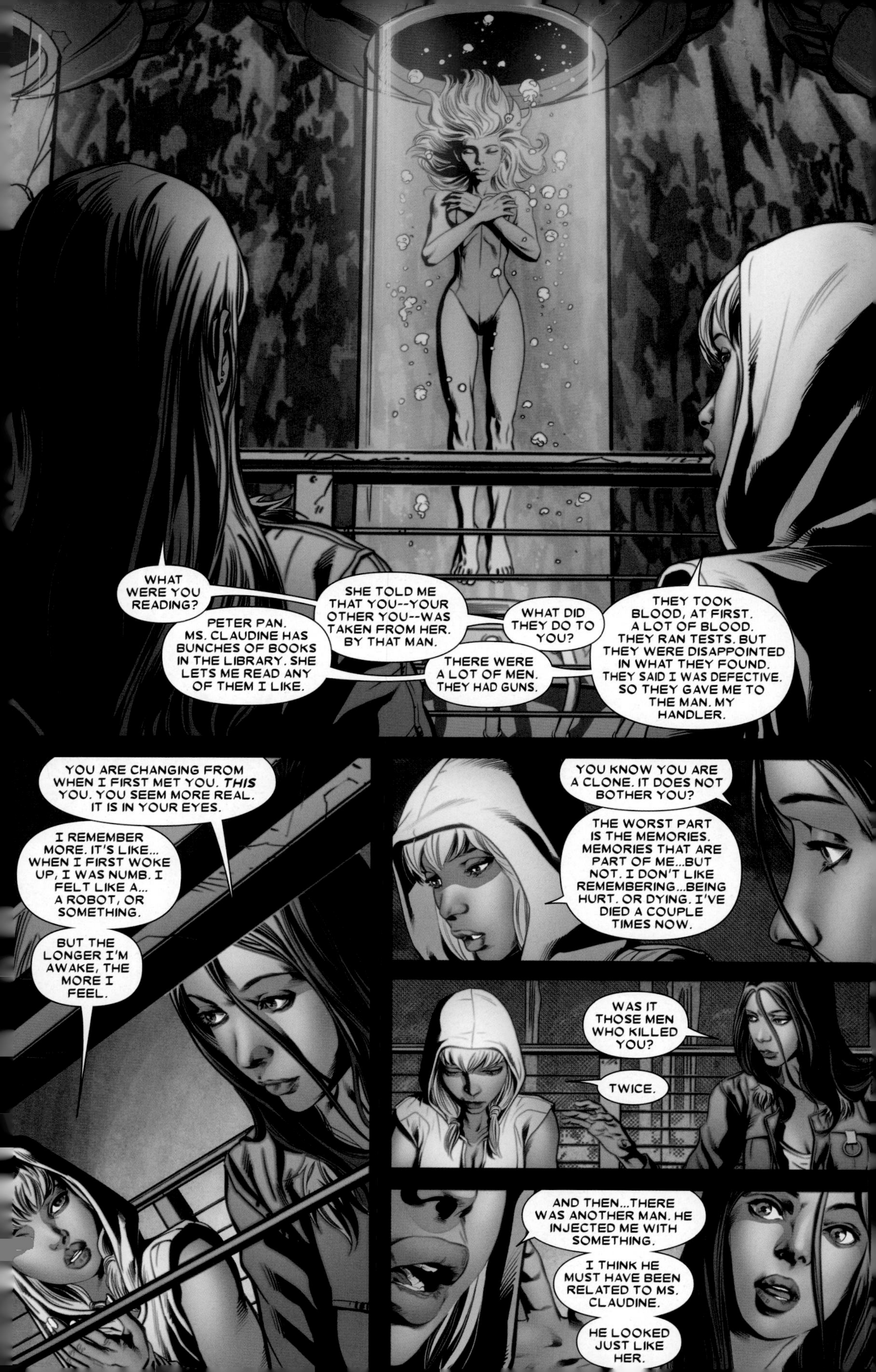
WHAT WERE YOU READING?
PETER PAN. MS. CLAUDINE HAS BUNCHES OF BOOKS IN THE LIBRARY. SHE LETS ME READ ANY OF THEM I LIKE.
SHE TOLD ME THAT YOU--YOUR OTHER YOU--WAS TAKEN FROM HER. BY THAT MAN.
WHAT DID THEY DO TO YOU?
THERE WERE A LOT OF MEN. THEY HAD GUNS.
THEY TOOK BLOOD, AT FIRST. A LOT OF BLOOD. THEY RAN TESTS. BUT THEY WERE DISAPPOINTED IN WHAT THEY FOUND. THEY SAID I WAS DEFECTIVE. SO THEY GAVE ME TO THE MAN. MY HANDLER.
YOU ARE CHANGING FROM WHEN I FIRST MET YOU. *THIS* YOU. YOU SEEM MORE REAL. IT IS IN YOUR EYES.
I REMEMBER MORE. IT'S LIKE... WHEN I FIRST WOKE UP, I WAS NUMB. I FELT LIKE A... A ROBOT, OR SOMETHING.
BUT THE LONGER I'M AWAKE, THE MORE I FEEL.
YOU KNOW YOU ARE A CLONE. IT DOES NOT BOTHER YOU?
THE WORST PART IS THE MEMORIES. MEMORIES THAT ARE PART OF ME...BUT NOT. I DON'T LIKE REMEMBERING...BEING HURT. OR DYING. I'VE DIED A COUPLE TIMES NOW.
WAS IT THOSE MEN WHO KILLED YOU?
TWICE.
AND THEN...THERE WAS ANOTHER MAN. HE INJECTED ME WITH SOMETHING.
I THINK HE MUST HAVE BEEN RELATED TO MS. CLAUDINE.
HE LOOKED JUST LIKE HER.

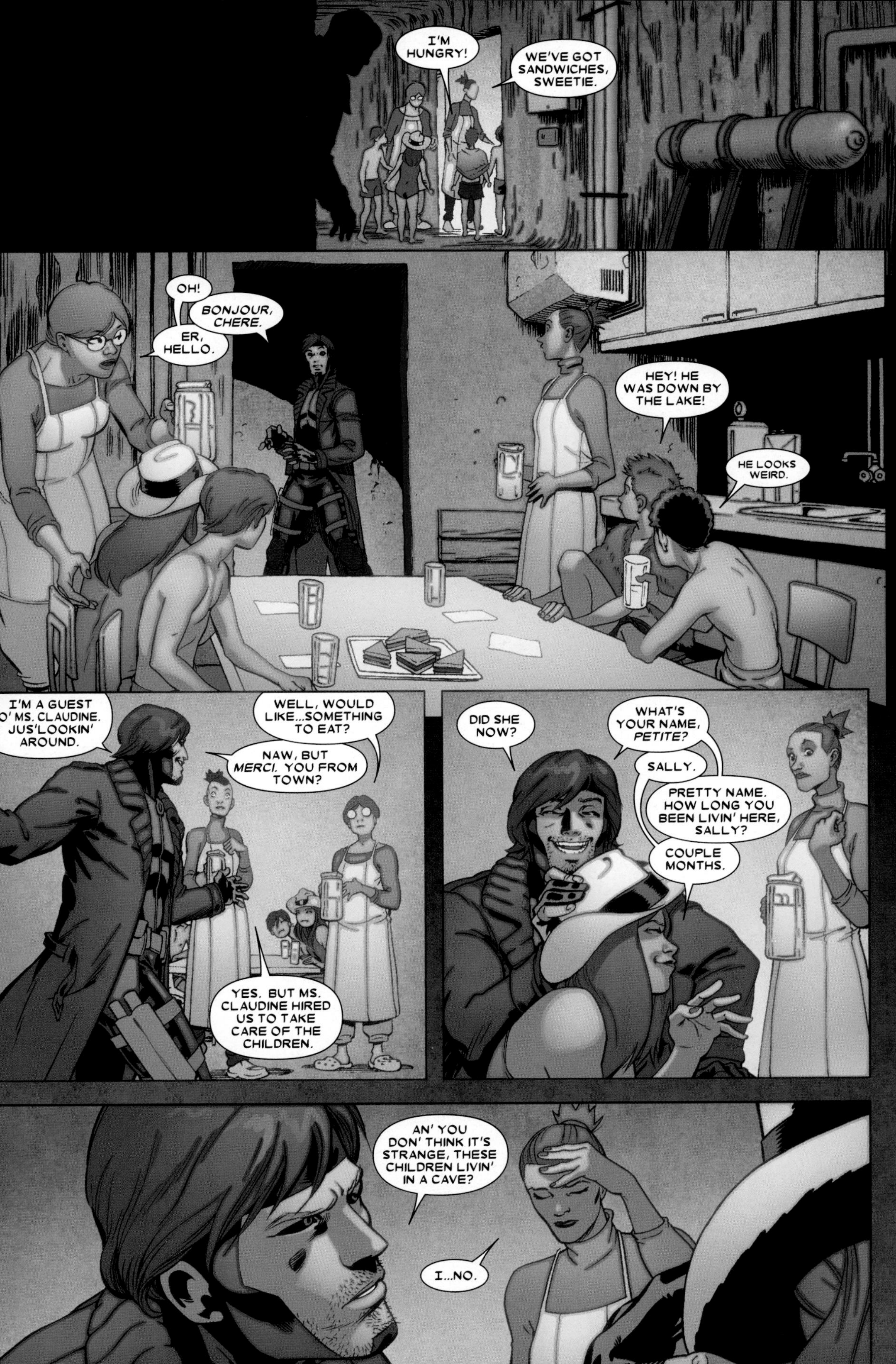
I'M HUNGRY!
WE'VE GOT SANDWICHES, SWEETIE.
OH!
BONJOUR, CHERE.
ER, HELLO.
HEY! HE WAS DOWN BY THE LAKE!
HE LOOKS WEIRD.
I'M A GUEST O' MS. CLAUDINE. JUS'LOOKIN' AROUND.
WELL, WOULD LIKE...SOMETHING TO EAT?
NAW, BUT MERCI. YOU FROM TOWN?
YES. BUT MS. CLAUDINE HIRED US TO TAKE CARE OF THE CHILDREN.
DID SHE NOW?
WHAT'S YOUR NAME, PETITE?
SALLY.
PRETTY NAME. HOW LONG YOU BEEN LIVIN' HERE, SALLY?
COUPLE MONTHS.
AN' YOU DON' THINK IT'S STRANGE, THESE CHILDREN LIVIN' IN A CAVE?
I...NO.

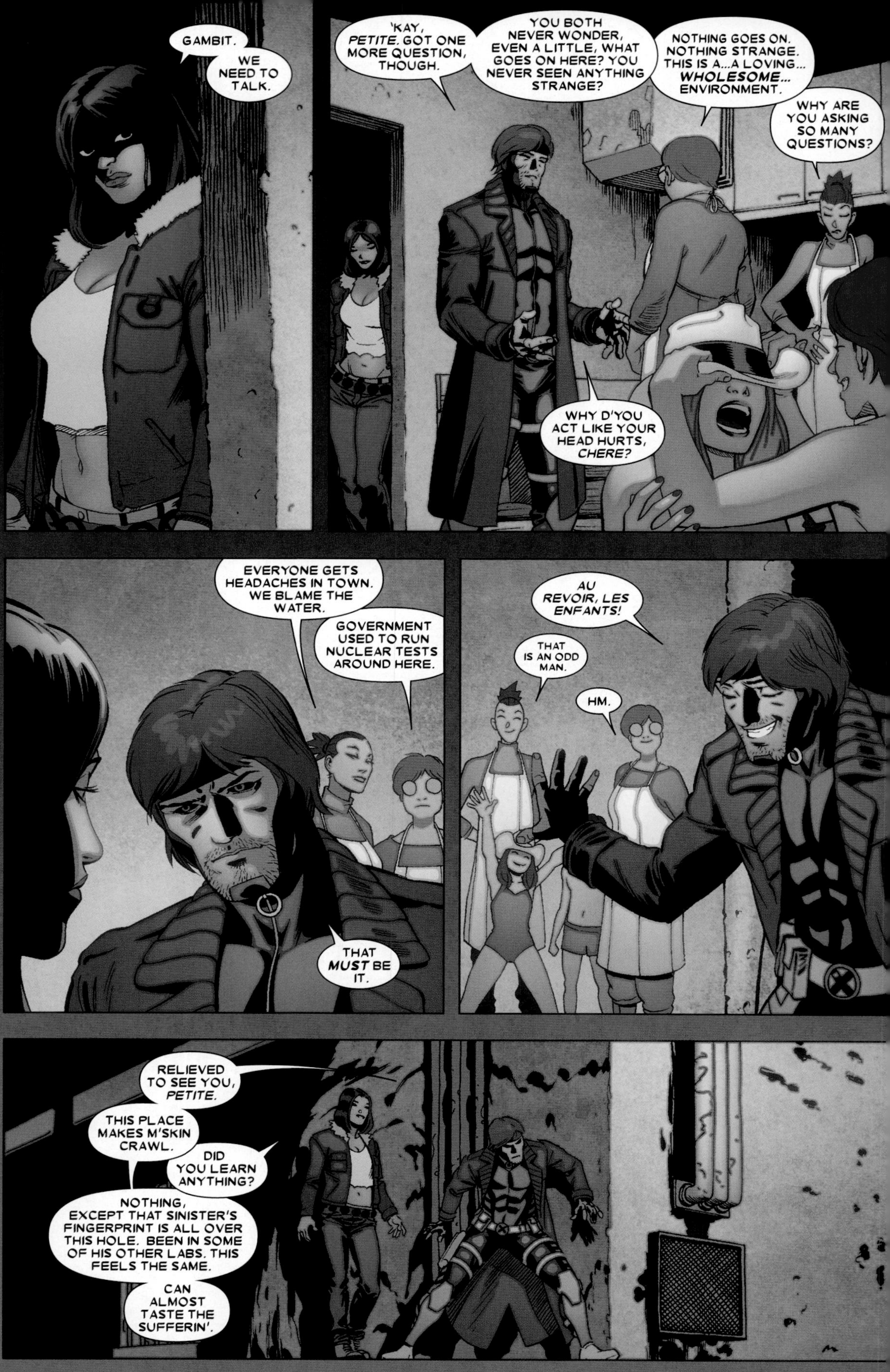
GAMBIT.
WE NEED TO TALK.
'KAY, PETITE. GOT ONE MORE QUESTION, THOUGH.
YOU BOTH NEVER WONDER, EVEN A LITTLE, WHAT GOES ON HERE? YOU NEVER SEEN ANYTHING STRANGE?
NOTHING GOES ON. NOTHING STRANGE. THIS IS A...A LOVING... WHOLESOME... ENVIRONMENT.
WHY ARE YOU ASKING SO MANY QUESTIONS?
WHY D'YOU ACT LIKE YOUR HEAD HURTS, CHERE?
EVERYONE GETS HEADACHES IN TOWN. WE BLAME THE WATER.
GOVERNMENT USED TO RUN NUCLEAR TESTS AROUND HERE.
THAT MUST BE IT.
AU REVOIR, LES ENFANTS!
THAT IS AN ODD MAN.
HM.
RELIEVED TO SEE YOU, PETITE.
THIS PLACE MAKES M'SKIN CRAWL.
DID YOU LEARN ANYTHING?
NOTHING, EXCEPT THAT SINISTER'S FINGERPRINT IS ALL OVER THIS HOLE. BEEN IN SOME OF HIS OTHER LABS. THIS FEELS THE SAME.
CAN ALMOST TASTE THE SUFFERIN'.

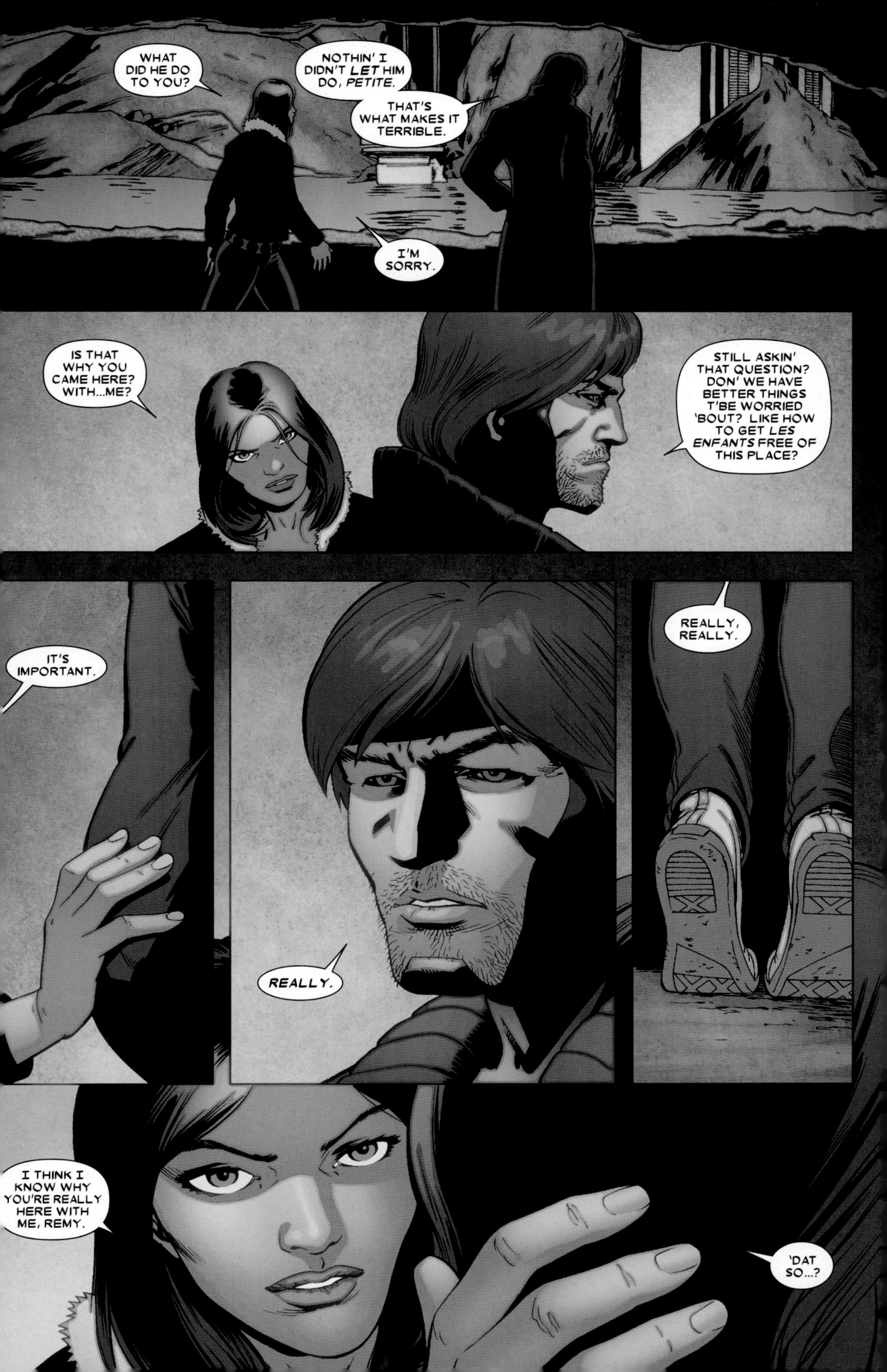
WHAT DID HE DO TO YOU?
NOTHIN' I DIDN'T *LET* HIM DO, *PETITE.*
THAT'S WHAT MAKES IT TERRIBLE.
I'M SORRY.
IS THAT WHY YOU CAME HERE? WITH...ME?
STILL ASKIN' THAT QUESTION? DON' WE HAVE BETTER THINGS T'BE WORRIED 'BOUT? LIKE HOW TO GET *LES ENFANTS* FREE OF THIS PLACE?
IT'S IMPORTANT.
REALLY.
REALLY, REALLY.
I THINK I KNOW WHY YOU'RE REALLY HERE WITH ME, REMY.
'DAT SO...?

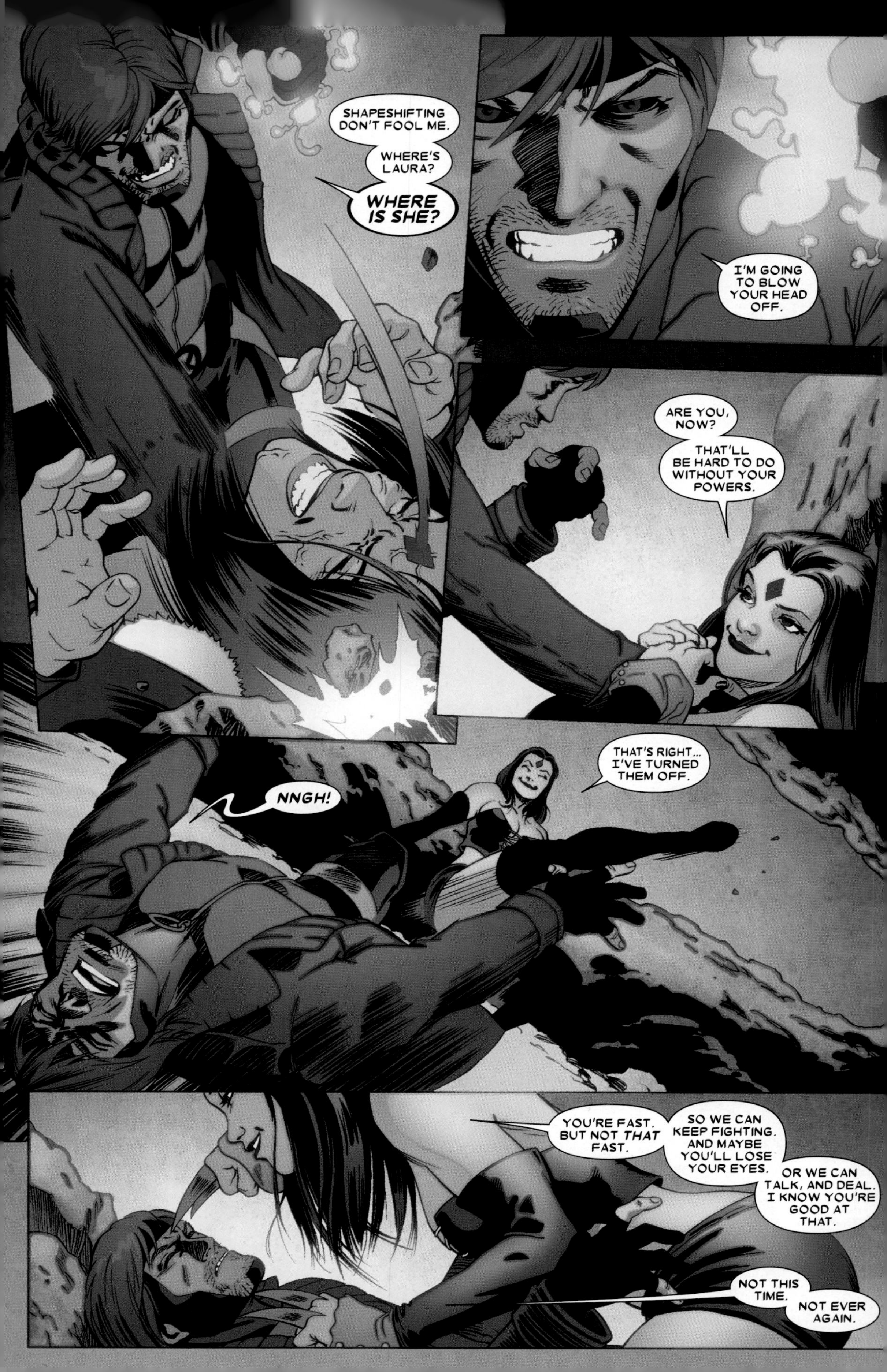
SHAPESHIFTING DON'T FOOL ME.
WHERE'S LAURA?
WHERE IS SHE?
I'M GOING TO BLOW YOUR HEAD OFF.
ARE YOU, NOW?
THAT'LL BE HARD TO DO WITHOUT YOUR POWERS.
THAT'S RIGHT... I'VE TURNED THEM OFF.
NNGH!
YOU'RE FAST. BUT NOT THAT FAST.
SO WE CAN KEEP FIGHTING. AND MAYBE YOU'LL LOSE YOUR EYES.
OR WE CAN TALK, AND DEAL. I KNOW YOU'RE GOOD AT THAT.
NOT THIS TIME.
NOT EVER AGAIN.

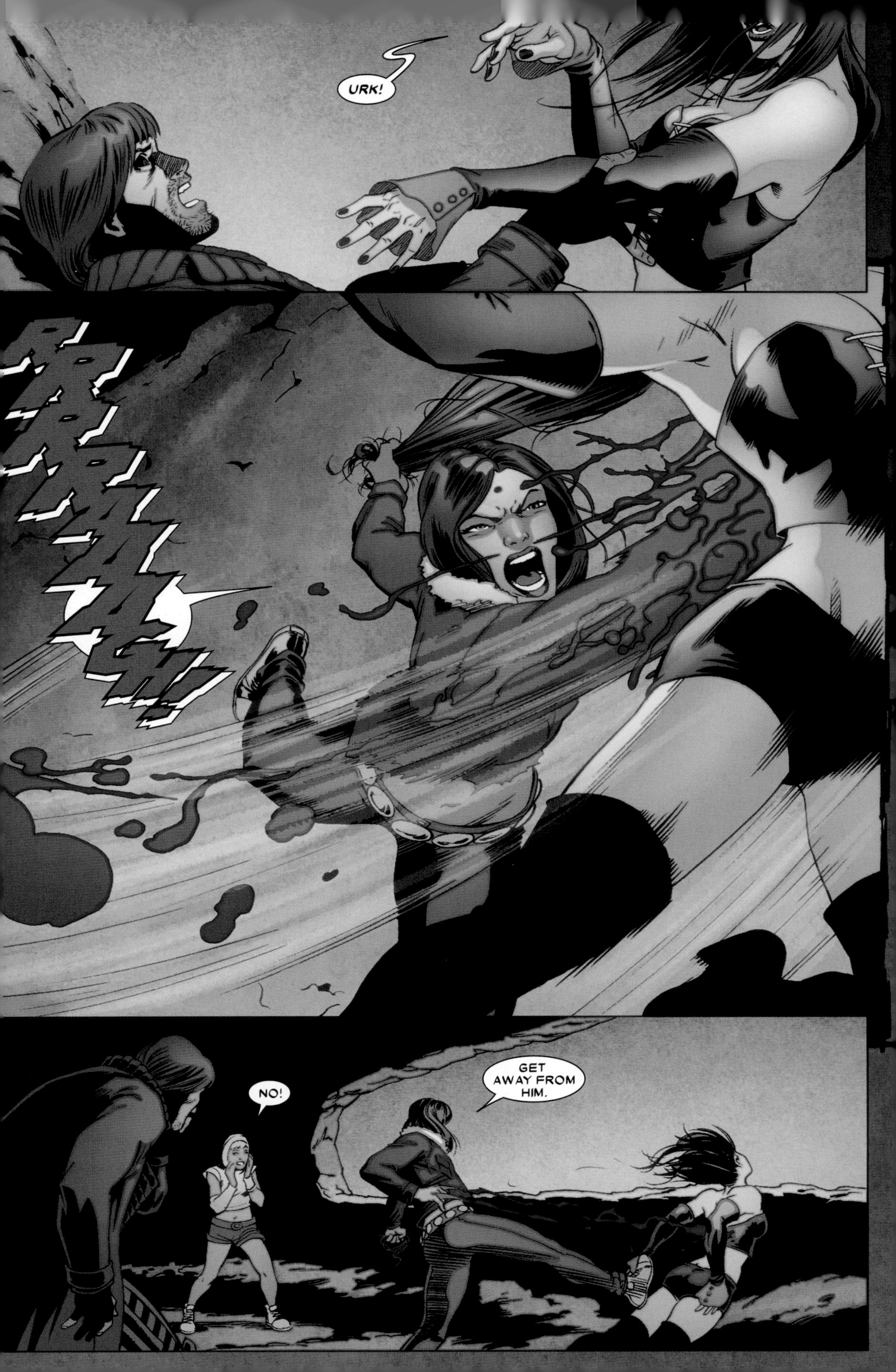
URK!
NO!
GET AWAY FROM HIM.

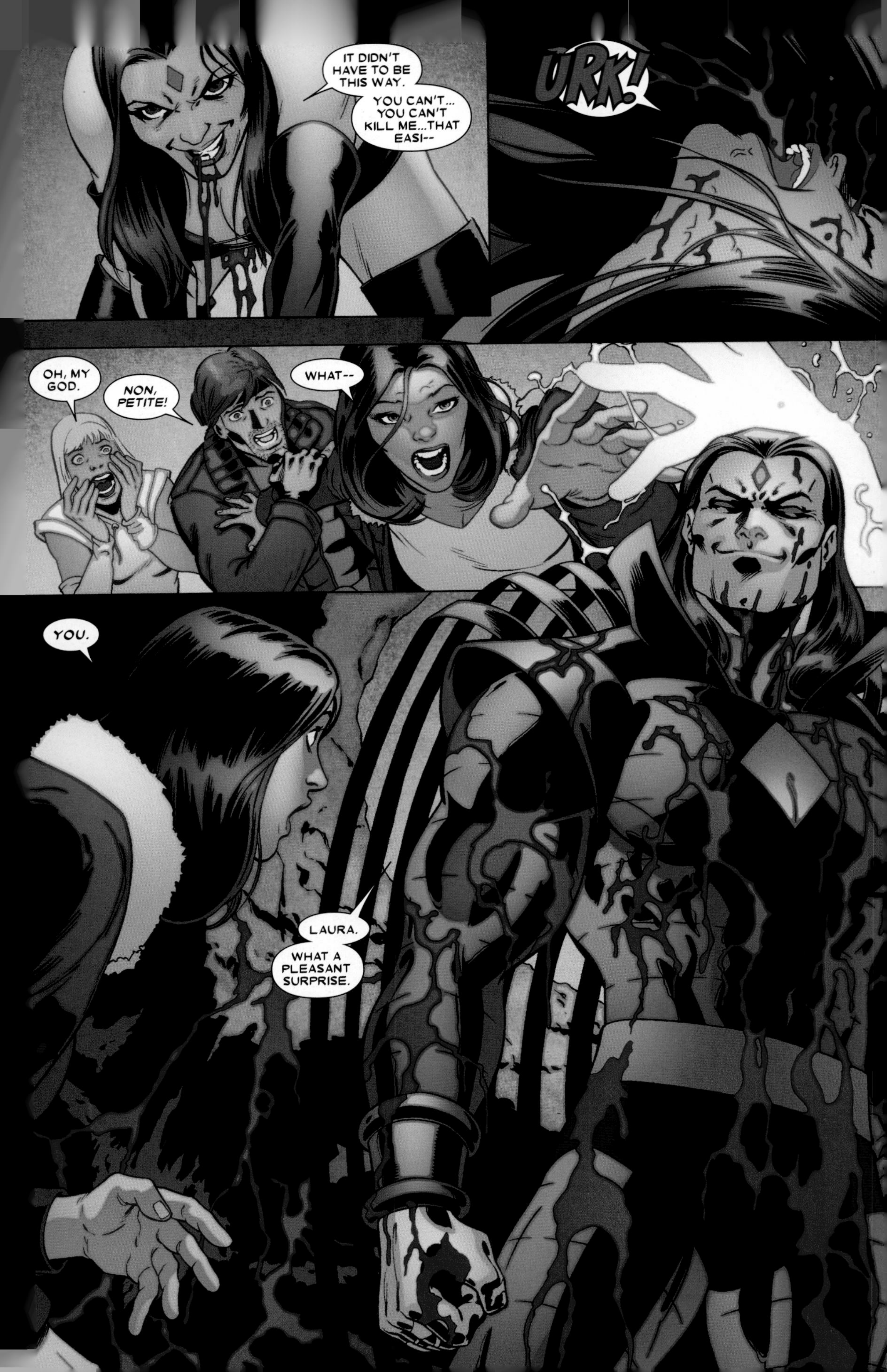
IT DIDN'T HAVE TO BE THIS WAY.
YOU CAN'T... YOU CAN'T KILL ME...THAT EASI--
URK!
OH, MY GOD.
NON, PETITE!
WHAT--
YOU.
LAURA.
WHAT A PLEASANT SURPRISE.

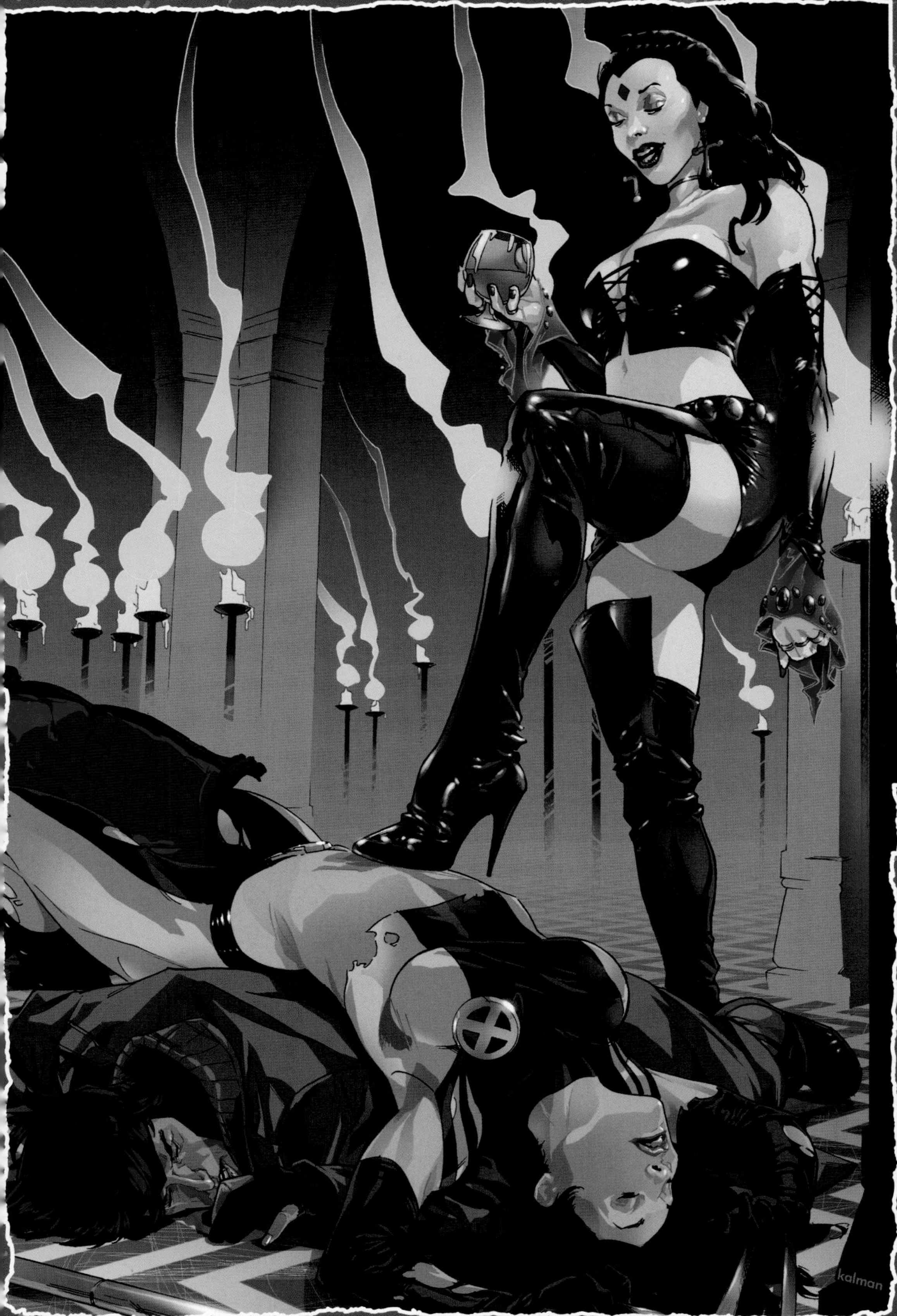
kalman

SIX

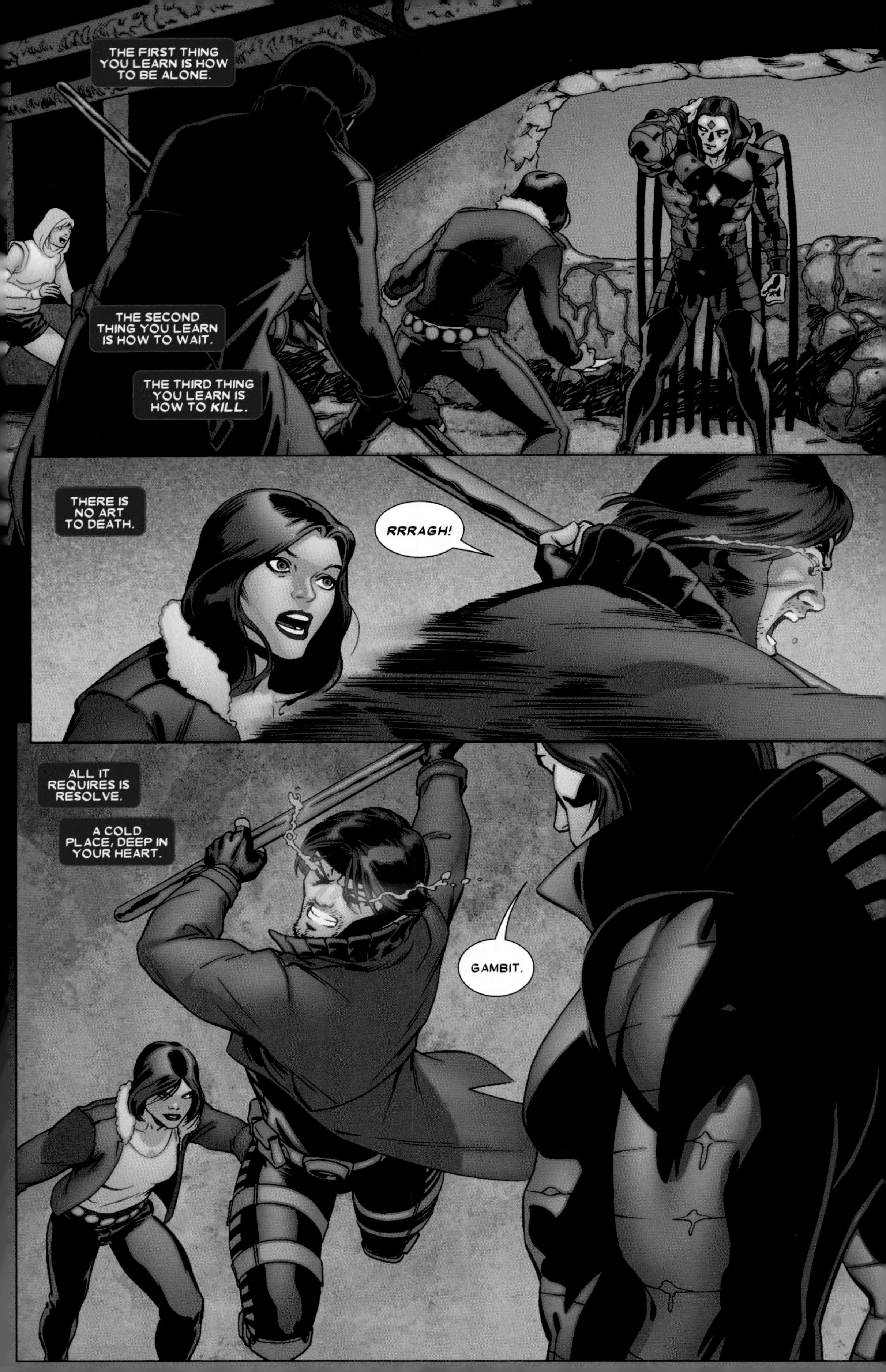
THE FIRST THING YOU LEARN IS HOW TO BE ALONE.
THE SECOND THING YOU LEARN IS HOW TO WAIT.
THE THIRD THING YOU LEARN IS HOW TO *KILL*.
THERE IS NO ART TO DEATH.
RRRAGH!
ALL IT REQUIRES IS RESOLVE.
A COLD PLACE, DEEP IN YOUR HEART.
GAMBIT.

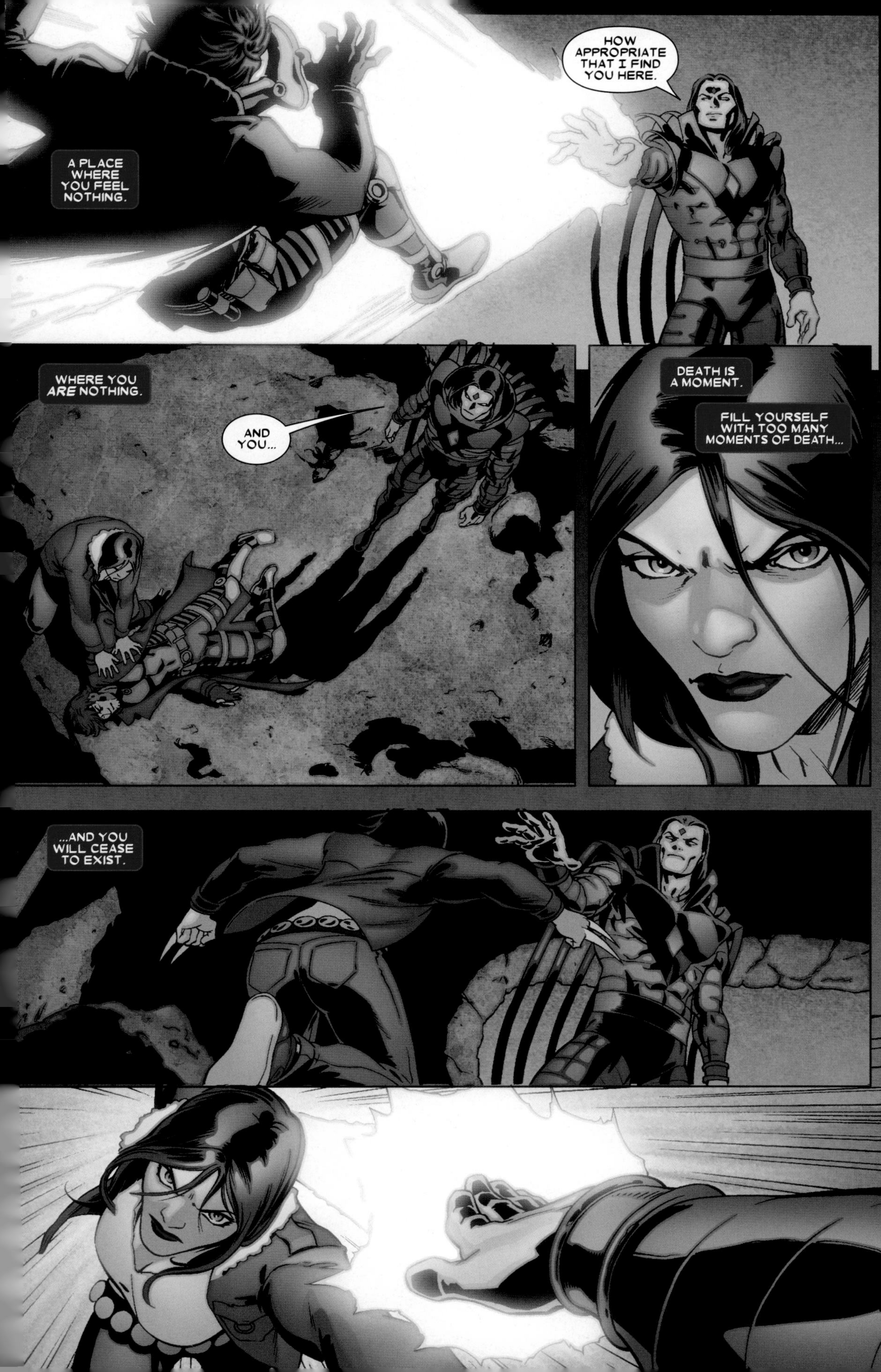
HOW APPROPRIATE THAT I FIND YOU HERE.
A PLACE WHERE YOU FEEL NOTHING.
WHERE YOU *ARE* NOTHING.
AND YOU...
DEATH IS A MOMENT.
FILL YOURSELF WITH TOO MANY MOMENTS OF DEATH...
...AND YOU WILL CEASE TO EXIST.

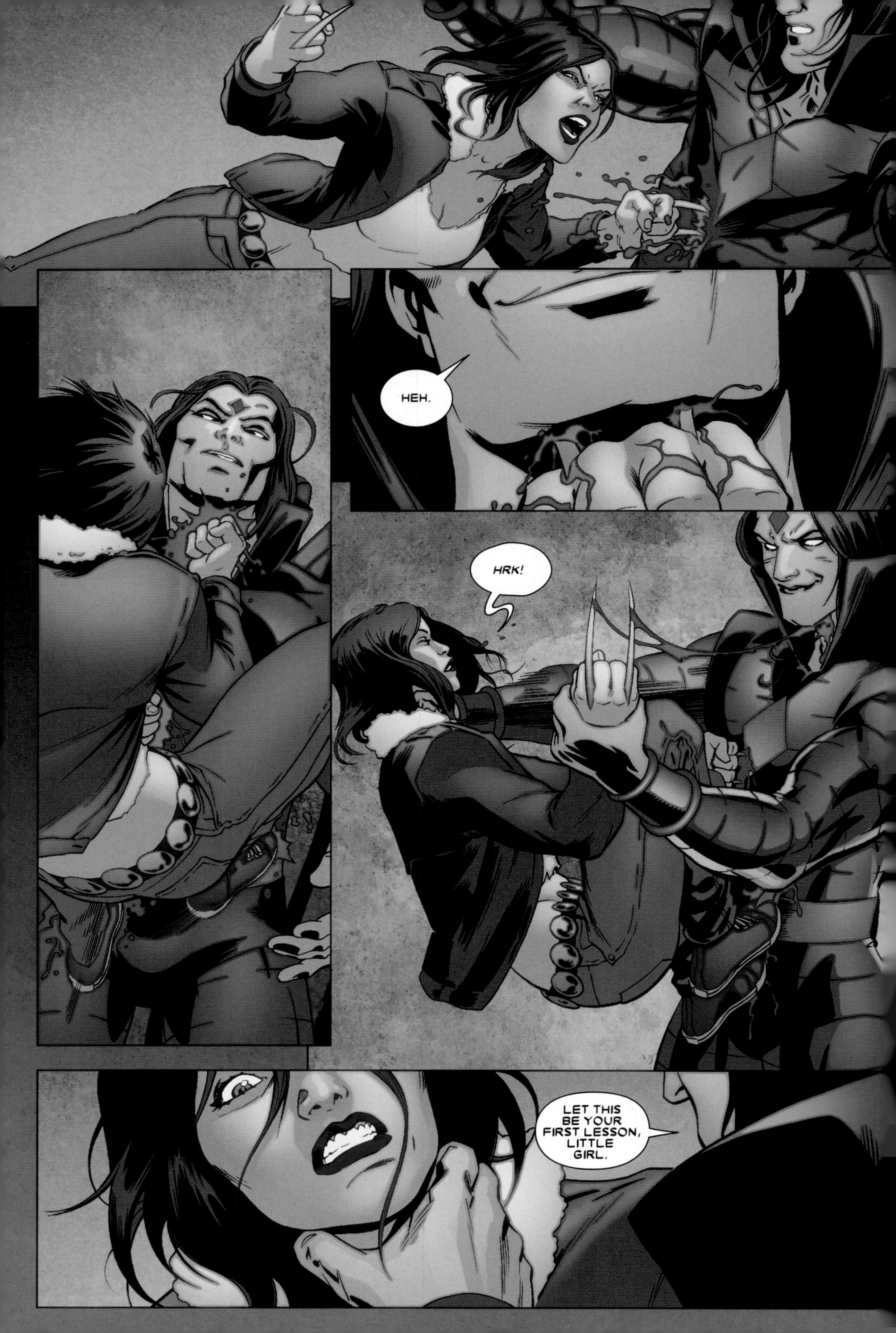
HEH.
HRK!
LET THIS BE YOUR FIRST LESSON, LITTLE GIRL.

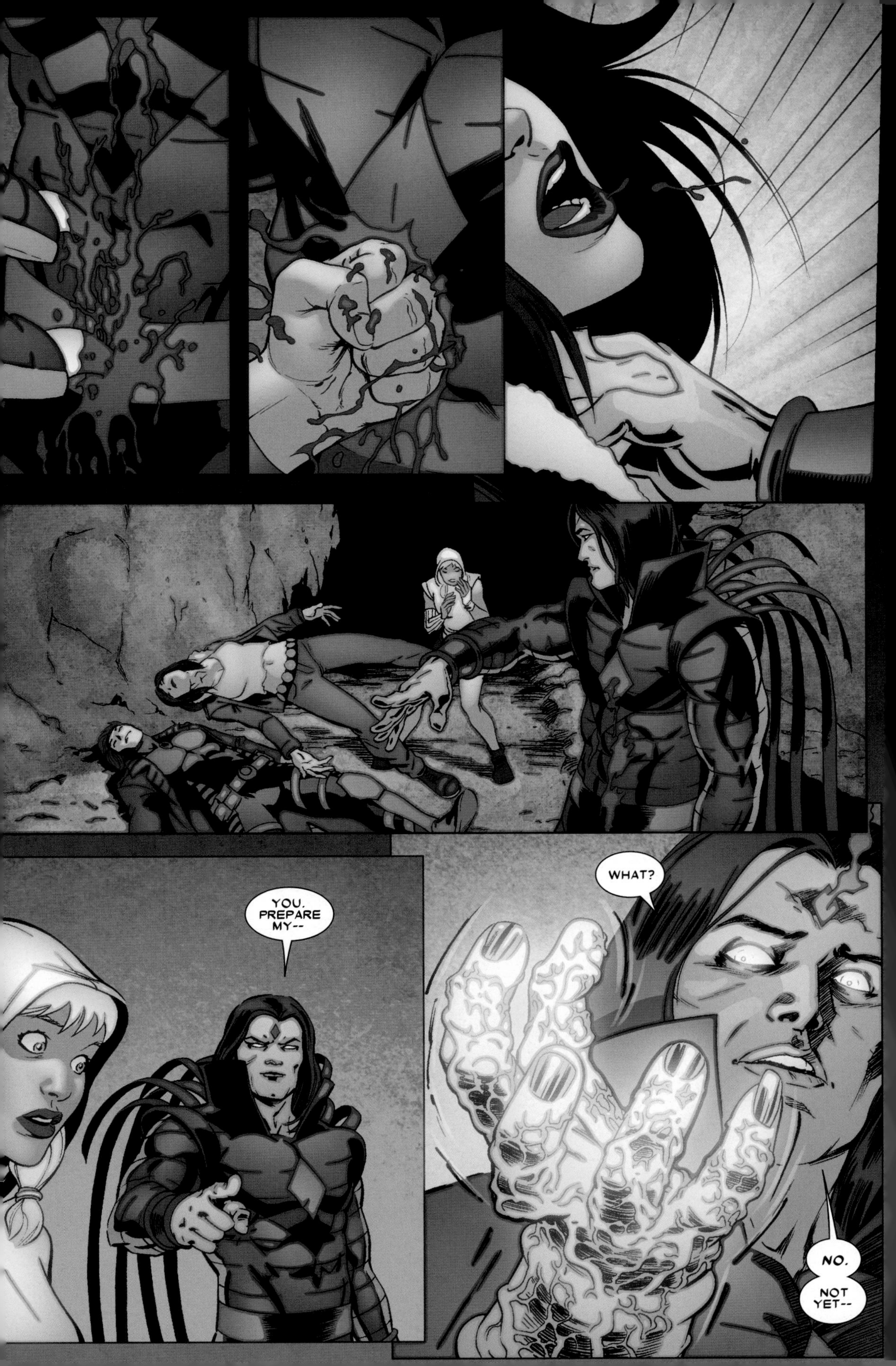
YOU. PREPARE MY--
WHAT?
NO.
NOT YET--

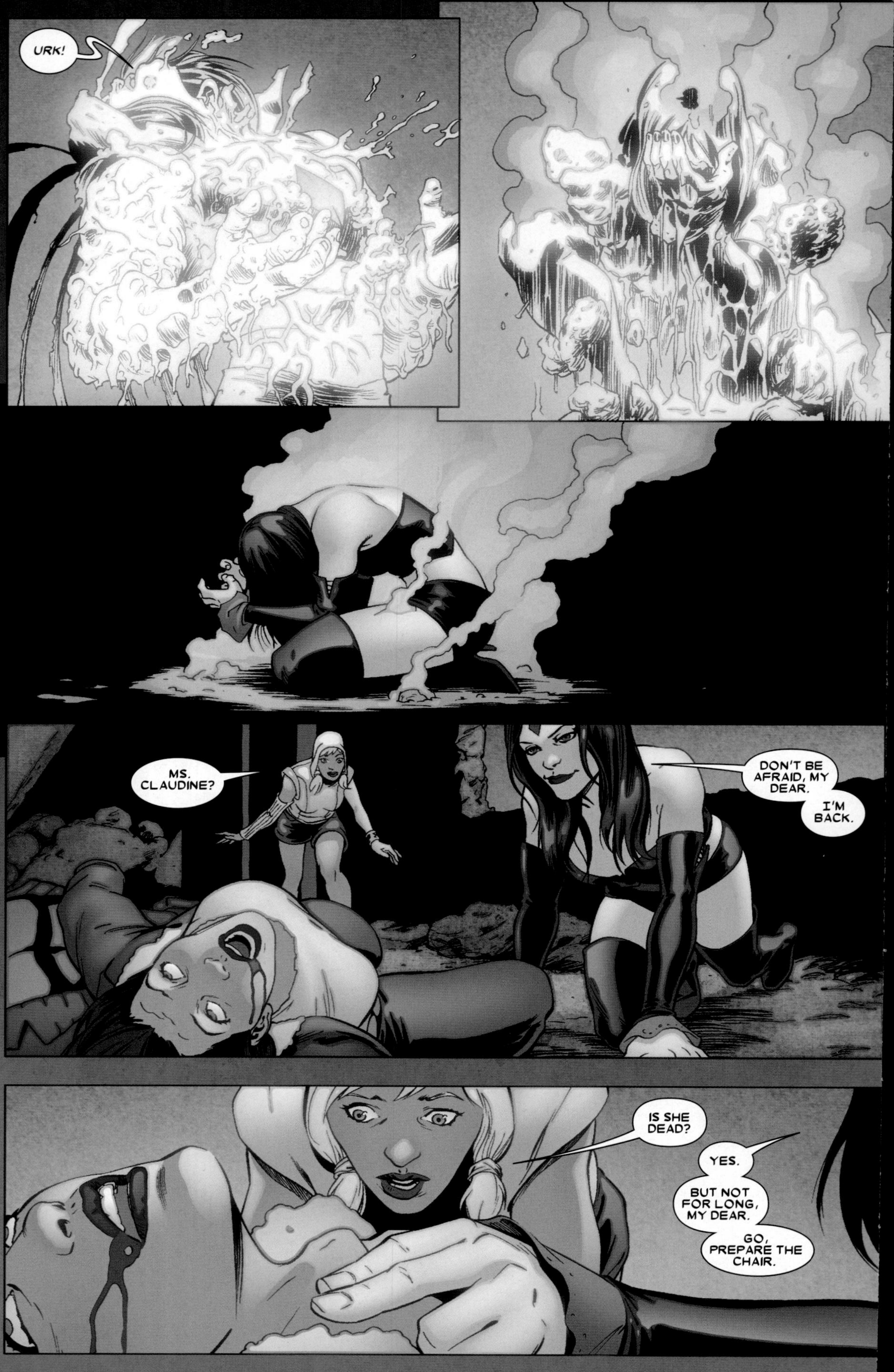
URK!
MS. CLAUDINE?
DON'T BE AFRAID, MY DEAR.
I'M BACK.
IS SHE DEAD?
YES.
BUT NOT FOR LONG, MY DEAR.
GO, PREPARE THE CHAIR.

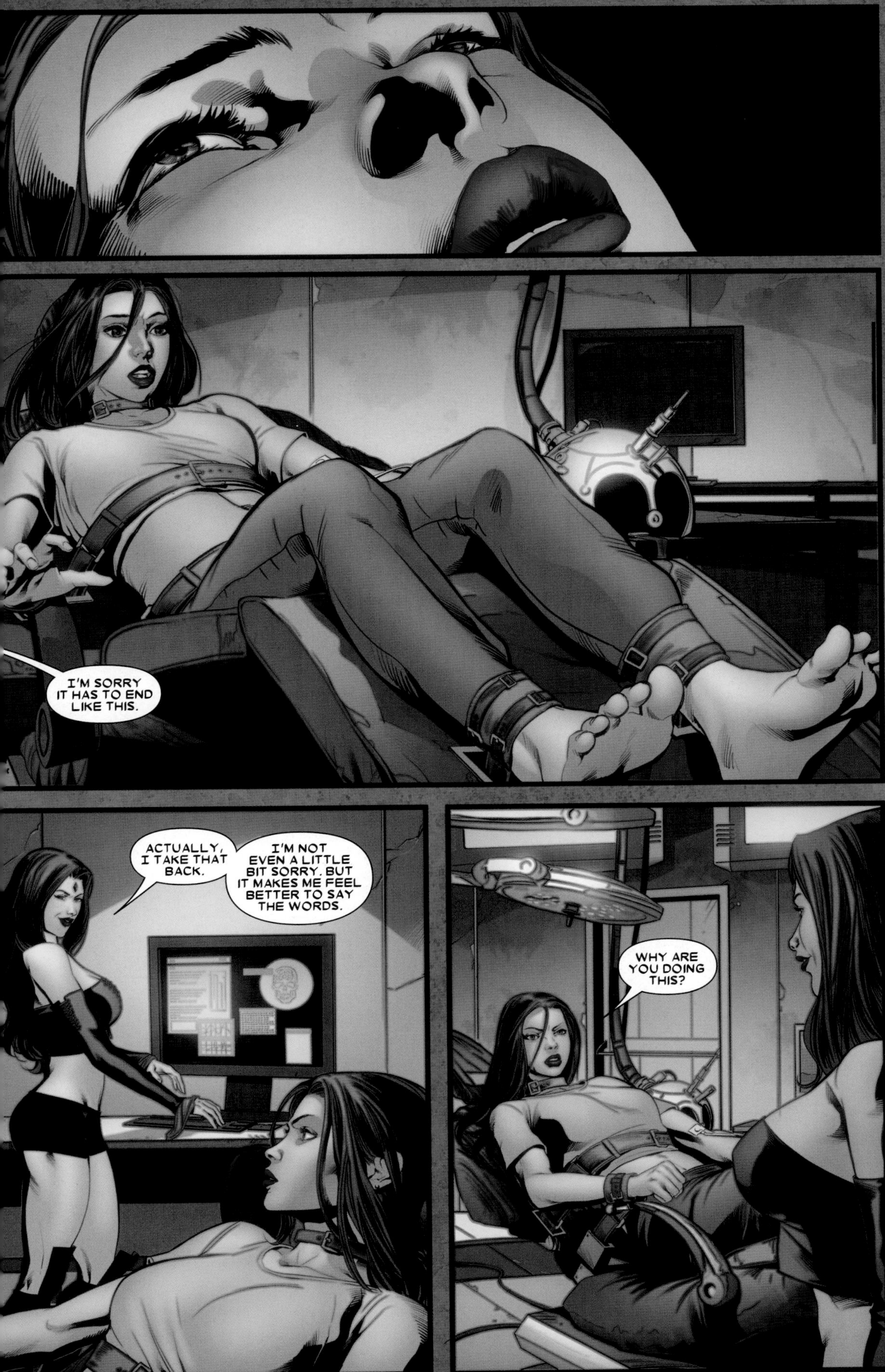
I'M SORRY IT HAS TO END LIKE THIS.
ACTUALLY, I TAKE THAT BACK.
I'M NOT EVEN A LITTLE BIT SORRY. BUT IT MAKES ME FEEL BETTER TO SAY THE WORDS.
WHY ARE YOU DOING THIS?

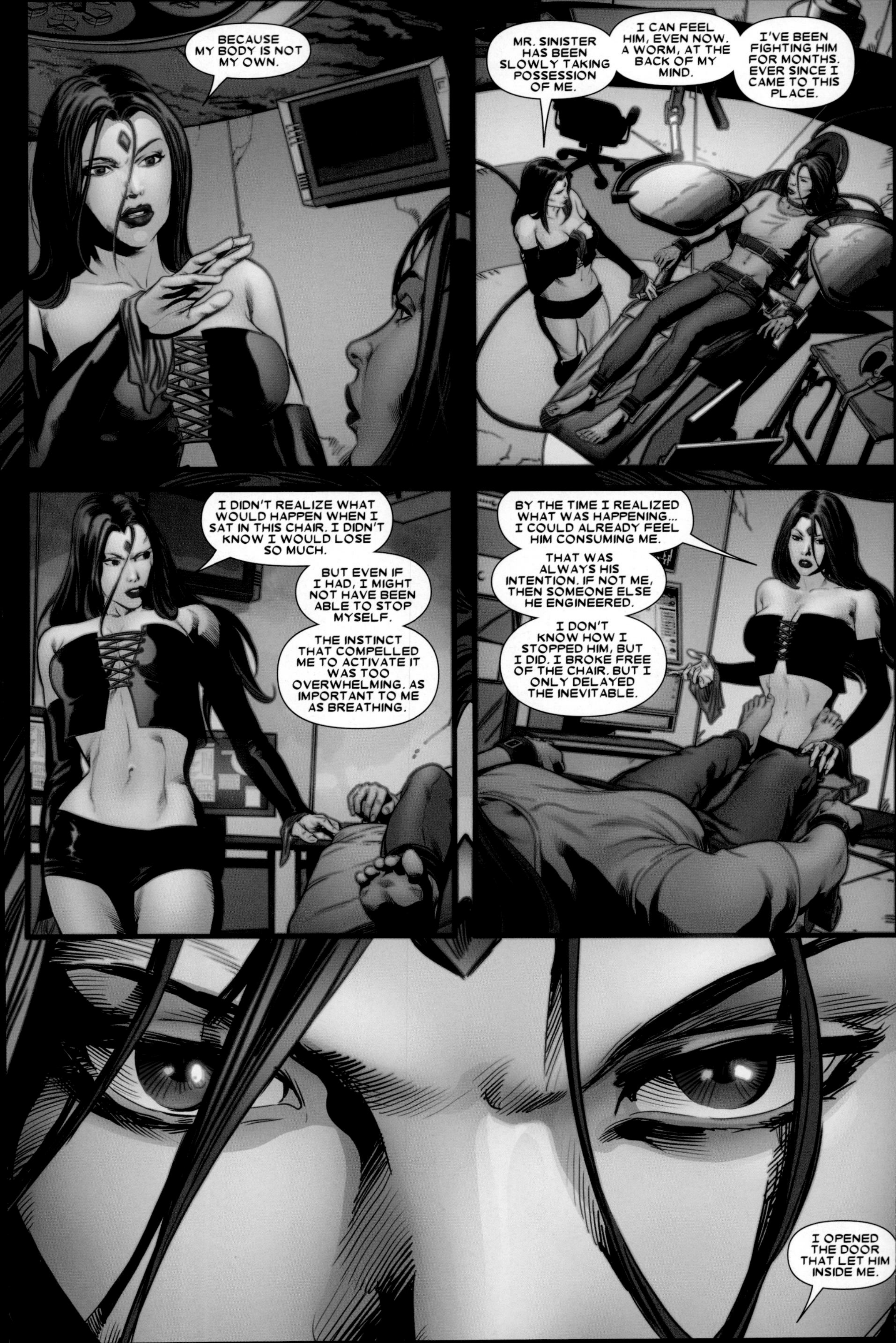
BECAUSE MY BODY IS NOT MY OWN.
MR. SINISTER HAS BEEN SLOWLY TAKING POSSESSION OF ME.
I CAN FEEL HIM, EVEN NOW. A WORM, AT THE BACK OF MY MIND.
I'VE BEEN FIGHTING HIM FOR MONTHS. EVER SINCE I CAME TO THIS PLACE.
I DIDN'T REALIZE WHAT WOULD HAPPEN WHEN I SAT IN THIS CHAIR. I DIDN'T KNOW I WOULD LOSE SO MUCH.
BUT EVEN IF I HAD, I MIGHT NOT HAVE BEEN ABLE TO STOP MYSELF.
THE INSTINCT THAT COMPELLED ME TO ACTIVATE IT WAS TOO OVERWHELMING. AS IMPORTANT TO ME AS BREATHING.
BY THE TIME I REALIZED WHAT WAS HAPPENING... I COULD ALREADY FEEL HIM CONSUMING ME.
THAT WAS ALWAYS HIS INTENTION. IF NOT ME, THEN SOMEONE ELSE HE ENGINEERED.
I DON'T KNOW HOW I STOPPED HIM, BUT I DID. I BROKE FREE OF THE CHAIR. BUT I ONLY DELAYED THE INEVITABLE.
I OPENED THE DOOR THAT LET HIM INSIDE ME.

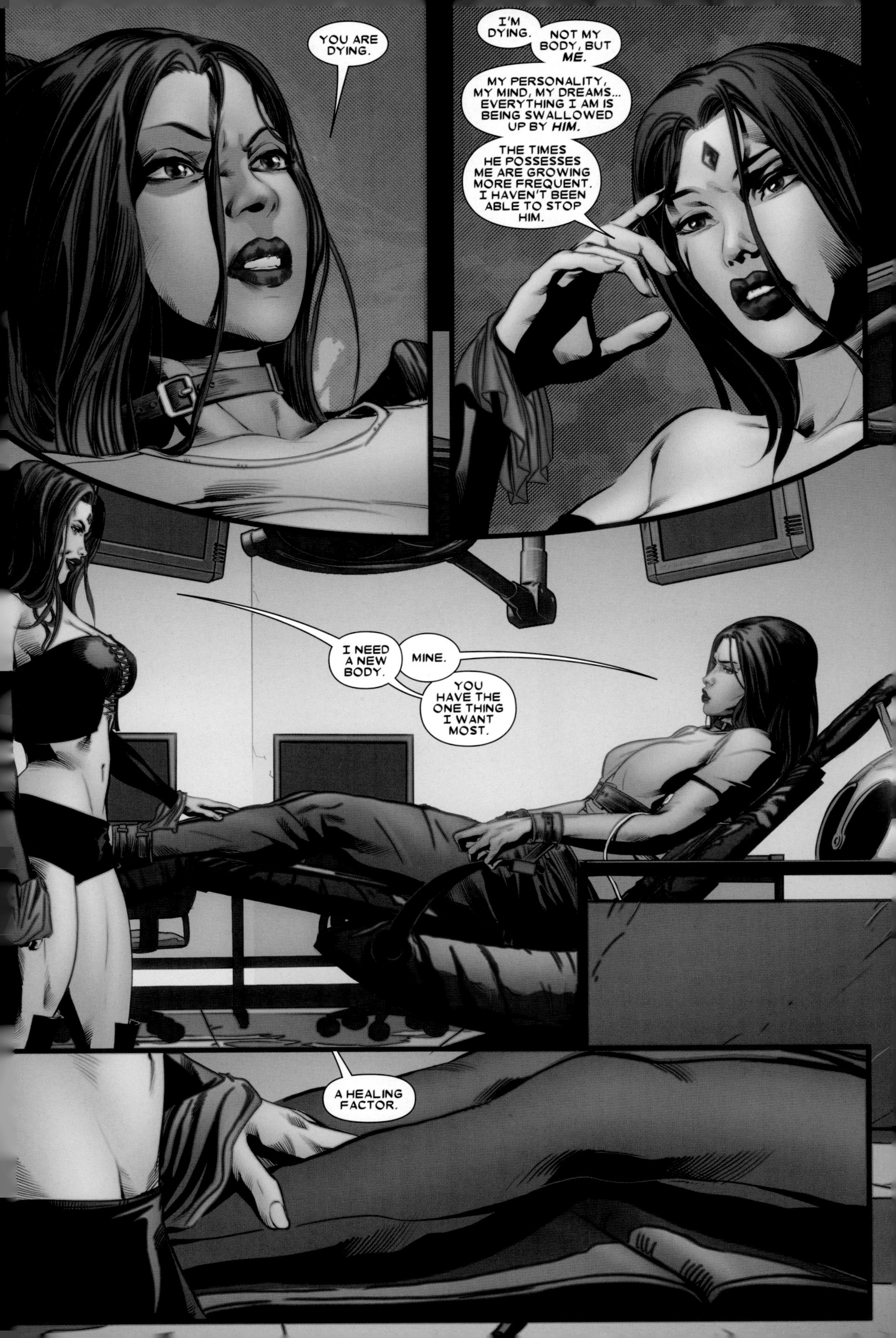
YOU ARE DYING.
I'M DYING.
NOT MY BODY, BUT *ME.*
MY PERSONALITY, MY MIND, MY DREAMS... EVERYTHING I AM IS BEING SWALLOWED UP BY *HIM.*
THE TIMES HE POSSESSES ME ARE GROWING MORE FREQUENT. I HAVEN'T BEEN ABLE TO STOP HIM.
I NEED A NEW BODY.
MINE.
YOU HAVE THE ONE THING I WANT MOST.
A HEALING FACTOR.

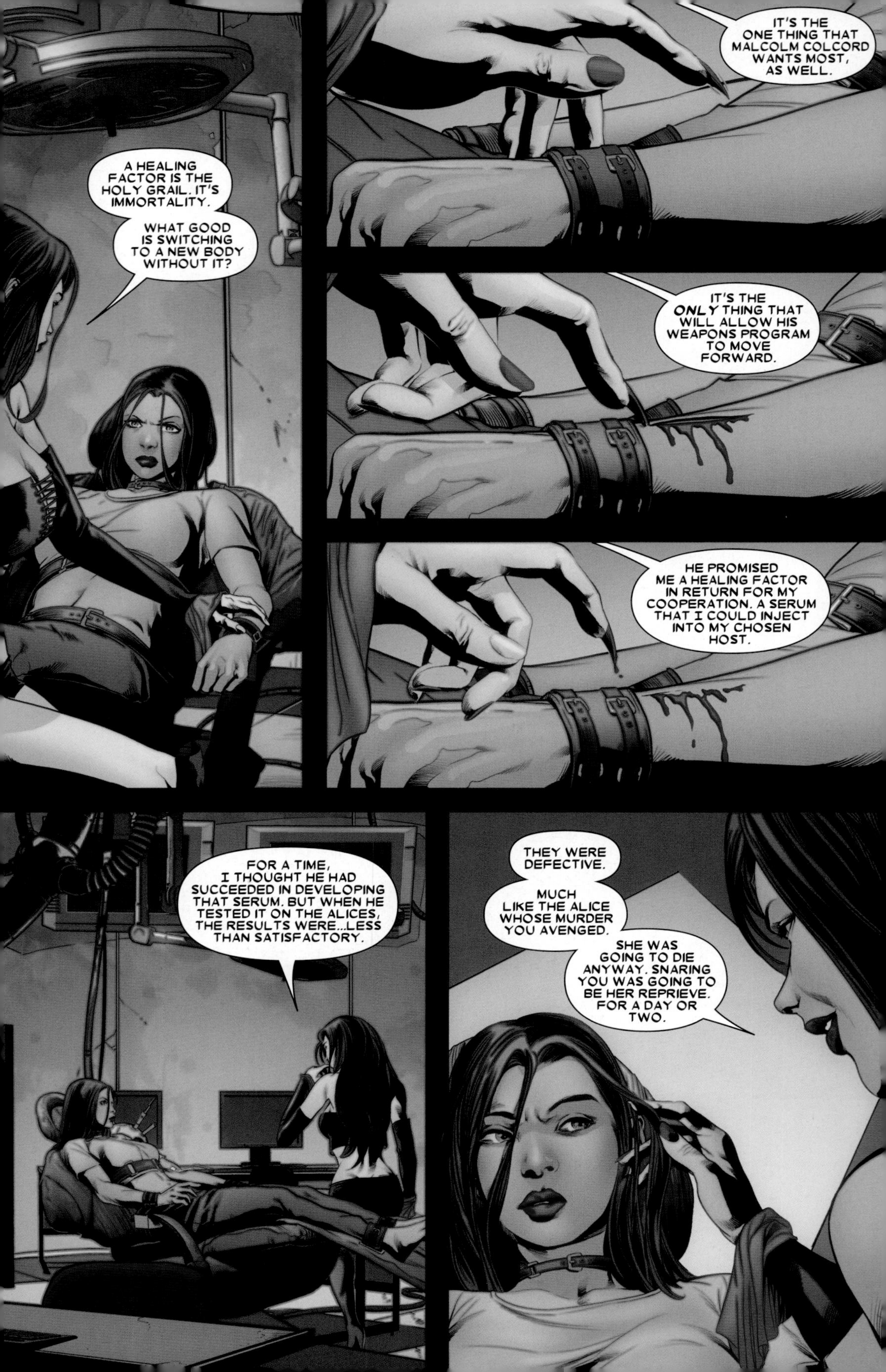
A HEALING FACTOR IS THE HOLY GRAIL. IT'S IMMORTALITY.
WHAT GOOD IS SWITCHING TO A NEW BODY WITHOUT IT?
IT'S THE ONE THING THAT MALCOLM COLCORD WANTS MOST, AS WELL.
IT'S THE *ONLY* THING THAT WILL ALLOW HIS WEAPONS PROGRAM TO MOVE FORWARD.
HE PROMISED ME A HEALING FACTOR IN RETURN FOR MY COOPERATION. A SERUM THAT I COULD INJECT INTO MY CHOSEN HOST.
FOR A TIME, I THOUGHT HE HAD SUCCEEDED IN DEVELOPING THAT SERUM. BUT WHEN HE TESTED IT ON THE ALICES, THE RESULTS WERE...LESS THAN SATISFACTORY.
THEY WERE DEFECTIVE.
MUCH LIKE THE ALICE WHOSE MURDER YOU AVENGED.
SHE WAS GOING TO DIE ANYWAY. SNARING YOU WAS GOING TO BE HER REPRIEVE. FOR A DAY OR TWO.

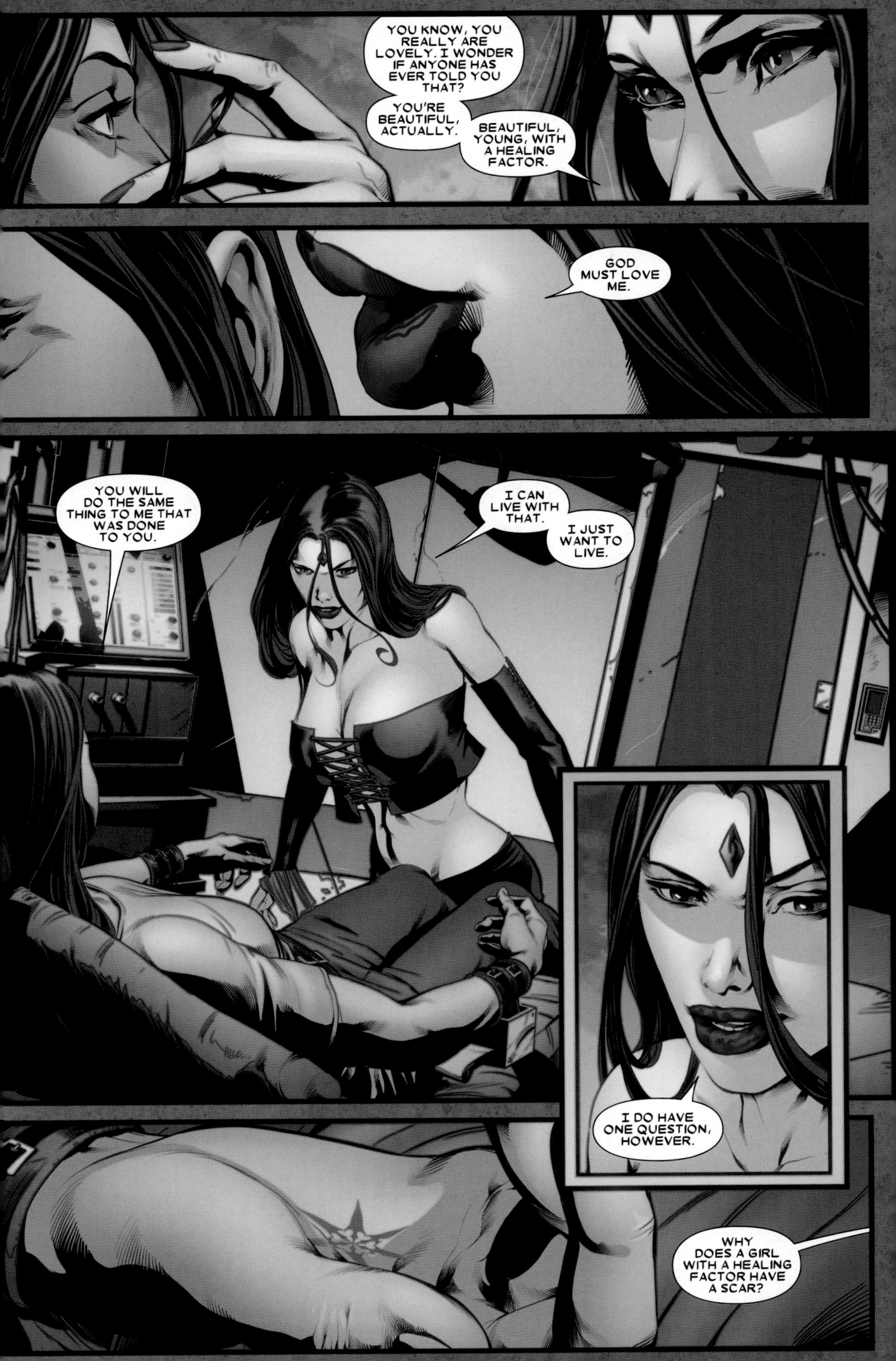

YOU KNOW, YOU REALLY ARE LOVELY. I WONDER IF ANYONE HAS EVER TOLD YOU THAT?
YOU'RE BEAUTIFUL, ACTUALLY.
BEAUTIFUL, YOUNG, WITH A HEALING FACTOR.
GOD MUST LOVE ME.
YOU WILL DO THE SAME THING TO ME THAT WAS DONE TO YOU.
I CAN LIVE WITH THAT.
I JUST WANT TO LIVE.
I DO HAVE ONE QUESTION, HOWEVER.
WHY DOES A GIRL WITH A HEALING FACTOR HAVE A SCAR?

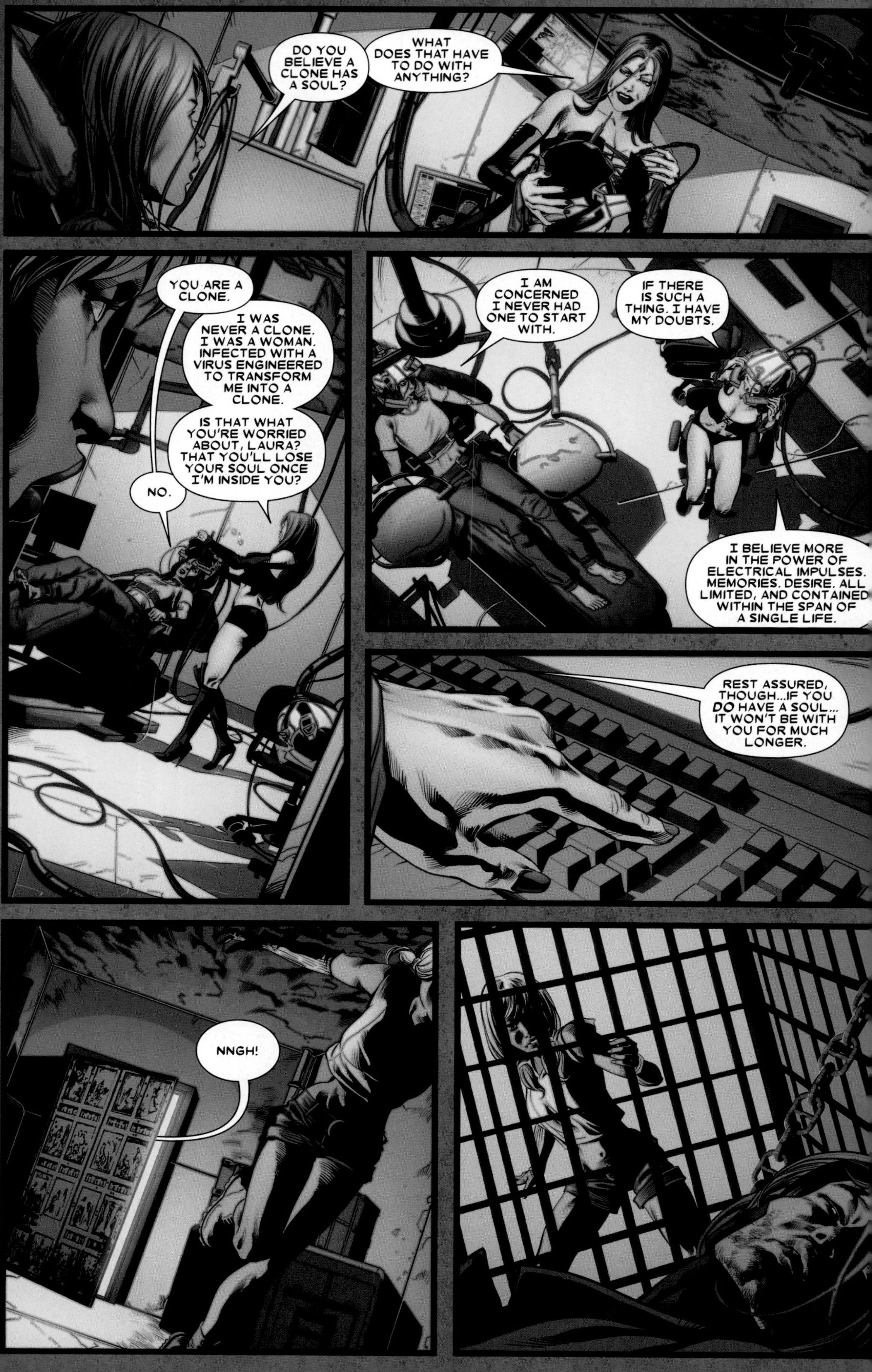
DO YOU BELIEVE A CLONE HAS A SOUL?
WHAT DOES THAT HAVE TO DO WITH ANYTHING?
YOU ARE A CLONE.
I WAS NEVER A CLONE. I WAS A WOMAN. INFECTED WITH A VIRUS ENGINEERED TO TRANSFORM ME INTO A CLONE.
IS THAT WHAT YOU'RE WORRIED ABOUT, LAURA? THAT YOU'LL LOSE YOUR SOUL ONCE I'M INSIDE YOU?
NO.
I AM CONCERNED I NEVER HAD ONE TO START WITH.
IF THERE IS SUCH A THING. I HAVE MY DOUBTS.
I BELIEVE MORE IN THE POWER OF ELECTRICAL IMPULSES. MEMORIES. DESIRE. ALL LIMITED, AND CONTAINED WITHIN THE SPAN OF A SINGLE LIFE.
REST ASSURED, THOUGH...IF YOU DO HAVE A SOUL... IT WON'T BE WITH YOU FOR MUCH LONGER.
NNGH!

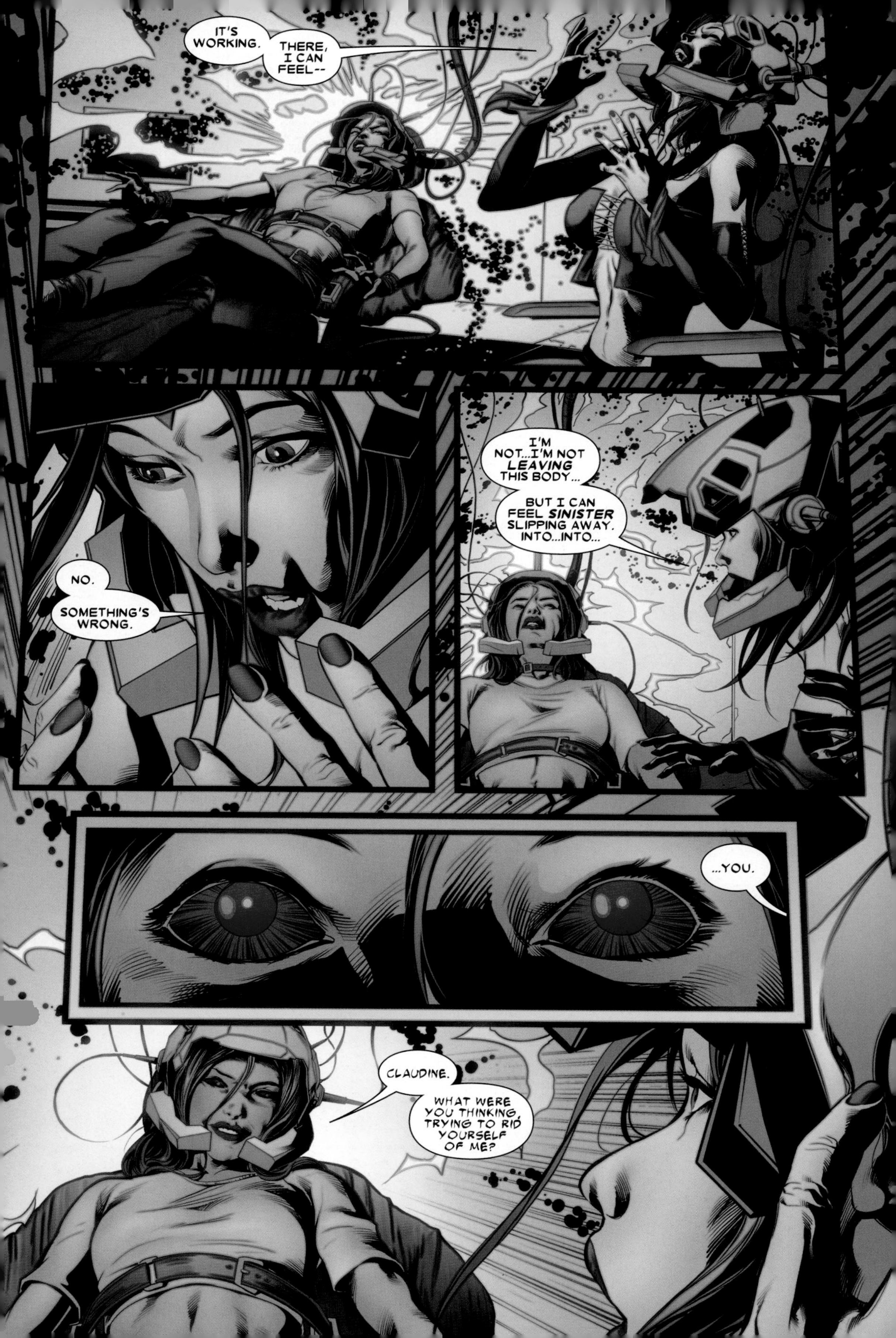
IT'S WORKING.
THERE, I CAN FEEL--
NO.
SOMETHING'S WRONG.
I'M NOT...I'M NOT LEAVING THIS BODY...
BUT I CAN FEEL SINISTER SLIPPING AWAY. INTO...INTO...
...YOU.
CLAUDINE.
WHAT WERE YOU THINKING, TRYING TO RID YOURSELF OF ME?

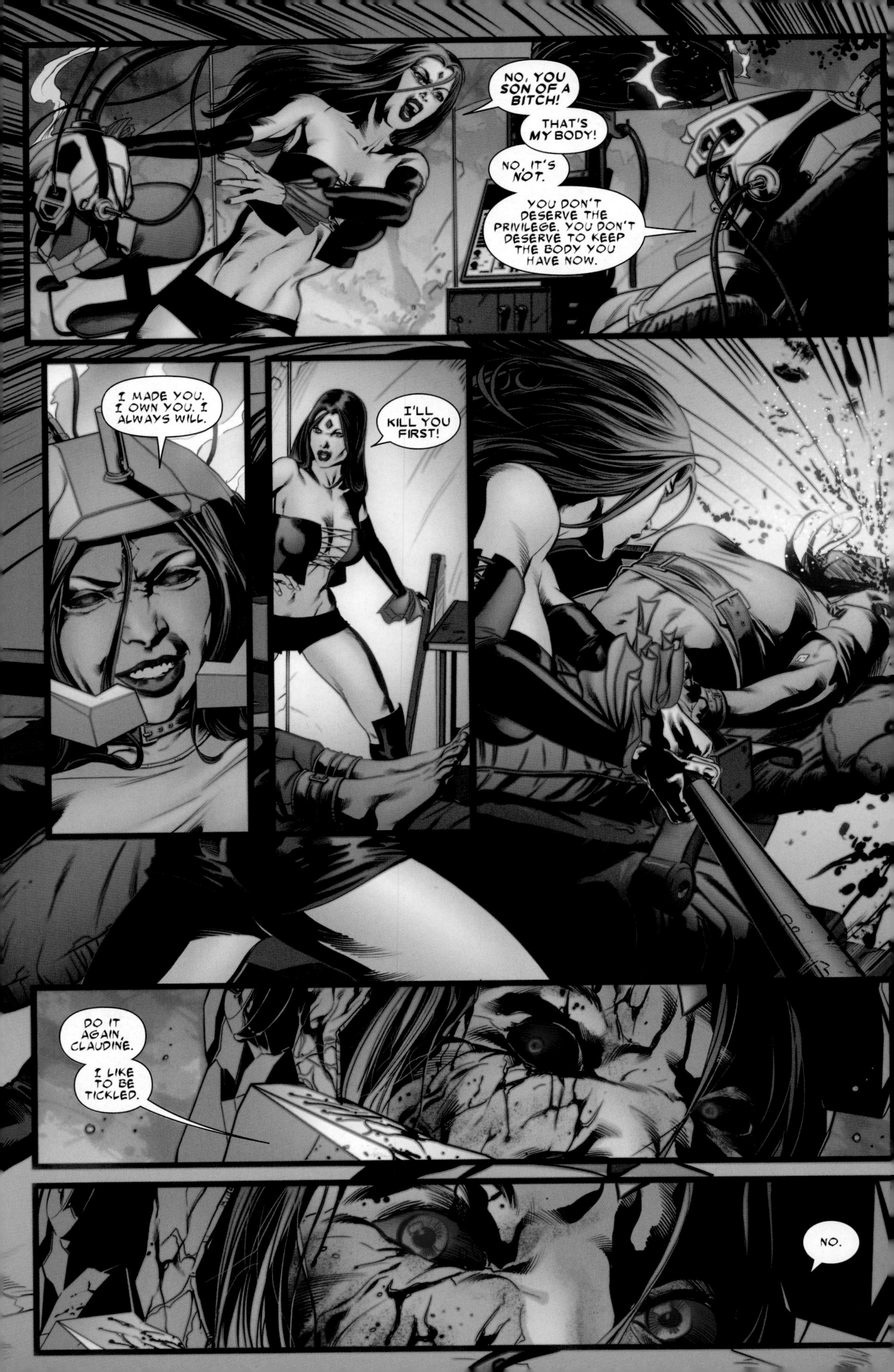
NO, YOU SON OF A BITCH!
THAT'S MY BODY!
NO, IT'S NOT.
YOU DON'T DESERVE THE PRIVILEGE. YOU DON'T DESERVE TO KEEP THE BODY YOU HAVE NOW.
I MADE YOU. I OWN YOU. I ALWAYS WILL.
I'LL KILL YOU FIRST!
DO IT AGAIN, CLAUDINE.
I LIKE TO BE TICKLED.
NO.

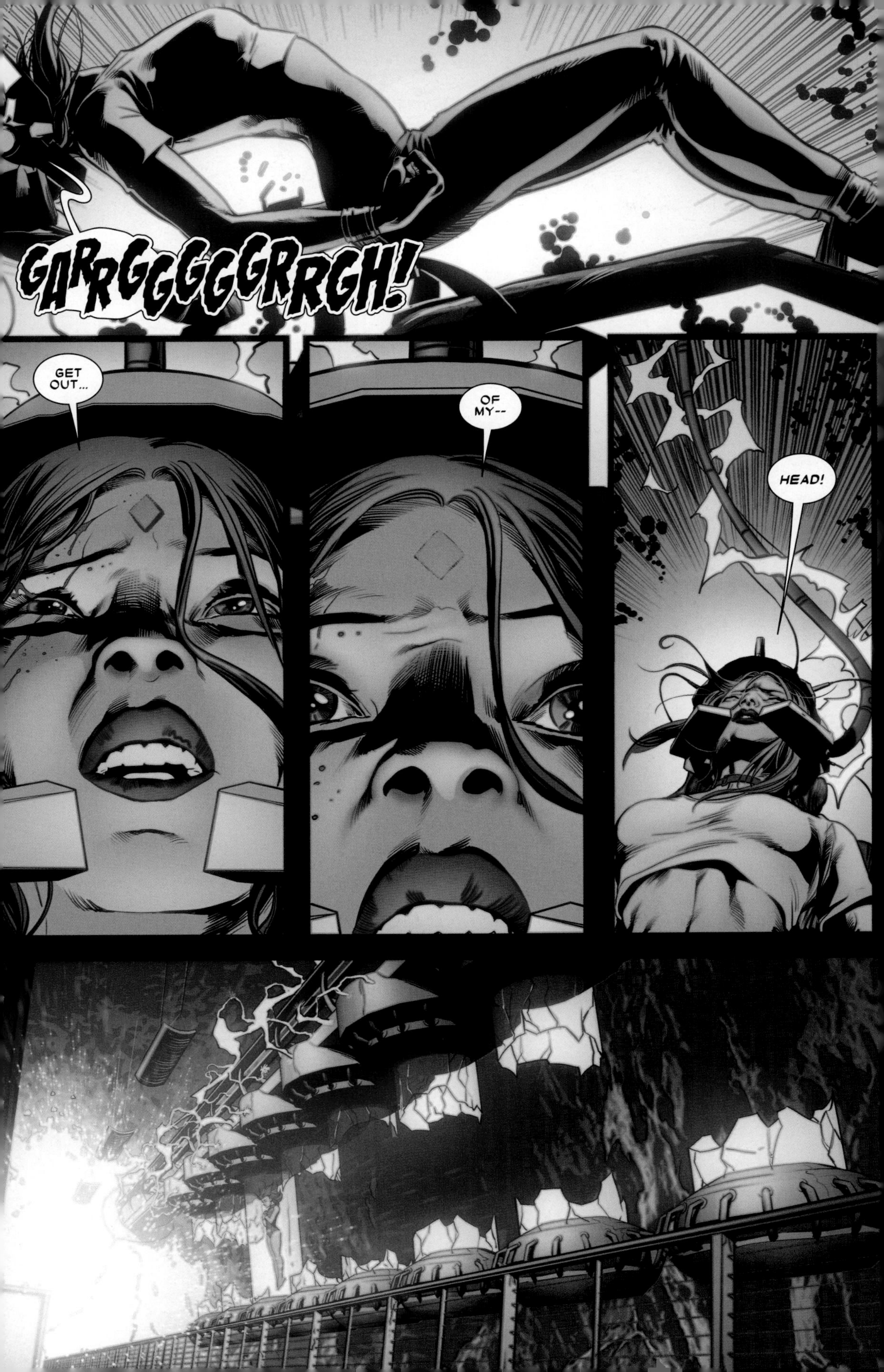
GARRGGGGGRRRGH!
GET OUT...
OF MY--
HEAD!

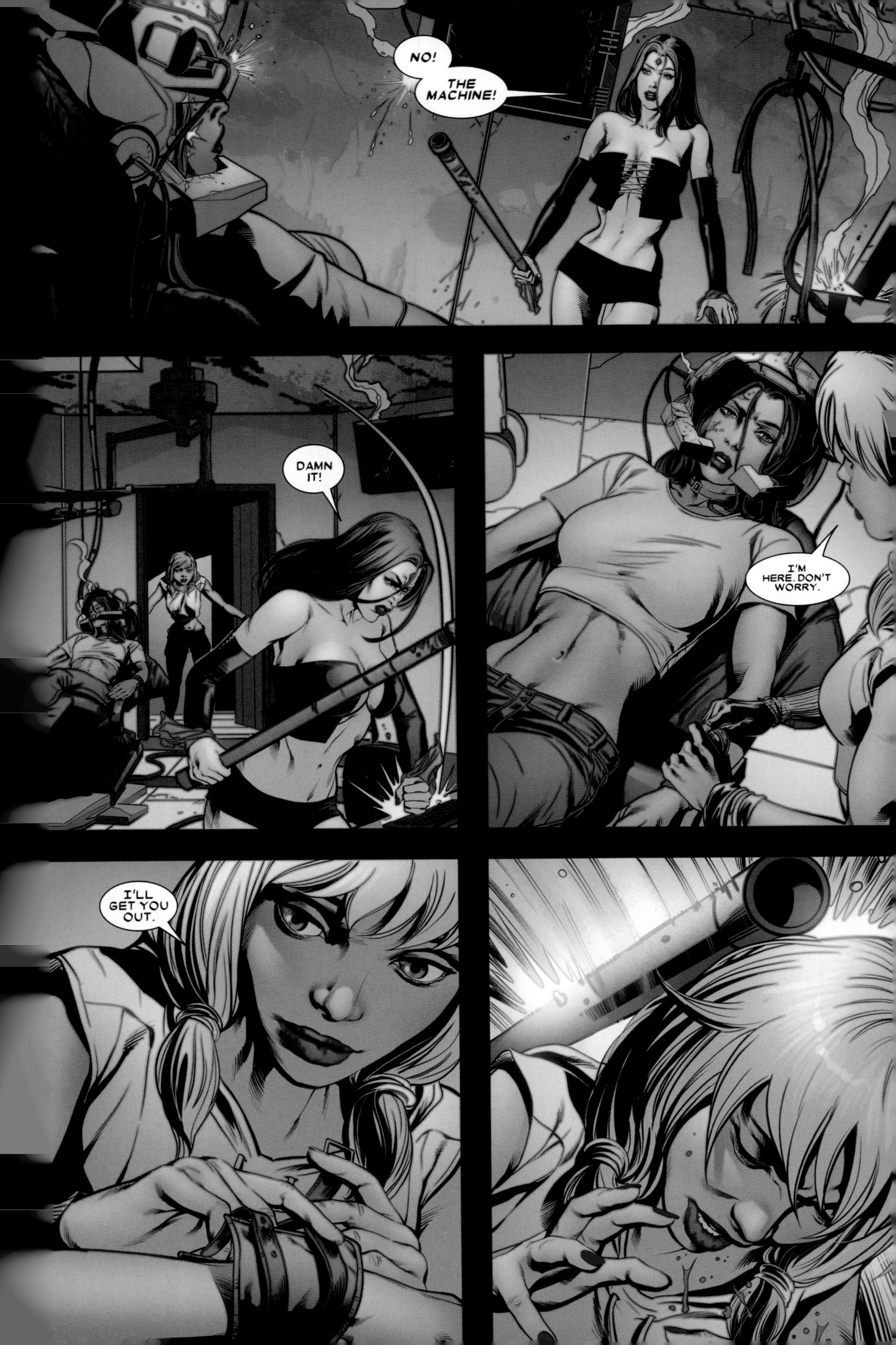
NO!
THE MACHINE!
DAMN IT!
I'M HERE. DON'T WORRY.
I'LL GET YOU OUT.

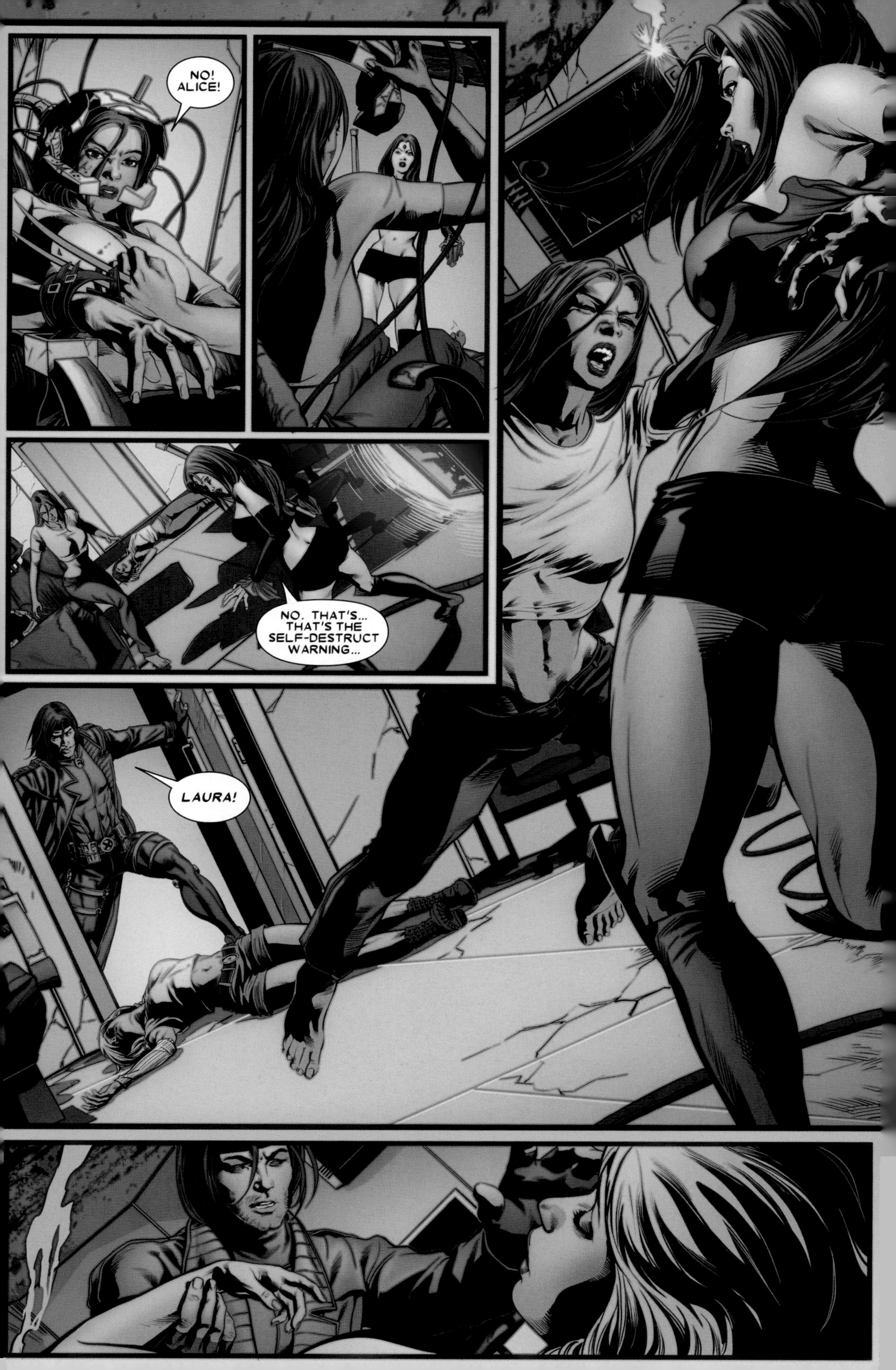
NO! ALICE!
NO. THAT'S... THAT'S THE SELF-DESTRUCT WARNING...
LAURA!

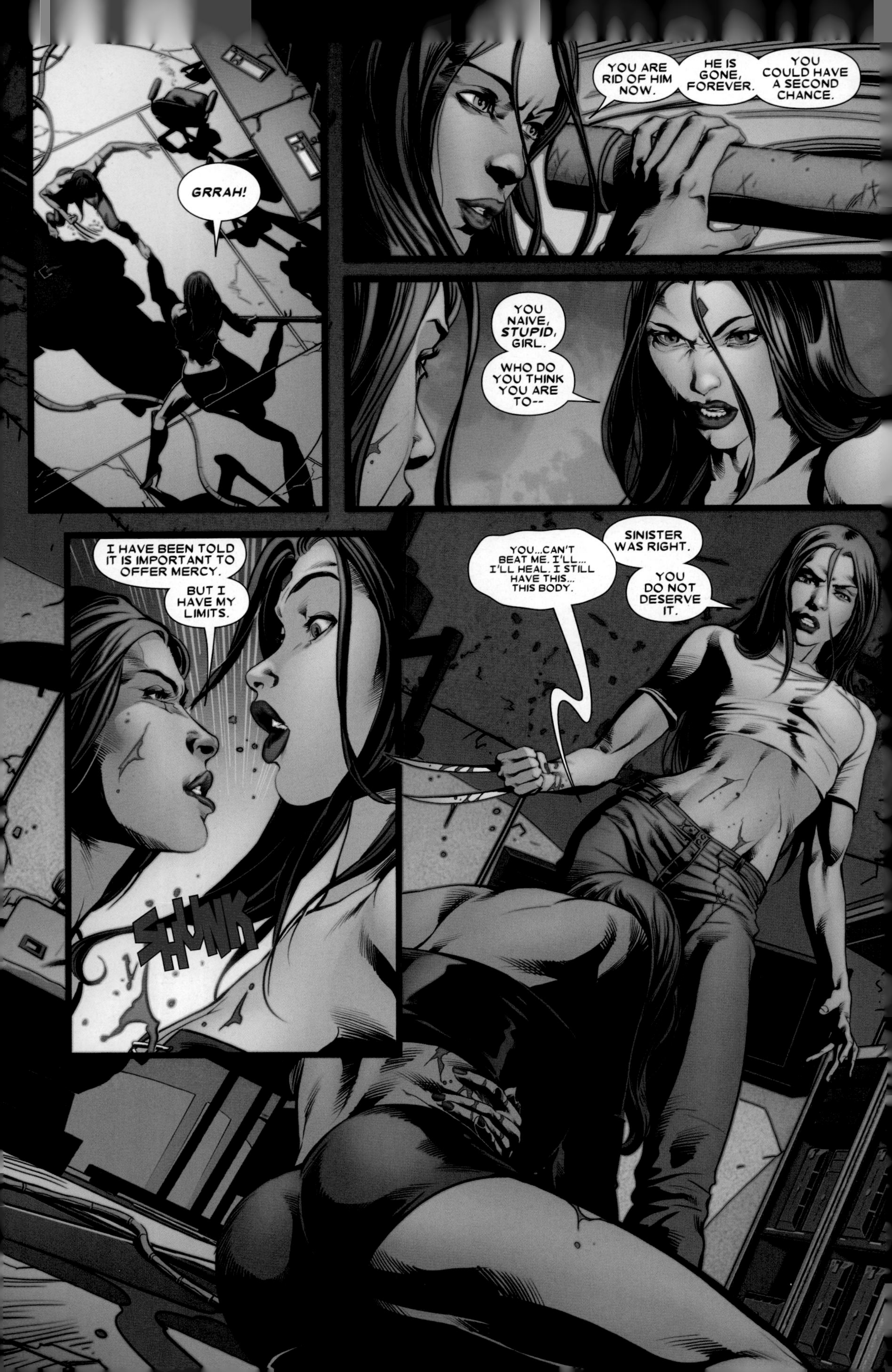
GRRAH!
YOU ARE RID OF HIM NOW.
HE IS GONE, FOREVER.
YOU COULD HAVE A SECOND CHANCE.
YOU NAIVE, STUPID, GIRL.
WHO DO YOU THINK YOU ARE TO--
I HAVE BEEN TOLD IT IS IMPORTANT TO OFFER MERCY.
BUT I HAVE MY LIMITS.
SHUNK
SINISTER WAS RIGHT.
YOU DO NOT DESERVE IT.
YOU...CAN'T BEAT ME. I'LL... I'LL HEAL. I STILL HAVE THIS... THIS BODY.

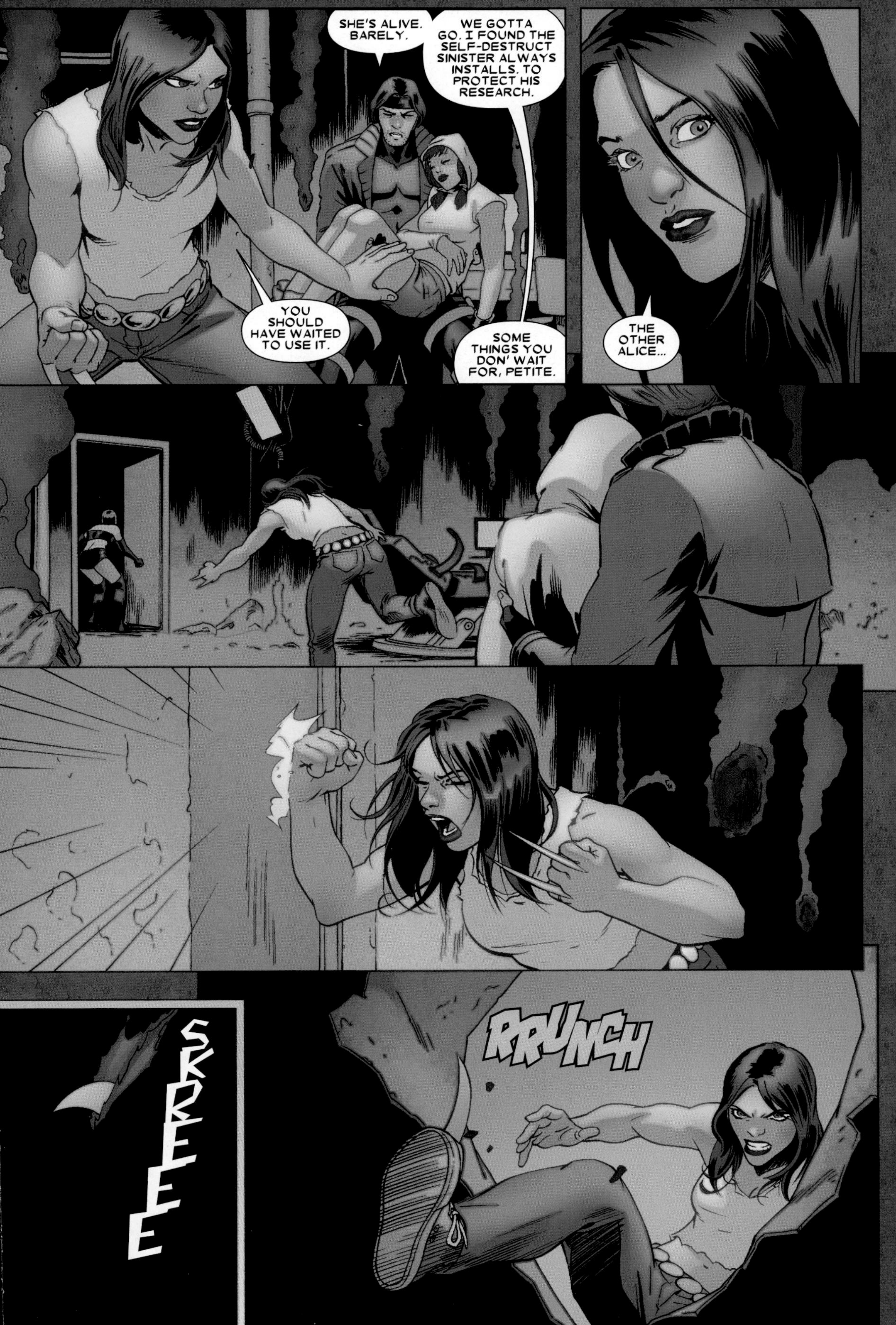
YOU SHOULD HAVE WAITED TO USE IT.
SHE'S ALIVE. BARELY.
WE GOTTA GO. I FOUND THE SELF-DESTRUCT SINISTER ALWAYS INSTALLS. TO PROTECT HIS RESEARCH.
SOME THINGS YOU DON' WAIT FOR, PETITE.
THE OTHER ALICE...
RRUNCH
SKREEEE

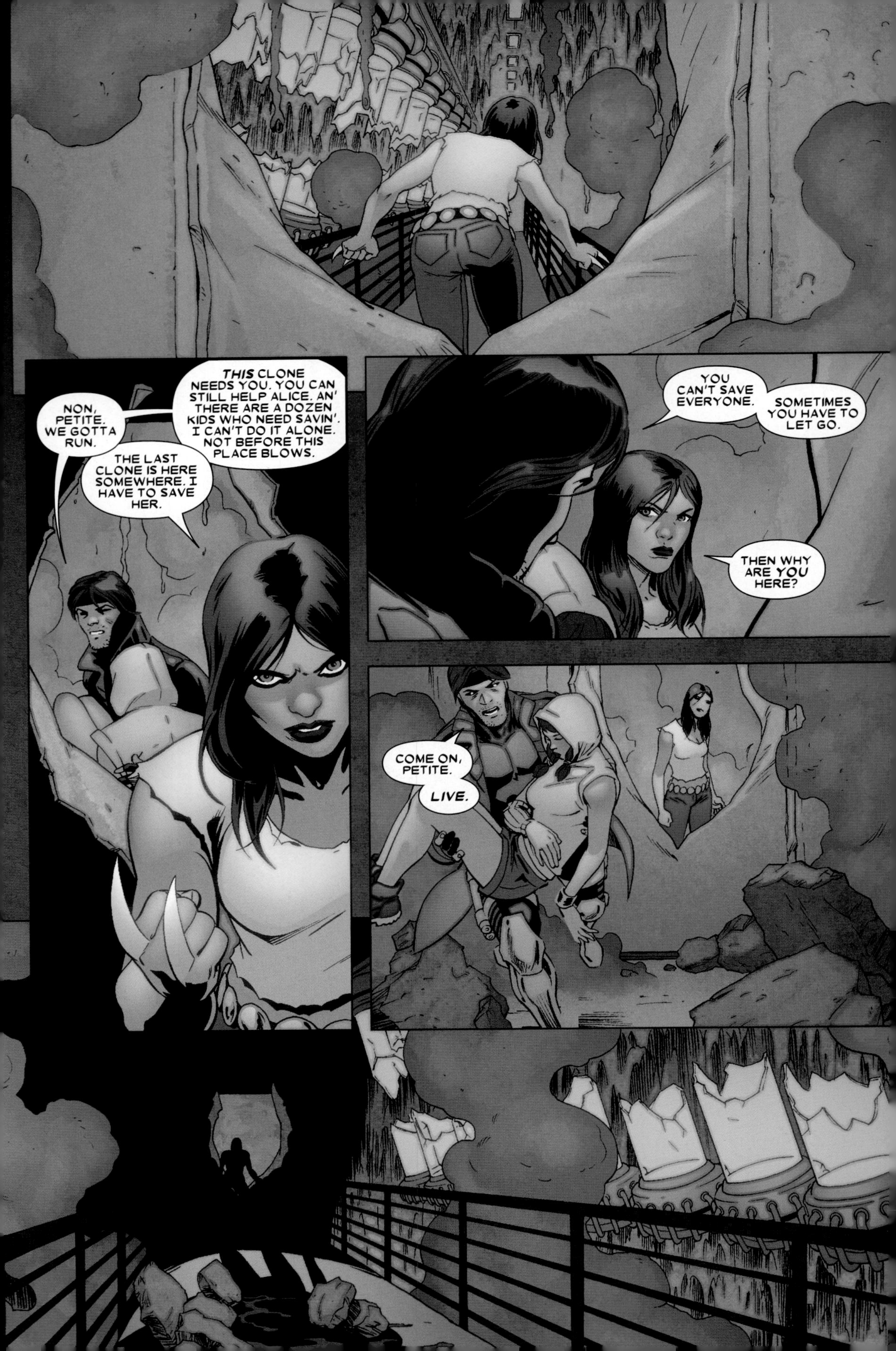
NON, PETITE. WE GOTTA RUN.
THE LAST CLONE IS HERE SOMEWHERE. I HAVE TO SAVE HER.
THIS CLONE NEEDS YOU. YOU CAN STILL HELP ALICE. AN' THERE ARE A DOZEN KIDS WHO NEED SAVIN'. I CAN'T DO IT ALONE. NOT BEFORE THIS PLACE BLOWS.
YOU CAN'T SAVE EVERYONE.
SOMETIMES YOU HAVE TO LET GO.
THEN WHY ARE YOU HERE?
COME ON, PETITE.
LIVE.

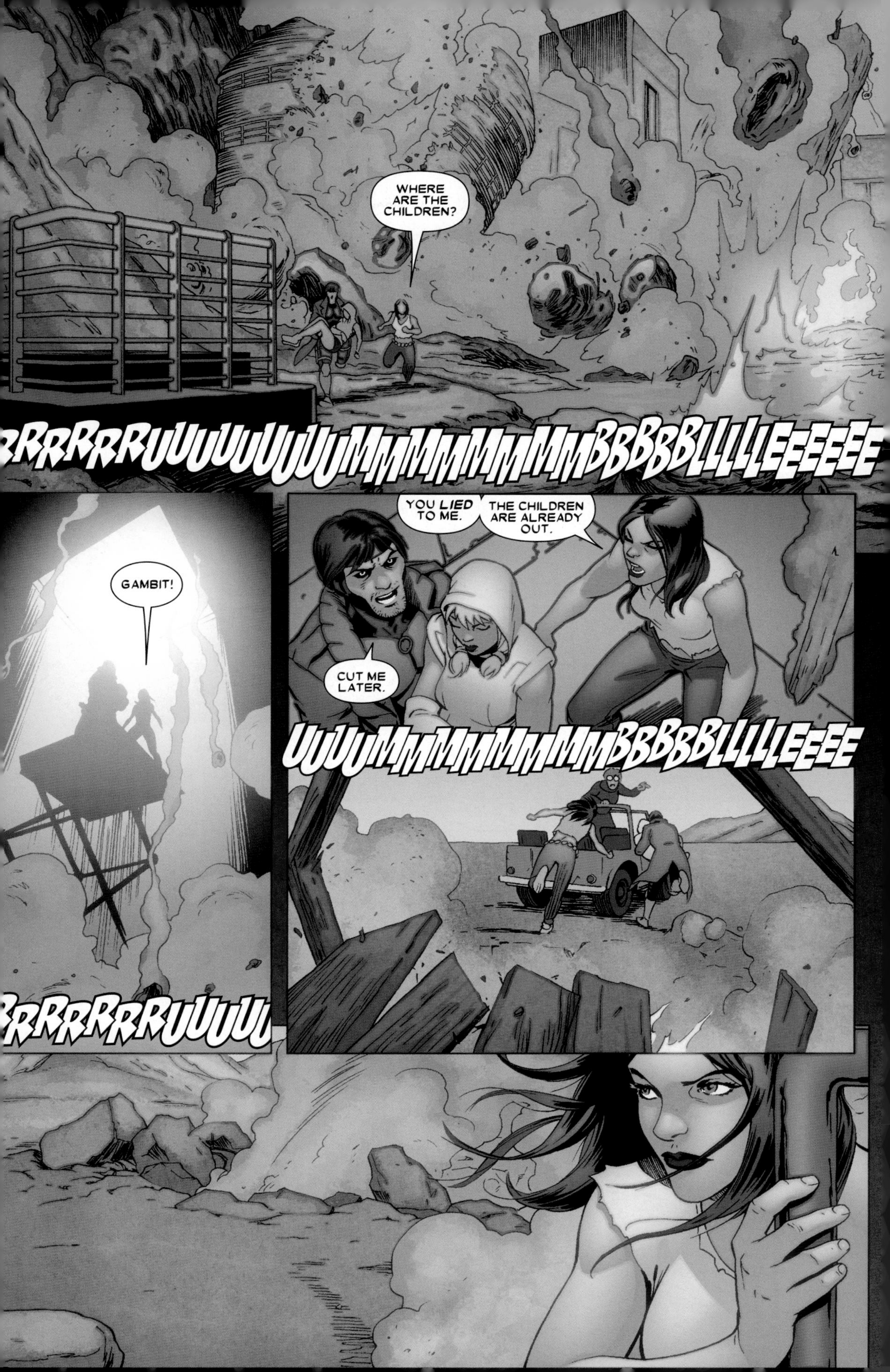
WHERE ARE THE CHILDREN?
BRRRRRUUUUUUUUMMMMMMMMMMMBBBBLLLLLEEEEEE
GAMBIT!
BRRRRRRUUUUU
YOU LIED TO ME.
THE CHILDREN ARE ALREADY OUT.
CUT ME LATER.
UUUUMMMMMMMMMMMBBBBLLLLLEEEE

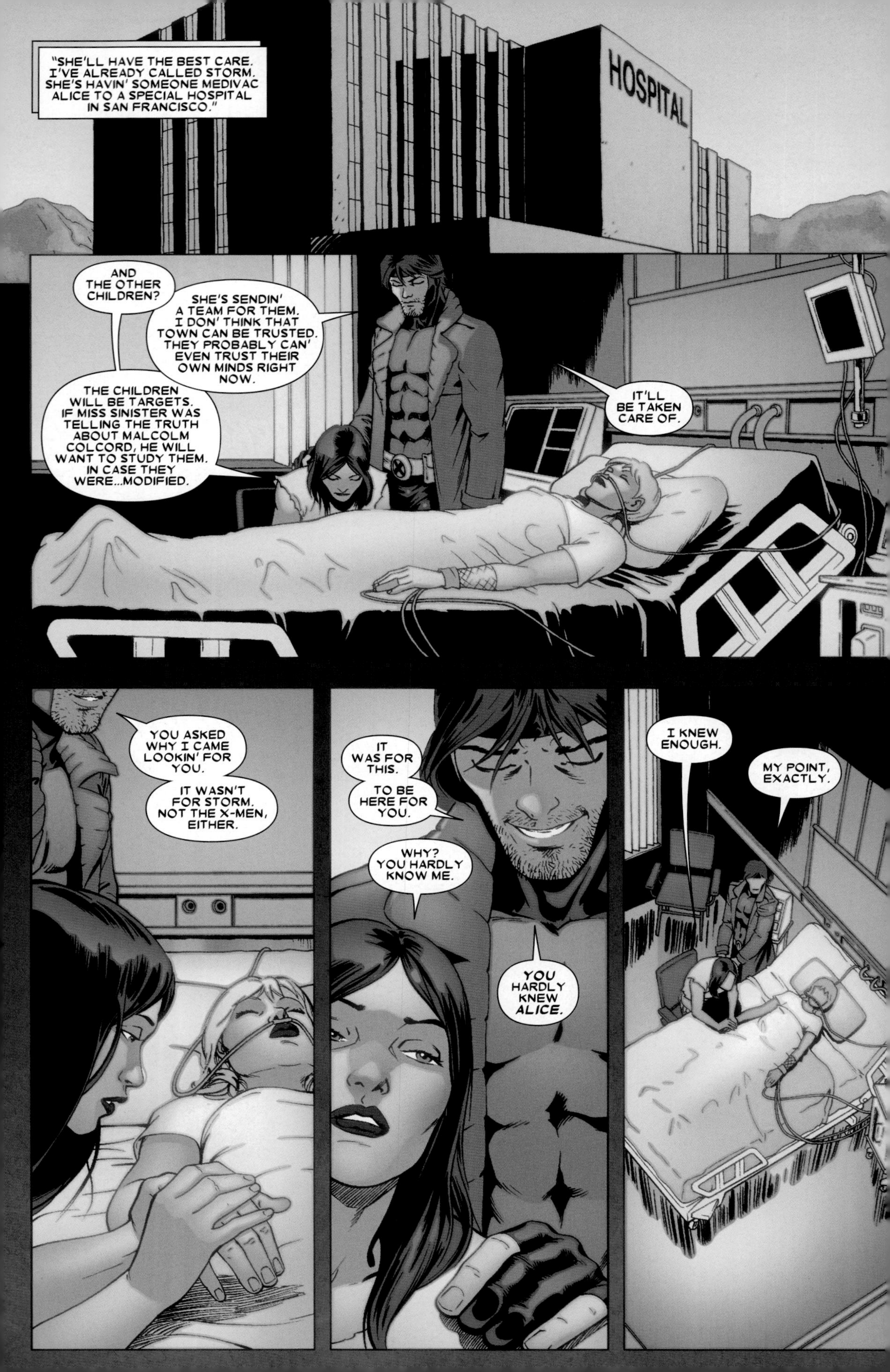
"SHE'LL HAVE THE BEST CARE. I'VE ALREADY CALLED STORM. SHE'S HAVIN' SOMEONE MEDIVAC ALICE TO A SPECIAL HOSPITAL IN SAN FRANCISCO."
HOSPITAL
AND THE OTHER CHILDREN?
SHE'S SENDIN' A TEAM FOR THEM. I DON' THINK THAT TOWN CAN BE TRUSTED. THEY PROBABLY CAN' EVEN TRUST THEIR OWN MINDS RIGHT NOW.
THE CHILDREN WILL BE TARGETS. IF MISS SINISTER WAS TELLING THE TRUTH ABOUT MALCOLM COLCORD, HE WILL WANT TO STUDY THEM. IN CASE THEY WERE...MODIFIED.
IT'LL BE TAKEN CARE OF.
YOU ASKED WHY I CAME LOOKIN' FOR YOU.
IT WASN'T FOR STORM. NOT THE X-MEN, EITHER.
IT WAS FOR THIS.
TO BE HERE FOR YOU.
WHY? YOU HARDLY KNOW ME.
YOU HARDLY KNEW ALICE.
I KNEW ENOUGH.
MY POINT, EXACTLY.

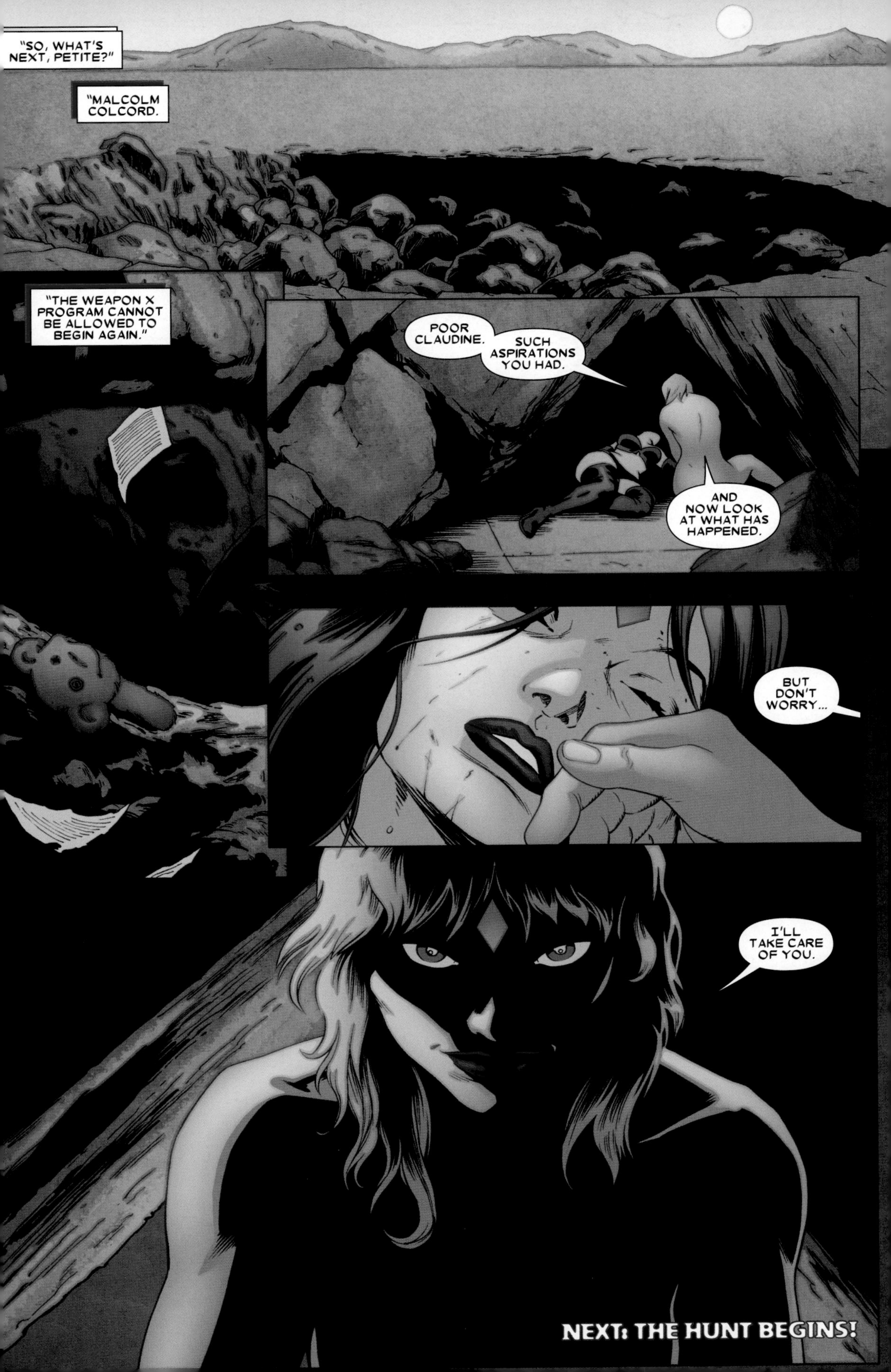
"SO, WHAT'S NEXT, PETITE?"
"MALCOLM COLCORD.
"THE WEAPON X PROGRAM CANNOT BE ALLOWED TO BEGIN AGAIN."
POOR CLAUDINE.
SUCH ASPIRATIONS YOU HAD.
AND NOW LOOK AT WHAT HAS HAPPENED.
BUT DON'T WORRY...
I'LL TAKE CARE OF YOU.
NEXT: THE HUNT BEGINS!

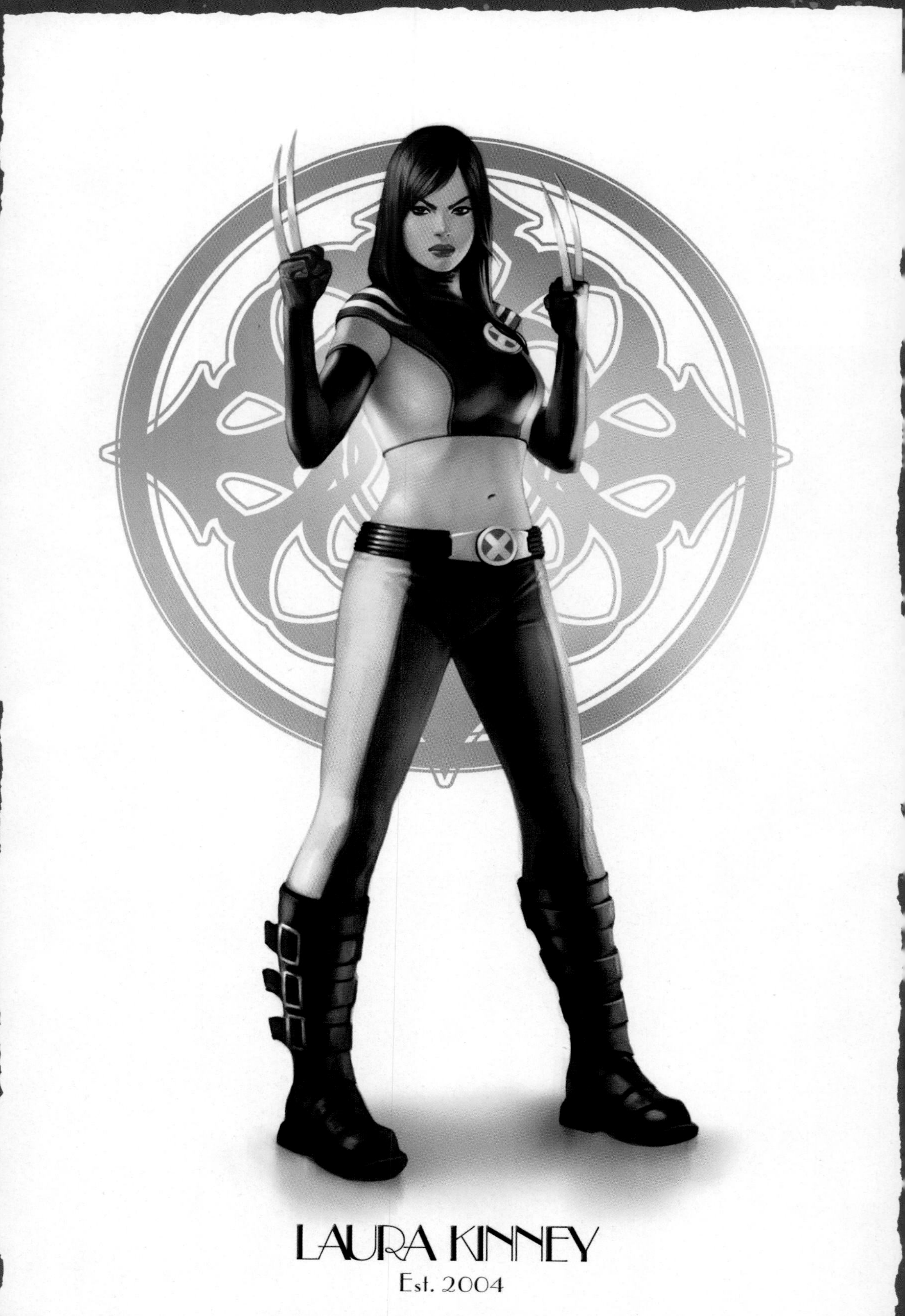
LAURA KINNEY
Est. 2004

#1 WOMEN OF MARVEL VARIANT BY
JELENA KEVIC DJURDJEVIC

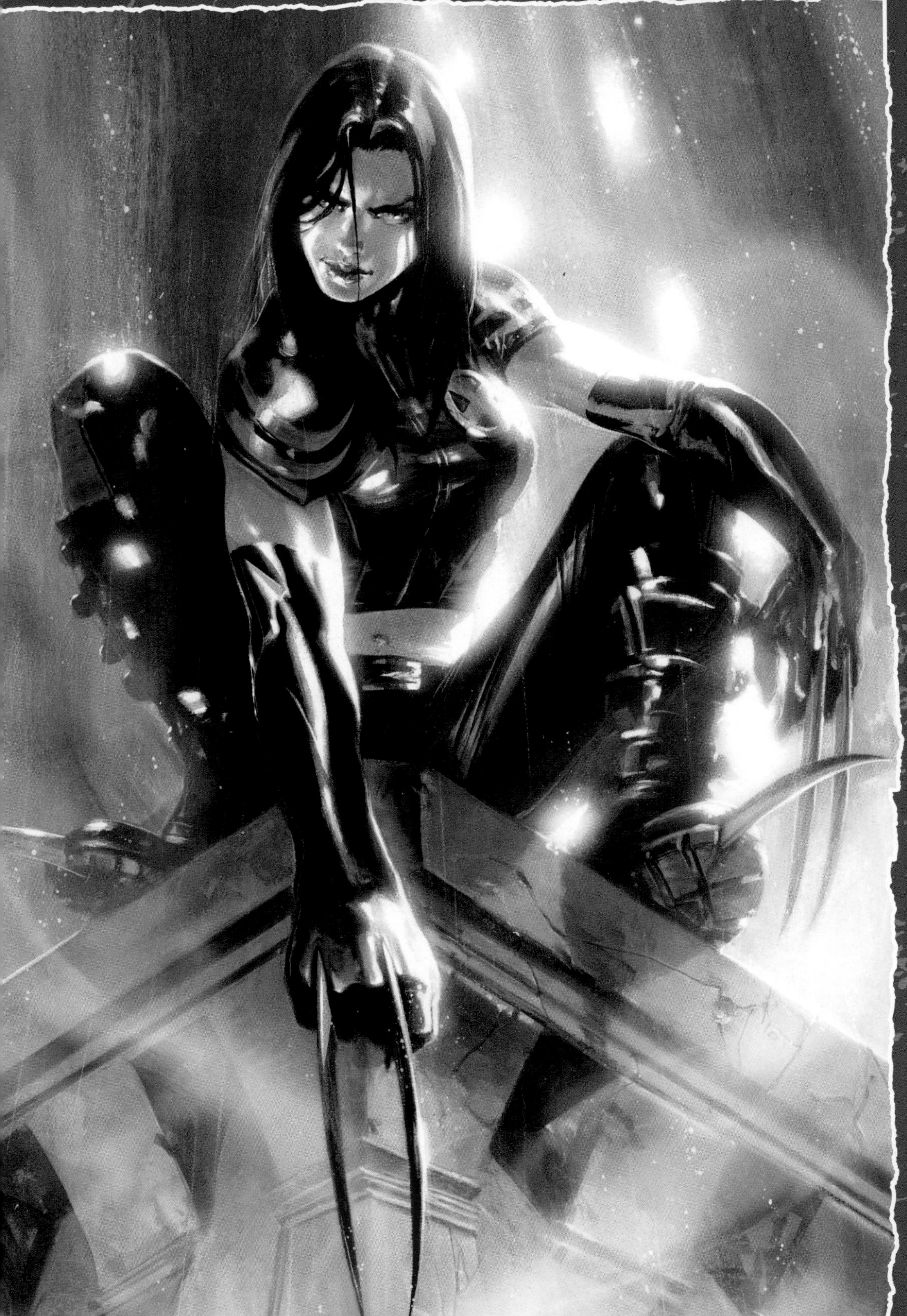

#1 VARIANT BY
GABRIELE DELL'OTTO

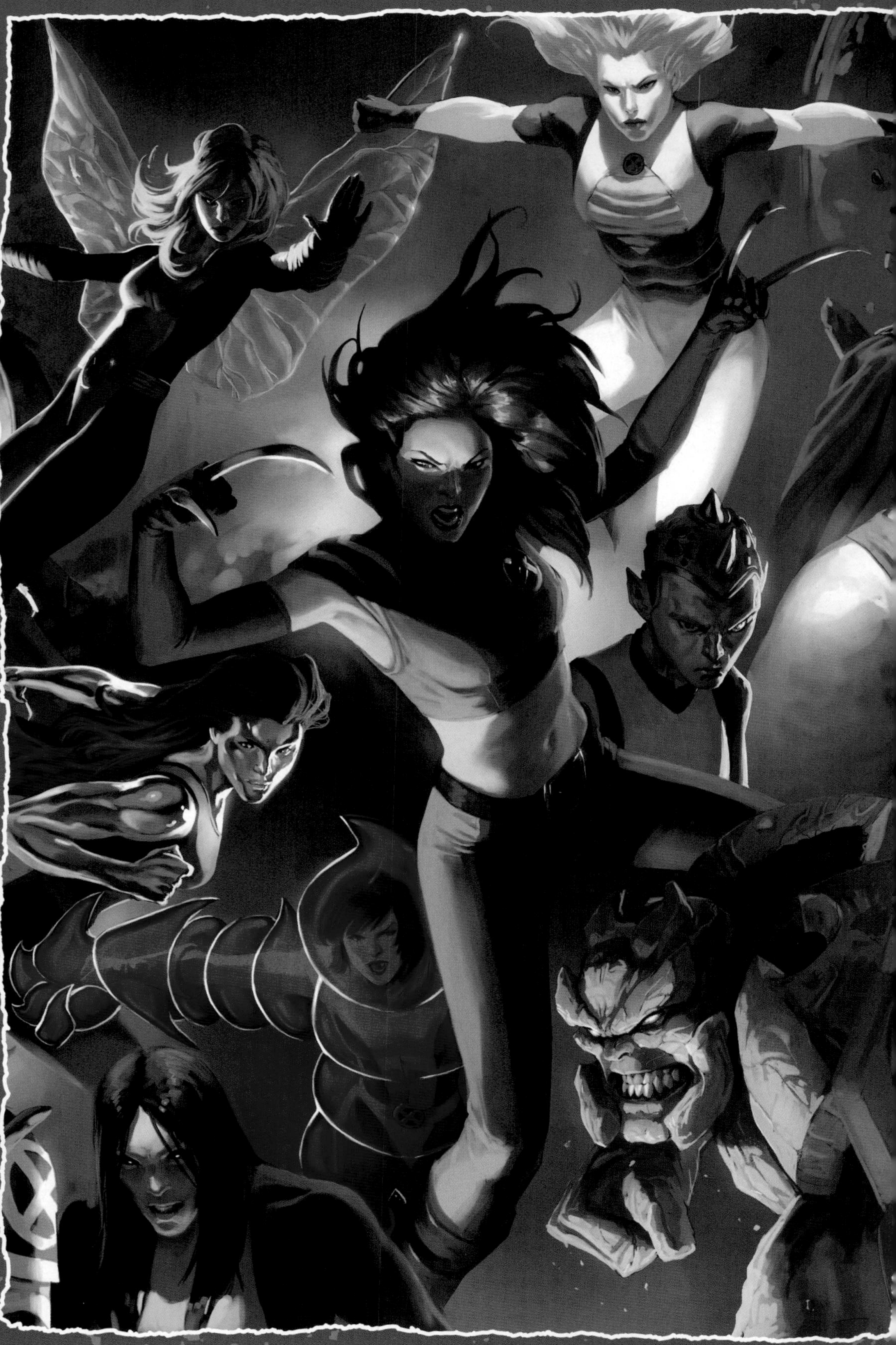

#1 VARIANT BY
MARKO DJURDJEVIC

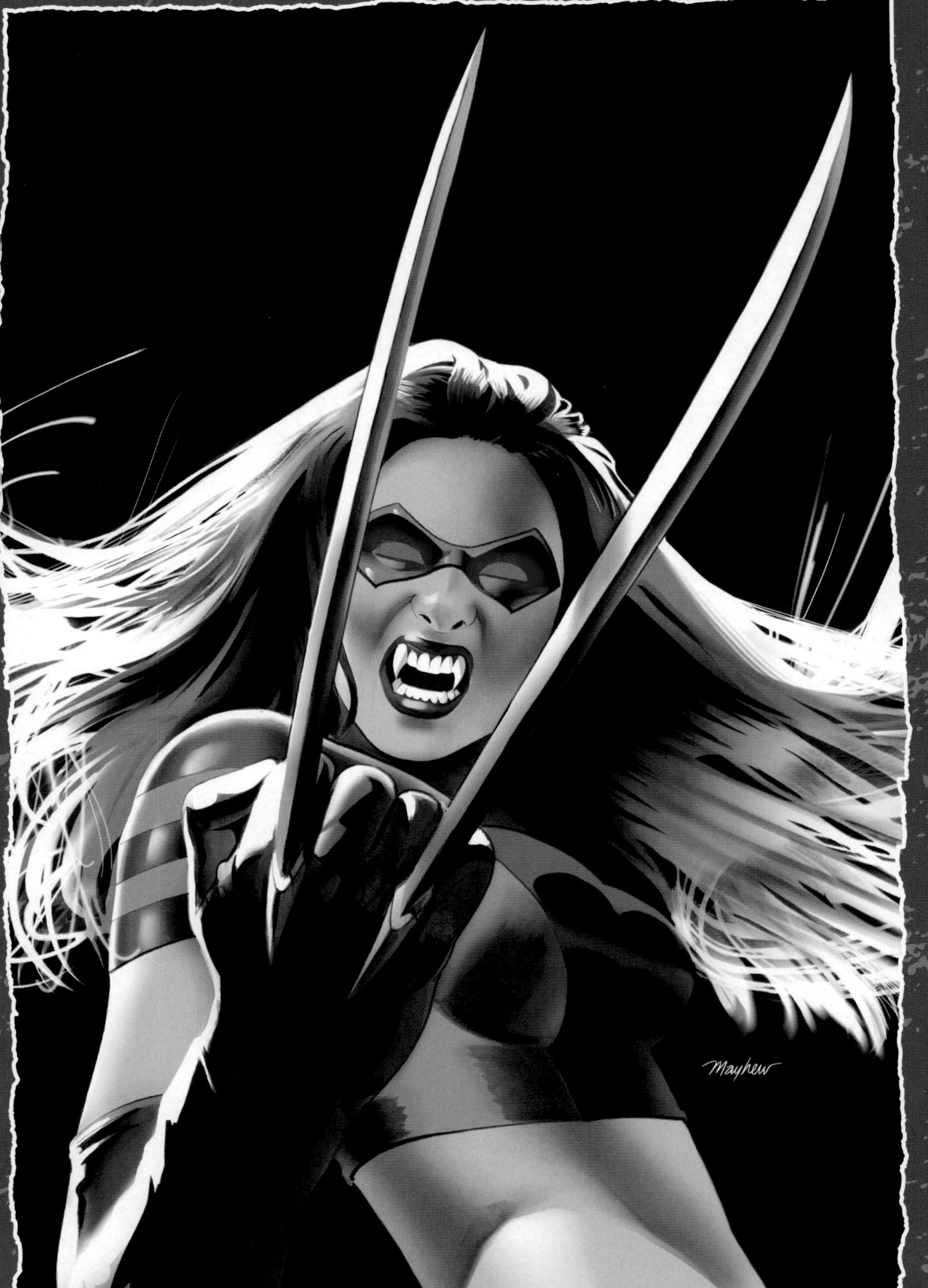
mayhew

#2 VAMPIRE VARIANT BY
MIKE MAYHEW

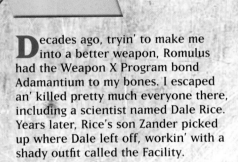

Decades ago, tryin' to make me into a better weapon, Romulus had the Weapon X Program bond Adamantium to my bones. I escaped an' killed pretty much everyone there, including a scientist named Dale Rice. Years later, Rice's son Zander picked up where Dale left off, workin' with a shady outfit called the Facility.

They wanted to clone me, an' mold the clone into an assassin-for-hire. But the genetic sample they had was damaged — scientist Sarah Kinney could only salvage the X chromosome, so she created a female clone. The 23rd embryo was viable — an' Sarah ended up servin' as the surrogate mother for project "X-23."

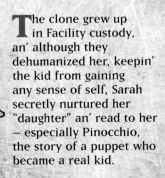

The clone grew up in Facility custody, an' although they dehumanized her, keepin' the kid from gaining any sense of self, Sarah secretly nurtured her "daughter" an' read to her — especially Pinocchio, the story of a puppet who became a real kid.

At age seven, X-23 began martial arts training, and the Facility soon developed a "trigger scent" that would kick-start a mindless killin' fury in the poor kid. She developed claws in her hands and feet, an' the Facility coated them in Adamantium.

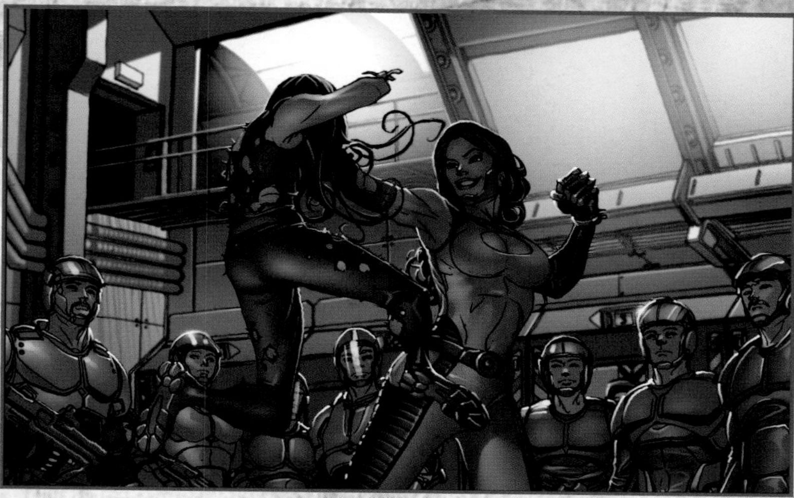

Zander hated me for killin' his dad, an' took it out on X-23. He engineered an indestructible sadist, Kimura, who brutally punished X-23 for even the smallest mistake. X-23 began to cut herself, though her healing factor fixed the damage instantly.

X-23's combat an' spy training intensified. They tagged her sensei with trigger scent — an' when X-23 slaughtered him in blind rage, they knew she was ready for field work. Her first assignment was to assassinate Presidential candidate Greg Johnson. Posin' as a disabled kid, she murdered him an' everyone nearby with ease an' skill.

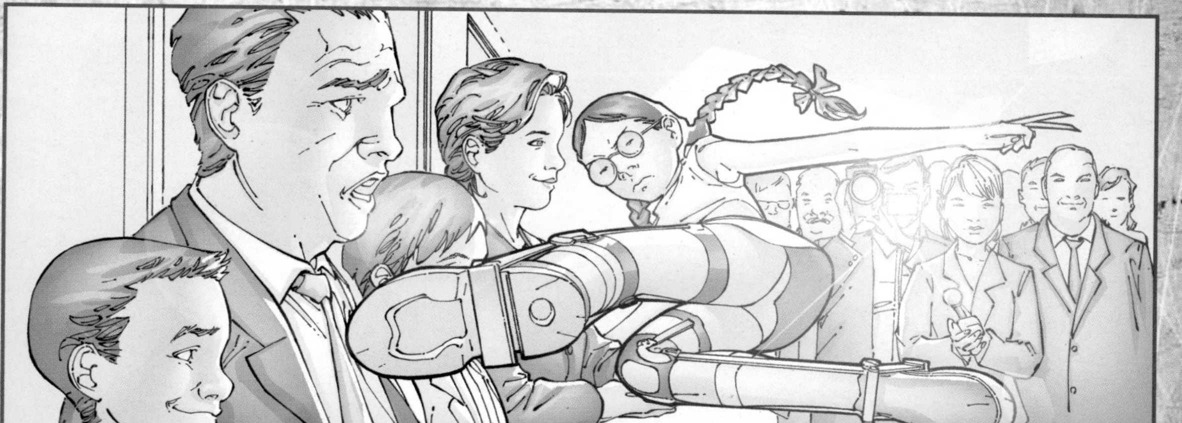

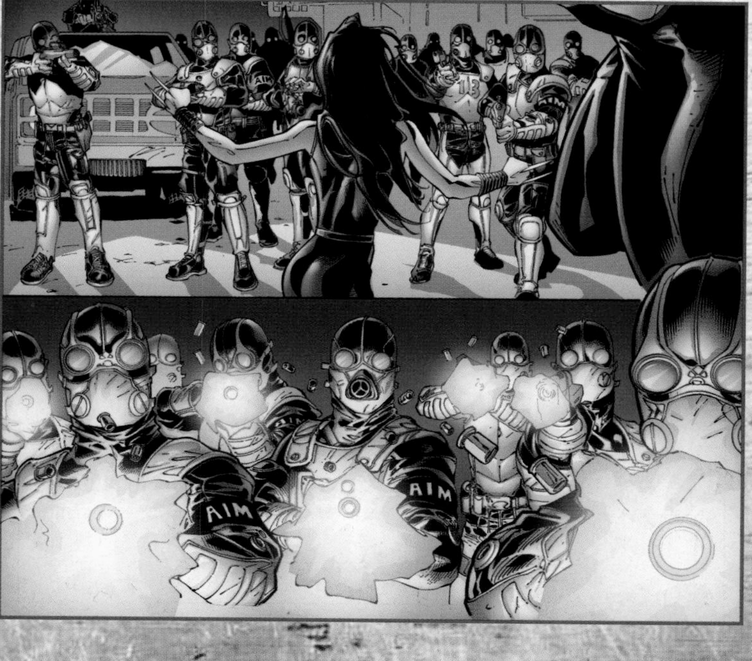

X-23 killed targets all over the world for three years, with no emotions or moral qualms. She became one of the Kingpin's favorite assassins. But on a mission against an AIM lab, Zander left X-23 behind, an' AIM's troops nearly killed her. When she finally made it back to the Facility, Zander lied an' Kimura punished her again.

When Sarah learned that her niece Megan had been kidnapped, she snuck X-23 out of the Facility to help find her. Trackin' Megan's scent, X-23 successfully rescued her "cousin," but Facility head Martin Sutter was furious.

Zander had been having an affair with Martin's wife, an' was actually her son Henry's real father. Deciding to take control of the project, Zander began gestation of embryos X-24 through X-50, an' gave X-23 a new mission — to kill the Sutter family.

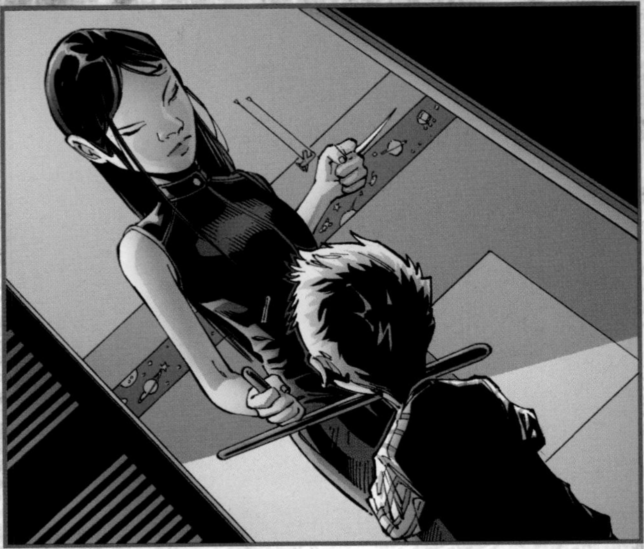

X-23 murdered Martin an' his wife, but couldn't bring herself to kill Henry. She spared him, an' smuggled evidence implicating Zander back to Sarah — the first sign of scruples an' morals she'd ever showed. A horrified Sarah gave X-23 her final mission: destroy the embryos an' kill Zander.

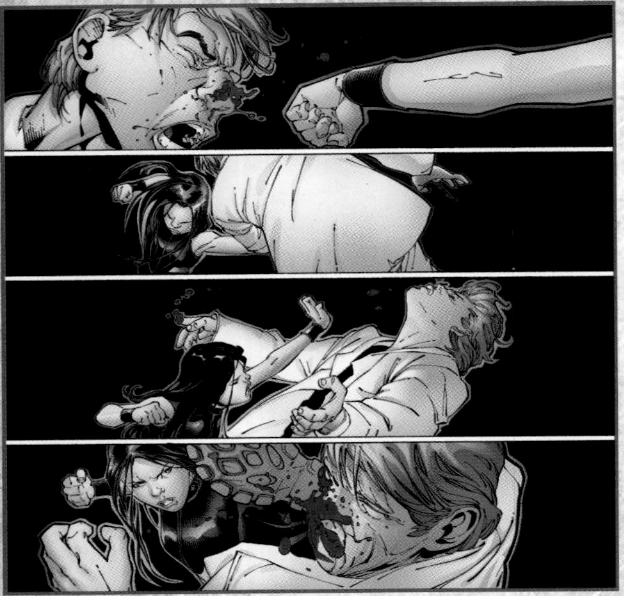

X-23 beat her lifelong tormentor badly, an' left him for dead as she blew up the lab. Sadly, Zander had planted trigger scent on Sarah before he died — an' it kick-started X-23's berserker rage. When she came out of it, her "mother" was dying in the snow...an' with Sarah's last words, she gave X-23 a real name: Laura.

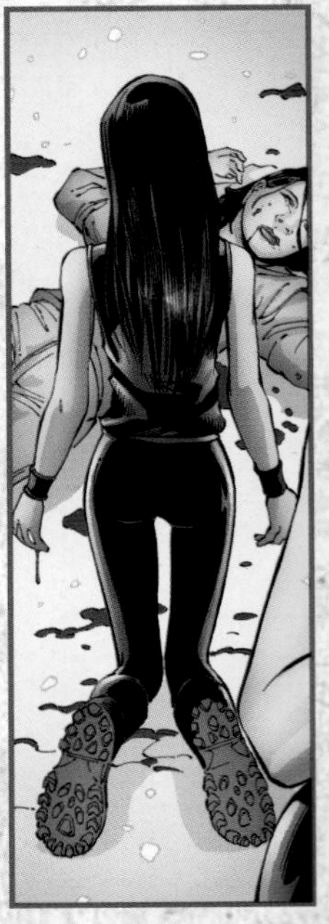

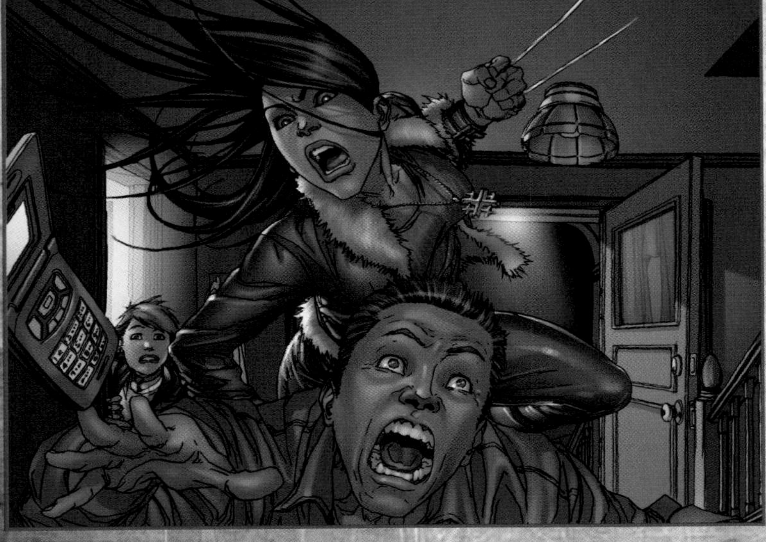

X-23 went to live with Megan an' her mother Debbie, but Debbie's boyfriend was a Facility spy. He dosed her tea with trigger scent — but it spilled on everyone, an' while X-23 snapped an' killed him, Megan an' Debbie fled to the shower and washed it off just in time.

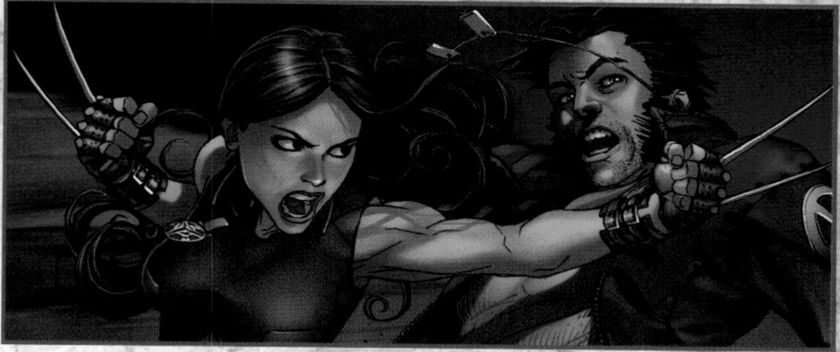

When Kimura attacked their house, X-23 fled with Megan an' Debbie, givin' them fake IDs an' sendin' them far away for their own safety. Then X-23 sought me out — we fought for a bit before I calmed her down, but Captain America showed up an' arrested her for multiple murders. Cap soon realized she was a victim too, though, an' let her go.

X-23 soon found herself on the street. Taken in by the pimp Zebra Daddy, she turned kinky tricks for guys who liked gettin' cut. When one John killed himself, X-23 found herself blamed an' on the run — an' fell in with a group of mutant runaways, ultimately killin' Zebra Daddy an' his goons when they came for her.

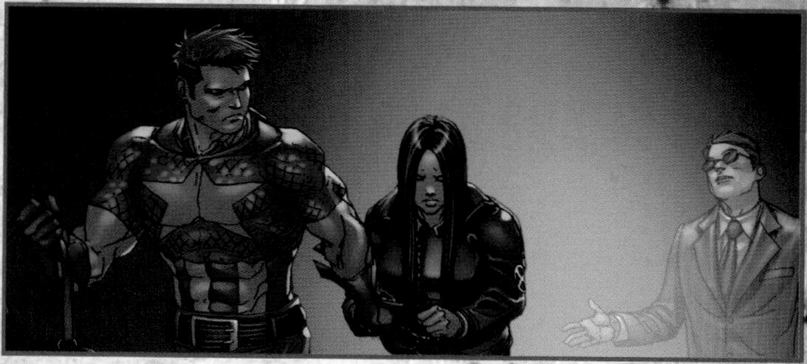

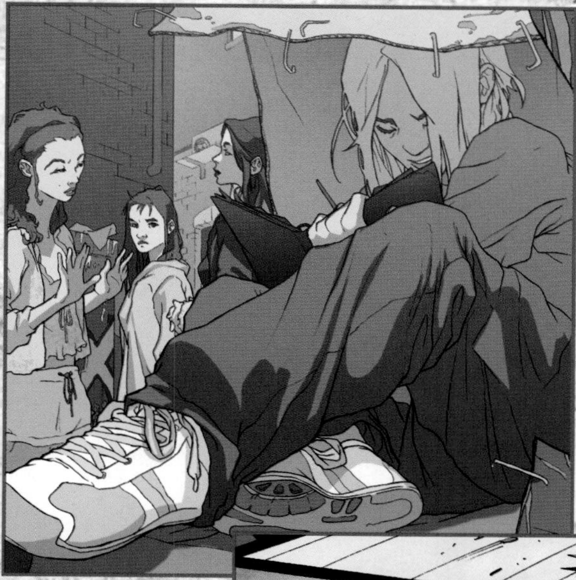

When X-23 killed some gangsters who tried to kidnap one of her friends, the X-Men investigated, an' foiled a scheme by the mercenary Bacchae. X-23 ended up paroled into our custody, an' although she tried to fit in at the school, her social skills still needed work.

Followin' me on a mission, X-23 teamed up with Psylocke an' the Savage Land Mutates to rescue the other X-Men from the saurian Hauk'ka race. She sensed the Mutates' leader Brainchild's treachery an' saved the Savage Land, but decided to leave the school shortly afterward.

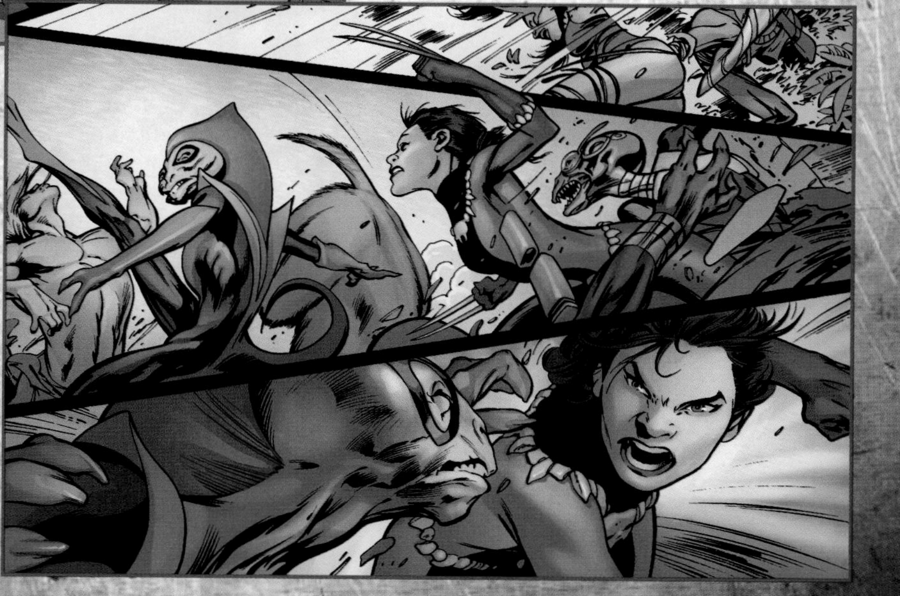

After M-Day, though, I convinced her to come back. Mutants had just taken a huge hit an' she needed to be somewhere safe, but she scared most of the remaining students. Hellion in particular was downright nasty to her, an' headmistress Emma Frost wanted her gone, worried that X-23 might snap at any moment an' kill someone.

X-23 wound up briefly possessed by the alien Uni-Power when she stumbled upon some AIM troops huntin' it, an' its cosmic abilities helped her destroy all of AIM's records on it. Soon after, Emma had the remaining students battle each other to stay on the active roster. She ordered Hellion to take X-23 out, but he hesitated, an' Cyclops made sure X-23 made the cut.

Reverend Stryker an' his fanatical anti-mutant Purifiers soon attacked the school, killin' 42 former mutants. X-23 saved her roommate Dust from Stryker's trap, an' helped the students determine that Nimrod, the super-Sentinel from the future, was helpin' him.

The New X-Men squad snuck out an' battled Nimrod, but although they defeated it, X-23 was badly injured — more than her healin' factor could handle. Hellion telekinetically flew her back to the mansion an' got her to the healer Elixir, an' X-23 started to develop a crush on Hellion.

When the Facility engineered mutant-eating Predator X creatures, Kimura kidnapped X-Men student Mercury to use her metal skin to coat the beasts. X-23 an' Hellion went to Mercury's rescue, an' Hellion dealt with Kimura by simply tossing her miles away. The X-Men arrived an' helped X-23 kill all the Predator Xs but one.

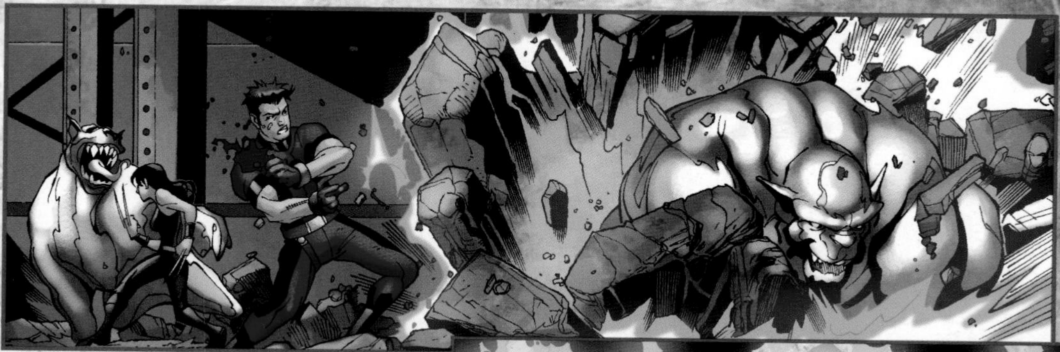

The demonic Belasco soon abducted the entire student body to Limbo, lookin' for his former protégée Magik. He repeatedly killed an' resurrected X-23, tryin' to scare the other students into cooperatin' – but Magik attacked with the other New X-Men an' defeated the demonlord.

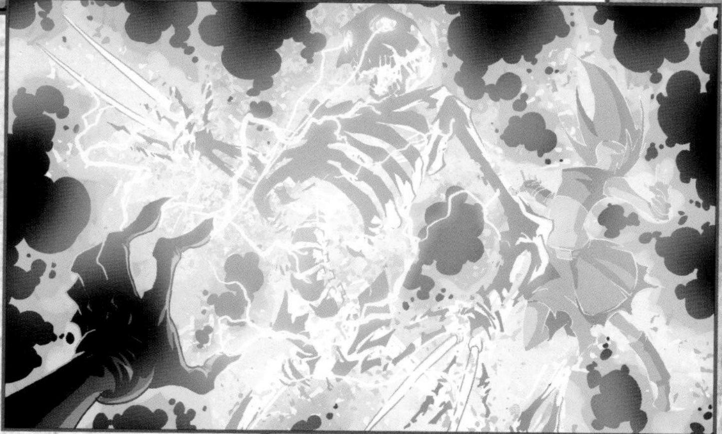

When things started gettin' really bleak for mutants, Cyclops put together X-Force, a black-ops squad to handle the X-Men's dirty work. I protested strongly about puttin' X-23 on the team – I wanted her to have a normal life, not to keep bein' someone's assassin – but Cyclops overruled me.

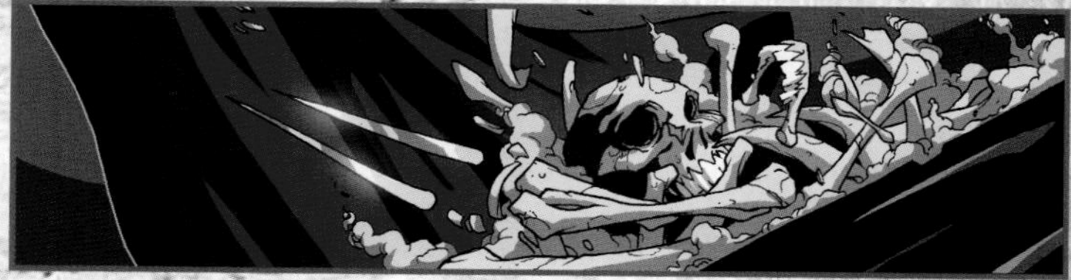

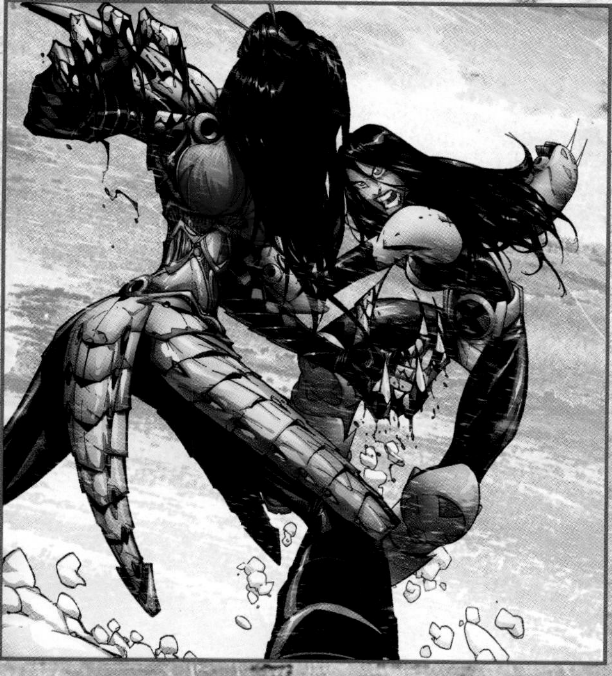

X-Force helped save the first mutant baby born in months, an' when Lady Deathstrike nearly killed Hellion, X-23 returned the favor. X-Force then battled the Purifiers, killin' hundreds of 'em – but with every life that X-23 took, I worried she was gettin' farther an' father away from her newfound humanity.

When X-Force went to destroy a sample of the mutant-killin' Legacy Virus, X-23 got infected. She intended to complete the mission by jumping into molten metal — but Elixir managed to heal her, purgin' the Virus.

X-Force was sent to the future to protect the mutant baby, Hope, who Cable was raisin' in the timestream — but found that we were stuck there thanks to the time powers of a future version of Kiden Nixon, one of X-23's old runaway buddies. X-23 couldn't bring herself to kill her friend — but Domino did it for her, an' we were able to go home.

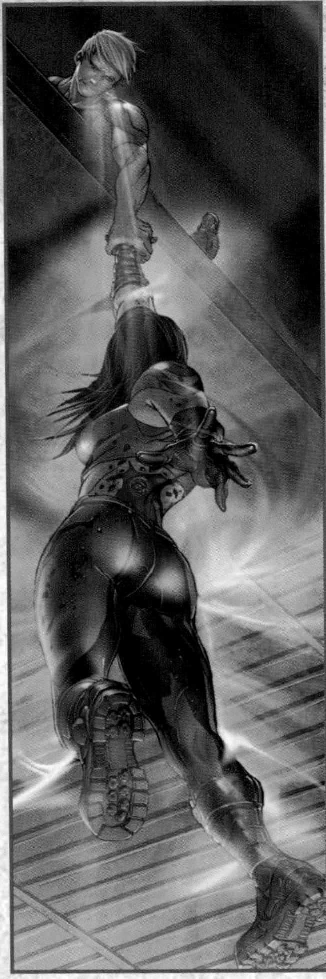

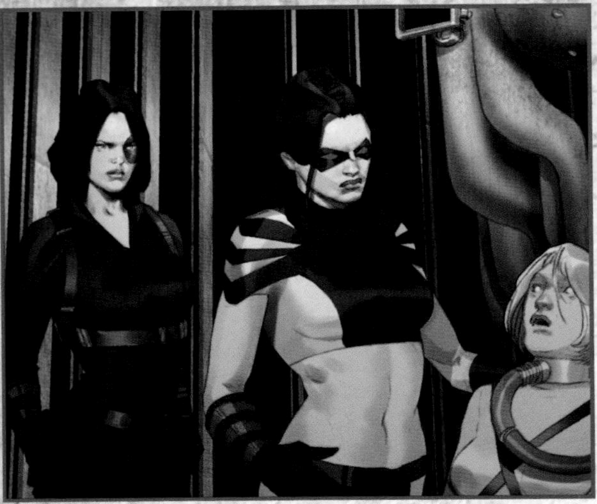

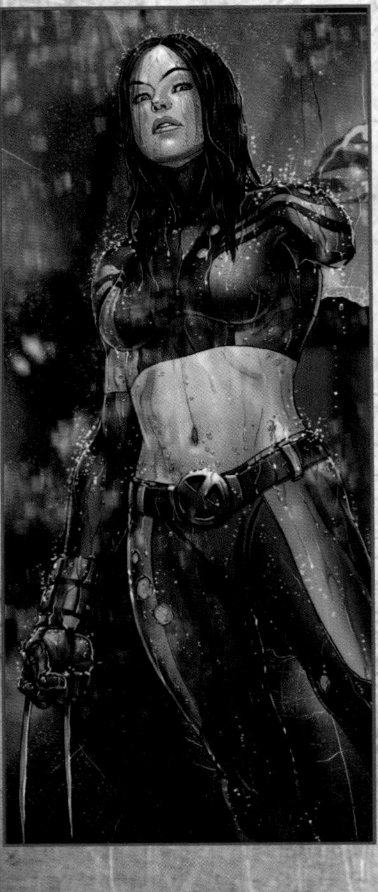

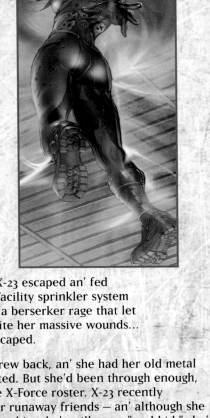

The Facility soon recaptured X-23, an' Kimura sadistically chopped off her arm. X-23 escaped an' fed trigger scent into the Facility sprinkler system — deliberately causing a berserker rage that let her kill everyone despite her massive wounds... except Kimura, who escaped.

X-23's arm soon grew back, an' she had her old metal claws re-implanted. But she'd been through enough, an' I took her off the X-Force roster. X-23 recently reconnected with her runaway friends — an' although she knows that, like Pinocchio, she's still not a "real kid," she's now determined to overcome her past an' earn a normal life for herself.

Text by Jeph York

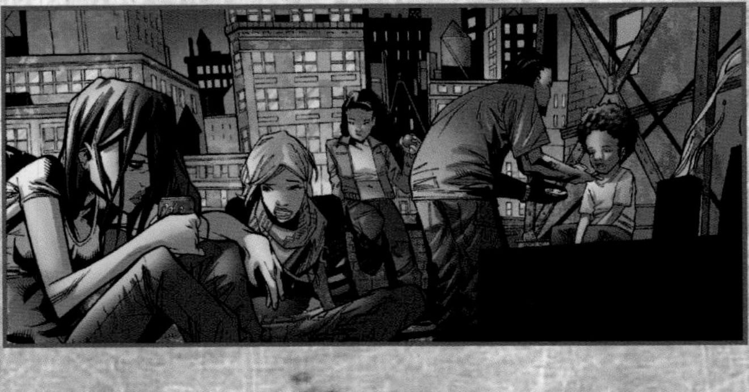